RESOLVED

"Ban Ki-moon has had an extraordinary and inspirational life, not least given the extreme poverty in which he grew up. You admire his ambition, tenacity, and patience in achieving global consensus for the incredibly important Sustainable Development Goals. But you also appreciate the golden thread that weaves its way through this book—his humanity. A true public servant, whose compassion shines throughout."

—Tony Blair, former prime minister of the United Kingdom

"This is a warm, readable account by Ban Ki-moon of his ten-year term as UN secretary-general and of his aim from the beginning to prioritize the climate crisis. At a time of increasing skepticism, his humble humanitarian concern and intense dedication should do much to restore confidence in the core values of the UN."

—Mary Robinson, former president of Ireland, former UN high commissioner for human rights, and chair of The Elders

"Can we not only imagine but actually build a better world? In this book, a farsighted global statesman not only says yes—but also shows us how."

—Graham Allison, author of *Destined for War: Can America and China Escape Thucydides's Trap?*

"In his momentous memoirs, Ban Ki-moon leads us through the exciting exchanges, communication, and interaction among world leaders, prominent personalities, citizens, and advocates as they craft a global agenda. This is a must-read for all interested in knowing the workings of the United Nations and its dedicated secretary-general."

—Ellen Johnson Sirleaf, former president of Liberia and recipient of the Nobel Peace Prize

"Ban Ki-moon describes a lifetime of service to Korea and to the world as the eighth secretary-general of the United Nations, where he put climate change at the top of his agenda. He provides fascinating details of the diplomacy and politics of what he describes as the ultimate threat to peace and security."

—Joseph S. Nye Jr., author of *Do Morals Matter? Presidents and Foreign Policy from FDR to Trump*

"Ban Ki-moon offers an incisive account of his history-shaping tenure as UN secretary-general. With his unswerving commitment to human dignity and the common good, Ban reminds us of the harrowing risks to humanity of narrow-mindedness, abuse of power, militarism, and vast disruptions of economic and technological change."

—Jeffrey D. Sachs, author of *The Ages of Globalization: Geography, Technology, and Institutions*

Resolved

UNITING NATIONS IN A DIVIDED WORLD

Ban Ki-moon

HarperCollins *Publishers* India

First published in the United States in 2021 by
Columbia University Press

This edition published in India by
HarperCollins *Publishers* 2021
A-75, Sector 57, Noida, Uttar Pradesh 201301, India
www.harpercollins.co.in

This English-language reprint edition is a complete reproduction, specially authorized by
Columbia University Press for publication and sale throughout South Asia

2 4 6 8 10 9 7 5 3 1

P-ISBN: 978-93-5489-419-0
E-ISBN: 978-93-5489-308-7

Cover design: Milenda Nan Ok Lee
Front cover photo: UN Photo/Marco Castro
Author photo: UN photo

Printed and bound at
Thomson Press (India) Ltd

HarperCollinsIn

MIX
Paper
FSC FSC® C010615

This book is produced from independently certified FSC® paper
to ensure responsible forest management.

I, Ban Ki-moon, solemnly swear to exercise in all loyalty, discretion and conscience, the functions entrusted to me as Secretary General of the United Nations, to discharge these functions and regulate my conduct with the interests of the UN only in view and not to seek or accept instructions in regard to the performance of my duties from any government or other authority external to the Organization.

Ki Moon Ban

—December 14, 2006

CONTENTS

Preface

War and peace—these are the guiding words of the United Nations and also the defining experiences of my formative years. War—the Korean War broke out in 1950 when I was just six years old. Peace—the United Nations was our savior, bringing peace to a divided nation. The images of bombs raining down on my village will forever be seared in my memory. But so is the sight of the United Nations flag flying high, signaling that we were not alone. As long as that blue banner waved, we would be safe. I will never forget the hope that this flag engendered decades before I came to head the United Nations and serve the organization that saved me and my country from ruin.

My devotion to the United Nations was reinforced when I was just twelve years old. I sent a letter, on behalf of my classmates, to then Secretary-General Dag Hammarskjöld, urging him to help the young people in Hungary who were fighting for freedom from the Soviet Union. I could never have predicted that the young boy who sent this appeal to the UN secretary-general would, fifty years later, walk in his shoes.

Having grown up surviving on UNICEF provisions and learning from UNESCO textbooks in the rubble of war, I can think of no greater honor than the privilege of serving as the United Nations secretary-general. When I was elected in October 2006, I pledged to exert my best efforts to create a better world for all people. I leave it to future historians to judge my efforts, but I take comfort in the knowledge that I have done everything I could to be a voice for the voiceless and a defender for the defenseless. I was one of them—and I know from experience that international solidarity is a matter of life and death. It saved my country, and I will never stop believing that it can save our world.

Even today we hear the cries of many millions of refugees, the painful images of boys and girls helplessly seeking assistance, the plight of widows struggling against oppression to find a bit of food for their children—all this suffering still keeps me awake at night. That is why I keep pointing out the urgent need for world leaders' political will along with a readiness to partner with others. And I continue to stress that this effort must be guided by an enhanced sense of our common humanity rather than a belief in barriers and barbed wire.

Today I am more concerned than ever about the divisions among countries, the dangerous rhetoric of hate spewing from some world leaders, and the threats to multilateralism. Some countries are balking at their commitments under UN-sponsored accords such as the Paris Climate Agreement, while others struggle with human rights.

As secretary-general, I was in constant contact with political, business, and civil society leaders—around the clock and around the world. I was guided by my strong conviction that open-minded and compassionate approaches with those concerned would help me steer through the turbulence of international politics. I tried to show respect and humility in my dealings with counterparts. Unfortunately, this was sometimes misunderstood as weakness. My guiding approach was to be flexible but strong like water, which can flow steadily around obstacles at times and have a fierce impact at other times. I believe that speaking is a revelation of knowledge, and listening is a source of wisdom. One of the greatest sources of conflict in today's world is the lack of understanding and appreciation among different cultures, countries, and regions.

Many others will judge my tenure, but I am proud that 2015 will go down in history as the year the United Nations delivered two of the most ambitious visions for the world's people: the Paris Climate Agreement and the 2030 Agenda with seventeen Sustainable Development Goals. On those two occasions, I heard the thunderous applause of world leaders inspired by their unity in the face of major threats facing humanity. Those standing ovations were proof that leaders at odds with one another can transcend their differences for the greater good.

I hoped that the sense of unity embodied by those two moments could last forever. But five years later, it's clear that we need to redouble our efforts with input from businesses, civil society, and ordinary citizens to make progress on both goals. I watched in sadness as the global recession and the coronavirus reversed much of our progress against poverty. Every region of the world is suffering from the irrefutable evidence of the climate crisis, yet we are not slashing carbon emissions with an urgency equal to the threat. In addition to achieving these two landmark goals, I devoted my time and energy to empowering women and young people. The creation of UN Women was hailed as an important reform.

My commitment to public service in Korea naturally grew into a commitment to public service for our world. I could never express how much I owe to so many people around the world for extending to me and all Koreans their strong, unconditional support and friendship. During the difficult moments when I faced complex crises, their voices have been a source of energy boosting my own limited capacity.

I hope people around the world will make the most of their own capacities, focusing on small improvements and concrete, long-term gains. Civic engagement is the future of our shared lives. We need the environment to sustain us, health to strengthen us, peace to inspire us, and the future to motivate us. I say "us" because we cannot attain these universal conditions working alone.

This book is not chronological, nor does it cover all that I experienced during my tenure. That would be impossible in this restricted space and time. It is informed by my personal perspective, which is naturally limited. Countless stories of selfless devotion by the tens of thousands of staff and peacekeepers also deserve to be told.

PART I

A Child of War, a Man of Peace

The Foundations of a Diplomatic Life

Chapter One

EARLY LIFE

From Tragedy to Strength

I was a child of war, but I became a man of peace.

My journey began in Korea. I was born in 1944 in humble Eumseong County, known for producing the fiery red chili peppers (*gochu*) that are inseparable from Korean cuisine. At that time, the Allies were liberating Western Europe in some of World War II's bloodiest battles. But that was far away, and my young parents were focused on making a living and starting a family. When I was still too young to talk, we moved to the city of Cheongju, where my father worked for an agricultural firm.

Just two weeks after my sixth birthday, soldiers from the Communist North invaded the South, sparking the Korean War. Some days we could hear the fighting in the distance. There was little doubt that North Korean soldiers were approaching, and with them, destruction. I don't know how I knew this because my parents were careful not to show fear around me, but they could only protect my brother and me so far. We were living in a crucible of fear.

After six months of anxious torment, the war abruptly changed, and invading forces came barreling toward us. More than half a million Chinese soldiers joined with the Northern army in early January 1951, pushing down the Allied forces with brutal strength.

It didn't take long for my parents to sift through our belongings and join the exodus from Cheongju. My mother, nine months pregnant, moved slowly and heavily as our neighbors raced past us in their exodus. My father, worried and ashen with fear, took food for the journey, clothes, and some things my mother would need after the birth. And I, only six years old, carried what I could and struggled to keep up as we trotted over the ground. Tears welled up, but I tried to be brave.

Our sacks felt heavy even though we left almost everything behind.

RACING INTO LABOR

Even before the war, giving birth was one of the most dangerous things a woman could do. The sanitary system wasn't good, and most parts of Korea lacked hospitals. Midwives were experienced in birth but had no medical training. Families could only light some incense or offer a prayer and hope that nothing would go wrong.

We were on the roadside when my mother went into labor, and we hurried to the nearest house we could see. Fortunately, the family took us in and my mother was attended to in one of the bedrooms. I had never heard screaming like that, each cry so loud and long and unrestrained. Her sounds pierced me to the bone. It was absolutely terrifying, and I cried so hard the tears chapped my cheeks. I understood she was in pain. I knew it had to do with the baby, and I knew her pain was very serious by the way my father held his face in his hands. I had never seen him so still, yet his shoulders shuddered every little while. When he turned to me, urging me to stop sobbing, his face looked so pale and drawn that it frightened me all the more. My brother Ki-sang, only four years old, cried as hard as I did.

My sister Ban Jeong-ran was born January 6, 1951, during the chaos of the infamous January 4 Retreat, when the Chinese army forced UN and South Korean forces below the 38th parallel. My mother was pale and wobbly, exhausted by her labor, but just three days after the delivery she marched on with the new baby clutched tightly in her arms. Jeong-ran was swaddled in our extra clothing and cried whenever she was not sleeping.

At the time, childbirth was dangerous for both mother and baby. My legal birthdate is June 13, 1944, but I was actually born one month earlier. My parents, as so many others, waited to register my birth until they were sure I would survive. As we were walking, I was terribly curious about this tiny child, who was even smaller and more helpless than I felt. I knew I had to be even braver now that my sister had arrived.

We walked as quickly as my mother could go, stopping frequently to rest. Safety was just fifteen miles away, but we traveled on foot—a journey that would take two days. I wore thin rubber shoes that did not protect me from rocks, brambles, or even the mud that covered the rough paths we hurried along. With bloody feet, little food, and constant walking, followed by an exhausted but shallow sleep, I was miserable. Having my parents so close was reassuring, but I was too frightened and cold to sleep.

Decades later, I felt this same terror whenever I visited refugee camps. Hundreds of thousands of refugees born in sometimes massive camps grew up knowing nothing but life in tents. Most of these refugees lived in dry, dusty regions, not the frigid Korean Peninsula. But, like mine, their lives were upended by the political and economic forces that drive people and nations to war. Many of these families have experienced the savagery and poverty that has now forced more than thirty million people from their homes. For these refugee children, the boundary of the camp represented the end of their world.

A CHILD OF WAR

My maternal grandparents lived on a mountainside at the edge of a forest, a safe place to wait out one of the most vicious conflicts of the twentieth century. Ki-sang and I watched as fighter jets strafed the towns and villages we had walked through. We cried in fear even though the bombardment was far away.

We stayed in my grandparents' small house in Jeungpyeong for a few months, but it felt so much longer! We passed the time mostly by searching for food and, for respite, playing with the baby. She must have felt how distressed everyone was because she cried all the time. There were no toys or even pencils, and I was bored. I remember playing a few pranks, but there wasn't much else for me to do.

We were focused on survival. My father and grandfather were running here and there, searching for food. We had just enough to eat, but rarely enough to fill our stomachs. It was poor food, potatoes and so on. We could not even buy rice! I was hungry all the time. Everyone was.

We finally returned home in the spring of 1951. The fighting was still going on, and everyone—civilian and soldier—was desperate with hunger. We had been eating so little for so long that the occasional egg was a treat. Signs of war were all around us, but we quickly worked to rebuild our homes and our lives. Parts of Cheongju had been damaged during the war, but my family's home was fine.

After the armistice in July 1953, the countryside again became frightening. North Korean and Chinese soldiers were withdrawing, and the mountainsides were filled with North Korean soldiers trapped below the 38th parallel.

When the war was over, we moved to Chungju, a city near Namsan Mountain. I lived there until I left to study at Seoul National University, but the rest of my family stayed including my mother, until her death at age one hundred in June 2019.

No society wants children to be exposed to the horrors of war. We don't want them to grow up into adults who think such atrocities are normal. But children are always caught up in the trauma and fear of armed conflict.

And so I became a man of peace.

RESCUED BY DISTANT NATIONS

The United Nations enshrines the dignity of human life by protecting children first and foremost. Special protections for the youngest are included in all international human rights documents, from the bedrock text of the 1948 Universal Declaration of Human Rights through the 1990 Convention on the Rights of the Child and beyond.

The importance of the United Nations to the Korean War is hard to overstate—simply put, the organization saved our lives and our country. The UN soldiers stopped the war. Humanitarian agencies gave us food and books. The blue-and-white flag, with a globe cradled by the olive branches of peace, gave us hope.

The United Nations Command (UNC) consisted of more than three hundred thousand troops from sixteen nations, with five more nations providing medical teams. It was a peace enforcement mission, which was conceived as a robust international military response to an armed aggression. U.S. President Harry Truman supported a muscular peace enforcement operation, because the United States did not want to plan and fight a new war alone so soon after World War II. Nonetheless, U.S. troops accounted for about 90 percent of the foreign forces. Still, the UNC suffered heavy losses: nearly forty thousand foreign troops died, more than thirty-six thousand of them Americans.[1]

The first time I saw Americans was among the ranks of the UNC. Each of the sixteen armies wore their national uniform, and at that age, I admit I had trouble separating the United States from the United Nations. We would shout "Hello!" to them, waiting to be showered with little trinkets and candies by the soldiers, who even tossed their rations on the side of the road as their trucks rumbled by. This is one certain way to impress a small child, but the Americans were only part of a multinational effort.

I could not know the importance of the United Nations at that time, but I knew its presence meant I could harbor a small sense of hope. Certainly, it meant friends around the globe were helping us. To the world, we mattered.

The United Nations gave us more than candy and toys. Schools were built to replace those damaged and destroyed by the war. The organization even tried to overcome the loss of thousands of teachers. I remember students carrying out a chalkboard every day and placing it under the trees that served as our classroom. Amid all the rubble, we sat on rocks for chairs. We brought sacks to class, at the urging of teachers, and carried home powdered milk donated by the UN. Food and clothing were most important, but I remember nothing as fondly as the textbooks we were given. In that barren landscape, we were introduced to reading, mathematics, and science, and to the world outside Korea. I devoured this knowledge as fervently as I did the rice bars.

On the last page of each textbook was written, "this textbook was printed with generous assistance from the UN Korean Reconstruction Agency (UNKRA) and the UN Educational, Scientific, and Cultural Organization (UNESCO)." I was so deeply grateful to both, and I was very curious about UNESCO. I never dreamed that I would someday personally thank the organization for teaching that impoverished boy to read and waking him to the world outside Korea. When I initiated the Global Education First Initiative (GEFI) in September 2012 with former UK Prime Minister Gordon Brown as the UN Special Envoy, I told this story to the member states.

A few weeks later, having heard my story, the Korean National Commission for UNESCO searched the old bookshops and uncovered several textbooks of the type we had used in those days, and they gave one to me in a ceremony held during a youth forum in Yeosu, Korea. It is the most treasured gift I have ever received. They also donated two of them to Irina Bokova, then director general of UNESCO, who permanently display them at UNESCO's Paris headquarters. I hope that children today, and in the future, also see the beacon of hope that the UN represents.

As we sat in those makeshift classrooms, we knew that one day we would be able to pay back the world for its assistance in our darkest hour. We would make the fastest transition in history from a nation in need to a nation able to give. This goal launched my trajectory and shaped my purpose. I vowed to become the best person I could be and to invest whatever skills or gifts I could acquire in my country.

A NUCLEAR FAMILY IN THE POSTWAR WORLD

We didn't have much money, no one did. All we had was nature. When I was young, the country was a source of wood for fires, grass for compost, and water for drinking and bathing. The water was delicious then—cold, clear, fresh, and sweet. I'd scoop it up into my mouth or just lower my head and drink as much as I could straight from the stream. I can clearly see the connection between these early walks through the forest and my commitment to fighting climate change more than fifty years later.

We grew barley and rice for our own meals and often had enough to sell or barter. No one could afford fertilizer, so each family used the composted grass and human waste from the outhouses in the corners of our yard.

As the eldest and a boy, I had the job of cutting the logs into firewood. I was very good with an axe. Half, then half again; each log cut into four pieces. At first, the axe was heavy and awkward in my hands, and I didn't trust it more than I would a weapon. But soon the motions became familiar—lift, aim, swing, and chop—over and over and over again. I grew to like the axe's heft and the sound of the wood splitting. My upper body grew muscular, and my hands—that until now had mostly held books—began to become calloused. I think I still have splinters! This was not about fitness, nor was it meditation, exactly. This was for my family, for our survival.

Like everyone else I knew, my family lived in poverty. All of us—parents and children—slept in one room, on the floor, as was the style in Korea. It was very close, and I sometimes ached for privacy. My parents were a source of strength. They met for the first time only on their wedding day. Weddings were arranged by matchmakers. It was very rare for young men and women to meet each other and decide to get married on their own. People used to marry early, often as young as age fifteen, but my father was about twenty when my parents married. Their parents decided they would make a good match, and they did indeed: they remained married until my father died fifty years later.

Korean fathers are strict, but mine was a good man, softhearted and compassionate. My father, Ban Myung-hwan, didn't discipline us or even say anything when we were naughty. He wasn't a big talker, but my father knew right from wrong and made sure his six children did as well. I learned from him my love of nature and a devout belief in caring for the stranger as well as one's family. He died too early, in a car accident. But my father must have been at ease because he knew that he had passed on a strong character to his children. I have always strived to live up to his example.

My father wasn't very good with money, always losing the money he lent to friends who couldn't pay him back. He just couldn't say no! He invited friends to stay with us, and they would eat and stay for a long time. He even invited one of his friends with leprosy. I had to stay with him in my bedroom for several months. I used to wash with water many times to make sure that the basin was clean and safe. I always felt uneasy and even worried about becoming infected. My mother grew very angry! "Why are we always poor?" she would yell.

My mother Shin Hyun-soon was always sick, surely because of all her pregnancies. I was the oldest of six siblings, but two children had died even before I was born. My mother was a woman of fortitude. I am proud that I inherited her capacity for hard work, resilience, and determination. She survived unbearable circumstances to live to her one hundredth birthday and, although uneducated, learned to read and write.

When her headaches and heart condition became too much for her, she would lie down in dim light, and it fell to me, as the oldest male child, to take care of the family. I learned to cook rice and simple stews. But I was in high school then, and I didn't like it! I had discovered the endless worlds inside books and wanted to be with my friends.

Women in the neighborhood would often help out, which gave me more time to spend with my books. In fact, they liked to come over because my mother was very popular—she was a bit of a gossip and a very good storyteller. Women would come to her when they had something personal to discuss. I rarely overheard their confidences and couldn't understand them when I did.

Despite her illnesses, my mother was a vivid presence in conservative Korean society, which was heavily influenced by Confucianism. In this teaching, women are accorded little agency or independence, and I had seen from an early age how grandmothers, mothers, wives, and daughters were treated. I knew, intrinsically, that this was wrong. I saw how the women around me rebuilt our villages and restored our lives. Despite their second-class status, Korean women were the backbone of our country's postwar rebirth.

My mother inspired me to empower women at the Korean Foreign Ministry, within the ranks of the United Nations and, especially, through UN programs around the world. I never needed studies to tell me that all of society benefited when women were given opportunities for an education, a sewing machine, or microloans.

My mother spent a lot of her time going to temple to pray for her children's good health and happiness.

Korean people used to believe that a woman would dream on the night she conceived, and that dream would affect the baby's life. My mother dreamed of a large pheasant, a symbol of good luck and happiness. She tried to catch it, but the bird was already in flight. My determined mother dashed after it and caught the bird with her skirt. Pheasants, with beautifully colored feathers, symbolize diversity and creativity, fortune and happiness. People often asked her about the dream, and I heard this story many times. Everyone said it was a good, strong dream.

My mother's own heartbreak in pregnancy and lack of care in childbirth has made me sensitive to the risk women take to give birth. Poverty, maternal health complications, and child mortality are universal concerns, and only a fraction of the world's countries have learned to make childbirth as safe as possible. As secretary-general, I traveled in many developing countries, particularly in Africa, and I always spoke about my mother's pain and strength. People were moved by her story, which was often so similar to their own. I found it helpful to share my memories, connect with people, and give them a sense of hope.

THE AMERICAN EXAMPLE

When the Soviet Union invaded Hungary in 1956, my life was changed again. Within days, tanks were pulled up to government buildings and soldiers were shooting at students. My schoolmates and I were deeply affected by the assault, in which 2,500 people were killed and 17,500 were injured. Hungary had been growing more democratic, making this a special loss. We decided to send a letter to UN Secretary-General Dag Hammarskjöld, urging the United Nations to resolve the crisis, and I drafted it. I read the letter out loud and clear to the students gathered in the playground, hoping that the message would be heard by the UN secretary-general and the children in Hungary.

Exactly fifty years later, on October 13, 2006, I was elected secretary-general. While delivering my acceptance speech, I expressed my hope that I would not have to receive that kind of letter from the world's young students.

I was pleasantly surprised to be decorated with the Medal of Hero of Freedom, hurriedly awarded by the Hungarian government.

I studied the traditional subjects in school but especially applied myself to learning English. I took every opportunity I could to speak it. When I was eighteen, my teacher encouraged me to enter a contest for an international students' program sponsored by the American Red Cross. The judges grilled me on questions about the English language, and how I would explain Korean culture to outsiders. I felt confident until the talent contest began. Competitors from much more prestigious schools showed off their prowess with musical instruments. All I could do was to sing—my voice was not great, but I did manage to convey enthusiasm.

I was surprised to be one of the four students selected to represent Korea in the program called VISTA (Visit of International Students to America). Here I was, a country boy from an unknown school, about to embark on a trip that would change my life in more ways than one. As poor as we were, the teachers from my school pooled their coins to buy me a suit so I wouldn't appear shabby beside the other delegates from around the world.

My first glimpse of the world outside Korea was electrifying from the start. On July 30, 1962, I left Kimpo International Airport with a sense of awe and hope. All my family members, parents, uncles, and friends saw me off. My first airplane ride was momentarily forgotten when I traveled across the Golden Gate Bridge in San Francisco and was transported to a land of impossible progress. I was surrounded by cars and supermarkets and was riding on the wide, modern Highway 101. As I took this in, I thought maybe my homeland could be modernized too. I resolved in my heart that Korea would attain similar development. I peered out the window, and in my excitement I knew that anything was possible and that I would do everything I could to make it happen.

California could have been overwhelming, but my "American mom," Libba Patterson, eased my transition. Libba and Robert A. Patterson welcomed me into their home in Novato, California, for a week, and they took care of me as if I was their own son. The whole Patterson family was curious about Korea, and the five of them were patient with my halting English conversation. I stayed in their son Bob's room. He was a year younger and taught me all about American life. He even coached me to play table tennis. Alayna and Maribeth were the younger daughters. I remember the day we visited the seaside and I splashed in the Pacific Ocean, falling asleep on the drive home. Libba slipped a blanket over me, and I felt deeply warmed by her kindness.

The Patterson family and I have stayed in touch throughout our lives. In fifty-five years, we have never lost contact, keeping in touch mostly through letters but also with mutual visits. I invited Libba and Maribeth to Seoul in 2004, when I became foreign minister, and I invited the whole family to the United Nations for my swearing in as secretary-general. They were all so proud of me. I have visited Novato many times, most recently on April 29, 2017, for Libba's one hundredth birthday party. It was a surprise visit, although everybody knew Soon-taek and I would come. My American mom was so surprised she began to cry, hugging me like her own son. That was my last visit with her; she passed away the following year.

Experiencing California was already monumental, but the American Red Cross arranged for us to travel from Novato to Portland, Oregon, and Spokane, Washington, beautiful cities in the Pacific Northwest. Finally, we traveled to Washington, D.C., where we met one of the most powerful leaders in the world—U.S. President John F. Kennedy. We would only be in the U.S. capital for seven days, but I was determined to see as much as I could. I needed to thank the Americans for saving our lives and to expand my knowledge and experience. I had no idea how to express my gratitude.

I met all the other foreign students in the Red Cross VISTA program on the South Lawn of the White House. It was August 29, 1962, and I was secretly relieved that I was not the only one from a less developed country. Although many of their nations were now at peace, I was aware that we barely had an armistice with the North and that their warring words could signal another invasion at any time. I momentarily worried that this might happen while I was in the United States.

Many participants had survived a war, but that was not what we talked about. We were all enthralled by the U.S. president, whom we could see from thousands of miles away was handsome, strong, and principled. I had been reading about President John F. Kennedy. We had very different families and lives, but he had known war too, as a member of the U.S. Navy during World War II. I yearned to talk to him myself and hear his wisdom in his own voice. And I knew every other young man and woman on the grass felt the same way. Then he joined us on the South Lawn.

President Kennedy called out our countries, and we raised our hands to show where we came from to the others. When he called out "South Korea," my heart was beating loudly, and I thought I would cry with pride. At that time, I had never even met the mayor of my small town. What a huge change and honor.

I did not understand everything, but it was clear that he held high expectations for us, no matter on which side of the Iron Curtain we lived. He instilled in us the importance of not succumbing to nationalism or to letting boundaries restrict us. We were one human family, and national boundaries shouldn't mean much. Then he said that only one question mattered: "Whether you are ready to extend a helping hand."

Those words would change my life. I decided there, on the White House lawn, that I would become a diplomat and help many countries reach development and prosperity. Korea needed my help, but I could serve my country while helping others. I returned home full of purpose, full of hope. Korea could come to know security and prosperity such as I had witnessed in the United States.

THE LOVE OF MY LIFE

I realize now that my life had changed even before I went to the ceremony at the White House. My whole town knew about me and about my trip to the United States, and everyone seemed to be as excited about it as I was. I understood I was the face of the new Korea, a country that now aspired to a place in the global community.

The Chungju-ju girls' high school was mobilized to embroider fifty or sixty small silk pouches in red, yellow, and blue thread—delicate gifts to bring to America. A girl of eighteen, Yoo Soon-taek was chosen by her classmates to be the student committee chairperson, and it was she who met me with the bag of pouches. I knew immediately she was sweet and smart and strong. Even in my excitement about the trip, and my fluster at meeting this young woman, I could feel Soon-taek's calm. This was the beginning of a pure love, and I was grateful to be introduced to her as a man with a future. I think she was interested in me too, but she was a very shy person and would never have said anything.

It was taboo for boys and girls to be alone together, but you could meet people from other schools at student activities. We began to see each other when we became college students in Seoul. She was studying to be a librarian, and I wanted to go into foreign affairs. We were both living alone, so we were more or less free and grown up enough that we were not expected to have a chaperone.

It was still difficult to see Soon-taek because there were no telephones. I had to write a letter inviting her to join me for a walk or a film, but I didn't know whether she would come or not. When I was lucky, she would get the note and would come. But if she didn't show up, I would wait until I was sure, and then I would have to go back. She sent me letters too, which in 1963 was very bold for a Korean girl.

FROM THE BARRICADES TO BUSAN

One of the smartest decisions I ever made in my life was to complete my compulsory military service after my sophomore year instead of waiting from university. In the early 1960s, students were staging pro-democracy protests, and classes at Seoul National University were repeatedly cancelled amid their strikes and demonstrations. I did sometimes go to the barricades, but I didn't feel the same passion as many others. I grew tired, then frustrated that political demonstrations were shutting schools down when I wanted to learn and get on with my life. I gambled that the school would be calmer in three years, and I was right. By the time I completed my military service, the domestic political situation had calmed down, and I was able to concentrate on my study of international relations at Seoul National University.

I served in the army as an enlisted man for two and a half years, beginning in April 1965. My role as an enlisted stevedore was to load and unload military supplies given to us by the U.S. government. I had to work all day and night at the Busan military wharf. Korean officers had to deal with many U.S. officers in the port, and I was often recruited to work as an interpreter. As the story of my English proficiency spread among officers, I was called to work for the commanding general, which made my life in the army a little smoother.

I proposed to Soon-taek when I came back from my military service and returned to school as a junior. I was twenty-five. The moment itself was not so special; what mattered to me was that she said yes.

Chapter Two

DIPLOMATIC LIFE

Sharing Korea's Traditional Values

India was my first diplomatic posting, and Soon-taek and I arrived in Delhi in October 1972. I served there for almost three years, first as vice consul of the Korean Consulate General, and once a full diplomatic relationship was established between Korea and India in December 1973, I served as second secretary of the Korean Embassy. It was such an exciting time in my life! I was twenty-eight years old, newly married, and on a diplomatic trajectory.

My daughter Seon-yong was just eight months old and my only son, Woo-hyun, was born in India on October 30, 1974. I used to joke with Indian people that my balance sheet with India is perfect because my son was born in India and my youngest daughter, Hyun-hee, is married to an Indian man. Even now, nearly fifty years later, I tell the Indian people that half of my heart belongs in their country.

The work was challenging but fascinating to a young diplomat. Our primary goal was to win full diplomatic recognition by India, a leader of the nonaligned group, which we did in December 1973. Koreans and many other diplomats felt that elevating consular relations to the ambassadorial level was a turning point in diplomatic relations. India was among the largest nonaligned states that recognized both Koreas.

I rose up the diplomatic ranks steadily, working in Seoul and at world capitals to advance my country's international relationships and development. I held more than a dozen foreign ministry positions after my posting to Delhi, and with each one I advanced. Even so, I was surprised and concerned to hear that many of my colleagues thought of me as a "fast flyer." At that time, the Korean foreign service was a bureaucracy that respected hierarchy, and it was uncomfortable to be promoted over the heads of others who had been there longer.

One of my most important mentors was Lho Shin-yong, who later became foreign minister and then prime minister. He was a respected diplomat with a far-reaching vision and a strong character who is still remembered as a charismatic leader. In 1987, Prime Minister Lho unexpectedly promoted me to a senior rank. I had worked for him when he was ambassador in New Delhi, and he had deep trust in me. The promotion was a surprise to my peers, and especially to many senior officers. This advancement was not due to a personal connection, as was often the case, but rather because he noticed my hard work and sincerity. At night, after work, I hand-wrote letters to my peers and senior colleagues, asking for their understanding and vowing to do my best to meet their expectations as a senior diplomat. It took almost a month for me to go down the list of at least 120 diplomats.

I know my earliest experiences drove my ambition to serve Korea and the world beyond the peninsula. Over my thirty-seven-year career in the Korean government, I oversaw most aspects of Seoul's relationship with the United Nations and the United States—both pivotal partners since the Korean War.

In 1978, I was posted as first secretary to Korea's Permanent Observer Mission to the United Nations in New York. Korea was not yet recognized as a sovereign member state by the UN General Assembly because the recommendation for membership must come from the Security Council. The communist Soviet Union and the People's Republic of China had both threatened to veto the resolution. Although Korea had no vote in any of the UN bodies, our diplomats were always busy, and our time was well spent. I learned the intricacies of the UN system and gained experience in multilateralism that would serve me throughout my career. We prepared carefully for every meeting, energetically lobbying member states to take the "South Korean" position rather than one favoring Pyongyang. North Korea also tried to sway delegations; it was a fierce diplomatic battle without guns.

We would not achieve full membership until September 17, 1991, when the General Assembly simultaneously admitted the Republic of Korea (South Korea) and the Democratic People's Republic of Korea (North Korea). This was a global recognition that the peninsula was now two countries, not one. Despite my sadness that our division was now official, this was one of the most monumental moments in South Korea's history since the end of the war. I joined the celebration for the Koreas' admission to the UN. I thought about my days working as a junior diplomat of an Observer Mission to the UN in the 1970s, and I was proud of my country and my small role in achieving this momentous day.

A ROUNDED EDUCATION

By this time, I often felt I was missing something important for my diplomatic career. I had been working hard as a public servant, but I could not cultivate much vision. I thought I needed to deepen and broaden my intellectual capacity. After having served as director of the UN Division, I wanted to broaden my perspective for my future career.

I discussed my career with then Deputy Minister Gong Ro-myung, who was later appointed foreign minister. He advised me to study abroad and allowed me to apply to graduate schools. I first applied in 1983 to the London School of Economics and Political Science for an international law course. Unfortunately, I was not admitted. They said I did not have enough of a legal background, which may have been partially true, but I had a very good academic record in the international law course at Seoul National University. I next applied to the John F. Kennedy School of Government at Harvard University for a master's degree in public administration, and I was thrilled to be admitted. I earned my master's in public administration from the Harvard Kennedy School in 1984, graduating with the prestigious Littauer Fellow award, a recognition of my academic achievements and contribution to the Harvard community.

I worked hard and was proud of my grades, but I was especially proud of graduating from the school named for my hero, John F. Kennedy. I even earned a nickname at Harvard: "JFK." When I first introduced myself to fellow students, I joked that my name was "JFK—Just From Korea." Everybody laughed. Later, former Dean Graham Allison often introduced me as JFK in forums. When I was elected secretary-general, there were many reports about my meeting with President Kennedy. While I was preparing to assume the position of secretary-general, Senator Edward Kennedy visited me in New York and gave me an unforgettable gift, a picture of me taken with President Kennedy. Under the picture he wrote, "JFK meets JFK." This was a deeply meaningful gift.

During the courses, I participated in the debates with professors and fellow classmates and expressed my views on many global issues. One memorable experience for me was playing the role of Vice President George H. W. Bush in an international crisis game. Professors were firm that the U.S. president would not read any policy memo longer than two pages. It was critical for all students to be able to explain our policy recommendations briefly and to the point! This discipline later helped me a great deal when I served as the national security advisor for two Korean presidents, a foreign minister of Korea, and later as UN secretary-general.

While taking a cross-registered diplomatic history course at the Tufts University Fletcher School of Law and Diplomacy, I challenged the professor's presentation of the history of the Korean War. The professor taught that there were two theories about who started the Korean War, one suggesting southward aggression and the other northward aggression. I raised my hand, asking, "Professor, what do you mean by 'northward aggression'?" It is a historical fact that North Korea began the war against South Korea on June 25, 1950. The UN Security Council adopted a resolution that same day, determining that the attack on the Republic of Korea "constitutes a breach of the peace" and calling upon "North Korea to withdraw their armed forces to the 38th parallel."[1]

The professor said that there could be different historical theories. I challenged him again, saying that these theories could not dispute historical fact. There might be theories, I said, when something happened many thousands of years ago. The argument continued, and I finally challenged him by saying that his presentation about Korea was "biased." The professor, angered and feeling humiliated by me, asked me how he could become unbiased. I asked him to give me the opportunity to explain the situation in detail. Fair and broad-minded, he invited me to give a guest lecture, which I did the following week. After the guest lecture, I visited his office and expressed my regret for challenging him in public, but I could not ignore this error because students might wrongly understand Korean history. He accepted my personal apology.

After graduating from the Kennedy school, I returned to government service. The United States was, of course, our most important ally, and I was appointed consul general in Washington, D.C. from 1987 to 1990. In June 1990, I was unexpectedly appointed director general of the American Affairs Bureau and returned to Seoul. I began to make high-level contacts within the U.S. government, nurturing relationships that would last my entire diplomatic career. I received one of my life's greatest shocks during that time when U.S. intelligence and military officials came to Seoul and organized a briefing of startling depth and clarity—North Korea was pursuing nuclear ambitions. I and everyone around me were momentarily silent when the presentation was over, each of us trying to find holes in the argument or evidence that would refute this horrifying news. But there was none.

DUTY AND RESPONSIBILITY

I worked on the nuclear files as one of five negotiators charged with convincing North Korea to abandon its nuclear ambitions. Heading home on December 30, 1991, after a late evening of nuclear negotiations with the North, I felt like we were making progress, and I was feeling good about our efforts. But when I walked in the door, something was clearly wrong.

My father had been hit and killed by a speeding car while riding a bicycle. His death was unexpected and shocking, and it felt like the sky would collapse and crush me. Momentarily I did not know what to do. My wife and I drove to Chungju to pay our last respects. It was a mentally and emotionally exhausting visit. The first challenge for me was how to handle these very important national affairs in the midst of this great sorrow.

I am a proud public servant and had always put my official duties before personal responsibilities. As the eldest son, however, my traditional responsibilities included arranging the funeral ceremony. My uncle Ban Pil-hwan, the respected deputy mayor of Chong-won County—himself a dedicated lifelong public servant—understood and said he would take care of the funeral arrangements. My uncle urged me to go back to Panmunjom, the "peace village" inside the DMZ where most of our negotiations with the North took place.

I stayed until well past midnight the night of my father's death, and Soon-taek drove all night from Chungju back to Seoul so I would be at Panmunjom early in the morning. She was concerned about my health and hoped I would sleep in the car. I couldn't. I went to the peace village with the other delegates, and late in the evening on that very day, December 31, 1991, delegates from both the North and the South agreed on the historic denuclearization declaration. It came into effect on February 19, 1992. Even now, twenty-eight years after adoption of the declaration, I feel privileged to have had a part in that historic negotiation.

This assignment raised my diplomatic profile, and I was able to expand the scope of my activities, meeting many U.S. government officials and academic leaders who later became a great source of support in my career as vice minister and foreign minister. They also helped secure my ultimate position as UN secretary-general. Kim Young-sam became president the following year, and he appointed me deputy foreign minister for policy planning in 1995 and later for political affairs. He came to trust my judgment and asked me to be his chief of protocol, and then I served as his national security advisor until the end of his presidency.

Korea was a severely wounded victim of the 1997 Asian financial crisis, and initially we had little success negotiating terms for a bailout with the International Monetary Fund (IMF). The Korean deputy prime minister and his team made every effort, but the IMF led by President Michel Camdessus would not budge. He was so implacable that he asked outgoing Korean President Kim Yong-sam to collect written pledges to comply with IMF mandates from all the candidates to succeed him. I saw President Kim's face harden.

President Kim entrusted me, then a national security advisor, to negotiate more acceptable terms with the IMF. I had not been engaged in the negotiations up to this point, and it was awkward for me to enter at the final phase. I did everything within my capacity, but I was not successful. As a result, in December 1997 Seoul signed a humiliating bailout agreement worth nearly $60 billion. The country had been successful for so long that this loan was a shocking symbol of how quickly prosperity could evaporate. The country lost hundreds of thousands of jobs and every community felt the pain. The Korean ship of state was sinking.

Just one year later, in February 1998, under the leadership of the new president, Kim Dae-jung, the entire nation acted as one to clear this debt. Koreans are hardworking and understand sacrifice, but the situation required even more than anyone expected. The government needed gold. When called upon, the Korean people put patriotism before sentiment and brought their jewelry and trinkets to special collection points. I remember almost tearing up as I watched people waiting in long lines to donate war medals and wedding rings to ensure the future of our country.

After very little discussion, Soon-taek and I decided to contribute our own modest wedding rings to save our country. We both believed in Korea and had grown up around countless examples of service and sacrifice. In retrospect, I'm surprised I didn't feel the loss of our rings more deeply. Even today, neither of us wears a wedding band.

It is customary to give a Korean baby a small gold ring on his or her first birthday, a gift we call *doljanchi*, or "anniversary." Doljanchi turned out to be a lifeline for my country as families parted with items whose sentimental value far outweighed their karats. The government collected more than 226 metric tons of gold, which was melted into ingots and sold on the international market. Korea repaid the loan in full in December 2001—four years early.

Kim Dae-jung was internationally admired for his lifelong struggle for democracy and freedom. In fact, he was awarded the 2000 Nobel Peace Prize for his example. He had been imprisoned, tortured, and sentenced to death by South Korea's military regime, but freed under international pressure. He was admired for his lifelong struggle for democracy and freedom. Elected president in 1997, Kim won the 2000 Nobel Prize for his Sunshine Policy to engage North Korea.

For the first time in Korean history, the conservative political atmosphere tilted toward more liberal politics. This did not bode well for me, a prominent conservative diplomat and civil servant. Despite my senior position, I was given a relatively minor post later that year, representing Korea as ambassador to Austria and Slovenia. I was also Korea's permanent representative to the international organizations in Vienna, where I cultivated my diplomatic career in the multilateral diplomatic arena. I presented my credentials to then-UN Secretary-General Kofi Annan through his representative at the UN headquarters in Vienna. A few months after my arrival in Vienna my portfolio expanded again when UN member states elected me chair of the Vienna-based Preparatory Commission for the Comprehensive Nuclear-Test-Ban Treaty Organization (CTBTO). I felt passionate about the work, but I served only twenty months as Korea's ambassador.

In January 2000, President Kim Dae-jung summoned me back to Seoul and appointed me vice foreign minister—the number two person in the entire Korean Ministry of Foreign Affairs. I often participated in cabinet meetings and represented the foreign minister when he was traveling. But the angel was not always smiling for me. Some people say that God might sometimes be jealous of somebody who flies too high or too smoothly. Sure enough, I was caught up in a diplomatic blunder that became a bilateral crisis between the administrations of newly elected U.S. president George H. W. Bush and Kim Dae-jung.

The 1972 Anti-Ballistic Missile Treaty (ABM Treaty) was hailed as a cornerstone of international peace, and Korea had always supported it. Unfortunately, we failed to understand that President Bush had campaigned on abolishing it. On February 27, 2001, in Seoul, President Kim and President Vladimir Putin of Russia issued a joint statement reaffirming the importance of the ABM Treaty. We didn't know that the new Bush administration was about to cancel it, although Moscow certainly did. Several newspapers covered the joint communiqué, warning that Korea, a staunch U.S. ally, was starting to tilt toward Russia.[2] This was an unfortunate mistake. We would never have criticized the United States so publicly. Washington was a vital partner, and a humiliated President Kim was forced to issue a public apology.

It got worse.

President Kim was soon leaving for Washington, D.C., where he was scheduled to meet the newly inaugurated U.S. president for the first time. The White House strongly urged President Kim to delay his visit for at least six months to give President Bush time to get up to speed on major international issues. But President Kim, a Nobel laureate, was anxious to brief or even lecture the new U.S. president before he could change the U.S. position on North Korea. President Bush reluctantly received President Kim early in March, only his second state guest.

At a joint press conference, President Bush told reporters he had a good meeting with "this man," an exceptionally casual way to address a Nobel laureate and senior statesman. The Korean people were infuriated by this perceived slight, and I was sure President Kim must have felt humiliated. The U.S. ambassador to Korea, Thomas Hubbard, had to explain that "this man" was just a plain English phrase, used when addressing friends with affection. Although President Bush was known for his "folksy" nature, the Korean public remained unconvinced.

A BUMPY ENDING AND AN UNIMAGINED FUTURE

As expected, both Foreign Minister Lee Joung-bin and I were dismissed when President Kim returned. It appeared that the president had already decided to fire the two top officials in the Korean Foreign Ministry. I was not offered a diplomatic position, and I found myself without a job for the first time in my life. I was completely unprepared. I had never imagined the financial implications and personal shame of being unemployed at age fifty-six. Many of my friends took me to lunches and dinners to console me during those days, and I admit I tried to ease my pain and anger with drink. Fortunately, that self-defeating phase did not last long. In that dark time, I couldn't have known that getting fired would allow me to take on the most challenging position of my life so far.

Korean Foreign Minister Han Seung-soo had been nominated by UN's Asian Group as the candidate for the presidency of the fifty-sixth UN General Assembly, and he tapped me in mid-2001 to be his chief of staff. I could not have been more surprised and relieved. I had been dismissed from the

Foreign Ministry only four months earlier, and now I had landed squarely in the middle of the most stimulating assignment. Soon-taek and I packed up in June and moved, once again, to Manhattan. My wife enjoyed New York, and I felt a surge of energy and optimism. We quickly settled into a sixteenth-floor apartment at Donald Trump's newly built residential tower across the street from the United Nations.

As the senior-most aide to General Assembly President Han, I oversaw the official calendar, slipped ambassadors in for a quick meeting, and much more. I also painstakingly built support for many of the 512 resolutions the General Assembly (GA) adopted during its fifty-sixth session. I worked from early in the morning until midevening, often stopping by one or even two diplomatic receptions on my way home. Most of these gatherings looked like fancy cocktail parties, but in fact they were hard work. It was possible to strike up a conversation with senior diplomats from a dozen nations in a little more than an hour and discuss a different subject with each one.

I would return home from these receptions with a spinning head and pockets full of business cards. I used these gatherings to meet many ambassadors of all the regions, and in the three months before I officially assumed my job at the GA, I had met most of the important permanent representatives. I couldn't know it then, but this was excellent training for my tenure as secretary-general. About one hundred presidents, prime ministers, and a few monarchs participated in the annual General Assembly debate every September, and I attended many of President Han's meetings.

The United Nations will always have my deepest respect and gratitude for saving my family and so many others from war and famine. The three UN pillars—human rights, peace and security, and development—were also Korea's goals. I had long appreciated the organization as a global meeting place where all nations, including the smallest islands and least-developed countries, had a voice and a vote equal to those of the most influential states. True, the Security Council passed resolutions with the force of international law, but a consensus in the GA carried the moral weight of no other organization. I was grateful for the opportunity to give back.

Shortly after I returned to Seoul in 2003, the newly elected president, Roh Moo-hyun, chose me to be his foreign policy advisor. I received the letter of appointment on the very day of his inauguration. I had never met him, and it was a bit of a surprise for me, a conservative, to be appointed to such a high position by a liberal president. My first meeting with President Roh was a working lunch in the Blue House on the afternoon of his inauguration.

The table was set for four and included the newly appointed chief of staff and the national security advisor. We discussed foreign affairs priorities, including North Korea, the United Nations and, of course, our relationships with the United States, China, and Japan. Although I took part in the conversation with ease and confidence, I marveled to be included in this exclusive meeting, especially with a leader known for his liberal views.

"Thank you for your confidence in me," I told President Roh.

"Have we ever met before?" he asked.

"No," I said, surprised by such a casual question from a Korean president.

"I have been advised by many people to appoint you as foreign minister," he told me in a low voice. "I already have someone in mind. Please work hard. Let us see. Who knows?" I was so stunned, so happy, by this informality that I immediately phoned my wife.

In March 2003, just one month into the Roh presidency, Moody's informed the Korean government that it intended to downgrade Korea's national credit rating by two grades. Kim Jin-pyo, the deputy prime minister and minister of finance and economy, failed to persuade Moody's to spare us this blow. I was again assigned to use my diplomatic skills to convince Moody's—as well as Standard & Poor's and Fitch—not to downgrade Korea's rating. I led the Korean delegation—Lieutenant General Cha Young-koo, deputy defense minister for policy at the Ministry of National Defense; Kwon Tae-shin, director-general at the Ministry of Finance and Economy; and Choi Jong-ku, director general of International Finance and Economy (MOFE)—to New York to meet Moody's executives in person. We were an able group; Kwon later became minister of government policy coordination in the prime minister's office, and Choi became chairman (ministerial) of the Financial Services Commission.

I explained that downgrading Korea's credit rating on the ground that the economy is struggling will only further damage our ability to recover. Moreover, the downgrade would impact Korea's external credit and capacity for national security. This, in turn, could compromise the U.S.-Korea strategic alliance. My team also met with Standard & Poor's and even flew to Hong Kong to make our case with Fitch. We also met the CEOs of Lehman Brothers and Goldman Sachs. While we were in Hong Kong, Moody's informed us that it no longer planned to downgrade Korea's credit rating. Our team members jumped up and down and embraced each other, and I felt a big sigh of relief. I felt immensely proud that the Korean ship of state was saved once again.

Although I was not one of President Roh's closest aides, I tried to have direct access to him as often as possible. I briefed him on a number of sensitive issues, usually in private. We discussed a host of diplomatic issues, in particular, Korea-U.S. relations. After only one month in office, the president asked me to be his "private tutor," and I did my best to "educate" him about Korea's relationship with the United States, China, Japan, and Russia, providing detailed historical background and perspectives. He was particularly interested in positioning Korea among the major powers surrounding the peninsula. On several occasions, in senior meetings included ministers, the president referred me as "a walking dictionary," a "genius," and a "Jack of all trades," making it clear that I was one of his favorites. I was a bit worried that the president's confidence would make officials uncomfortable with me, but in fact his remarks strengthened my status and enabled my voice to be heard by other senior advisors in the Blue House.

My diplomatic efforts must have made a lasting impression on President Roh because he appointed me foreign minister on January 17, 2004, in recognition of my thirty-four years of service to Korea. It was an immense honor, and I believe he recalled visiting the United Nations three years earlier, where I was widely known for my General Assembly position.

TRAGEDY IN IRAQ

I was only foreign minister for five months when the country experienced a tragic foreign policy crisis. Kim Sun-Il, a Christian missionary, had gone to Iraq in early 2003 to work as a Korean-Arabic interpreter for Gana General Trading Company, one of the many Korean suppliers to U.S. military camps. Shortly after he arrived in Iraq, Islamic militants were alerted to his evangelical activities. Apostasy is a terrible offense in Islam, and his efforts to convert Iraqis was a grave mistake indeed. In fact, I don't think he should ever have been sent overseas. On May 30, 2004, Kim was kidnapped by Islamic militants who threatened to behead him unless Seoul removed 660 Korean troops from the country and canceled our commitment to send three thousand more. Although his employer knew about his abduction, the company waited several weeks to inform our small consular staff in Baghdad. Most of us learned about Mr. Kim's kidnapping only in late June. On June 21, Al Jazeera aired a videotape of Kim, blindfolded and frantically pleading for his life. Islamic militants favored the Arab-language cable news network, and I later learned they had sent the organization all manner of monstrosities.

The Korean people were shocked by the utter barbarity of the threat. The video—so personal, so anguishing to watch—generated an uproar. At least a dozen TV news crews set up in the Kim family's house, where his elderly parents wept and displayed a graduation picture of their son. I immediately dispatched a senior ambassador-at-large to Iraq, Chang Jae-ryong, a former deputy foreign minister, but he was too late. The following day, the militants dressed Kim in an orange jumpsuit, the same one Guantanamo prisoners wear, and beheaded him on camera. Ambassador Chang was still in air when it happened.

U.S. officials had tried to intervene but did not have the contacts to reach the group. A U.S. Army patrol found Kim's desecrated body in a bag on the main road between Fallujah and Baghdad. A State Department official informed us immediately, and the slain interpreter's house was besieged by mourners and media. The horror was not over. Al Jazeera soon informed us that they had received the grisly tape of Kim's murder, but they promised not to broadcast the final moments. In fact, we were scheduled to send a military division to northern Iraq in just a few months, and the murder rattled Korean support for the deployment. Nonetheless, the majority of the people supported our modest presence in Iraq and believed we should continue to expand our participation. Although this was difficult and controversial, President Roh vowed to deploy our troops.

Criticism of the government was rising hour by hour, particularly in the foreign media, and I thought I should resign to quiet the public sentiments. On Sunday morning, I contacted the presidential residence and asked for a brief meeting with President Roh Moo-hyun. Unexpectedly, the Blue House was quite quick to arrange a meeting. That morning I offered President Roh my resignation, which I hoped would spare the government some of the loud criticisms. I told him I didn't want this episode to tarnish his administration.

But the president said he did not think Kim's death was my fault. He admitted that several close aides had advised him to fire me, or at least to reassign me. "If you were the foreign minister," the president challenged them, "what would you have done to save Kim?" I never belonged to the president's inner circle, mostly liberal-leaning politicians and policy experts twenty years younger than I was. But this was one of many times that I felt the president respected my experience and judgment, and I was reassured by his confidence.

Chapter Three

ELECTION OF THE SECRETARY-GENERAL

Seeking a Mandate to Lead

The four steps to the General Assembly podium would soon become effortlessly familiar, but on December 14, 2006, when I was sworn in as the eighth secretary-general of the United Nations, they seemed unusually steep. My breath was shallow, but my hands were steady. I took the oath of office with my hand on a copy of the UN Charter, the first secretary-general to do so. As only seven men had done before me, I promised to serve the institution with loyalty, conscience, and discretion.

I believe wholeheartedly in the UN Charter, and I had read it so many times during my diplomatic career that I had almost memorized it. I vowed to myself that I would "reaffirm faith in fundamental human rights, in the dignity and worth of the human person, in the equal rights of men and women and of nations large and small."[1] As I stood before the soaring gold leaf wall emblazoned with the emblem of the United Nations, I promised member states that I would focus my aspirations on improving the world we live in and the organization I would now be leading:

> I have witnessed at first hand the high level of professionalism, dedication, and know-how that exists throughout the United Nations. Armed with that knowledge, I look forward even more to working with the able and courageous men and women who serve this organization every day, often in difficult circumstances, sometimes in dangerous ones.

I gazed out over the vast chamber, imagining the weight of the matters that are brought here for resolution, for renewal, for action, for justice. I vowed to invigorate and challenge the UN staff, uphold the highest ethics and standards, and strengthen the three pillars of the organization: security, development, and human rights. I wanted member states to expect new life, new energy, and new ideas from my administration. I wanted to reestablish trust after years of allegations. I asked them for their patience and support:

> We cannot change everything at once. But we can build progress in a few areas, and so make way for progress in many more. That will require intensive and continuous dialogue. It will require us to work together transparently, flexibly, and honestly. And it will require us to start with an open mind. Today, I ask both colleagues and member states to work with me in that spirit. You have the right to expect the same of me.

Kofi Annan, the outgoing secretary-general, was sitting on the high dais behind me. He had restored urgency and vitality to the United Nations, and the respect and affection people felt for him was genuine. Soft-spoken and charismatic, he was awarded a Nobel Peace Prize, created the Millennium Development Goals, and defied the United States by trying to prevent and then criticizing its 2003 invasion of Iraq. The job requires the support of members states, not just diplomacy and will, and no one could do this job perfectly. The UN under Kofi Annan became ensnared in the boondoggle of the Iraq oil-for-food program, and his valiant effort to reform the UN human rights body was derailed by the despotic regimes that won seats. Nonetheless, I deeply admired his lifelong commitment to the United Nations and its ideals. Speaking directly to him, I said:

> You have led the organization through challenging times and ushered it firmly into the twenty-first century. You have given the United Nations new relevance to the people's lives.[2]

My speech lasted only about twenty minutes, less time than it took for me and my wife to leave the General Assembly chambers. The aisle between us and the exit was lined with ambassadors who were eager to shake my hand, offer congratulations, and pledge their support. Photographers jostled and cameras flashed.

We had scaled the distance from rural Chungju to the General Assembly. We had come so far.

OPPORTUNITY KNOCKS

My road to the post of UN secretary-general began in January 2004, when I was appointed foreign minister by President Roh Mu-hyun. Seoul had been weighing whether to contest for the secretary-general's post or seek a nonpermanent seat on the UN Security Council. Eventually, the government decided to field a South Korean to succeed Kofi Annan on December 31, 2006. I was not their favorite candidate.

In early 2006, after long and heated discussions among top-level Korean ambassadors and advisors, the Korean government decided to withdraw its candidacy for a nonpermanent seat in the Security Council despite significant support from member states. We thought we might have another chance later for the Security Council seat, but it seemed like the last and the only chance for a Korean citizen to be elected secretary-general of the UN. By custom, we could not simultaneously contest for the Security Council seat and the office of the secretary-general. This job, among others, is passed around the world on the basis of an informal principle of geographic rotation, and there was almost unanimous agreement that it was "Asia's turn."

By 2005, two or three former foreign ministers and an influential newspaper publisher were among those lobbying under the radar to be chosen by the Blue House as Korea's candidate for the UN job. Hong Seok-hyun, publisher of the influential daily *Joong-ang Ilbo*, was rumored to be the administration's favorite, and he had been installed as ambassador to the United States to give him some diplomatic experience before the campaign. When an inner circle politician came to see me and proposed appointing Hong as Korea's ambassador to Washington, I was surprised but recommended him to President Roh. This influential politician, a cabinet minister at that time, later insisted that Hong be nominated as a candidate for the next UN secretary-general. I strongly disagreed, arguing that it was not right in principle and was discourteous to the U.S. government. In my next private meeting with President Roh, he did not mention Hong as a candidate for the UN post.

Unfortunately, Ambassador Hong was soon implicated in a slush fund scandal and forced to resign as ambassador. Over the next several months, for reasons political or personal, the remaining Korean candidates dropped out, and there was no one left. It reminded me of the Confucian saying, "A large mountain with no one climbing it." Soon after Hong was summoned back to Korea for a criminal investigation, President Roh invited me to a breakfast meeting for a tête-à-tête. He suggested that I assume the ambassadorship in Washington and consider being a candidate for the secretary-general's post.

It was totally unexpected, and I momentarily had no idea how to answer. I warned him that a Korean candidate would have only a slim chance of becoming secretary-general because we have a military alliance with the United States, which could draw a veto from China or Russia. I shifted the conversation back to the ambassadorship, telling the president I would, of course, accept the assignment to Washington. I also cautioned him that Korea should consider changing its usual practices of sending high-powered former ministers and political leaders to Washington because the U.S. government normally treats foreign ambassadors at the rank of assistant secretary of state or occasionally undersecretary of state, but no higher. Some of our former prime ministers or foreign ministers have been frustrated by their limited role. President Roh immediately understood and asked me to stay on as foreign minister. We agreed to discuss the candidacy issue later.

I could not quite get the idea out of my mind. The secretary-general of the United Nations is, effectively, the voice of morality and peace. The secretary-general must behave impeccably in all professional and personal dealings and hold himself and all around him to the highest principles of peace, human rights, and development. As the world's top diplomat, he (and someday she) maintains political neutrality while trying to resolve international disputes that lead to conflict. There is no job description, but the job has hundreds of responsibilities. In addition, the secretary-general must have administrative skills to run an organization with headquarters on every continent, six official languages, and at least a dozen peace operations at any one time.

I was cautious, even pessimistic, that Korea would continue to contest for the secretary-general job, but if Seoul was still interested, I began to honestly consider whether I could become a candidate. I felt more cautious than confident, but I knew I could serve as a bridge between nations, having learned so much as Korea developed from a war-wracked country to an industrialized nation in record time. Why try? What did I think I could bring to the job, to the UN, and to the world?

President Roh gave his first speech to the General Assembly September 14, 2005, on the occasion of the sixtieth anniversary of the United Nations.[3] Roh considered the visit his official duty, but I was looking forward to walking the building again and seeing familiar faces. As it happened, this was a pivotal day for me. My president saw how many foreign ministers, ambassadors, and even UN staff greeted me warmly. No one seemed to recognize President Roh until I introduced him. He was often alone, and it was awkward.

Later that day President Roh and I were in his limousine creeping along in clogged traffic. It is usually a ten-minute drive between the United Nations and the Waldorf Astoria Hotel, but during UN events such as the annual General Debate, hundreds of police officers block streets and impose checkpoints. Normally we would be discussing speeches and our contacts with other dignitaries, assessing who would be our likely allies on North Korea–related issues. But President Roh was unusually quiet. To fill the silence, I explained that the dump trucks parked around the UN campus were filled with wet sand to block attackers and, if necessary, absorb the blast waves of a car bomb. UN security is always a dramatic topic, but I was not sure he was even listening. He had already seen the bomb-sniffing dogs and the crush of bodyguards. Although we weren't supposed to notice them, I pointed out the sharp shooters on nearby roofs and undercover officers lining the route.

"Minister Ban," he said, "will you run for the post of secretary-general? I would strongly support your candidacy."

I was not expecting this extraordinary moment. Not now. I felt surprised, excited, and light of heart. My heart and breath jolted me. Then my ego quickly chimed in, telling me I had been redeemed and was being rewarded for my service. The Blue House valued me, trusted me, and I reveled in this pride. I strive to be humble, but I admit that I liked this feeling. I experienced conflicting emotions, but I had no doubt about my answer.

"It would be my honor," I said, with the formality the moment required.

I was elated but not sure how much of a chance I would have, a Korean coming from a divided nation, and one with a military alliance with the United States. However, I thought I had no alternative but to proceed. "I will accept your offer, but will you let me stay in New York for a few days? I need to stay here and touch water," I said. This is a Korean expression that means sounding out the bigger powers. He immediately agreed, and my mind was already racing toward a strategy.

"I suggest we keep this confidential, don't announce it," I said. "Not until I test the temperatures of key member states." The most important soundings I would take were, of course, the five permanent members of the Security Council, whose vetoes could crush my candidacy. Fortunately, I had good relations with most of the ambassadors dating back to my days in the General Assembly.

I knew that Korea already had two strikes against it: The country was both bitterly divided between the South and North, and the South was a close military ally of the United States. The connection to Washington would trouble many capitals, particularly Moscow and Beijing. In addition, I was worried that we were getting a late start in a crowded field. The earliest and most promising candidate at that moment was Thailand's deputy prime minister Surakiart Sathirathai, who had been chosen by ten nations to be the consensus candidate of the Association of South East Asian Nations (ASEAN).[4]

At the presidential suite, I asked President Roh to speak to presidents George Bush of the United States, Hu Jintao of China, and Vladimir Putin of Russia. These three leaders were to visit Korea to participate in the upcoming Asia-Pacific Economic Cooperation (APEC) summit in Busan that November, and their support was vital to any candidate.

When I returned to Korea, I told Soon-taek that I had been asked to stand as Korea's candidate for secretary-general. My wife is always calm and did not say much in response to this news. She is in all things gentle and supportive. Soon-taek had been with me through thirty-five years of foreign service, and I was grateful for her acceptance. Nonetheless, I was already thinking about how much our lives would change. They would possibly even be endangered.

I reflected later that she must have been feeling happy, or glad, but also concerned. Neither of us discussed the subject again for some time.

THE CAMPAIGN BEGINS

The Security Council nominates one candidate to the General Assembly, whose members traditionally ratify the choice after little debate. Although the Charter does not say this, those fifteen nations—or, more specifically, the five members with veto power—choose the secretary-general. The process has never been fair, and by the end of my term as secretary-general, discussions had intensified to begin reforming this process.

After the talking with President Roh, I immediately began my own consultations with the United States, starting with UN Ambassador John Bolton whom I had known for years. I explained my vision as a candidate, including my pledge for reform, and emphasized the importance of American support. Ambassador Bolton, the unusually plain-spoken U.S. ambassador from 2005 to 2006, responded positively. He welcomed a candidate of such high stature and would immediately report to Secretary of State Condoleezza Rice, who was still in New York. I felt a chill of anticipation. This was real.

The following day I requested a tête-à-tête with Secretary of State Condoleezza Rice, and we met in private the following afternoon. She said she had received favorable recommendations from Ambassador Bolton. "You know the position of the U.S. government is not to say anything in public about the election of the secretary-general. But you have my full confidence," Secretary Rice said with characteristic poise. She advised me to reach out and get support from other member states. We agreed to keep our discussion confidential, with the unspoken understanding that announcing U.S. support too soon would be a strategic blunder—normally called "the kiss of death."

While in New York, I reached out to the foreign ministers or deputy ministers of the five permanent members of the Security Council. Russian Foreign Minister Sergei Lavrov, whom I had known since 2001 when he was the UN ambassador, said with an unreadable poker face that he would not oppose my candidacy. French Foreign Minister Philippe Douste-Blazy was attentive to my overtures but reserved. He recommended I learn French, saying that his government had never supported any candidate who does not speak "the language of diplomacy." In fact French and English are the two "working languages" of the UN Secretariat, and Paris has made proficiency, if not fluency, a requirement of sorts. Despite some lessons thirty years ago, I was not able to express myself in French and immediately hired a French tutor when I returned to Korea.

Having gone through initial consultations with the P5 (the permanent members of the Security Council), I reported to President Roh that I was cautiously optimistic about our chances but wanted to keep news of my candidacy strictly confidential. I discussed the matter with the head of the National Security Council, Lee Chong-suk, seeking his support. He agreed to keep my candidacy a secret for the time being, but he soon met the Foreign Ministry press corps and told reporters that the president had nominated me as an official candidate and placed a strict embargo on the news. I was impressed that media honored this request for the full four months until the announcement. I personally contacted all the diplomatic staff reporters and senior editors in several rounds of meetings, asking for their cooperation in keeping the news under wraps.

I felt that quiet diplomacy was still the most effective strategy at this stage. I also knew instinctively, from my lifetime in public service, that the first man up the ladder is the easiest to attack. That philosophy was not widely shared. The thirty-four members of the Asia Cooperation Dialogue (ACD) agreed to field a consensus candidate at the June 21–22, 2004, ministerial meeting in Qingdao, China. That's interesting, I thought, mentally assessing my competition. Thai Prime Minister Thaksin Shinawatra said he would "sacrifice" himself by releasing Foreign Minister Surakiart to be the common Asian candidate. That was an unwelcome surprise and a direct threat to my largely unknown aspirations. But I was not yet an official candidate, and no one would have thought to look for my reaction. I was embarrassed and crestfallen, but I refused to show any response that would arouse the interest of anyone around me.

It was clear that the Thai foreign minister was getting off to a fast start, and no one else had declared a candidacy. I thought again about the first man up the ladder and realized that a stealthy start was even more important than I thought! Prime Minister Thaksin's proposal received enthusiastic applause, and right in front of Chinese Prime Minister Wen Jiabao! By prematurely presenting Minister Surakiart as a fait accompli candidate, I thought the Thai government was trying to win the support of extremely influential Beijing.

Immediately after the opening ceremony, the foreign ministers gathered in a closed meeting. When the chairman proposed endorsing Surakiart as the Asian consensus candidate, Foreign Minister S. Jayakumar said Singapore agreed with Prime Minister Thaksin's proposal to present a consensus Asian candidate but suggested choosing that person later. His own country, he added, might have a candidate. The rest quickly agreed to delay the decision.

In December 2005, I was in Slovenia to participate in the ministerial meeting of the Organization for Security and Co-operation in Europe. I was delighted to see Luxembourg Foreign Minister Jean Asselborn, who kindly introduced me to a number of European foreign ministers. I was quite encouraged by their responses.

There is a breathtakingly beautiful church on a small island in the middle of Lake Bled, with a bell in a very tall tower. Ring the bell, the legend goes, and your dearest wish will come true. The catch is that the bell is on the end of a very heavy loose rope, and the only way to ring it is by using the right proportion of strength and balance. As my host, Foreign Minister Dimitrij Rupel, looked on, I took a deep breath and heaved that rope with all my mental and physical courage. When I heard the deep peel, I knew I had a good chance of success.

Just three weeks before I announced my candidacy, as a courtesy, I sent personal letters to the foreign ministers of all UN member states except

North Korea informing them of my candidacy and seeking their support. Many ministers expressed their appreciation and encouragement. The news embargo was lifted with an official announcement of my candidacy on February 14, 2006.[5] Surprisingly, this was not big news in Korea. As foreign minister, I nearly had to break the news myself, but the government decided to tell reporters at the ministry's weekly press briefing. Vice Foreign Minister Yu Myung-hwan announced that I was Korea's candidate and then turned the room over to me. I had a few brief remarks prepared.

> The Republic of Korea established its government with the help of the UN, and since then our country has developed into an exemplary nation which has realized the settlement of peace, security, economic development, democracy, and human rights, all of which are the ideals and goals pursued by the UN.

Then I pivoted to the news from North Korea.

GAINING MOMENTUM

The first European endorsement came from German Foreign Minister Frank-Walter Steinmeier, who later became the president of Germany. He publicly announced his country's support during a joint press conference in Korea on February 19, 2006. I was overjoyed—it was only five days after Seoul had announced my candidacy. Germany works closely with the United Nations and enjoys excellent relations with South Korea. At home, we often say the Germans and Koreans have the same work ethic. I hoped Germany's diplomatic and political weight would influence other European governments.

Weeks later President Islam Karimov of Uzbekistan pledged his support during a state visit to Korea. He even offered to recommend my candidacy to the Russian president Putin. But the Russian position was not clear, and the messages coming from Moscow were mixed. Thai Prime Minister Thaksin had recently visited Putin seeking his endorsement, but it was impossible to know whether he was successful. During a state visit to Korea in November 2005, President Putin told President Roh that he had already endorsed Surakiart. Russia would be supportive, "if the situation changed," he said. I was disappointed, but I also knew that President Putin kept his opinions quiet and his options open.

Smart and gregarious, Surakiart was endorsed by the ASEAN countries, but I had a feeling that the group's support was not solid. I had heard from several foreign ministers who were not enthusiastic about the gregarious Thai, even though they showed solidarity with the others in the bloc.

Korean President Roh paid a state visit to Egypt in March 2006, and during a joint press conference President Hosni Mubarak said his country would support my candidacy, and that news spread quickly among both Arab and North African blocs. Algerian President Abdelaziz Bouteflika's and Nigerian President Olusegun Obasanjo's subsequent support was also a boost.

Despite outward appearances, I was not blind to the United Nations' shortcomings and outright failures. Many constituents had lost faith in the organization, frustrated or furious with peacekeeping's deficiencies, seemingly toothless resolutions, and the perceptions of waste, fraud, and mismanagement. I knew there was a tremendous amount of work to do. Yet optimism came naturally to me, and this made me feel that perhaps I was the right candidate for the job. Korea was a model country, rising quickly from the ashes to become a member of the Organization for Economic Cooperation and Development (OECD).

I spent much of 2006 flying between individual capitals and arranging for state visits by leaders who wanted to visit Korea. My schedule was hectic. On one memorable six-day trip, I traveled from Tokyo to Lima, Buenos Aires, Auckland, and Canberra and then back to Seoul. Prime Minister Helen Clark of New Zealand, whom I would later appoint as administrator of the UN Development Program, one of the organization's largest agencies, met me at the Auckland airport when I was transiting to Australia. I was deeply moved by her courtesy.

I refined my campaign pledges around these issues: make the United Nations more efficient, effective, and transparent; address climate change; seek a solution for the atrocities in Darfur; and focus on extreme poverty by extending the Millennium Development Goals, which were set to expire in 2015. I emphasized the protection of civilians during wartime by championing the International Criminal Court and advocating for the Responsibility to Protect, which holds governments legally and morally responsible to protect civilians from gross human rights violations.

To overcome reservations about my nationality, I spoke about Korea's transformation from crushing postwar poverty to a thriving and peaceful democracy. Korea fully shared the challenges of the poor developing countries, and this history helped me understand how to bridge the gap between the developed and the developing world. I was steeped in its lessons, and I told many foreign ministers about my own experience as a young boy in a war-torn country. I had watched with awe as foreign countries and organizations raced to support our reconstruction after the devastating occupation by Japan and war with North Korea aided by China. At the same time, my government took steps to ease rural poverty and move the nation from agrarian poverty to the economic expansion of industrialization. Korea was the only country that had moved from abject poverty to become an OECD country. I emphasized Korea's unique experience and said that I and my country would be bridge builders between the rich and the poor.

By now there were two other Asian candidates for the job of secretary-general: Surakiart Sathirathi, who had been promoted to the post of Thailand's deputy prime minister, and Sri Lankan diplomat Jayantha Dhanapala, who served as the undersecretary general for disarmament affairs. Shashi Tharoor, an Indian author and longtime UN official, joined soon afterward. The well-respected Jordanian ambassador and former UN peacekeeper Prince Zeid Raad al-Hussein was briefly an early favorite. Years later I appointed him to be the UN High Commissioner for Human Rights. Zeid is highly admired (now one of the Elders) and was widely considered a high-performing high commissioner. Thailand's candidate, Surakiart Sathirathi, was the only one that felt like a real rival to me at that time. Tharoor and Dhanapala did not have the strong support of their governments and perhaps overestimated the appeal of their UN service to world leaders.

Eastern Europe, which is not technically a UN bloc, coalesced around Latvian President Vaira Vike-Freiberga. She wasn't from Asia, but she was the only woman to contest at a time when drafting a female secretary-general was starting to gain currency. She was positioned as a protest vote. U.S. Ambassador John Bolton must have emboldened the region when, speaking on behalf of the United States, he told reporters, "It is our view that we should pick the best qualified person, whatever region of the world the person comes from."[6]

The final candidate to declare his interest was former World Bank official Ashraf Ghani of Afghanistan. He did not place well, but he was elected president of Afghanistan just a few years later. At the time, President Hamid Karzai assured me of his continued support and indicated that he didn't have much confidence in the official Afghan nominee.

As I began my formal campaign, I first approached the former secretaries-general Perez de Cuellar of Peru and Boutros Boutros-Ghali of Egypt. The latter gave me invaluable advice for achieving and carrying out the role of the world's top diplomat. Boutros-Ghali advised me to attend regional summits, and he introduced me to Amr Moussa, the shrewd and long-serving secretary general of the League of Arab States. He personally invited me to the group's next summit meeting and, of course, I went.

Taking Boutros-Ghali's advice, I then called on the African Union chairman, Alpha Omar Konaré, the respected former president of Mali.

"Mr. Minister," he said. "I understand you are in the running to be the eighth UN secretary-general." He looked pleased.

"Mr. President," I answered. "That's true, and although there are many able candidates in the field, I would like to ask for your support." We spoke about my chances and Korea's role as a bridge between African nations and developed countries.

"Of course, you won't have time to travel to all the African capitals," Mr. Konaré said, promising to mobilize African support for my candidacy. He then invited me to address the upcoming African Union summit. It is impossible to achieve anything in the UN General Assembly without the support of the African and Arab states, whose membership numbered a slightly overlapping 53 and 21 votes out of 191. Knowing them both well is crucial.

At the invitation of Secretary General Moussa, I attended the League of Arab States summit in Khartoum, Sudan, in March 2006. I found this trip energizing rather than exhausting as well as very efficient. It would have been impossible to travel to each country to meet each leader separately, and asking for a government's support does not have to take a full day. I prepared for the meeting and addressed their issues as I made my case for their vote.

I expected the other candidates for secretary-general to be at the meeting. When I entered the conference room, I saw a line of chairs in the front with the names of the candidates. Although momentarily disappointed to find that I was not the only one invited, as I sat and waited for my rivals, I grew curious about their absence. Who would fail to engage with the Arab nations? What could be more important? Chairman Omar al Bashir, the Sudanese president, announced that the summit would listen to the visions of the candidates for UN secretary-general, but I was the only one to present my ideas. I still vividly remember the embarrassment on the face of Amr Moussa when the chairman kept calling the names of the candidates. The Sudanese strongman would later fight me ferociously over the creation of a peace operation in Darfur, and in 2009 he was indicted by the International Criminal Court for genocide.

In my official capacity as foreign minister of Korea, I met with presidents, prime ministers, and foreign ministers, and these leaders complained that other candidates had not come. More than one questioned their respect for the Arab League and said, "You are our candidate! You have our support."

The scene was quite different during the African Union's July 2006 summit in The Gambia. Having heard what had happened in Khartoum, all the candidates came to Banjul.

Talking to Beijing was the most delicate of my discussions. China had supported the North during the most brutal offensives of the Korean War. Our nations had only established diplomatic relations in 1992, and economic ties were growing. Both governments had been trying to keep relations smooth. I traveled to China's capital on June 27, 2006, and asked Chinese Foreign Minister Li Zhaoxing for his government's support. It would be a key endorsement because China was a powerful member of the Security Council and had significant influence in Asia. As I had expected, Minister Li did not give me clear encouragement. During the meeting, I quietly said, "I understand you are favorably considering the Thai candidate, but I would appreciate it if you also support me whenever an opportunity arises."

Minister Li's demeanor was impossible to read. "We welcomed his candidacy," he told me. "Welcome is different from support." I heard the message and felt relieved.

After the formal meeting, the minister steered me into a private corner and presented me with a most meaningful gift: a bronze statue of Pegasus with a small bird under one of its feet. "This is a flying horse," Minister Li said quietly."It flies so fast and high, it can catch even a flying swallow. Please keep this in your office when you are elected secretary-general." The Chinese consider Pegasus to be a symbol of wisdom and fame. I was deeply moved by such a subtle expression of support. Of course, I gave the statue pride of place in my official UN residence and enjoyed explaining the story to visitors.

I was optimistic for a number of reasons. I knew I had made a positive impression as a diplomat and a crisis manager. Five years earlier, during a brief UN duty, I had shepherded through the General Assembly a resolution condemning the September 11 attacks. I knew the Republic of Korea was well thought of, and I made many high-level contacts as foreign minister. However, there were some unfounded allegations that South Korea was trying to buy votes for me through official development assistance (ODA) to the world's poorest countries.

I was deeply concerned and angry. Believing that one of my opponents might be playing a dirty trick, I asked the Korean ambassador to the UN, Choi Young-jin, to call the reporter who broke the story. I met with Colum

Lynch, the *Washington Post* UN correspondent, and explained the longtime policies of the Korean government not to interfere in this way. He understood the allegations were not credible, and the story died down.

Security Council members conducted their nonbinding first straw poll on July 24, 2006. I was in Singapore and received a call at 5:20 a.m. from the Security Council president, Ambassador Jean-Marc de La Sablière of France. He informed me in French that I had received twelve "encourage," one "discourage," and two "no opinion expressed." He repeated in English the number twelve to make sure I understood. I was excited to be the frontrunner.

But who had cast the negative vote?

Japanese Foreign Minister Tarō Asō, who later served as prime minister, assured me that his government had cast a vote of encouragement. But many people suspected that Japan had cast the negative vote. In his 2007 memoir, *Surrender Is Not an Option*, U.S. Ambassador John Bolton stated that Tokyo had cast the vote of discouragement. The Japanese government was embarrassed. When Ambassador Yukio Takasu requested that Bolton correct the error, the American diplomat retorted that he was in the room at the time, saw the vote, and invited Ambassador Takasu to write his own memoir.

The results of the first straw poll follow; the numbers are, respectively, encourage: discourage: no opinion expressed.[7]

Ban Ki-moon (Republic of Korea)	12:1:2
Shashi Tharoor (India)	10:2:3
Surakiart Sathirati	(Thailand) 7:3:5
Jayantha Dhanapala (Sri Lanka)	5:6:4

The results exceeded my expectations. I was the latecomer, but I was now the frontrunner. The path to the UN secretary-general's thirty-eighth floor office began to glimmer into focus. But I could not get rid of the worry that the negative vote had come from a permanent member of the Security Council. It was rumored that Shashi Tharoor did not enjoy the Indian government's support, but the fact that he received ten votes made me anxious. I was sure that the "no opinion expressed" came from Peru because President-elect Alan García had asked the incumbent, Alejandro Toledo Manrique, to abstain until the presidential inauguration. In fact, President Toledo gave me his full support in person when I visited him in Peru.

WHITE HOUSE SUPPORT

I was in Washington, D.C. with President Roh on September 14 when the Greek ambassador, Adamantios Vassilakis—September's president of the Security Council, a position that rotates monthly—phoned to tell me that I had received fourteen "encourage" votes and one "discourage" in that morning's poll.[8] It was an overwhelming result, and if not for the one "discourage" vote, I would have been officially elected that day!

Ban Ki-moon (Republic of Korea) 14:1:0
Shashi Tharoor (India) 10:3:2
Surakiart Sathirati (Thailand) 9:3:3
Jayantha Dhanapala (Sri Lanka) 3:5:7
Prince Zeid al-Raad al-Hussein (Jordan) 6:4:5

My spirits soared, even as I wondered which country had cast the "discourage" vote. If, as some thought, it was the UK or France, that would severely undermine my chances.

When President Roh and I stepped inside the Oval Office, President Bush greeted me warmly, saying," I wish you good luck. I am closely following you. You know what I mean." He must have been briefed about the results of the second straw poll that morning:

Once we were settled in the Oval Office, President Roh asked for Washington's endorsement. "He is a good man," President Bush said. "I hope he will be elected. I think he will be elected." Then he asked me, "Why do you want to do the most difficult job in the world?"

Although the question was asked lightly, I explained my vision to build a more stable, peaceful world. This was a private audience with President Bush, along with Vice President Dick Cheney, Secretary of State Condi Rice, Defense Secretary Donald Rumsfeld, National Security Advisor Stephen Hadley, and some other officials. Having heard my presentation, President Bush declared, "You are the right man. He is our candidate!"

Personally, I was honored when President Bush put his hand over my shoulder and led me to the door. But I tried to take his hand off my shoulder and told him to walk with President Roh, who was following behind. It was embarrassing for me because I felt it was disrespectful to President Roh. As usual, President Bush paid no attention. "You did a remarkable job,"

President Roh told me as we walked out of the White House. Despite the chill, my coat was unbuttoned. I was walking on air. It felt like a golden day for my future.

Two weeks later, Ambassador Bolton telephoned to say that there had been a meeting of the foreign ministers of the Council's five permanent members before the third straw poll and that the P5 foreign ministers had agreed to elect me as the next secretary-general. According to a U.S. diplomat who attended the small meeting at the Waldorf Astoria Hotel during the General Assembly, Secretary Rice suggested that they agree on a candidate. She asked Chinese Foreign Minister Li Zhaoxing to start. Minister Li, without hesitation, said China would support Ban Ki-moon, to which Condoleezza Rice agreed. The remaining permanent members concurred.

DISSENT, HAPPINESS, AND DISAPPOINTMENT

The results of the third straw poll, conducted on September 28, were a disappointing surprise. I received only thirteen "encourage" votes and one each for "discourage" and "no opinion expressed."[9] I could not understand what had happened. However, I was the only candidate who received more than the nine-vote minimum to win. The other candidates had lost votes: Shashi Tharoor had eight votes, losing two positive votes, and Surakiart, stung by his support of Thailand's recent military coup, received only five votes.

Just before the vote went to an excruciating fourth straw poll, I learned that France had cast the vote against me. As a veto-wielding council member, that vote would have killed my candidacy. My French was getting good by this point, and I was tempted to use it. I telephoned Foreign Minister Phillip Douste-Blazy to ask—in English—for an explanation. He asked me outright to appoint a French national to head the UN Department of Peacekeeping Operations, an important, highly visible job that Secretary-General Annan had filled with a succession of Frenchmen. France had taken the lead on peacekeeping in part because they still had good relations with many former African colonies, as well as the nations that host, contribute, or support UN troops. Also, they are a P5 member and were in a position to make demands.

Nonetheless, I was uncomfortable with the assumption that Paris had a lock on any position. Perhaps my reticence made me play a stronger hand. I responded that I was just a candidate and that he should elect me secretary-general. Then I would consider his request. I ultimately won the support of France and did, in fact, choose three consecutive Frenchmen to run the peacekeeping operation. I retained Jean-Marie Guéhenno and appointed Alain Le Roy and Hervé Ladsous, and all of them did an exemplary job.

On October 2, I received fourteen "encourage" votes and one "no opinion expressed." The others withdrew their candidacies, assuring my success.[10] After nearly thirty-seven years in diplomacy, I was poised to win what was widely known as the most impossible job on Earth. I often think I have a wooden heart. My mild reaction on that night would disappoint many, but I am stoic by nature. It was not like you see in the movies, with jumping and dancing, I just quietly accepted the news. My children, in their homes in the United States and Africa, called to congratulate me. My wife was by my side, and I knew she was proud.

Many South Koreans were excited by this news, which we learned shortly after midnight, in the first hour of our National Foundation Day. Korean media carried large headlines, but my news was quickly overtaken by events. At 6 o'clock that evening, North Korea announced it would soon test its first nuclear weapon. I felt more concerned than celebratory. I was horrified by the development, and regretted that it happened on such a happy day.

A TOUGH BEGINNING

One week later, on October 9, Pyongyang detonated its first nuclear weapon, jeopardizing peace and security on the Korean Peninsula. People everywhere were shocked by this terrible development. The world had suddenly become a much more dangerous place.

Later that night I watched the Security Council meeting, and its members unanimously nominated me to succeed Kofi Annan as secretary-general of the United Nations. After the president for the month of October, Ambassador Kenzo Oshima, gaveled my election, I raced to a press conference in the Foreign Ministry building. More than one hundred Korean and international reporters were there to cover my election, even though it was after midnight. "Thank you for your patience over this long campaign," I told the reporters. "I would be overjoyed at this moment, but no one can be excited when our neighbor has just tested a weapon of mass destruction. I am proud that the United Nations has shown the world that these provocations will never be accepted."

Many member states concluded that North Korea was sabotaging the process to stop a South Korean from leading the United Nations. Pyongyang was widely considered to be capable of anything. I'm sure that the leadership felt threatened when I became the secretary-general of the United Nations. Kofi Annan had largely taken a hands-off approach, but they did not know whether or how a South Korean would use the power of the United Nations to engage the regime. I couldn't predict how I would handle individual crises, but I had been clear from the beginning that I wanted to address human rights and development while strengthening the organization and its ability to adapt to unprecedented threats to peace and security.

This may well have been North Korea's attempt at a blunt message that we must all take them seriously. It was also a stark reminder that there would be many tough challenges ahead of me.

TOUCHING HISTORY

Member states reelected me to a second five-year term in June 2011, many months earlier than usual. Rather than waiting until the end of my first term, the General Assembly decided to hold my official swearing-in immediately. I wanted to do something special to celebrate.

The U.S. National Archives had never before released the original Charter of the United Nations, a small but precious document with an incalculable moral force. But the archives agreed to let me take the Oath of Office on the bound volume, and they delivered the precious package to the United Nations under armed guard. In my office, the pages were carefully turned by an archives curator wearing protective gloves. It was an extraordinary moment to see and even touch the precious document that created this indispensable institution. I was permitted to handle only the cover, but it was still a thrill.

On June 21, 2011, General Assembly President Joseph Deiss of Switzerland administered the Oath of Office for my second term. With my left hand on the original UN Charter, I promised to honor the United Nations with loyalty, discretion, and conscience.

Chapter Four

DANGER

The Risk Is Real

When most people imagine a diplomat, they see a man in a dark suit or a woman in a conservative jacket and skirt. That's not wrong, but it's not always true. I traveled about one-third of every month, and my attire could include a bulletproof vest, a state-of-the-art jumpsuit against the cold, a lightweight shirt, or several pairs of latex gloves. None of this would have looked right on the podium of the General Assembly.

Over my decade as secretary-general, I learned that danger comes in many forms. Threats can be as big as a mortar or as small as a virus. There are no places to hide when crowds get out of control, and no source of cover on a deserted airstrip. We all assume a degree of risk, but to be UN secretary-general today is to be an international target.

When I joined the United Nations in 2007, there was no question that I would be living inside a twenty-four-hour bubble. A highly trained security detail escorted me through the halls of the United Nations and across the world. They set up a command post just inside the door of my residence. They installed a metal detector outside my office. For ten years I was forbidden to go anywhere alone, and on one occasion I even traveled with a decoy. My wife and I had a difficult time adapting to the guards, cameras, and other precautions that can constrict life—or maybe extend it. I was grateful for my diligent protectors, but however unobtrusive they were, it was a constant reminder of mortal threat.

BAGHDAD, IRAQ: A MOUTHFUL OF DUST

I was completely unprepared for the mortar that interrupted my Green Zone press conference on March 22, 2007. I was standing beside Iraqi Prime Minister Nouri al-Maliki as I told journalists that my one-day visit was proof of Iraq's returning stability. Within minutes there was a loud boom, a shaking room, and a whoosh of dirty wind. I instinctively hunched behind the podium, and I didn't quite remember what had happened immediately afterward. My mouth and eyes were instantly filled with dust, but I was more shaken than scared. Militants had fired four rockets into the heavily fortified Green Zone, and one had landed just ninety yards away from the prime minister's office. I trembled for hours.

Of course, the press conference was televised live and later posted on YouTube, but weeks went by before I finally watched it. Would I feel scared? Embarrassed? Lucky? I was relieved to see that I didn't panic, only my mouth was puckered with surprise. I was proud to see how quickly I straightened up and shook off the daze. But my cool was no match for Iraqi sangfroid; Prime Minister Maliki had barely flinched, and the interpreter who was translating my statement into Arabic paused only a few short moments before continuing.

"How did you stand so calmly?" I later asked the prime minister.

"This happens a lot," he said.

It turned out that the militants were alerted to my unannounced visit by the press conference itself. The UN made a terrible mistake in allowing it to be broadcast live. I was later informed that no visiting VIPs announce their visits until they have already left the country. In fact, UN protocol is for me to convey travel plans only by telephone, directly to the president or prime minister. I had done so, but even that precaution is not foolproof.

BAGRAM, AFGHANISTAN: A THREATENING CALM

My plane stopped for refueling in Tbilisi, Georgia, en route to the international donors' conference in Afghanistan in July 2010. My private jet suffered a very hard landing, cracking the windshield. It was a jarring experience, tossing me sharply against my safety straps and rattling my bones. That seemed like enough danger for one trip, but this day was not yet over.

Georgian authorities found us another plane, and forty minutes later Swedish Foreign Minister Carl Bildt and I resumed our journey to Kabul.

We arrived to find the airport closed down, and huge searchlights and flares pierced in the sky. It was very strange, and my stomach felt that this wasn't good. I relaxed only slightly as we circled for a while at high altitude before corkscrewing our landing at Bagram Airfield. We learned the next day that the Taliban had fired on the airport at the time I was scheduled to land. I was horrified; someone in the president's office had leaked my schedule.

Bagram is the headquarters of the U.S. military and, presumably, some of the best-guarded land in Afghanistan. But when we touched down, the airfield was unmanned and seemed to be unnaturally quiet. Literally empty. Foreign Minister Bildt and I stood alone on the tarmac waiting for American soldiers to arrive. Although we must have been given permission to land, we looked like unauthorized visitors, and I was afraid we might be shot. After the cracked windshield and whatever had happened at the Kabul airport, I joked that we might have run out of luck. But it was fine.

After a while a couple of sleepy-looking American soldiers in cargo shorts came to see what was happening, and they looked as surprised to see us as we were to be there. I asked them for a helicopter to take us to President Karzai's compound, and soon we were in a Blackhawk, flying dark, two soldiers with machine guns watching the ground intently.

I seemed to have a run of bad luck with airplanes, including two UN flights in which the plane's landing gear would not retract. In March 2011, the day before NATO began air strikes in Libya, the landing gear problem was discovered just after takeoff from Madrid. Luckily, I was able to fly with Spanish Prime Minister José Luis Rodríguez Zapatero who was also going to Paris for the same meeting. The same problem happened again the very next day, flying from Paris to Cairo! We had to spray off our jet fuel before landing to minimize the danger from flying sparks. This time, French President Sarkozy was kind enough to provide his own special aircraft for me. I was grateful that this arrangement was made even on Sunday in France.

The staff was dead silent until we landed. I don't know what occupied their thoughts, but I was thinking about Dag Hammarskjold, whose airplane crashed half a century before in Zambia. Upon my return to New York, I called Susana Malcorra, Under Secretary General of the Department of Field Support, the office that arranged my trip. "Would you allow me to become the second Hammarskjöld?" I asked. Of course she apologized. She was otherwise very good at her job, and I later appointed her as my chief of staff.

Inconvenient, unnerving, and deadly—we had a lot of trouble with UN-maintained aircraft while I was in office. The deterioration of UN peacekeeping planes, in particular, I believe is the fault of Western member states, whose budget constrictions force us to accept the lowest bidder regardless of its performance.

DRESS FOR DISTRESS

Safety isn't all about firepower or even manpower. Sometimes the right deterrent is 100 percent cotton. Clothing is excellent camouflage and protection. I appreciate the reliable beauty of a well-tailored dark suit, but it belongs in the General Assembly, not on the muddy paths of eastern Congo. Every visitor, regardless of nationality or rank, must wear an ice suit in Antarctica and a lightweight shirt in Haiti. I wore multiple layers of rubber and plastic to shield me from the Ebola virus in Guinea, but I would not have gone to parts of Mali or Syria without Kevlar.

Of course, it takes more than clothing to stay safe around crime, crowds, and assassination attempts. Sometimes it requires an army escort. Or a body double.

BEIRUT, LEBANON: THE DECOY

Prime Minister Rafik Hariri was assassinated in a Beirut attack widely assumed to be the work of the Syrian regime on February 14, 2005. This massive car bomb killed twenty-two people, wounded more than two hundred, and left a swimming pool–sized crater on Beirut's famed Corniche. Forensic investigators concluded that the bomb contained approximately one thousand tons of TNT. I was Korea's foreign minister at the time, and I was shocked. I watched the clip of the aftermath, which cable news showed over and over.

Years later I visited Lebanon early in my first term as secretary-general, and my security detail was understandably nervous. They decided that my longtime aide, Kim Won-soo, would ride in a second car as a decoy. There were very few Koreans in Lebanon, and we thought we looked enough alike. Kim got out of his car first, and when no one began shooting, security let me disembark as well. I have known Kim for many years, and I'm sure he accepted this assignment with a sense of duty. But I can't imagine what it felt like to stand there in such a dangerous situation. I was profoundly grateful for his loyalty.

Two years after my retirement from the UN, I was surprised to learn that the Lebanese government had arrested three Palestinians, known to be members of Da'esh, or the Islamic State, who planned to assassinate me during my visit to Lebanon in 2012.

The Lebanese military court tried them in a plot to murder the UN secretary-general during a daytrip to South Lebanon. That attack, said Lebanese authorities, was likely foiled by my last-minute decision to take a helicopter rather than drive.

I have still not checked with authorities to see whether they were found guilty.

SVALBARD, THE ARCTIC CIRCLE: SHIPBOARD

Danger is not only about violence—sometimes it's just a simple task gone wrong. In July 2015, Soon-taek and I sailed the Arctic on a small Norwegian research ship, boarding in Svalbard, well inside the Arctic Circle. It was not luxurious. That night, as I climbed down from the upper bunk bed, I fell and hit my head and shoulder on a chair. I was in pain, but I did not want to distract anyone on the expedition. Nor would I discomfort Norwegian Foreign Minister Børge Brende, who accompanied us. I didn't want the minister to cancel the trip out of concern, and I certainly didn't want my entourage to be overly solicitous so I said nothing about it. I moved carefully, minimizing my movements as much as I could, and Soon-taek hovered slightly, keeping people from jostling me on the left side.

I saw a doctor as soon as I returned to New York, and a CT scan found signs of minor fractures on two ribs on my left side. There was nothing they could do for me; I had to wait for nature's healing. I moved very carefully for the next two months, walking slowly and willing myself not to cough. Despite my stiffness, few people noticed anything strange. I was grateful I did not injure my right side because then I might have had trouble shaking hands with visitors—sometimes three dozen times a day! This happened just a little over a month after John Kerry had broken a leg while taking a bike ride in Geneva during the Iran deal negotiations.

CAIRO, PORT-AU-PRINCE, DARFUR, AND TOO MANY OTHER PLACES: THE THREAT YOU CANNOT REASON WITH

There is safety in numbers—until there's danger. Diplomacy is not a useful skill in large, disorganized groups. Crowds are the one thing that scare me. They are unpredictable, emotional, and cannot be persuaded. It's remarkable how quickly a situation turns dangerous. One frustrated person will multiply into dozens. A few journalists can become a competitive scrum with sharp microphones and heavy cameras. Demonstrators sometimes stampede.

I was in Port-au-Prince days after the January 2010 earthquake nearly leveled the Haitian capital. I was on the street, speaking calmly to a young woman who grew increasingly emotional as she told me about her home, destroyed with everything she owned inside. The specter of life on the street terrified her. As her voice rose and carried, more people pressed close to hear us. Now they were clustered tight all around my security detail, shouting in Creole. My guardians had me loosely by the arms and were waiting for an opportunity to swing clear of the angry circle. I know the Haitians meant us no harm, but now there were dozens of people shouting and crying—their anger, fear, and frustration crowding out the air at the center of the pack. Their voices grew louder, ringing from all sides. Finally, the security detail quickly bustled me away. I know, intellectually, that we were not in danger. but that much emotion in such as small space was frightening.

A year later North Africa simmered through the early months of the Arab Spring, and Libyan strongman Muammar Gaddafi was barely hanging onto power. By then, Libyans frequently and sometimes violently demonstrated against his long and brutal rule.

The League of Arab States held an emergency meeting in Cairo on February 3, 2011, to condemn Gaddafi for his bloody crackdown and discuss the imposition of a no-fly zone to protect civilians from bombardment. After the meeting, my security detail and I were walking to my car when about fifty Gaddafi supporters rushed me in the parking lot, chanting slogans against me and waving pro-Gaddafi placards. I was surprised and alarmed and I ran, threading my way behind and between cars as they chased me. Egyptian security ran after me, catching up before the protestors did. We circled back into the building, and I took shelter in the office of Arab League Secretary General Amr Moussa. I stayed for fifteen or twenty minutes while security made sure it was safe for me to come out again, and I exited through a rear door directly into the back seat of my car.

A group without a leader is unpredictable because no one can focus its attention or lower its energy. Later that night I wondered if the crowd in the parking lot was, in fact, all that dangerous. The next morning one of the newspapers carried the story, along with a large photograph of an Egyptian security officer running beside me. My eyes are wide. He is reaching for his pistol. At the time I hadn't noticed that he was drawing his weapon. I felt a buzzy shiver, invisible beneath my suit.

UN HEADQUARTERS, NEW YORK: LIVING WITH AN ENTOURAGE

I understand that the United Nations has enemies, and its leader is a highly visible, vulnerable symbol. The UN security office does as well, and for two generations it has treated the secretary-general as a precious, fragile package. My close protection detail was a multilingual and multitalented team, small but fierce. These armed officers would go days without sleeping or eating properly, traveling often, far from their families, and standing squarely in harm's way. History may never show the many times they saved me from danger, but I will always remember. I could not possibly thank them enough.

My security team was led for a decade by Captain Bernard "Robby" Robinson, who came to Korea in November 2006 to escort Soon-taek and me to New York. I saw him almost every day. When I left New York after ten years of service, it was Captain Robinson who escorted us back to Seoul and, with elaborate care, handed me over to Korean security.

Safety and security ruled our lives in New York, where precautions included unmarked sedans and uniformed armed guards. Two security officers were always stationed in my residence. When something especially controversial happened at the United Nations, the New York Police Department deployed SWAT teams around the residence. When that happened, I wondered whether my Sutton Place neighbors appreciated my presence in this tranquil enclave.

I never much minded the security detail, but I am disappointed that I rarely played with my grandchildren on the residence's idyllic green lawn. It made me uncomfortable to know security cameras were watching us. I became accustomed to the guards' discrete presence, but Soon-taek did not. My wife had enjoyed the city when we lived there in 2001, with many activities and friends. But as the wife of a secretary-general, she was unable to go shopping alone or play bridge without security nearby, although she did manage to give her guards the slip once. I don't know where she was headed that day, but I think she just wanted to feel free. When she returned, they politely and firmly told her never to do that again!

Knowing that the guards would be in trouble if she were to disappear again, I doubt she did.

SEOUL, KOREA: IN THE SHADOW OF A THREAT

I will live in the bubble for the rest of my life. The Korean government has been providing me with a security team to accompany me nearly round-the-clock since I returned home in 2016. Seoul and the UN Department of Safety and Security decided protection was necessary to prevent retaliation for my many condemnations of the Islamic State and other terrorist organizations. In my second term, UNDSS discovered an Islamic State website instructing followers to harm or kill me. There is some evidence that at least a few had tried. So there is that.

I can't say that I never think about assassination, but fear certainly does not curtail my life. I still go out with friends and frequently accept speaking invitations or attend meetings several hours' drive from Seoul. Before Covid-19, I traveled two weeks a month, on average, seeing to a dozen climate change- and development-related events and meetings. I also visit the Ban Ki-moon Centre for Global Citizens, which opened in Vienna in January 2018. You see, I'm not exactly hiding.

Even in my retirement in my own country, I travel everywhere with plainclothes officers led by Police Senior Inspector Han Young-eun. I am often recognized in public, and people walk up to me to talk and have their pictures taken. Most reach out to shake my hand or boldly stand beside me, even on the street. In restaurants, my group must take a private room, and when that's not possible, my courteous guardians sit as unobtrusively as they can at the next table. Secretly, I'm delighted and don't mind a few minutes of local fame. But even friendly crowds make my security detail uncomfortable. Worse, people often hand the agents their mobile phones to take pictures with me. They are too kind to refuse, but you can see that these officers don't like it. It narrowly focuses their vision when they need to keep a wide angle on the environment.

Close protection feels more invasive at home than it did in New York. The security makes impulse impossible, and it's isolating in even the smallest ways. I am aware that I will probably never again drive a car. And I will never get lost. Soon-taek and I now refrain from taking our quiet after dinner walk because of the effort that goes into even a neighborhood stroll. I still do a lot of flying, but unlike the old days, I wait quietly in the airport lounge until the flight is called, and then I am usually the last one to board.

I know some of this sounds like a luxury, but remember that I cannot turn it off. These lovely gentlemen in neat blue suits are my constant reminder that someone, possibly someone nearby, might try to harm me.

I am not exactly a free man, but I am not complaining.

Chapter Five

NEGOTIATION

Flow Like Water

Every stage of my diplomatic career has involved negotiations. Some have been relatively simple, convincing both parties to give up something small for a win-win deal. But others are tense and contentious, such as hammering out the Iran nuclear agreement. The most useful qualities in both the moderator and participants are flexibility and humility, backed up by strength and determination.

Throughout my diplomatic career, I have taken inspiration from water, the softest yet most powerful of the natural elements. Chinese philosopher Lao Tzu taught its virtues some twenty-six centuries ago: Water is clear, without taste, color, or shape, but it will extinguish fire, sweep away rocks, rust metal, and degrade wood. It can be as hard as ice or as soft as steam. Water is often underestimated; it gives life and flows around obstacles instead of confronting them. This teaching—that "the highest virtue is like water"—is so important to me that I carefully drew a Chinese calligraphy of it for U.S. President Barack Obama for his birthday. The best negotiators are fluid—always moving, always adapting, always finding a way over or around an obstacle—they are nonconfrontational but brook no belligerency.

Diplomacy is the art of the possible, and negotiation is diplomacy in action. My style is personal diplomacy with compassion, which means remaining humble and sustaining contact that builds confidence and respect. Even the briefest conversation can build goodwill, but not if every interaction is a transaction or criticism. This philosophy works well for me, but, of course, the downside of building personal relationships is the repeated turnover in world leaders. At each turnover, we have to build confidence in each other all over again.

Former UN Secretary-General Boutros Boutros-Ghali advised me to occasionally cancel engagements at the last minute or take an extra day to return a world leader's call. But my style is to emphasize trust and principles. This was particularly valuable in January 2009 when I traveled to the Middle East to try to end the devastating war between Hamas and Israel, Operation Cast Lead. This was shuttle diplomacy by definition and deed: I flew thirteen times in seven days, visiting eight countries. The civilian toll was so high that world leaders met with me on very short notice everywhere I went. Even the Israelis, no fans of the UN, met me immediately. Both sides were ready to end the war and just needed a way to do it. Many agreements have failed due to loss of face, so smart negotiators make sure both sides leave the table with at least a small concession they can claim as progress or a victory.

Water can crash ashore with a storm's ferocity, or ripple with a soothing reflection of the sky. I always start with a calm and open mind and listen, listen, listen! I also approach discussions as a partner, not an opponent. Collaboration is nearly always better than confrontation—fresh ideas sometimes emerge, as do significant and legitimate concerns. If the parties cannot agree on the final outcome, a lengthy and painful process is required to map out effective incremental steps.

I've seen negotiators barge into discussions and try to browbeat the parties they think of as resistant. I am sorry to report that the big powers, in particular, often start discussions from a position of strength and even arrogance. This approach is far less productive than setting a positive example. I wish they could understand that respect is more sustainable than brute coercion.

Russian Foreign Minister Sergei Lavrov and U.S. Secretary of State Condoleezza Rice could reflexively slip into opposing positions. I watched them spar in meetings of the Quartet, an advisory group created by the United Nations, the European Union, the United States, and Russia in 2000 to develop a road map to peace in the Middle East. Minister Lavrov, a brilliant former UN ambassador, knew and remembered everything about negotiations and the region. Secretary Rice, a specialist on the Soviet Union, was also well prepared, and she was tenacious. It was a duel between these two most persuasive diplomats, and I found myself energized and enlightened as I listened to them.

I attended my second Quartet meeting in Berlin in February 2007 and was startled when the two immediately crossed swords. The Palestinians had just agreed to form the National Unity Government, but there was a disagreement in the room about the role of Hamas. Secretary Rice repeated Washington's demand that Hamas leader Ismail Haniyeh publicly denounce violence and acknowledge Israel's right to exist. "I don't underestimate the importance of the implicit recognition of Israel," Minister Lavrov said, but "I disagree with maximalist demands."

I soon learned that they would disagree—eloquently, rationally, and passionately—on many aspects of the road map. But they blocked each other every time they clashed. Friction between the positions of Washington and Moscow was not the only reason the Quartet had a do-nothing reputation—the Palestinians and the Israelis bear some of that blame as well—but these disagreements contributed to our gridlock.

Some people are natural diplomats. Former U.S. president Bill Clinton, the UN Special Envoy to Haiti after the massive 2010 earthquake, won people over with star power and charm. When Secretary of State Hillary Clinton came to the United Nations, she was trailed by cameras and diplomats. They were both celebrities around the UN: people wanted to talk to President Clinton and expected Secretary Clinton to make news.

Populist bullies are perhaps the least effective diplomats. These leaders, often egotists, give away their strategies and boast about their outcomes—the antithesis of international diplomacy. U.S. president Donald Trump repeatedly promised Americans that North Korea would surrender its nuclear weapons program, strengthening Kim Jong-un's hand by showing how important a deal was to him personally. Recip Tayyip Erdoğan vowed to drive the Kurdish army from Kobani, triggering a military escalation that prolonged Syrian suffering throughout the winter of 2014. Hezbollah and Hamas know they can count on Iran's support. Hungarian leader Victor Orbán's disregard for the European Union and criticism of NATO weakens international cooperation. The influence of dictators on the UN Human Rights Council radiates permission for autocratic leaders to abuse domestic freedoms.

I admit that diplomatic language is often vague and maddening to people who demand specificity. Urging "the parties" to disarm is the beginning of a gradual process. Listen closely and you'll hear diplomats express "concern," "deep concern," and finally "grave concern" about actions taken or avoided. It doesn't sound like much to people on the outside, but I assure you that diplomats hear the difference. We feel the urgency, especially in conflict.

Deployed thoughtfully, strategic ambiguity gives us room to increase the pressure and a little extra time and space in which to negotiate. Words can send subtle messages in addition to their meaning. For example, I have rarely expressed "frustration" on any issue because that might give the impression that the UN has no capacity to resolve the crisis.

No government wants to be publicly criticized, and more and more countries are growing immune to public pressure. "Naming and shaming" can still be an effective tool in the human rights sector, but today it more often makes leaders defensive. In my televised address the day before the 2014 Sochi Winter Olympics, I called on Russian president Vladimir Putin to change his government's persecution of homosexuals; nothing changed. Indeed, Israel and the United States ignore repeated condemnations, and Indonesia, the Philippines, Zimbabwe, and Burundi, among others, have all refused to admit UN human rights investigators more than a dozen times.[1]

UN diplomats are among the best in the world, and I respect them deeply. Some have significant experience in their own governments, and others have come up through the UN system. I couldn't possibly name them all. It's important to truly understand the issues and the history of the matter at hand, as well as the personalities of those in charge who sit across the table. During active conflicts and negotiations, the UN Department of Political Affairs continually briefed me on the issues we were mandated to mediate. I have learned that shutting down the conversation is rarely a successful tactic. Ideally, an agreement is win-win *and* lose-lose. Both parties must win concessions to save face, and they must yield to a few demands. In a good negotiation, both sides can feel the sting but also claim a victory.

Former Algerian foreign minister Lakhdar Brahimi and Nobel laureate Martti Ahtisaari, a former president of Finland, have been deployed all over the world to defuse political and armed conflicts that many thought intractable. As mediators, they are subtle, experienced, and wise. Brahimi is patient and kind, and his Arabic was a plus when he was the UN-Arab League Joint Special Envoy in Syria. Ahtisaari has devoted his life to peace, and his accomplishments give him great stature in negotiations. Both diplomats now serve as members of the Elders.

The success of UN diplomacy depends on resolutions, personalities, and timing, and it isn't always a perfect fit. In fact, if the UN envoy pushes too hard, or embarrasses the host government by speaking unguardedly, the envoy could be declared persona non grata and be expelled. Senior representatives in-country have sometimes been expelled, and others have gotten too close to the government. Most often, though, our diplomats are able to walk the fine line of diplomacy.

The newly independent South Sudan was a particularly tricky example. By the spring of 2014, there was no easing the turbulence between President Salva Kiir and my special representative Hilde Johnson, a former Norwegian minister for international development. They complained about each other privately and even in public, and this friction was impeding peace operations. Finally, the somewhat autocratic leader, a former freedom fighter who never renounced violence, demanded that I replace her. The host country cannot select or reject the secretary-general's special representative, and I urged President Kiir to do South Sudan a favor and treat Johnson with as much respect as he would show to me. And I reminded Johnson that it was essential that they work together closely and professionally. But neither did. Clearly, this relationship could not be salvaged, and I needed a strategy to make a seamless transition. I insisted that the president praise my special envoy in public, so people would not think there was a problem. When he finally complimented her work at a press conference, I reluctantly replaced her.

Negotiations sometimes require pressure from many sides, including the threat to use force, the imposition of sanctions, or sustained censure. When I added my voice, it was often in private because this is more effective than outright public condemnations, which often are refuted publicly by the parties concerned.

THE BACK CHANNEL

On March 23, 2007, the Iranian navy intercepted the British navy's HMS *Cornwall* in the narrow Strait of Hormuz, saying it had sailed into Iran's territorial waters. Authorities detained as possible spies the *Cornwall*'s fifteen-person crew and the Royal Marines on board. Tehran refused to release them even after a thorough inspection of the ship turned up nothing unusual.

Later the following week I discussed the matter with Iran's foreign minister, Manouchehr Mottaki, on the sidelines of the 2007 Arab League Summit in Saudi Arabia. The British government had satellite images and was convinced the ship was in international waters. I was just three months into my job as secretary-general, and it was my first meeting with any senior Iranian officials. I was a bit anxious, but I appealed to Mottaki not to further strain Iran's international relationships by detaining ships, even if they accidentally slipped from international to territorial waters. "Iran must be seen as helpful, not a problem country that holds foreigners who are clearly not a threat," I advised him. I was deeply gratified that Tehran let the naval personnel go just a few days after we had spoken. Sometimes one's voice carries farthest in public, and sometimes it is more commanding in confidence.

On July 31, 2009, three young American hikers were apprehended on—or possibly just near—the Iranian side of the Iraq-Iran border. Sarah Shourd, Josh Fattal, and Shane Bauer, all in their late twenties and early thirties, were imprisoned and eventually charged with spying on the Islamic Republic of Iran. It was a frightening time for their families. The parents were unable to contact their children, and they could not find out what was happening in the jail or in the court. Rumors expanded into the vacuum: they were held in solitary confinement, they were pawns in the negotiations over weapons inspectors, or they would be traded back to the United States in a prisoner swap.

The American people were watching the case closely and with horror. It should have been evident to Tehran that these young people were on vacation, not on assignment for the CIA. But direct communication between the two governments was complicated by decades of mistrust and the absence of diplomatic recognition. I had my spokesman read a statement stressing my support for dialogue and an expectation of fair treatment. "Can you explain how they intended to harm the country?" I asked Iranian ambassador to the UN, Mohamad Khazaee.

I pointed out how much ill-will had been stirred up by the arrests. "How does Iran benefit by holding them? Why don't you release them immediately?" I asked the ambassador to relay my message to President Mahmoud Ahmadinejad, explaining that "it would give him leverage with the American government and would help me to help you."

I kept up gentle diplomatic pressure from New York. I have had good relations with Tehran, and the leadership trusted me. The American and British governments, by comparison, are quick to criticize and condescend. Tehran finally set Sarah Shourd free on September 14, 2010, on humanitarian grounds. But Josh Fattal and Shane Bauer remained in custody.

In August 2011, they were sentenced to eight years in prison for "espionage" and for entering the country illegally. There was an international outcry, and the two men were unexpectedly set free in September, after twenty-six months of confinement and just days before Iranian president Mahmoud Ahmadinejad arrived in New York for the UN General Assembly debate.

The president all but confirmed that he had hoped to exchange the young hikers for Iranians held in U.S. prisons. Did Tehran need a face-saving reason to let the three Americans go? Did President Ahmadinejad fail in an attempted prisoner swap? Possibly all of the above. Complex negotiations have many moving parts. Were these people spies? No, I don't believe so. Espionage is an effective charge to discredit critics and silence inconvenient foreigners, such as journalists. People with dual nationalities are particularly vulnerable under Iranian law, which does not recognize dual citizenship.

As secretary-general, I worked closely and quietly with diplomats and intermediaries to win the release of detainees, nearly all from Iranian custody. Hostage negotiation is a time-honored UNSG task—Dag Hammarskjöld achieved a great reputation for his daring attempt to negotiate the freedom of U.S. airmen in Chinese custody. Some had already been convicted in a show trial or in secret. Their crimes: drifting over an Iranian border or asking too many questions.

I worked behind the scenes to help free a number of reporters and broadcasters. Freelance journalist Roxana Saberi, a U.S. and Iranian citizen, was convicted in a one-day secret trial of spying for the United States. I pressed her case with Iranian officials, and she was released after serving one hundred days in prison. When she came home, Saberi thanked me in a call and then a card.

Iranian and Canadian journalist, human rights advocate, and documentary filmmaker Maziar Bahari, a reporter for *Newsweek*, was arrested in June 2009 after covering a rally protesting President Ahmadinejad's tainted reelection. Charged with "acting against national security" and "disturbing public order," he was convicted in a show trial along with many of the demonstrators. I asked Ambassador Khazaee to convey my message to President Ahmadinejad, and Bahari was released on October 17, just two days after I issued a scathing report on Iran's violent crackdown on free speech and assembly during the election period. I was pleased that *Newsweek* did not mention my involvement in its cover story because I almost always conducted my negotiations behind closed doors. But I was happy when Bahari came to visit me.

I was deeply concerned by the July 22, 2014, arrest and detention by the Iranian authorities of the *Washington Post*'s Tehran bureau chief, Jason Rezaian, a citizen of both the United States and Iran. I was in Washington, D.C. for a meeting at the White House when a number of *Washington Post* editors and Jason's brother came to see me. It was autumn, and they were extremely concerned about the safety of Rezaian and his wife Yeganeh Salehi, an Iranian journalist who had also been arrested. They asked for the

UN's help to get the couple released and, almost as important, find out what they had been charged with.

I spoke to Iranian foreign minister Javad Zarif, whom I knew well as his country's former UN ambassador. I forcefully urged his government to release Rezaian and other political prisoners and said I was anxious about their human rights. I also asked him to convey my message to President Hassan Rouhani. The minister assured me that he was familiar with Rezaian's work but said that Tehran had reasons to be concerned. It was clear to me that other journalists in Iran also had reason to be worried. After months of appeals and private conversations with Iran's leaders and influential officials, the *Post* reporter was freed in January 2016, ending eighteen months of difficult confinement. Like the BBC, the *Post* handled his confinement publicly, enlisting dozens of entertainers, American lawmakers, reporters, and other notables. In the end, he was released in a prisoner swap.

I met Jason Rezaian in Cambridge, Massachusetts, in 2017. I had just retired from the UN and was a Special Fellow at the Harvard Kennedy School. I was giving a presentation for Nieman Fellows and was surprised when he introduced himself to me after class. I was so happy to meet him! We embraced. A few days later we met again in my office to piece together what had happened. Parts of his story were very difficult to hear. Rezaian had served a total of 544 days in Iran's Evin Prison on a scurrilous charge of espionage, and he had been tortured while in custody. On November 22, 2019, the U.S. District Court for the District of Columbia awarded Rezaian and his family a $180 million judgment against Iran for illegal detention and abuse. Tehran did not present a defense in court and scoffed at the judgment. The journalist's next negotiation will likely be convincing the U.S. government to pay the award out of the $4 billion to $5 billion in frozen Iranian assets.

I was not the only person working for the release of these journalists and other Westerners, but I do think I helped Tehran make the right decisions. The position of UN secretary-general is widely respected as moral and apolitical, independent and impartial. The secretary-general, the Elders, and other international figures must act as a collective conscience rather than an extension of the great powers. To do otherwise would betray the office and jeopardize its integrity. I conducted my efforts at the highest levels, working quietly and privately. I tried to be as transparent as water—mostly unseen and unheard, yet forceful.

Iran was not the only country to arrest foreigners for financial or political gain, but it was among the worst. Perhaps the most terrible, though, were the militant groups. The BBC went public when Gaza correspondent Alan Johnston was abducted by the Army of Islam on March 17, 2007. The global community mobilized every resource at its disposal, which turned out to be significant. Officials, organizations, and prominent journalists around the world demanded that the reporter be set free, and many others, myself included, worked behind the scenes. In an unexpected development, London and Hamas engaged in secret talks, their first direct contact and a confidence-building measure that might still be beneficial today. BBC UN correspondent Laura Trevelyan asked me to record a live televised appeal for Johnston's release, which was translated for the Arabic Service and broadcast on the fifth week of Johnston's captivity.

My role in these kinds of negotiations was a combination of public demand and private persuasion, of coalition building and finger-pointing. Johnston was released on July 4, and the BBC celebrated. It held a reception for dozens of people—reporters who had also been detained or kidnapped, as well as the many people who had worked for his release. I was pleasantly surprised by a special "thank you" to the United Nations. When I left the party, I was overwhelmed to see that the news organization had projected a ray of UN blue on the crown of a neighboring building.

THE TEN-YEAR CONVERSATION

How do you reconcile a disagreement or conflict when there is no time limit; negligible financial, political, or military pressure; and little appetite for compromise? That's the problem I and five of my seven predecessors had faced when trying to bring a lasting peace to Cyprus. The beautiful Mediterranean island has been cleaved since Turkey's incursion in July 1974.

Cyprus might not strike people as a lingering confrontation because it doesn't look like other UN peace operations. The people who live along the Green Line buffer zone are not under threat from the other side. In fact, the UN Peacekeeping Force in Cyprus (UNFICYP) is one of the few ongoing missions that fits the original definition of UN peacekeeping: acting as guarantor of a durable cease-fire. With Turkish soldiers reinforcing the UN boundary from the north, there is virtually no threat of violence.

Even on a warm and vibrant border, we must negotiate to end divisions. After decades of inertia, I thought the time was right to work forcefully for peace. Greek Cypriot Demetris Christofias was elected president early in my term, and I had a positive relationship with longtime Turkish Cypriot leader

Mehmet Talat. Both told me that they were ready to resolve outstanding issues, including governance and power-sharing, property, the economy, and joining the European Union. Although leaders from both sides had been saying that for forty-five years, I decided to be optimistic.

The two leaders were certainly talking, and that alone made this dispute seem more reconcilable than many. There had been tantalizing possibilities over the years, but the United Nations and our partners remained unable to forge a political solution to this low-level conflict. One of the few things on which the earlier leaders had agreed was that nothing was agreed upon until everything is agreed upon. I hoped a change of scenery might help the atmosphere in negotiations, which were usually cordial but had produced few significant results. On January 25, 2012, I invited the leaders to meet with me in Greentree, a beautiful and cozy estate that its former owner had pledged to peace. Located just an hour outside of Manhattan, Greentree has been a valuable resource for the United Nations, and I'm grateful it exists. In fact, it reminds me of the U.S. presidential retreat at Camp David.

A thick January snow had fallen just before we arrived, and there was nothing for Christofias and Talat to do but eat and sleep and drink and talk. But the two men strengthened their personal relationship over this two-day retreat, making it easier for them to discuss their differences. I felt emboldened and changed the venue to Geneva, at UN headquarters and in the Swiss resort town of Mont Pèlerin. In continuing efforts to find common ground over my ten years at the United Nations, I convened trilateral negotiations with both leaders five times in New York and Switzerland, and I met each individually a dozen times. My special advisors, Alexander Downer and then Espen Barth Eide, former foreign ministers of Australia and Norway, respectively, were constantly engaged. But I'm not sure how much we have to show for our efforts. The turnover in leadership certainly didn't help. There were five different leaders during my UN tenure, and the amiable relations and goodwill we'd built with each other had to be developed anew with each one.[2]

It is tempting to think that if we can just get the two parties in conflict to talk to each other they will work out their differences. But mere conversation is not enough to correct history nor to suture the divisions. And, frankly, there is little anyone can do if the leaders themselves do not feel any urgency to end the conflict. I wasn't expecting to make a breakthrough, but I did hope we'd get somewhat further along on elements of an agreement. Until Turkey relaxes its demands and Greece offers some concessions, Cyprus will remain divided. We know what has to happen to create a united Cypriot federation, but how can a threshold of political will be fostered to overcome complacency, habit, and the entrenched interests that benefit from division? What is the alchemy that produces unity?

My first visit to Cyprus was on Sunday, January 31, 2010, a date that still stands out in my mind. I traveled from the south to the north through the Ledra Street Crossing in central Nicosia. The border, which divides the main shopping district, is symbolic to both sides because it is the most direct of six checkpoints on the island. When I stepped through Ledra and onto Turkish Cypriot soil, I was surrounded by thousands of people on the street and leaning out of their windows shouting "resolution now!"—a reference to reunification. Women were throwing carnations, and the street was electric with desire and hope. My thoughts would return to Ledra during many Cyprus conversations, and I would think, "your people are telling you what to do! Stop talking and listen."

As I stood there at the Ledra crossing, having taken a small but immensely symbolic step, I thought how wonderful it would be to visit North Korea through the peace village, Panmunjom. Unlike Cyprus, there is no easy crossing there. Our families and cultures have been divided for more than seventy-five years. I felt the differences between the Cypriot and Korean divisions, and I felt them deeply. The scene at Ledra was beautiful, but to me it was also sad.

THERE ARE PEOPLE WITH WHOM YOU WILL NEVER AGREE

Western Sahara is a windswept desert on Africa's Atlantic coast, beset by uncompromising heat, thick fog, and dust-filled siroccos that wrap the Sahrawi people with stinging winds. Its hardships are evident, but the territory's wealth is nearly invisible. Beneath the sands and sunbaked villages are some of the globe's richest deposits of phosphate, a vital component of scores of products from toothpaste to chemical weapons. Recent exploration suggests the possibility of game-changing offshore oil as well.

The Moroccan government annexed Western Sahara in 1975 when Spanish colonial rule ceded the land to neighboring nations. Morocco has convinced Algeria and Mauritius to relinquish their claims, but that has not led to peace. Morocco has rejected international criticism for more than forty-five years, saying it cannot occupy land that is already Moroccan. The United Nations brokered a cease-fire in 1991, and the UN Mission for the Referendum in Western Sahara (MINURSO) has been deployed there ever since, mandated to reduce tensions within Western Sahara and on its Moroccan border.

From the early days of my tenure, I had tried to go to Western Sahara to visit MINURSO and thank peacekeepers personally for their efforts. I also wanted to try to resolve the disputes between the Sahrawi Polisario government and Morocco. But Morocco intentionally delayed permission to enter the 75 percent of the territory under its control, insisting that King Mohammed VI himself wanted to personally welcome me to Western Sahara but that my proposed dates were never convenient for him. Officials never offered alternatives times.

Near the end of my second term and frankly frustrated, I went to the region anyway. Wherever I travel, I make it a priority to visit refugee camps, and the Sahrawis' conditions were inhospitable. They lived without relief from the blazing heat and abrading sandstorms. There is no arable land and no water, which rules out farming, firewood, and much of the hardscrabble economy. The people of Smara camp, like most of the refugees that have settled in the Tindouf area, must rely on foreign humanitarian assistance for all their needs, including food. The displaced are among the most vulnerable people in the world. My heart went out to the Sahrawi refugees, who live in terrible conditions with no end in sight. So many hundreds of children were born in these camps, and so many more would grow up here before the referendum would finally be held.

One of my first stops was to be the 17 June School at the edge of the Smara refugee camp. A tight crowd of refugees was waiting for me, as many as twenty thousand people according to some estimates. They lined the road around my motorcade. I have visited refugee camps around the world, and with few exceptions, most are welcoming. But a great many men and women Smara refugees wanted me to see their anger. I saw their pent-up indignation at having to live in these rough camps, and their fury that the United Nations had failed to end their struggle against Morocco.

I was surprised and embarrassed to see so many angry young men holding signs such as "No to 40 years of occupation!" and "UNfair!" I could hear the protesters chanting and shouting, some rushing up against the vehicle to show me pictures of bloody bodies. My security officers told me to stay inside the bulletproof car, and I did not argue. U.S. diplomat Christopher Ross, my personal envoy to Western Sahara, did get out to check the situation. Meanwhile, stones began bouncing harmlessly but loudly against the reinforced doors and windows.

Algerian and UN security agreed that we had to cancel the visit, but I insisted that we proceed. We drove through the camp without stopping. More refugees surged toward our convoy, but we kept moving, driving quickly through a hellish vista of dirt and tarp tents surrounded by young children who should have been in school. I needed to make a quick decision whether to cancel this trip and return to the airport. But the tumult decided for us.

UN security officers and local law enforcement were running beside the car and hanging off the sides. It was chaos, and people crowded into the road to see what was happening. Upon the recommendation of Ross and my security officials, the meeting was canceled and we turned our convoy around. As the car picked up speed, two UN security guards who were swinging from the running boards fell away from the vehicle, landing hard. Mohammad Abdul Hussein hurt his shoulder and José Lawrence damaged his hand. I was horrified to discover later that they both would need months of physical therapy.

I was touring the region eighteen years after Kofi Annan's 1998 visit, which took place near the beginning of his term. The Moroccan government had waited a long time between our visits, I thought, likely to avoid the attention that accompanies our travels. Despite my emotion and exhaustion, we proceeded directly to the press conference that had been scheduled. "I was very saddened to see so many refugees and, particularly, young people who were born there," I said in response to a reporter's question. "The children who were born at the beginning of this occupation are now forty or forty-one years old." "Occupation." I knew the word was very sensitive to the Moroccans, but I was so moved by what I had experienced that afternoon and so emotional that I had spoken without censor. In fact, I had spoken the truth.

My words were widely reported, and I immediately realized this would have serious repercussions. I alerted the UN press office, which quickly issued an official statement, with my approval, saying that the remarks were my own opinion and not the position of the United Nations. I doubted that would mollify the Moroccan government, and I was right. King Mohammed quickly denounced me and described the use of the word as "premeditated." Ultimately, my visit to the region was counterproductive. King Mohammed chose to withdraw Moroccan peacekeepers from MINURSO and halt its $3 million annual payment. Its brief expulsion of dozens of international civilian staff severely curtailed the mission and was widely criticized. After I left the region, well-organized protests were staged throughout Morocco, complete with signs, loud shouting, and speakers to keep the crowd enthusiastic and angry. The Moroccans estimated the size of the protests, held in every city and major town, at more than one million people.

March 15, just days after I returned to New York, Moroccan foreign minister Salaheddine Mezouar came to visit me at the United Nations. I received him even though I knew he was in New York to protest my unintentional words, which he had done publicly many times already. But I was startled when he directed me to apologize to his government and King Mohammed. I would not. I told the foreign minister that in my decade of service to the United Nations I had never seen or even heard of such unacceptably rude behavior by any member state following a secretary-general's spontaneous and genuine emotion. I also pointed out that I had already expressed regret.

The UN press office issued another strong statement at my instruction conveying in barely diplomatic language my astonishment at statements made by Moroccan officials and my "deep disappointment and anger" over the demonstrations that targeted me personally. The statement also noted that such attacks were disrespectful to the secretary-general and the United Nations. My relationship with King Mohammed VI was not to be repaired. In fact, Moroccan officials never fully recovered from my candor, but I was not sorry to have spoken the truth.

In November 2016, just six weeks before my retirement, I visited Marrakech for a climate conference and met with King Mohammed in his palace. Our conversation was brief, polite, and superficial. I met the king again in December 2017, a year after my retirement, during the One Planet Summit in Paris. French President Emmanuel Macron hosted a luncheon, and it would have been awkward if we didn't shake hands. So we did, politely and without much talk.

We may come across each other in the future, probably at a conference on climate change or youth initiatives. But I don't know when, if ever, we will reconcile. We cannot reach people who don't just disagree but also refuse to hear us. Nothing can be achieved with such people, and it is important to know when to just stop trying.

PART II

Peace and Security

Conflict, Disaster, and Global Politics

Chapter Six

NORTH KOREA

The Difficult Cousins

North Korea has cast a dark shadow across my entire life and career. Throughout my decades working on North Korea, I have never let myself forget the cruelty inflicted on its people by the regime. The utter heartlessness and disregard for human rights and suffering are difficult to fathom, much less describe. I have never stopped believing in the reunification of our divided lands, but I am uncertain of prospects for unity in my lifetime. The current thaw may not last. In fact, during my five decades of public service, numerous foreigners have asked me if or when the reunification will take place. I am getting more and more pessimistic.

The Korean War shattered my childhood. In the immediate aftermath of war, I often saw the bodies of suspected North Korean fighters and sympathizers displayed in the streets as a warning to traitors. I was never able to erase that haunting memory. Young though I was, I intuitively sensed that if these were the spoils of war, truly there were no winners. This lesson left an indelible mark, and more than half a century later it shaped my work as UN secretary-general. Belligerents throughout time cling to the idea that they will achieve a military victory, but I know from personal experience that war only generates loss—of resources, blood, and even the will to live.

The other lesson I drew from my childhood memories concerns not war but peace, specifically the power of international solidarity. My hometown, Chungju, and much of Korea was in complete ruins. But soldiers bearing the United Nations Command insignia came to help us. These soldiers were not from one but from twenty-one countries, including five countries (Sweden, India, Denmark, Norway, and Italy) that sent humanitarian teams. They came from the five continents and from the far-away countries of South Africa, Ethiopia, and Colombia. I was overwhelmed to learn that so many countries were willing to give us a helping hand.

The role of the United Nations in the Korean War was precedent setting, marking the first time the UN reacted to aggression with a decision to use armed forces—a much more robust response than the usual peace operations. In what is now viewed as a strategic blunder, the Soviet delegation had been boycotting the Security Council over the issue of replacing Taiwan with the People's Republic of China, a switch that had been opposed by the permanent Western powers of the United States, the United Kingdom, and France. This left the other members to forge the unity needed to approve Security Council Resolution No. 83 on June 27, 1950, which authorized military intervention to repel North Korea's invasion of the South.[1]

When the Soviet Union finally returned to the Security Council in August 1950, they were quite angry that members had taken important decisions even in their absence and wrote a vehement complaint against the first UN secretary-general, Trygve Lie. The UN Charter does not permit the secretary-general to overturn Security Council resolutions. Nonetheless, Moscow refused to work with Secretary-General Lie, aggressively undermining and humiliating him. By November 1952, he felt he had no choice but to tender his resignation in favor of someone with better relations with member states.

Secretaries-general have long grumbled that "SG" stands for "Scape Goat."

ETERNAL GRATITUDE

No South Korean could fail to be moved by the thought of people from distant lands sacrificing their lives for our freedom. In only three years, some forty thousand foreign troops, an almost unfathomable 217,000 South Korean soldiers, and one million civilians lost their lives.[2] The bodies of 2,282 of these fallen heroes are buried in the world's only UN Memorial Cemetery, in Busan, Korea, on the southeastern part of the Korean Peninsula. It was originally a bare field with white crosses, with the graves organized behind a line of flags of the nations whose men were buried there. However, when I became director of the United Nations Division of the Korean Foreign Ministry in 1981, I oversaw a major renovation of the site.

As secretary-general, I visited the cemetery, calling for remembrance of all who had died, as well as the millions of civilians and soldiers still suffering the senseless pain of war. When I returned to Korea after my decade of service at the UN, I again visited the cemetery to pay my respects to the UN's fallen soldiers. Their sacrifice calls to us all, reminding us that those who receive assistance should return the favor when others are in need. I have met hundreds of Korean War veterans from Ethiopia, Greece, Turkey, the United States, the United Kingdom, Australia, and New Zealand. I told each one that I was grateful for their service and sacrifice. Many spoke movingly of how surprised they were that Korea had developed so much, and they were proud of helping us achieve this transformation.

Those faces and words have never left me. I never forgot the sad beauty of the cemetery as I moved up in the ranks of government service and delved deeper into the tangled North Korea file. I often recalled it in difficult times as a symbol of the brotherhood of humanity that can be relied on in the direst of situations.

SHOCKWAVES

Early in 1990, when I was director general of the American Affairs Bureau, officials from the U.S. Central Intelligence Agency (CIA) traveled to Seoul for a secret meeting. I knew it was not the usual briefing because it took place in the National Defense Ministry, not the Foreign Ministry. I was intrigued. These officials had highly confidential intelligence proving in irrefutable detail that Pyongyang had been trying to develop nuclear weapons. The CIA had satellite images of activity in the Yongbyun area, photographs and cables. North Korea was developing a military nuclear program.

This was the first any of us had heard of this, and we were shocked. Some hoped Washington's intelligence was wrong. I was astounded—by both the news and the detail of proof. We had no suspicions, but the CIA's presentation was quite credible. My thoughts cascaded during the briefing and again afterward: Could Pyongyang go all the way to developing a viable nuclear weapon? Would they point it at us, their cousins and brothers? Was my own family less safe now than it was yesterday? A year ago? I felt anxious and apprehensive.

It was not just the North-South equation that had changed. The news also had deep regional and global ramifications because North Korea's destructive power could soon reach far beyond the peninsula, destabilizing the region and the world. Now we knew that the regime had been investing in nuclear war instead of seeking peace.

CONFRONTATION, NOT CONVERSATION

We assembled a joint South Korea-United States task force in response. As the head of our American Affairs Bureau, I became the focal point for the Korean side, working closely with counterparts in the U.S. State Department as well as with Korea's Unification and Defense Ministries and intelligence community.

In 1991, my involvement was formalized; I was appointed to be one of the five South Korean negotiators. Our first-ever talks with the North Korean government were held at the border area of Panmunjom, the peace village. Seoul knew this would not be an easy or straightforward negotiation where both sides fundamentally agree on the outcome, but I did not have the faintest idea that negotiations with the North would drag on for three decades and seven South Korean administrations.

The North made it clear from the beginning that it would not curtail its nuclear program. The regime's primary tactic was to drag out the talks, effectively playing for time while work on the nuclear plants continued. This led to some surreal negotiations. I was confounded by the North's manipulations, which began with the furniture itself. These kinds of negotiations are usually conducted with a standard conference arrangement. The delegations sit along each side of a rectangular table in order of seniority, with each participant facing his or her counterpart. During tea breaks, negotiators would often murmur privately among themselves, away from the table, brainstorming new approaches.

From the beginning, the atmosphere had soured. In Korea, it is customary to provide hospitality to guests, and there was no exception in Panmunjom. But when the North was hosting talks, their manipulations knew no limit. The North would provide copious amounts of water along with sugary and salty foods that forced repeated bathroom breaks. A contest was implied: the stronger side would not give in to "nature's call." Being relatively young at the time, I did not suffer much during this unspoken war of wills.

THE ELEPHANT HUNTER

Over three decades of peace talks, we could count on one thing: the conspicuous arrogance of North Korean Major General Kim Yong-chol. General

Kim, the highly visible right-hand man of Kim Jong-un as he had been for his father, Kim Jong-il, led denuclearization talks with the Trump administration until the February 2019 Hanoi summit suddenly broke down, leaving Kim Jong-un humiliated before the world. The summit could have led to an easing of international sanctions, but it collapsed with worsened relations and no clear follow-up.

It was said that General Kim knelt down before Kim Jong-un in the train heading back to Pyongyang and was demoted to a less visible position upon their return. General Kim had turned up in official photographs for years, usually in the elaborate military uniform of a four-star general. He is not tall but appears powerfully built, and he carries himself with the disdain of an indispensable advisor. In fact, until 2019 he was one of Kim Jong-un's trusted aides, an enforcer.

In the early 1990s, Kim Yong-chol's outspokenness and fierce rhetoric quickly brought to my mind a poisonous snake, and that is how I came to think of him. The regime clearly condoned his impertinence, which further underlined my suspicion about the regime in Pyongyang. Although Kim wore a military uniform with one star on each shoulder, he was the most junior member of the five-man negotiating team. In fact, he sat at the far end of the table, a position that rarely speaks. Yet he was a disruptive presence from the beginning, for example, challenging the remarks of South Korea's second man, Lee Dong-bok. Whenever Lee challenged the wrong facts presented by the North Korean chief negotiator, Major General Kim would intervene saying, "Mr. Lee must be from Korean CIA. Who, except KCIA, would dare speak when the chief negotiator is not speaking in the South?"

Serious psychological warfare was always part of the negotiations. Once, during a break, Kim Yong-chol approached our delegation with an unexpected question. "Have any of you ever hunted an elephant?" An elephant, I thought, as in Rudyard Kipling's *The Elephant's Child* poem? There were no elephants on the Korean Peninsula except a few in the zoo, and I found the question bizarre and devious. Given the tension in the room, this was certainly not an innocent conversation starter. "Well, usually an elephant is a difficult beast to kill even with a machine gun," he said with disconcerting pleasure. "But there is a way to kill it with a single bullet, you see." The silenced room listened attentively. "If you shoot it right between the eyes, the beast will collapse immediately." It was clear that the elephant he was referring to was the United States, and the single bullet was meant to be a nuclear weapon. Kim was clearly not focused on building an enduring peace and didn't care that we knew it.

Kim was particularly fond of reminding us that North Korea had the power to annihilate Korea and her allies. Such blatant and consistent behavior was intended to incite our delegation, and it was an eye-opening experience for me. But our meticulous preparation blunted the power of his provocations.

RISING HOPES, PLUMMETING ODDS

We sat down to work on a road map to denuclearize the Korean Peninsula. A draft was prepared with both sides agreeing to mutual inspections at a time and place to be agreed upon. For me, this mechanism—the "challenge inspection"—was the critical element of the agreement because it provided the transparency needed to begin accumulating the trust long lost amid the rivalry and hostility.

In September 1991, President George H. W. Bush announced his decision to withdraw all tactical nuclear weapons from the South Korean territory, saying they were no longer needed to protect the U.S. ally. The U.S. ambassador to Korea, Donald Gregg, informed me of this decision, which was immediately reported to my foreign minister, Lee Sang-ok, and to President Roh Tae-woo. On November 8, 1991, President Roh publicly declared that "there are no nuclear weapons in Korea, in the territorial sea, air, and the land." This gave our delegation strong leverage to negotiate with the North Koreans. Now we could say our hands were clean and free, without nuclear weapons.

On December 31, after a series of meetings in the last stretch of negotiations, both Koreas finally agreed to the historic South-North Joint Declaration for Denuclearization of the Korean Peninsula.[3] The international community hailed the agreement along with the Korean people. It was the first-ever concrete, comprehensive agreement in the history of divided Korea. This was one of my happiest and proudest moments.

A POWERFUL PROHIBITION

The Joint Declaration came into effect on February 19, 1992. Both sides pledged that they "would not test, manufacture, produce, receive, possess, store, deploy, or use nuclear weapons." There were strong but premature expectations that the Korean Peninsula would soon be denuclearized. I felt cautiously optimistic, as did everyone, but I soon became frustrated.

To verify compliance, in March 1992, both sides established the South-North Joint Nuclear Control Commission (JNCC). I was named vice chairman of the South Korean delegation, and in that position I conducted most of the negotiations. The chairman was Gong Ro-myung, who later became foreign minister. As usual in any bureaucracy, as a vice chair, I engaged in intense and often emotional months-long negotiations with North Koreans to make sure they would implement the eight pledges in the Joint Declaration.

This agreement was far more specific than the "complete denuclearization" President Moon Jae-in and Chairman Kim Jong-un agreed to on April 27, 2018. Unfortunately, President Moon's team, without a clear understanding of the previous process of negotiations with the North, continued to reiterate the vague wording of "complete denuclearization" found in the Panmunjom declaration.

I remain concerned that South and North Korea and the United States have not been able to clarify the exact definition of "complete denuclearization." However, even the U.S. government has been changing its position from "complete, verifiable, and irreversible denuclearization" (CVID) to "final, fully verifiable denuclearization" (FFVD). President Trump has said that the United States would be happy if there were no testing, suggesting that his priority is the safety and security of the American people. This is of great concern in Asia because it shows that the United States is thinking about the impact of North Korean missiles on North America, not their impact here in the region.

JNCC negotiations convened from March to December in 1992, and I returned home one night with my spirits and body totally exhausted. "Honey," Soon-taek told me, "I was disappointed by your attitude, shouting at the North Korean delegates." I did not realize that the beginning of our talks had been broadcast by the media. Normally, we would make the usual exchange of pleasantries in a "camera spray" for more than a dozen journalists. I must have thought all of the media had gone, and I was embarrassed that this became the lead item in Korea's 9 p.m. newscast, the most watched primetime news program in Korea.

My response to my wife was, "Honey, how could I bear such imprudent and brazen arguments by the North?"

CHALLENGING NEGOTIATIONS ON CHALLENGE INSPECTIONS

The South-North talks became difficult almost immediately. Seoul's priority was to adopt challenge inspections, in which both sides would be given only a few hours' notice before international inspectors visited a suspected nuclear facility. We were so committed to the challenge inspection that we included the U.S. Army bases, where the nuclear weapons were deployed. The North had initially agreed but soon called for different terms and conditions. Specifically, they insisted that both sides must agree on time and place, a demand that would buy them weeks or even months of notice before each proposed inspection. This would render the scrutiny meaningless. Eventually, the talks stalled on this point. North Korea abandoned the negotiations after thirteen rounds of meetings in late 1992.

Since then, the regime has completely shut the door, refusing to engage South Korea on the subject of denuclearization. Seeing the efforts of all those painstaking preparations and exasperating negotiations evaporate without progress, I experienced my first genuine frustration with North Korea.

Pyongyang did not return to nuclear diplomacy until 1994, when the United States engaged the North Korean government in Geneva. I believe the regime felt its very survival was threatened as communist governments toppled, including the Soviet Union. When President Bill Clinton publicly considered surgical strikes, the regime was finally forced to engage with the Americans. I still believed that the 1992 Joint Declaration on Denuclearization of the Korean Peninsula was possible because of imminent threats Pyongyang felt from the rapidly changing international political environment. The Soviet Union fell apart into fifteen states as nine former Eastern European and five Central Asian states declared independence, plus Russia. Yearnings for freedom and democratic rule were spreading like wildfire. North Korean leader Kim Il-sung must have been anxiously watching how this would affect North Korea. The threat of democratization must have tempted North Korean leadership to engage in the talks, but only to buy time.

Unfortunately, the Geneva talks left Seoul on the sidelines. By the summer of 1994, we had been shut out of direct negotiations with our own neighbor, and the capital was filled with frustration. The South managed these unpleasant circumstances by dispatching senior ambassador Kim Sam-hoon and his able staff, who met every evening when U.S.-North Korea talks were over and conveyed the Korean government's position. We now take such an approach as normal, and it is still regarded as a good partnership. But at the time this signified a huge shift in Washington's policy toward North Korea.

In Korean foreign policy circles, people became preoccupied with the selection of the U.S. negotiator. Two names were floated as potential candidates: Winston Lord, assistant secretary of state for Asia-Pacific affairs and a former U.S. ambassador to China, and disarmament expert Robert Gallucci, assistant secretary of state for political-military affairs. We preferred Lord, believing that he had a deeper understanding of regional dynamics. We also hoped he would minimize the damage of sidelining us from the negotiation in which we have an inalienable stake. Ultimately, Gallucci was appointed to lead negotiations with North Korean Vice Foreign Minister Kang Sok-ju. The American had a fine reputation and intellect, but his manner could be brusque, especially for a diplomat.

THE PRICE OF SUCCESS

Kim Il-sung died suddenly of a heart attack on July 8, 1994, forcing the North Koreans to shut down the nuclear negotiations for a month while the country plunged into mourning for the eighty-two-year-old Great Leader. Disarmament circles buzzed with speculation: Would his son and successor Kim Jong-il be more committed to the nuclear talks? Would he simply walk away and allow North Korea's weapons programs to continue unhindered by global fears? Seoul felt the impact as well. The North Korean leader had been scheduled to meet with President Kim Young-sam only seventeen days later, the first time in history two Korean leaders would sit down to talk. Now all hopes were shattered. The government considered sending a delegation to the funeral but ultimately did not when the specter touched off so much domestic controversy.

The disarmament talks resumed several weeks later, after President Bill Clinton applied strong military pressure on the North. The tactic was successful, and on October 21, 1994, negotiators announced they had hammered out the Geneva Agreed Framework, which would freeze the North's existing nuclear programs, adopt the safeguards of the International Atomic Energy Agency, and take other moves to further normalize relations on the peninsula.

North Korea reaffirmed its commitment to abandon its quest for fissile material, and in return, the U.S. government would guarantee the provision of two light water nuclear reactors and provide 500,000 tons of heavy fuel oil annually. This agreement also left room for the United States and North Korea to discuss establishment of liaison offices in their respective capitals.

The agreement came with a price tag. The cost of the two nuclear reactors was to be shared by South Korea, Japan, and others, including the European Union. The United States would only provide the fuel oil. To facilitate the process, a multilateral institution was established, the Korean Peninsula Energy Development Organization (KEDO). The final cost was estimated to reach $4.8 billion, with South Korea paying 70 percent of the bill.[4] Seoul accepted this burden with a mixture of apprehension and bitterness. KEDO, with North Korean labor, began building its first light water reactor, which would generate nuclear power without the ability to enrich the uranium rods used in the process. It was, as much as possible, a "safe" nuclear reactor.

Despite this apparent progress, in his first State of the Union address on January 29, 2002, newly elected U.S. President George W. Bush named North Korea and Iran and Iraq members of the "axis of evil."[5] As I feared, Pyongyang was quick to return verbal fire, and tensions again rose on the peninsula.

In October 2002, U.S. assistant secretary of state James Kelly traveled to Seoul following his visit to Pyongyang and confirmed our suspicions: North Korea was still secretly pursuing uranium-enriched nuclear weapons as well as the plutonium-based programs. The Agreed Framework collapsed. It was a devastating blow to everyone involved, and I was personally crushed.

THE SIX-PARTY TALKS

In early 2003, George W. Bush and Chinese president Zhang Zemin agreed to bring together the two Koreas along with China, Japan, Russia, and the United States. This process was called the Six-Party Talks. I do not believe it was a coincidence that the talks came together when Vice President Dick Cheney had taken ill. Like most "neocons," a small but influential community of conservatives advocating a vigorous national defense policy, Cheney was known to oppose such multilateral arrangements. But in his brief absence, Secretary of State Condoleezza Rice built support for this new arrangement, even winning President Bush's endorsement. I wished Vice President Cheney a speedy recovery, but I was also amused to learn how furious his team became when they learned that the deal had been negotiated despite his opposition.

By September 19, 2005, the Six-Party Talks in Beijing were showing real progress. I was South Korea's foreign minister and coordinated closely with

Secretary of State Condoleezza Rice and Japanese Foreign Minister Nobutaka Machimura, who later became Speaker of Japan's House of Representatives. We were all in New York, monitoring our delegates' negotiations in Secretary Rice's suite at the Waldorf Astoria Hotel. Our negotiators showed heroic diplomacy. We three agreed to accept the laboriously negotiated Joint Statement, in which North Korea publicly committed to abandoning its existing nuclear programs and returning to the world's key nuclear agreements: the international Non-Proliferation Treaty and the International Atomic Energy Agency's Nuclear Safeguards.[6] This was monumental, and momentarily I thought it was a victory for all six governments. Several more rounds of talks continued while the North continued to drag out the implementation.

The Six-Party Talks collapsed less than a year later, when Pyongyang test-launched a satellite with nuclear implications.[7] Nobody, except the North Koreans, expected the North to test their first nuclear bomb just one year later, even before the ink had dried on the agreement.

THE SECRETARY-GENERAL AND THE HERMIT KINGDOM

By early October 2006, I was nearing the end of my year-long quest to become the eighth UN secretary-general. I was increasingly confident that the UN Security Council would elect me, despite its reluctance to award senior posts to individuals from countries in conflict.

A defiant North Korea, which had tried unsuccessfully to launch several missiles in July, tested a nuclear weapon on October 9. The timing was terrible for me, and I had to assume Pyongyang knew that. Nonetheless, twelve hours later, I won the Security Council's unanimous nomination, sending my name to the General Assembly for approval and appointment. The Security Council members were determined not to be threatened by the North's malicious tactics. I was honored by the decision, but my heart was heavy as a result of the events on the peninsula.

Despite Pyongyang's attempts to undermine my candidacy, I was committed to using my role to advance prospects for peace on the peninsula. I had been contacting the North Koreans since my early days in office, hoping to arrange a visit and use my new role to try to resolve old animosities. North Korea's UN Ambassador Sin Son-ho was an unusually gentle man and a courteous emissary compared to others from Pyongyang. In late 2009, he brought me an official invitation to visit North Korea, but I thought the timing was wrong. It was too close to the December climate change summit in

Copenhagen. Climate change was my signature issue, and the talks were in jeopardy. I did not want to be seen as wasting time while my main priority foundered.

As an alternative, I proposed to Pyongyang a visit in early 2010. I raised this at the climate talks in Copenhagen with U.S. Secretary of State Hillary Clinton and South Korean President Lee Myung-bak, and both agreed that a trip would be worthwhile. The visit was planned for January, but while I was still in Copenhagen, the North Koreans informed my deputy chief of staff Kim Won-soo that the trip would have to be postponed. Pyongyang did not provide any explanation for cancellation of the visit. I later learned that Kim Jong-il might have been planning to visit China. Whenever the North Korean leader leaves the country or even when hosting a visit, they close the borders. I hoped for another opportunity and was angry that they were changing the dates at will. I look back and wonder whether I should have pushed harder to go at that time. I failed to anticipate that relations would take an unexpectedly sharp turn for the worse just a few months later.

On March 26, 2010, North Korea attacked and sank the South Korean Navy corvette *Cheonan*, killing forty-six servicemen. I condemned the deadly provocation, as did other world leaders. Kim Yong-chol, by now North Korea's director of intelligence, was widely considered to have given the order. I told reporters it was deplorable that the incident took place at a time when talks remained stalled. Such an unacceptable attack, I pointed out, ran counter to international efforts to promote peace and stability in the region. Relations between North and South Korea were completely frozen. There was no room to negotiate a visit, but we painstakingly worked to restore trust.

Between 2003 and 2007, five rounds of high-level negotiations were conducted among the governments of the Six-Party Talks. No useful role was assigned to the UN, and China and the United States took the lead in discussions. They didn't even consult with the Europeans on the UN Security Council, and the Russians complained that they were kept in the dark. I was deeply disappointed, both professionally and personally. Disarmament is one of the United Nations' signal responsibilities, and peace on the peninsula has been my lifelong passion. These negotiations only addressed disarmament, leaving the country's internal issues to other venues. But the humanitarian conditions were appalling, and the regime's human rights abuses remain among the worst in the world.

It was all the more reason to do everything I could to help. I continued my unofficial communications with North Korean officials through their UN mission, and we agreed on a planned visit in May of 2015. I was to have an interim stop on the way to Pyongyang; instead of going directly to the capital, I was to make a one-day visit on May 21 to the Kaesong industrial complex, a rare site of economic cooperation between North and South Korea. Located in North Korea near the demilitarized zone, at that time the area allowed South Korean companies to employ fifty thousand North Korean workers. They commuted in big busses, arriving each morning like Rome's soldiers moving by chariots. They worked for two hundred to three hundred companies and were grateful for the jobs.

"The Kaesong project is a win-win model for both Koreas," I said two days earlier at a meeting of the World Education Forum in Incheon. "It symbolizes a good way to tap the advantages of South and North Korea in a complementary manner. I hope my visit will provide positive impetus to further develop it and expand to other areas."[8] I was to start my day with a tour of the facilities and conclude with remarks to the press. There was no doubt this would be a canned encounter—the North Korean workers would not dare speak out of turn. I was too realistic to hope for any spontaneous interactions. After all, I had been there before, in 2006, when I was foreign minister of Korea. Although I did not expect the trip to break the North-South stalemate, I considered it an interim step toward opening a dialogue that might restart that process.

While my team in New York was busy finalizing the details of this trip, I was approached by World Bank President Jim Yong Kim, who said he would like to join me should I decide to visit North Korea. I announced on May 19 that I would be going, making the first visit of any UN secretary-general since 1993, when Boutros Boutros-Ghali met Kim Il-sung. The news instantly blared across the headlines and airwaves. "All parties would benefit from renewed engagement and commitment to genuine dialogue," I told the press in Incheon. Keeping peace and security on the Korean Peninsula is one of the most important tasks of the UN secretary-general," I said, stressing that dialogue was the only way to solve the problems there. So it was with a well-honed grasp of the complexity of the labyrinth we would have to navigate that I pushed for dialogue. But I did not expect what happened next.

The day before I was to leave Incheon, following months of delicate and detailed preparations on both sides, the North Koreans canceled. No prior warning. No explanation. And certainly no apology. The chance to reflect was forced upon me at a moment of personal disappointment. As secretary-general, I felt angry and frustrated, and the downtime amplified my feelings. Far more wounding was the dashed hopes for the prospects of peace. I had to wonder, How did I arrive here? We had only shreds of information about which offices within the Pyongyang regime had made the decision. It would be months before we would be able to perform a full autopsy on the death of that particular initiative. We eventually realized that my reference to human rights had provoked the North Koreans to cancel. I suspect that my comments were widely reported in South Korea, and foreign media did not help the situation.

I made the announcement on live television, shocking the public and triggering headlines across Korea speculating on what had gone wrong. I offered the bare facts about the cancellation as we knew them, and I reiterated my long-standing pledge to try to break the impasse. "I, as the secretary-general, will not spare any effort to encourage the DPRK to work with the international community for peace and stability on the Korean Peninsula and beyond."[9] For the time being, it was all I could do.

In the months that followed, I continued informal consultations with North Korean Foreign Minister Ri Su-yong. I hosted him at a private dinner at my residence in 2015, with North Korean Ambassador Ja Sung-nam and my wife. We met again in Paris at the end of the year, during the climate change summit. Each time we agreed I should visit North Korea before the end of my term. I continued consultations with the North Korean ambassador to the UN, Ja Sung-nam, and all the arrangements were agreed upon. Ambassador Ja and I had the warmest relationship of the North Korean ambassadors with whom I had worked. He was kind, accessible, and friendly.

Within the United Nations, few people were informed of the visit. At the same time, we decided to keep in the loop a select group of global media, including the Yonhap News Agency of Korea. My spokesperson, Stéphane Dujarric, quietly contacted representatives of these organizations as he had done many times for secret trips where we invited the press.

In November 2015, during the G20 summit meeting in Antalya, Turkey, I told Korean president Park Geun-hye about the trip, and she agreed I should go. Her endorsement came as a surprise because her government had a strong stance against engaging North Korea.

I also spoke with U.S. President Barack Obama and National Security Advisor Susan Rice, who had served as UN ambassador in President Obama's first term. She, too, reacted with surprise. "What's the use?" she asked. "What do you expect at this time from North Korea?" But President Obama ruled in favor. Washington was on our side.

President Xi Jinping was very happy and supportive when we talked about the visit. He even suggested that I should come to China beforehand to discuss the trip, and he pledged to render all possible support. President Putin also wholeheartedly welcomed the Pyongyang visit and asked, "Are you sure you are going?"

"Almost," I replied. My caution was prescient. As we taxied on the runway for my flight to New York, Kim Won-soo phoned, out of breath, to tell me that the trip—for the third time!—had been canceled.

The news had leaked. *Yonhap* carried a story on November 15, citing a senior UN official and announcing "UN Chief Ban Ki-moon to Visit Pyongyang This Week."[10] This leak triggered huge interest among the Korean press outlets, and they demanded that I also raise human rights. I believe these articles must have inflamed the North Korean authorities. I was depressed, frustrated, and angry that they were canceling for the third time. It was easily one of the lowest points in my career.

Many people asked me why North Korea had canceled my visit three times, but of course I could not answer. I could think of two reasons that may have prompted Pyongyang to cancel my scheduled visits. First, I declined their invitation to pay my respects at the Kumsusan Palace, the Kim Il-sung Memorial. Second, according to a well-informed expert on North Korean politics, the government was not enthusiastic about giving the limelight to a potential South Korean presidential candidate, which it was speculated that I would become.

I cannot refrain from offering a sober analysis of the current situation. After U.S. President Donald Trump's three meetings with Kim Jong-un, North Korea has been rewarded for making promises that are far, far easier to keep than the eight pledges in the 1992 Joint Declaration. Having seen how difficult it was to enforce such a comprehensive and well-thought-out agreement, I am left with grave doubts that Pyongyang will make good on its word with so much less verification required and so much more at stake.

A CITIZEN STATESMAN

Shortly after I retired from the United Nations, the Korean Peninsula was under the worst strain I could remember. Over the months of 2017, both Pyongyang and Washington exchanged spiteful words, flaunting deep-seated mutual disdain in full view of the world. In the aftermath of the repeated nuclear tests by North Korea in January and again in September of 2016, the international community was focused on containing Kim Jong-un's regime in a tight seal of sanctions. But these measures only made Pyongyang more dogmatic and intractable.

Throughout 2017, President Trump's intimidation campaign intensified, reaching its climax as he warned North Korea that its threats against the United States "will be met with fire and fury like the world has never seen." Kim Jong-un responded by conducting yet another nuclear test—the largest thus far—followed by the public announcement that North Korea had successfully tested a new intercontinental ballistic missile capable of striking the U.S. mainland.

It seemed that things were escalating out of control. There were reports that President Trump might soon annul the Joint Comprehensive Plan of Action on Iran's nuclear issues. I knew the North Koreans were watching the fate of the JCPOA, the delicately negotiated nuclear deal to halt uranium enrichment in exchange for sanctions relief.

Although I was no longer Secretary General, I decided to meet with UN Ambassador Nikki Haley in New York. "Do not underestimate the regime," I told her on October 12, 2017. "Pyongyang has been studying the Trump administration. Scrapping the JCPOA will send the wrong message to the North Korean leadership that the United States does not keep its promises."

I could tell she understood.

Meanwhile, the inter-Korean relationship had entered a new phase. Moon Jae-in, a liberal politician who favored engagement with Pyongyang, was elected in May 2017. It signaled a shift in our policies and, I feared, not all for the better.

LOW EXPECTATIONS FOR THE KOREAN SUMMIT

It is no secret that I had considered running for president of South Korea after leaving the United Nations. I had no political affiliation, but people generally saw me as a conservative and assumed I would join the ruling party. In fact, there was a widespread expectation among the Korean people that I would be a candidate. But that was not to be. By the time I returned home to Korea on January 12, 2017, President Park Geun-hye had been impeached for abuse of power and corruption. The conservative ruling party, Saenuri, was in crisis. Some senior members split off to create a new party, but I did not join them.

Nonetheless, I have often thought about how I would have worked with Pyongyang as the leader of South Korea. First, I would never use this position for personal or political gain. Second, I would be firmer, more principled, and less trusting of the North Korean leadership than I thought President Moon might be. It is no secret that I thought about running for president in 2017 after my UN tenure. Had I been president, it could have been my hand shaking Kim Jong-un's and my foot crossing the tile border into North Korea. Or perhaps that meeting would not have happened. A handshake means nothing if it is insincere.

The Moon administration is biased toward quick political victories, however short-lived they might be. I am concerned that the president is thinking about this monumental issue in the context of his political legacy. But he must understand that the North Korean regime would never destroy its own nuclear program. Never. This is the correct starting point for a relationship, not the manufactured potential for shared prosperity. I have warned Seoul for years not to take Pyongyang's apparent openness to disarming at face value. The North defines "complete denuclearization" as halting future development but holding on to its current stockpiles. South Korea and the United States expect a comprehensive disarmament in which North Korea renounces its nuclear programs and voluntarily surrenders its arsenal. This is an enormous difference, one requiring unwavering political commitment. Personally, I'm no longer sure the centrifuges will be dismantled even with full diplomatic recognition by the United States and a declaration of peace on the peninsula. The regime is not motivated by a desire for peace.

My doubts have never wavered. None of these leaders have experienced the brutality of the war years, nor sat across the table from North Korea's nuclear negotiators. In twenty-five years of engagement, I have rarely seen a genuine glimmer of cooperation or even goodwill. We need to be much more realistic and shrewd in our dealings with the North. By focusing its efforts on reconciliation, South Korea has already given up leverage that could easily be used against us or our neighbors.

TEAM KOREA

One of the most conspicuous outreach efforts was the invitation for North Korea to participate in the February 2018 Pyeongchang Winter Olympics. The International Olympic Committee (IOC), led by President Thomas

Bach, had been in contact with the North Korean authorities for nearly a year. For his part, President Moon reached out to Pyongyang unofficially after assuming his office, but he met with unresponsive posturing, leaving him quite nervous about the prospect.

Traditionally, the New Year's statements of North Korean leaders have been an important gauge of the state of inter-Korean relations. During the years of Kim Il-sung, who reigned between 1946 and 1994, they were delivered in his voice through a radio broadcast. His son Kim Jong-il—known to be an introvert compared to his father—preferred them to be transmitted via text in the form of an official directive printed in all major newspapers in North Korea, including the official publications of the party, the military, and the youth organization. Now into the third generation of the dynasty, Kim Jong-un resumed his grandfather's style with an added flair—a live televised speech. In his 2018 New Year's speech, Kim Jong-un informed his country that North Korea's nuclear and missile arsenals were operational. However, President Moon paid attention only to the leader's willingness to dispatch a team of Olympic athletes to Pyeongchang. Kim even suggested that the two governments discuss preparations. Eager to accept this proposal, the Moon government almost immediately released a statement welcoming the news. In my opinion, it might have been wiser for President Moon to delay a bit and give himself time to coordinate with Olympic officials and strengthen his negotiating position.

Throughout my term as secretary-general, I maintained a close relationship with successive heads of the IOC, including Jacques Rogge and Thomas Bach. I had worked with President Bach since 2013 to create the "Promoting Peace Through Sports" campaign, establishing a close personal bond in the process. At times, he would informally reach out to me for advice on matters related to North Korean participation in the Pyeongchang Winter Olympics, and I would lend whatever insights I had.

In the midst of negotiations between IOC and the authorities in Seoul over composition of the joint entrance of South Korean and North Korean athletes and the mixed women's ice hockey team, I had placed a telephone call to President Bach and asked him for maximum flexibility on the part of the IOC in determining the number of South and North Korean athletes to be accepted on the team. Of course, all conversations were kept low key, given the political sensitivity at the time. I am satisfied in knowing that I was able to play a small part in building the agreement that made the historic, unified Korea team possible in women's ice hockey.

It's true, the mixed women's ice hockey team was badly beaten on the ice. But the goodwill generated by their sportsmanship and mutual effort gave even the most dubious observers a glimpse of the possibilities.

KEEPING US ALL ON EDGE

Kim Jong-un's New Year's statement and subsequent North Korean participation in the Pyeongchang Winter Olympics turned 2018 into a landmark year for both inter-Korean relations and U.S.-North Korea relations. Counting the number of summit meetings alone, there have been four between the two Koreas, four between China and North Korea, and three between the United States and North Korea. Such a top-down mode of negotiation was unprecedented and generated a sense of security among Koreans, reducing tensions and building confidence.

One way to keep citizens engaged is through humanitarian projects, which I believe are vital to inter-Korean relations because they humanize the other side. But governments have important roles to play as well. These series of summit meetings certainly gave high hopes to the aging separated families residing in South Korea, hinting at the possibility of a much-awaited family reunion. It is unfortunate that despite, or because of, the façade of building a better relationship, urgent humanitarian matters such as family reunions are not making significant progress toward meeting the expectations of those who are waiting.

I am, of course, worried about the military front. By September 19, 2018, military agreement between the two sides had significantly weakened South Korea's aerial surveillance capabilities, a worrisome downgrade of its defense posture. Furthermore, I fear potential discord between the crucial allies of Seoul and Washington. The Trump administration's unconventional mercantilist view of U.S. alliances suggests deeper concerns over the value of the U.S.-Korea alliance as a whole.

The events that unfolded over the course of 2018 are worrisome because they have upended the functional definition of North Korea's nuclear disarmament issues, overturning a quarter-century of progress. Through a series of summit meetings, Kim Jong-un has succeeded in acquiring de facto nuclear state status by solidifying the idea that, in return for not developing additional nuclear weapons, his existing nuclear arsenal would remain in place. His image abroad has been transformed into somewhat of a state leader, on par with those he meets. However, the human rights situation in

North Korea—among the worst in the world by any standard—is no longer given the attention it deserves.

Kim's 2019 New Year's address did not mention giving up his nuclear weapons, arguing instead for weakening the U.S. presence in the region and railing against UN-imposed sanctions. Kim Jong-un's newly forged relationship with Chinese President, Xi Jinping, has added to my pessimism. I am not alone. For many South Koreans, the first U.S.-North Korea summit in Singapore on June 12, 2018, was a disappointing meeting in which the United States ceded crucial joint military exercises with its ally, South Korea, in return for vague language on denuclearization. It is completely unacceptable that President Trump did not share a single word with President Moon in advance of canceling the decade-long joint military exercises. The South Koreans fear that repeated concessions to North Korea will mean giving up on the long-held goal of the denuclearization of North Korea.

I was further troubled by the change in the Trump administration's rhetoric toward North Korea. What began as a strict insistence on "final, fully verified denuclearization" softened with the unlikely relationship between the American and North Korean leaders. Despite Mr. Trump's defeat in 2020, I worry that Washington is chiefly concerned with intercontinental strike capability. The prospect of any administration losing interest in eliminating North Korea's nuclear warheads, plutonium, and uranium, and instead focusing only on its delivery system implies that the U.S. government is only concerned about America's safety. This is an unacceptable position in an ally.

Finally, I am concerned about Donald Trump's lasting impact. His erratic negotiating style showed little respect for or knowledge of Korean culture. In March 2019, President Trump unilaterally lifted a number of newly imposed U.S. sanctions on North Korea, throwing his foreign policy advisors and senior treasury officials into turmoil. White House spokesperson Sarah Sanders told reporters that he eased the sanctions regime because "President Trump likes Chairman Kim and doesn't think these sanctions will be necessary."[11] I am wary of President Trump's unpredictable behavior, which has kept me and everyone else on edge. It has been clear to me that he is so hungry for a deal with Pyongyang that he would squander leverage in exchange for faint concessions.

Nonetheless, President Trump made a wise decision in Hanoi by rejecting North Korea's demand to lift a range of debilitating sanctions that have been choking the throats of the people and the regime. Although it is painful to watch, nonmilitary pressure is the only sensible weapon to compel Pyongyang to abide by the norms of the international community. I am sad to say that the poorly prepared Hanoi summit has harmed relations between the United States, South Korea, and North Korea. This will surely impede future progress.

However, President Trump was right to reject North Korea's demands for what it had to offer. After the talks were canceled, Foreign Minister Ri Yong-ho of North Korea insisted that, contrary to what President Trump had announced, the North Korean leader did not demand complete lifting of the UN sanctions. He argued that Kim Jong-un called for "lifting five of the UN sanctions imposed in 2016 and 2017." He insisted that the North wanted sanctions lifted that "hampered the livelihoods of ordinary people." In fact, among the eleven sanctions imposed on North Korea since 2006, those five sanctions are the toughest, choking the throat of North Korea. The trade volume fell by 48 percent and their GDP fell by 4 percent in 2018.[12] For North Korea, lifting those sanctions was vital for their economy and their people.

I'm sure it was a total surprise to Kim Jong-un when President Trump demanded the closure of productive nuclear facilities in Kangson. The North Korean leader had offered to dismantle only the antiquated nuclear facilities in Yongbyon in return for lifting "all the sanctions." The North Koreans obviously underestimated U.S. intelligence capabilities. Perhaps they really believed that President Trump would overlook transgressions because of his "love" for Kim Jong-un. For Kim Jong-un, it must have been a most shameful event during his nine-year leadership. It must also have been an embarrassment for South Korean President Moon Jae-in, who eagerly supported the success of the U.S.-North Korean summit. In anticipation of the successful outcome of the Trump-Kim summit, it was reported that he was preparing a grand plan to expand economic cooperation with the North through the New Korean Peninsula Peace Regime initiative, including reopening the Kaesong industrial complex and the Mount Kumgang tourism project.

AFTER HANOI

The four-month stalemate in U.S.-North Korea negotiations ended abruptly on June 30, 2019, with a surprise summit between U.S. President Donald Trump and North Korean leader Kim Jong-un. In fact, the bilateral meeting appears to have been something of an impulse. President Trump tweeted an invitation to Kim from the G20 meeting in Osaka and later told reporters he had just thought of it. President Trump—closely watched by scores of journalists, government officials, and audiences around the world—crossed the demarcation line at Panmunjom to become the first sitting U.S. president to step onto North Korean territory. Although no one saw this coming, it's fair to say that none were more surprised than the South Koreans. It was not clear whether Seoul was consulted prior to the meeting, and more important, Pyongyang did not appear to have had advance notice either.

After such an acrimonious conclusion to the Hanoi summit, the U.S. invitation startled much of the world, not to mention his own advisors and the Korean people. The hurriedly choreographed encounter of the three leaders was more than enough to excite the world's people and give them hope for a breakthrough in the long-stalled denuclearization negotiations. President Trump, as usual, starred in the spotlight while President Moon Jae-in was all but sidelined, a mere observer of the events that would impact South Korea more than any other country. I imagine he must have felt somewhat bitter watching the American and North Korean leaders smiling and shaking hands. From the start, President Moon had positioned himself as a "facilitator" rather than as "a directly concerned party." Of course, the Korean media and people were not happy to see him sidelined while the other two looked triumphant.

The two sides agreed to begin working-level negotiations within two weeks. Pyongyang, however, immediately began playing hardball. North Korea fired at least five short-range missiles over the downsized annual Korea-U.S. military exercises. President Trump chose to disregard these provocations, saying the missiles flew only short distances. Seoul was initially silent because officials stated that the launches didn't violate the September 19 military agreement, which calls for military cooperation and stops any provocations on the land, air, and sea, preventing unintended military conflicts. But many Korean people did not like the government's mild response, even after the Blue House expressed concern and urged the North to refrain from such tests. Many critics continue to oppose President Moon's cautious positions, which they say are calibrated not to be too harsh on the North.

What has been more troublesome to the South Korean people is that the North Korean official and affiliated media continued to slander and even ridicule South Korean President Moon in indescribably humiliating tones.

The South Korean people had grown used to the North's vulgar and abusive language, but this was unacceptable. Although mortified, the Moon administration was determined to ignore these jibes.

Much of the Korean public has grown frustrated with Seoul's response to our parlous neighbor. The global media speculated that President Moon has tried to achieve a historic rapprochement to bolster his popularity, or even to win the Nobel Peace Prize. Of course, they said the same thing about President Trump, who never denied asking Japanese Prime Minister Shinzō Abe to nominate him.

U.S. Special Representative for North Korea Stephen Biegun and North Korean Ambassador Kim Myong-gil met at the Villa Elfvik Strand in Stockholm on October 5, 2019—four months after the failed meeting in Panmunjom and only three days after Pyongyang launched a submarine launched ballistic missile (SLBM). The meeting ran all day but ended fruitlessly. There was speculation at the time that the Trump administration would be willing to relax the Security Council sanctions imposed on North Korea for three years to compel the country to comply with international norms. I don't know if that was true, but it would have been an unacceptable deal.

Visibly angry, Ambassador Kim blamed the failure on Washington, and even made a veiled threat: "The United States has failed to arrive at any calculus after the Panmunjom meeting. . . . If the U.S. is not properly ready, who knows what horrible disasters can occur. Let's see what happens." In marked contrast, the South Korean government, which had high expectations for the talks, responded to the breakdown with some dismay. Meanwhile, the U.S. State Department said that the North's remarks did not "reflect the content or the spirit of today's eight and a half hour discussion" and that "the U.S. brought creative ideas and had good discussions" with the North Koreans.

The breakdown of the preparatory negotiation in Stockholm only seven months after the collapse of the Hanoi summit raised concerns in many respects. I worried that the Trump administration—riven by scandal and facing another brutal election—would accept a half-done deal, allowing North Korea to keep its nuclear stockpiles despite Pyongyang's easily broken promise not to manufacture nuclear weapons in the future. I was pleased in December 2019 when the United States opposed a Russian-Chinese Security Council resolution to lift sanctions.[13]

I have spoken out for years trying to warn the world that North Korea would never abandon its nuclear weapon state.[14] The eight crucial words contained in Article 1 of the February 1992 Joint South-North Declaration on Denuclearization of the Korean Peninsula stating that neither side would "test, manufacture, produce, receive, possess, store, deploy, use" nuclear weapons are clear and unambiguous compared with the simple "complete denuclearization" contained in the 2018 declaration. President Moon should have demanded clarification on this phrase before signing the Panmunjom declaration on April 27, 2018.

Every South Korean government since 1953 has tried to figure out how to deal with one of the most resilient, dictatorial regimes on Earth. No administration has succeeded. North Korea continues to lumber down its solitary path, regardless of Nobel laureate President Kim Dae-jung's sunshine policy or decades of liberal ideas and conservative initiatives. President Moon Jae-in's passionate approach during the initial period seemed to gain unexpectedly smooth progress, but he had not fully understood the ultimate hidden purpose of Kim Jong-un. Under these circumstances, I do not know how Seoul and Washington, working in sync, will compel Kim Jong-un to move toward complete, verifiable, and irreversible denuclearization.

One important factor for the U.S.-Korean side is the rapidly deteriorating North Korean economy. By 2020 the country had endured eleven rounds of Security Council sanctions and was touching bottom. North Korea's official economic system is broken, smashed by poor governance, scant investment in development, and an isolation so deep that it precludes most international trade and aid. Only the United Nations provides boots-on-the-ground humanitarian relief.

In 2017, North Korea's official trade volume amounted to just U.S. $7 billion. By 2020, it was less than half that. Just one division of the Samsung Group (Samsung Electronics) earned more than seven times what North Korea did. This desperate fiscal condition imposed excruciating strain on the North Korean government and its citizens. Total trade volume of South Korea was four hundred times that of North Korea. When comparing the amount of export, that's a 2,500-times disparity. In these dire circumstances, people who are not privileged by the regime often depend on coping mechanisms such as the self-help "people's markets." Families bring whatever they have or don't need, and they barter or buy more useful items. Chillingly, even these markets are shrinking rapidly now.

Pyongyang continues to dodge international sanctions and raise money for its nuclear weapons program despite attempts to bar it from the global financial system. A 2019 report from the Panel of Experts of the UN Sanctions Committee on North Korea conclusively shows how Pyongyang capitalizes on an old method of sanctions-busting (smuggling) and a much newer one (hacking).[15] North Korea's use of ship-to-ship transfers continues to circumvent sanctions, and the country has been using increasingly sophisticated cyberattacks to steal funds from financial institutions and cryptocurrency exchanges. I am concerned by the hard-hitting tactics Pyongyang is willing to take. North Korean leaders traditionally have not taken responsibility for any failure. As Kim Jong-un declared in his New Year's statement, he might take a "new way" by testing nuclear weapons or firing ICBMs to coerce Washington into another round of negotiations with even higher stakes.

I do not know what the future will bring for North Korea's grotesque human rights violations, international alliances, or nuclear pursuits. But I do know that Washington and Seoul must show firm and principled positions if we are to avoid an escalation of tension. Without temperance and resolve, we cannot expect Kim Jong-un to behave as a responsible member of the international community.

UNSTEADY TRAJECTORIES

Unfortunately, cooler heads have been eclipsed by reckless emotions. Kim Jong-un and Donald Trump—who have insulted each other as "little rocket man" and "mentally deranged dotard"—were motivated by an ugly, dangerous pride. Moon Jae-in was leading with his heart. All were seeking unsustainable glory instead of long-term stability and trust.

On December 5, 2019, North Korea taunted the United States, saying it would send a "Christmas gift" and that it was up to Washington to select what kind of gift. The subtext, clearly, was that Kim Jong-un wanted to resume negotiations. Only two days later, North Korea's Academy of Defense Science announced it had conducted a "very important test" at its western satellite launching site. The results were so successful, the academy said, that it would alter the country's "strategic position." South Korean defense authorities believe Pyongyang was testing a fuel engine designed for an ICBM—a missile capable of carrying a nuclear device over long distances. This signaled to me that the North was, once again, deliberately provoking the international community.

I believe the Korean government should support U.S.-led efforts to eliminate North Korea's nuclear arsenal. This would be the most helpful course immediately, and it will send the right message to Pyongyang about international expectations. Kim Jong-un favors the stick, and President Moon has stuck with the carrot. He has been focused on reconciliation, particularly through economic means, to improve the inter-Korean dialogue. Unfortunately, there is little evidence to support this approach.

Washington briefly lifted some unilateral sanctions on North Korea in late 2018 when President Trump and North Korean leader Kim declared their first bilateral a success and, in Donald Trump's words, "we fell in love." That improbable ardor faded five months later, the minute the Hanoi summit collapsed without any agreement. U.S.-North Korea talks are currently in permanent suspension.

I have closely watched international negotiations over Iran's nuclear program, which is widely considered to be developing weapons as well as or instead of much needed energy. I dare say that Pyongyang is monitoring them at least as intently. As I told Ambassador Haley in October 2017, the North sees Iran's treatment as a preview. If the United States cannot be trusted to honor a carefully negotiated disarmament deal with Iran, then North Korea has even less incentive to forge an agreement.

Given the parallels, I was curious to see how the North Korean government and media handled the January 3, 2020, assassination of Iranian General Qasem Soleimani. I was not expecting to hear silence, but I think the strike resonated in Pyongyang, forcing the regime to reevaluate the Trump administration's willingness and ability to use force. The state media did mention the lethal drone strike three days later, but in unusually muted language. This reticence suggests that the regime has thought about its options and decided not to rile the United States. I interpret the mild response to mean that Kim Jong-un remains open to a dialogue with the United States. That is a hopeful sign. However, my long experience protects me from irrational optimism. Recent events are tantalizing, but I do not expect harmony and cooperation on the Korean Peninsula for a considerably long time to come.

Chapter Seven

SEPTEMBER 11, 2001

The Complexity of Consensus

Most people don't remember this, of course, but there was another target-rich building in New York City on the morning of September 11, 2001. Two planes hit the World Trade Center towers on the opening day of the UN General Assembly, a permanent UN body that changes leadership every September. As the chief of staff to the incoming president of the Fifty-Sixth Session of the General Assembly, I took responsibility for the welter of diplomacy, bureaucracy, and problem-solving the tragedy required.

Scores of foreign dignitaries were inside the customary prayer breakfast in the delegates' dining room when my staff informed me that a plane had hit one of the towers. I hurriedly jotted down "airplane hit the World Trade Center and it's on fire," passing the note to president-designate Han Seung-soo. The breakfast program, which included a keynote speech about the need for reconciliation, continued. When the second plane crashed into the towers just three miles south of the United Nations building, security guards interrupted the event and hustled everyone to the basement, a drab hallway leading to midsized conference rooms and a coffee shop. Everyone feared another plane. UN security ordered the evacuation of some five thousand UN staff members and hundreds of diplomats.

As Han and I raced across First Avenue to the Korean Mission, I thought about my wife, Soon-taek. We had just moved to New York for the year, renting a south-facing apartment on a high floor of the newly built Trump world tower. If she was looking out the window, she would see the disaster just forty blocks away. I worried about her peace of mind and wanted to go to her, but there was no opportunity to do so.

This was to have been a celebratory day for the Republic of Korea, which had been gradually taking on greater responsibilities on the world stage. The disaster, which we assumed was a terrorist attack, scattered my thoughts. I was buzzing with adrenaline but unsure of what to do with it. In a few hours, I would manage the world body's response to an unprecedented crisis, putting Korea on the diplomatic map for years to come.

DIPLOMACY UNDER PRESSURE

No one offers odds on the next General Assembly president because he or she is designated by their regional group as long as a year before the session begins. The position rotates geographically, and in September 2001 it was Asia's turn. However, member states don't vote for the president, twenty-one vice presidents, and the six committee chairs until the world body's opening day. The Republic of Korea's foreign minister, Han Seung-soo, was to be sworn in as president of the Fifty-Sixth Session of the General Assembly that afternoon in a ceremony rich in tradition and, of course, speeches. But the session was quickly canceled.

There is usually a one-day gap between the last meeting of the previous General Assembly and the beginning of the new one. But this year a disconcerting leadership vacuum was created, with one term ending before the next General Assembly was seated. There was no telling when the president and committee chairs would be formally elected, nor was the docket of work and the voting schedule finalized. It was nearly impossible to reach most of the 192 member states because most telephone lines were shut down, and police cruisers had blocked off streets near the United Nations.

Secretary-General Kofi Annan called a brief emergency meeting that afternoon with outgoing General Assembly President Harri Holkeri of Finland and incoming President Han, as well as their advisors. We were led by UN security through the abandoned Secretariat to the secretary-general's temporary basement office. I was to spend countless nights in the empty Secretariat building throughout the year, but no other night was as eerie as this one. Everybody looked stricken as we crowded into the small room. There was no small talk. The secretary-general suggested we open the GA session the following day under tight security. Our only order of business would be to elect the world body's new leadership, and to do it quickly.

Although telephone lines were down, his office had been able to establish email connections with member states and would communicate with the missions, as each government's office at the UN is called.

I returned to the Korean Mission, walking through the beautiful afternoon light. No racing this time. Workers had erected barriers around the United Nations, and with the sounds of sirens in the distance, I wondered how long these barriers would be in place. Finally, the magnitude of the attack landed on me: two ordinary airplanes, the buildings crashing down, the likely number of fatalities, and waiting for the next one. This was a shockingly inventive and heinous terrorist attack, and I feared it was the opening act of a new era in political violence.

I had no doubt the world was heading in a dangerous direction that would make the United Nations more important than ever. The organization is powerful because its near-universal membership represents every continent and every type of government. Small and underdeveloped nations have the same vote as the superpowers. The United Nations, I believed, should be a most effective forum in which to fight terrorism.

Han and I had no time to discuss the attack because we were developing a strategy for our first order of business: a resolution denouncing terrorism. The world body's credibility hung on our ability to condemn this horrifying act in clear, unambiguous language. As the designated chief of staff to the GA president, I convened an emergency meeting of the chairs of the UN's five regional groups: Asia, Africa, Latin America and the Caribbean, Eastern Europe, the catch-all Western Europe, and others. These ambassadors braved barricades, crowds, and possibly fear to get to my office.

Because there is usually unanimity within the regional groups, this was by far the fastest way to draft language that all nations could quickly agree upon. It was imperative that we pass a strong resolution on our first day of business or risk our relevance and respect. "This resolution should be a brief, strong, and unambiguous condemnation of this attack on the United States and the world," I told them. The ambassadors quickly agreed in principle, and I thought the drafting would be relatively simple. But I was wrong. Crafting a statement—even one as obvious as the denunciation of terrorism—can be very difficult with so many points of view. That's why so many resolutions are watered down. I shuttled between the groups, proposing language in increasingly frustrating negotiations conducted in meetings or, when possible, by phone. The process made me anxious and angry as I raced between the regional chairs.

On the streets of midtown Manhattan, some people were panicking, the news was still unthinkable, and the clock was ticking off wasted minutes. Despite the urgency, I realized that some groups were not feeling the pressure of time.

THE ROOT OF EVIL

The Arab countries and several others insisted that the resolution address the "root causes" of terrorism. In the language of the United Nations, this phrase refers to poverty and occupation, and, implicitly, to Palestine. The United States, in particular, hated the phrase, construing it as an obligation to increase development assistance as well as being openly anti-Semitic. Mentioning the supposed root causes of terrorism would be a roadblock to drafting what should be a short, sharp declaration. At the same time, I had been editing Han's speech, cutting it from thirty minutes by half, and later by half again, to meet the UN security directive that we spend as little time as possible inside the UN compound.

The antiterrorism draft advanced in painfully slow fits and starts, and in exhaustion. I began to question whether the member states could reach an agreement on anything if they were drawing out such a simple resolution. By the following afternoon, September 12, the attacks were already thirty hours old, and the secretary-general had long ago issued his statement of condemnation and condolence. The General Assembly had not yet agreed on language, but I was almost consoled when I realized that the Security Council, with only fifteen members, had not issued its statement yet either. I began to wonder if every resolution would be like this. My exhaustion crested, and I was tempted to rest my head on my arms for a few moments—but we did not have a few moments because all the delegates were waiting for the draft resolution.

"President Han," I said, handing him the latest draft of his remarks, "you must not dismiss the ambassadors and you must not end the session when you are done speaking. You must keep everyone in the hall so they can vote in favor of the resolution." I knew he was reluctant to draw out the meeting, but I told him that this was our only chance to vote. He understood: It was today, under heavy security, or never. But we still did not have a text.

The delegations were trying to cram too much into the resolution, and I emphatically told the five regional chairs that we need only condemn the attack now; we could work out other details in subsequent declarations. At last the Arab and many African nations dropped their demand and agreed to condemn terrorism without mentioning root causes. The resolution condemned the attack, conveyed condolences to the United States, and urgently called for international cooperation to fight terrorism. Short. Simple. Declarative. It was enough.

With only minutes before the 3 p.m. meeting to formally elect Han, I was informed that all GA resolutions must be translated into the six official UN languages at least twenty-four hours before a vote. Already hungry, I grew light-headed. I almost screamed at the Secretariat officials to print the resolution in English and waive the twenty-four-hour rule. I don't remember whether I was persuasive or pleading, but the exception was made. This meeting was our only chance to convene the General Assembly while a resolution was still timely.

By the time I got to the GA hall, the newly elected president of the General Assembly had, in fact, been sworn in and had delivered the remarks I had carefully shaved to only seven minutes. And, sure enough, the ambassadors were still in their seats. General Assembly aides were distributing the final draft of the resolution—in English only. We were almost ready to vote. I was nervous, and I think the president was too. In our haste, I had secured the consent of regional groups, but I hadn't contacted any of the individual delegations. I had an idea about which ambassadors would take offense and possibly refuse to join the consensus out of principle or pique.

I raced up to the podium, which sits in front of the soaring green marble dais and a wall of gold leaf. It is a very formal stage, befitting the decisions made here. It is also visible to all delegations and television cameras, so consultations up here are a rare event. "The resolution is being distributed now," I whispered to the new president, covering the microphones with a still-shaking hand. Considering the need for speed, I told him that the twenty-four-hour rule was being waived, as was translation into all official UN languages. My mind was focused, but my breath was labored from running through the UN's wide hallways. "When it's time for the vote, Mr. President, do not make eye contact with any ambassadors and be sure to pause for just a moment before bringing down the gavel." I cautioned him that "this was vital." Eye contact would embolden a delegation to raise a comment or an objection, and the pause gave ambassadors just enough time so they couldn't object later. As I left the stage, I heard him informing delegations that certain rules had been waived. With that, President Han introduced, paused, and gaveled GA Resolution A/RES/56/1.[1]

That's when the Cuban ambassador pushed his microphone button to speak. When the little light went on, my heart sank, and my empty stomach heaved. "The president should have followed the correct procedures," Rodriguez Parrilla said, referring to the translations and, more important, to consultations among the member states in advance. "However, I will not object because it is your first day." The first resolution of the Fifty-Sixth Session of the General Assembly was only 134 words long, and it was adopted by acclamation. I didn't realize I was holding my breath until I exhaled. Standing to the side of the hall, I felt proud that I had helped draft and negotiate the resolution. But I could not ignore the knot of apprehension in my shoulders. Why had it been so hard to get every nation to sign on to a resolution with which they all agreed?

No General Assembly resolution is passed until every delegation has dissected it with jewelers' tools, and that's how it should be. The critics are right; it *does* take too long for the General Assembly to come to a decision. A consensus resolution is weighty, and it has more authority than one split along regional lines. Bureaucracy is only part of the problem.

Was terrorism, despite its universal abhorrence, going to be especially contentious? Or was this the new paradigm? Al Qaida's attacks compelled us to postpone the annual General Assembly General Debate, the two-week meeting that typically draws more than 150 world leaders. Days later we decided to hold a compressed event beginning on November 10. It was a brief debate, with so many denunciations of terrorism that many other important issues were forgotten.

President Han and I didn't have much time to consider terrorism's rise and ramifications until after the General Assembly opening events. But we agreed that in the future the president should be officially elected by member states months in advance so there is never a repeat of this year's gap. I raised the proposed change with diplomats, suggesting a resolution to move the vote up by three months, and it was adopted in the middle of the session without fanfare. It was one of the most important procedural initiatives we passed that year, and a new president of the UN is now ready to handle its agenda even during crisis.

Drafting the terrorism resolution was ulcerous and exhausting, but the silver lining was revealed just five years later, during my campaign for secretary-general. Looking back, I think UN diplomats formed a good impression of me that day. They saw a man who would work hard, build consensus under fire, and avert crisis. That raised my profile as a powerful chief of staff and demonstrated my leadership ability. Many of the diplomats I worked with in 2001 have gone on to become ministers in their governments. As far as I know, most supported my candidacy at the highest levels. Sergei Lavrov, who later became the Russian foreign minister, and Jean-David Levitte, who would become France's ambassador to the United States and an advisor to President Nicolas Sarkozy, were among them.

More than one diplomat expressed surprise in 2005 and 2006 that I would want any more to do with the United Nations after so many divisive votes on so many anodyne topics. But by then I knew how to navigate the United Nations, and I felt profound respect for the organization and its ideals. This great organization had saved my life and, likely, my country, and I was sure I could improve the UN's effectiveness and reputation. I wish all nations would choose more passionately to uphold the United Nations' bedrock positions on universal human rights, world peace, and the importance of economic and social development.

Terrorism threatens us all. But if nations have to passionately disagree, I'm glad there's a peaceful forum for that as well.

Chapter Eight

PEACEKEEPING

Without 360° Agreement, Every Step Is a Battle

The Security Council—in reality, its five veto-wielding permanent members—writes the resolutions that authorize the use of force. They create the shape, size, priorities, and mandate of all UN peacekeeping operations, but it's the troop contributors that have the power. Those resolutions are just words until fully armed, trained, and equipped peacekeepers are deployed to the dozen or more peace operations the UN manages at any given time.[1] It's not easy to find the necessary troops, especially troops who can be sent with urgency as far away as South Sudan, East Timor, or Western Sahara. Every UN secretary-general has lain awake worrying about the demand for peacekeepers. New conflicts don't just replace old ones, they often add to the existing instability. I felt this keenly during my tenure as well.

In my first months on the job in 2007, the Security Council created five new peacekeeping and political missions: in Darfur, the Central African Republic and Chad, Lebanon, Nepal, and in Central Asia. Later in my tenure, two of the most challenging peace operations the UN has ever run were launched in Mali and the Central African Republic, each carrying many faceted mandates and equipped with thousands of troops. More than one hundred thousand Blue Helmets were deployed when I left the office, as well as numerous accompanying civilians. With the surge in troops, staff, and complexity, the peacekeeping budget rose from $5 billion to a record $8 billion while I was secretary-general—a staggering cost, although still less than one-half of 1 percent of global military spending.

This increase was a lot to ask of the UN Department of Peacekeeping Operations, which already handled everything needed by tens of thousands of troops as well as all military planning, budget, and personnel matters. And it was a lot to of ask of member states, many of whom were stretched thin by their UN dues and peacekeeping obligations.

It takes more than money and recruits to build any peacekeeping mission. I believe the most important element of any effort is political will, and that's one resource that has been dwindling for more than twenty years.

DIVISIONS OF LABOR

There is an informal saying around the United Nations: "There are those that vote, and those that go." I would add "those that pay" to that expression. Peacekeeping is a job that has fallen to the developing world. Ethiopia, Rwanda, Bangladesh, India, Nepal, and Pakistan send the most troops, anchoring nearly every mission. I can't put this more plainly: Without these troop contributors, there would be no UN peacekeeping. I remain grateful that so many countries are willing to put their own soldiers and civilians into harm's way to protect faraway regions. This willingness to sacrifice for the greater good is at the heart of UN ideals.

It is a political risk for governments to contribute troops for peacekeeping missions. Sometimes the troops are suddenly needed on their own home fronts. Other times it can be difficult to explain to a nation why its sons and daughters were killed in combat tens of thousands of miles away. I respect the leaders who are able to send the UN hundreds or even thousands or tens of thousands of troops, not to mention pilots, medics, and logistical experts, in the cause of peace.

It's easy to understand why some countries contribute companies and battalions to peacekeeping. Soldiers get combat experience they could not get at home, and they return battle-tested to teach others what they've learned. The UN reimburses troop contributing countries $1,428 per peacekeeper per month. That doesn't mean much in Europe, but for many developing nations that easily covers a peacekeeper's salary, sometimes with a little bit left over. This reliable source of hard currency is crucial for some countries.

It was understood that nations on the Security Council, particularly its five permanent members, would also contribute soldiers to the peacekeeping operations they create, but it doesn't work like that any longer. The United States, Russia, and Great Britain no longer send military troops in great numbers, although they do supply experienced military trainers to strengthen Africa's peacekeeping capabilities, advisers for commanders in the field, and analysts at headquarters. They also provide vital financial contributions and political support. The United States alone pays more than one-quarter of the peacekeeping budget.

Communication gaps grew between the Security Council, the troop contributing countries (TCCs), and the peacekeeping department. In fact, the "information silo" complaints were growing, as were suspicions. The TCCs, in particular, felt shut out of the decision-making process that directly affected their own troops. It was clear to me that the peacekeeping department could improve its briefings on strategies and evolving threats to improve their own decision-making. To heal the simmering communication gaps, I encouraged Security Council members to meet with troop contributors at least once a month to share plans and hear concerns.

WOMEN IN BLUE

I have worked hard to diversify the UN staff, and peacekeeping is no exception. In fact, gender was a priority given the ratio of male to female Blue Helmets. Although the number of female troops nearly tripled during my tenure as secretary-general, we never approached my goal of 20 percent. In 2018, women accounted for only 4,684 troops (5 percent of all peacekeepers). Only in the UN Mission in South Sudan (UNMISS) did women have a significant role.

Female soldiers and civilians are an asset to UN peacekeeping missions, and during my tenure we reached out to governments to request female troops, police officers, and support staff with special training. Some countries were able to answer the call, but they were the exception because women are not well represented in many national armies.

India sent the first all-female Formed Police Unit (FPU) to Liberia in 2007. The sight of 125 women drilling in formation in peacekeeper blue was an electrifying role model in a country where women had paid heavily during back-to-back civil wars. During night patrols, the unit has deterred sexual violence and helped rebuild safety and confidence among the population. I thought it was vital for civilians to interact with female peacekeepers as examples of gender equality. In addition, women and many men, too, were more comfortable talking about physical or sexual abuse with a woman.

But it was important to me, and to many in peacekeeping, to have women in command positions. In 2008, I appointed former Danish UN Ambassador Margrethe Løj as Head of Mission for the UN Mission in Liberia (UNMIL). This moderately dangerous operation with twelve thousand personnel was responsible for restoring order after two unusually brutal civil wars. They also supported the transition to peace by aiding UN experts on governance and human rights as they advised the new government. Ambassador Løj did such a good job that in July 2014 I transferred her to lead the UNMISS, one of our most complex missions.

DEATH AND REMEMBRANCE

There is a beautiful meditation room just off the visitors' entrance to the United Nations headquarters in New York. The narrow room is small and silent, with a few wooden benches; a six-ton block of iron ore, lit from above with a single white spotlight, sits in the center. When Dag Hammarskjöld designed the room, he chose iron because it can be used to make swords or ploughshares, war or peace. When I am in this quiet, Spartan room, I can feel my pulse slowing down and experience an inner stillness. The little vestibule outside the meditation room is the opposite. It is lined with scores of artifacts from UN peace operations that suffered grave losses. Both rooms are reminders of the danger and hardship UN staff and troops face in the field.

Two blue and white UN flags hang at the entrance. On the left is the dirt-begrimed flag that flew over the UN office in Haiti until the massive 2010 earthquake collapsed several of our buildings, killing 102 UN personnel. On the right, the ripped flag that once hung over the Baghdad office, which was destroyed by a truck bomb in the early days of the 2003 Iraq War. Plaques commemorate fallen UN staff and peacekeepers, and framed medals testify to their valor. More than four thousand troops have been killed in action since 1949, a grim reminder that the real cost of peace far exceeds its budget.[2]

More than forty thousand soldiers died in the 1950–1953 Korean War. As secretary-general, I met many retired soldiers in Ethiopia and Turkey and heard their personal stories from the Korean War. I was deeply moved when they told me that they had not known anything about Korea but had fought at the call of the United Nations. When I was a young boy, Turkish soldiers left an indelible memory for us. They were close to the Korean people, and many people my age remember a famous Turkish folksong, *Üsküdar'a*. When I sang this song during my visits as foreign minister and UN secretary-general, the Turkish people laughed with warm surprise.

Peacekeeping is an increasingly deadly job. Ninety troops were killed in 2007 alone, and that was the last time UN casualties measured in the double-digits.

POLICING OUR OWN

I think of myself as a man of peace, and UN peace operations seemed like a natural extension of my philosophy. During my tenure as UN secretary-general, I worked with troop contributing governments to improve how peacekeepers are vetted, trained, and if necessary, prosecuted. Every nation is obligated to prevent or punish their own soldiers' criminal or immoral actions in the field.

I knew that the only way to impose discipline for wrongdoing was to ensure that the entire chain of command would take complaints as seriously as headquarters did. I told the Security Council that I wanted to see responsibility flow up the chain of command, with officers in the field investigating allegations, particularly crimes against civilians. Superior officers need to be reminded that they are responsible for the actions of their troops, just as they are in any national army. But we don't have a lot of leverage. Complain about an issue too politely and nothing will change. But a more strongly worded rebuke might cause a government to withdraw its troops from that mission or others. For years our only tool was shame.

Each troop contributing country has a status of forces agreement (SOFA) with the host government and the United Nations to ensure that peacekeepers are charged or prosecuted only under their own country's laws. This can get complicated pretty quickly when, for example, a peacekeeper pays a local woman for sex. If prostitution is legal in his own country, has he done anything wrong? What if it is legal where the incident occurred? What if the other party says relations were consensual? The UN has a zero-tolerance policy on sexual exploitation and abuse, which effectively forbids any sexual contact.

For years, few peacekeepers were disciplined for what happened on a UN deployment. Investigations were not thorough, and trials, if there were any, were often perfunctory. The UN had to ask the concerned government to repatriate the soldier for investigation and, if necessary, prosecution and punishment. Peacekeepers are tried in accordance with their national legal system, but few nations took this seriously. Even if guilty, the soldiers often went free. Some governments sent these peacekeepers back to the UN for another tour of duty! That had to stop.

With no tribunal of our own—which I believe would ensure a detailed investigation, vigorous prosecution, and equal justice—we have to rely on governments to take allegations seriously. It has been a difficult process, but the peacekeeping department has strengthened our hand. New accountability measures allow the United Nations to withhold payment to a battalion if a country makes no effort to prosecute a peacekeeper accused of specific crimes. In 2012, sexual abuse of civilians in the Central African Republic was so bad that we had to repatriate an entire brigade.

The peacekeeping department has developed better systems of background checks and closer cooperation with militaries to ensure that bad peacekeepers don't return. The department has even refused troops with unacceptable records. Some peacekeeping units show poor performance in the field that necessitates removing them. In one instance, in the Democratic Republic of Congo, a platoon-sized patrol from an African country surrendered to just three or four armed rebels, giving up all of their assets, including weapons, uniforms, and vehicles. I ordered repatriation of the whole contingent. We could not tolerate this behavior. After a few months and many pleas from the government, we accepted most of those troops back, but only after a thorough inspection by the Department of Peacekeeping Operations.

Conflicts were growing more violent and diverse during my term, with the majority of peacekeeping operations taking on militias and guerrillas, not organized armies. This was a different kind of conflict, and it required a new approach.

PROACTIVE AND PROTECTIVE

As my second term began, Eastern Congo was again in spasm. Mercenaries of the M23 rebel group began blazing a trail of destruction through villages near the Congo-Rwanda border in April 2012. As the Kigali-backed army advanced, it grew larger, hungrier, bolder, and bloodier. The rebels' march was so decisive that more than a thousand Congolese soldiers defected, and the rest refused to fight. The Rwanda-backed group was initially composed of a few hundred former Congolese soldiers, but it absorbed brutal militias and more army deserters as it advanced, swelling to some five thousand fighters partially armed by and loyal to Kigali.

The fighters left a trail of blood and death behind as they sliced through Eastern Congo. I frequently denounced their human rights abuses, which included kidnapping, forced labor, sexual torture, and other acts of irrevocable violence. The UN Security Council and human rights bodies, as well as individual governments, repeatedly demanded that neighboring states halt their support of this group. I was in constant contact with the leaders of Congo, Uganda, and Rwanda, all of whom protested that they had no influence over the rebels but would see what they could do. These calls were maddening, and I paused a beat before hanging up so no one could say I was angry. But I hated these phone calls. To me they underlined the limitations of the UN rather than its strengths.

The United Nations Organization Stabilization Mission in the Democratic Republic of the Congo (MONUSCO) was another reminder of the UN's enervation. At its zenith, MONUSCO was one of the largest peacekeeping mission in UN history, but even eighteen thousand troops could not secure the widely spaced villages and settlements against rapacious militias. It was at best a porous buffer zone between villages and settlements and the militias that preyed on them.

Less than two years into the fighting, it became clear that the battalions were often too conflict averse to be effective even during nearby attacks. The mission was not loved; in fact, it was barely tolerated. Member states were reluctant to spend a billion dollars a year on a mission that had no peace to keep. Troop contributors did not relish sending their soldiers on such a dangerous mission. The Congolese people, the most outspoken of them all, complained that the UN was spending a fortune on troops that don't protect them. They wanted emergency assistance and development. Instead, they said, they were given peacekeepers who were afraid to fight.

By April 2012, a new threat was literally on our radar screens. Sadistic even by local standards, the May 23 movement (M23) was an informal collection of Congolese rebel soldiers, Rwandan fighters, and civilians who joined or were conscripted. At its height, it comprised hundreds of men, an unruly infantry without limits. The UN Operations and Crisis Center tracked M23's progress, and peacekeeping officials in New York were in constant contact with MONUSCO command. We watched in real time as the rebels advanced toward Goma, encountering little resistance when they cut through the junction city of Rutshuru and continued their southward march. We knew Congolese soldiers were in the region, but they either melted into the civilian population or crossed over to join the militia.

Satellite images and our UN staff in the region traced the M23 trajectory clearly—the militia was advancing unopposed on the provincial capital of Goma and drawing new fighters as it went. More than one million people were packed into the city and its environs, crowding that would make a shooting war as deadly as any in the Congo theater of operations. Everyone was on edge, watching what we feared would be a prelude to atrocities. Goma fell to the M23 rebels on November 20, 2012. The international community watched in horror as this band of hardened men and boys with guns paraded through Goma's main thoroughfare, whooping and hollering and shooting bullets and shells into the air as they hung off the sides of dilapidated pickup trucks.

The Congolese people, UN critics, and, painfully, those who believe in the UN were furious to see MONUSCO troops standing casually amidst the crowds, watching the M23 celebrate its victory. The rebels had raped, tortured, looted, kidnapped children, and burned villages. Why was the UN not taking action? Commanders said MONUSCO's mandate did not allow them to act unless a threat was imminent, and on this day they had no choice but to lay down their own weapons. Our commanders told us what was happening. Journalists and aid agencies told the rest of the world: The UN had failed to act. I could not disagree. This mission was a catastrophe.

Eastern Congo was more than a UN vulnerability, it was a tragedy and an embarrassment. Why didn't the UN do anything to protect people from the predators that obliterated villages overnight? Those attacks—with terrifying gunfire, desperate screams, acrid smoke, and the orange flare of burning homes—were impossible to ignore, they said, even from a few kilometers away. Many hundreds of thousands of local men, children, and especially women had been raped or slaughtered since the Congo mission was established in 1999.

Eastern Congo is a huge and ungovernable region suffering from the "resource curse." Incalculable riches in minerals, timber, gems, fertile land, and other natural resources have brought not prosperity but sickening waves of violence to this region. Whatever wealth the local or national governments obtained was eroded by corruption or squandered on weapons for soldiers who were always changing sides. It was difficult to tell who was winning this mutating conflict, but the Congolese people were clearly losing.

The Kivu provinces, on the border with Rwanda, were cross-hatched by gangs and mercenaries, many aligned with and even armed by the Rwandan and Ugandan governments. These fighters, many conscripted as children, were sadistic and persistent. They used fire, knives, and sexual torture to clear the land of settlements and witnesses, taking what they wanted quickly and without resistance. Critics rightly wondered if MONUSCO was unable to engage the militias or simply chose not to do so. Few understood that MONUSCO's initial mandate was limited to fighting combatants. Until the Security Council expanded its rules of engagement to include the protection of civilians, nothing would change. But the situation had to change, immediately, and I was resolute.

The last straw broke in January 2013, when MONUSCO failed to protect a nearby village against particularly bloodthirsty attacks. Peacekeeping officials in Congo said they could not help the doomed villagers because their rules of engagement do not allow them to protect civilians directly, only to support the Congolese Army's efforts. The same limited rules of engagement (ROE) prevented peacekeepers from chasing the fighters. The UN was widely and passionately criticized for MONUSCO's failure to act. It was a blot on the entire organization, and it absolutely could not keep happening.

After the Goma disaster, I called an emergency meeting with my senior advisors, including Under Secretary General for Peacekeeping Herve Ladsous, Under Secretary General for Political Affairs Jeffrey Feltman, Assistant Secretary General for Human Rights Ivan Šimonović, and Susana Malcorra and Kim Won-soo, my chief and deputy chief of staff. I was furious, and the meeting was not pleasant for anyone in the room. "Ask any people on First Avenue if they understand the Security Council mandates on MONUSCO," I shouted, one of the rare times I raised my voice. "The UN has to take all actions to protect civilians regardless of the mandate." I ordered them to draft rules of engagement that would allow peacekeepers to protect civilian populations.

Inaction by the UN forces was widely seen as indifference and even cowardice. I was furious about this, and I instructed Herve Ladsous to come up with a plan to present to the Security Council as soon as possible. In the meantime, I developed an idea of my own. I instructed Ladsous to draft the outlines for a small unit within MONUSCO to be empowered with first-strike capabilities. We knew the most dangerous individuals and groups operating in our battle space, but under the current mandate peacekeepers were not allowed to arrest them on suspicion. I believed their murderous ways justified preemptive captures or even casualties. I wanted this force intervention brigade (FIB) to be a highly trained unit that was authorized to make proactive targeted attacks on known militants, a revolutionary tactic for peacekeeping.

UN member states created peacekeeping seventy years ago to ensure that all sides to a conflict respected the terms of the peace plan to which they had agreed. As peace operations became more dangerous, UN troops were provided with armored personnel carriers and even attack helicopters. But until now, the Blue Helmets were mandated to prevent and defend, not to take the lead. Creating the FIB demanded that nations confront the limits of previous UN peace operations and take bold steps to expand their power. The FIB challenged nations to think anew about international peacekeeping.

As I had expected, the Security Council members had reservations. Guatemala and the United Kingdom were initially uneasy about using such unorthodox peacekeeping tactics and feared that preemptive strikes could lead to human rights abuses. Others warned that the attacks would shatter the aura of impartiality of the UN. But all acknowledged that something had to be done. Two months later, on March 28, 2013, the Security Council overcame the concerns of many nations and created the three thousand member force intervention brigade to "neutralize and disarm" known rebels.[3]

Three thousand FIB troops from Tanzania, South Africa, and Malawi arrived in Eastern Congo in the spring and did well in early, relatively minor skirmishes. Tanzanian General James Aloizi Mwakibolwa commanded the FIB. In late October, the FIB and the Congolese army advanced on the militia's North Kivu strongholds from the south, west, and north, driving thousands of M23 fighters across the eastern borders into Rwanda and Uganda. It took only four days to dislodge the thousands of remaining rebels and force them back to the negotiating table. But even the FIB later lost the will to fight, refusing to engage the militias, an attitude that by this point had infected most of MONUSCO.

I believe the FIB prevented attacks on civilians, and I'm deeply disappointed that nations lacked the will to contribute additional troops. I am even more disappointed in the Security Council members, who resisted authorizing proactive tactics for other missions.

40,000 NEW TROOPS IN SIXTY MINUTES

U.S. President Barack Obama gave peacekeeping a desperately needed lift in September 2015, convening a summit for the leaders of UN peacekeeping's largest funding and troop contributing countries. President Obama and his team marshaled their political clout to mobilize sixty-one nations to pledge more than forty thousand new troops, increase contributions for training and logistical support, and add air assets and medical facilities. These resources are impossible to value.

At the summit, held on the margins of the 2015 UN General Debate, I acknowledged that our peacekeepers—their sons and daughters—were now deployed to increasingly difficult environments. "The situations into which peacekeepers are deployed have never been more challenging, as tasks multiply and we face extremists, criminal groups, and others who show no regard for international humanitarian or human rights law," I told the world leaders. The United States announced it would increase technical and logistical support, including air- and sealift and engineering capacities, and contribute millions of dollars to training for civilian police and improvised explosive device (IED) detection.

"Too few nations bear a disproportionate burden of providing troops, which is unsustainable," President Obama said, overlooking his own country's very light footprint in peacekeeping missions. But it was President Xi Jinping who drew applause with China's pledge of eight thousand highly trained soldiers, a standing force ready for immediate deployment. Most of these troops had the specialized "enabling" expertise—such as medicine, logistics, and engineering—that every mission requires. Beijing also pledged $1 billion over the next decade, part of which is being used to train African peacekeepers. I was overjoyed. China fielded the globe's largest army by more than one million troops and its enthusiastic support of peacekeeping would go a long way.

The troop contributors' meeting was brief, but I knew it marked a new era for member states, reinforcing their commitment to collective security and making a strong linkage between peace, human rights, and development. Dozens of nations increased their resolve to contribute to peace operations this day. The commitment of heavy support by wealthier nations would speed up deployments, and investment in training and logistics would yield long-term benefits. In addition, developing nations pledged to send more troops to UN missions. It was a great day for the United Nations.

TOO LITTLE PEACE TO KEEP

UN peacekeeping operations are likely to grow even more perilous in the coming years. Attacks on Blue Helmets have multiplied as missions grow larger and are more effective. A flood of cheap weapons has galvanized aggressors ranging from armies to insurgents. Over the past fifteen years, the traditional battle space of opposing armies has been entered or hijacked by religious extremists in Mali, organized crime in South Sudan, criminal gangs in Haiti, and smugglers in the Congo, among many other conflicts. These and other "bad actors" are loyal to nothing and have no compassion for the unarmed civilians whose lives they shatter. These groups will never negotiate a peace treaty, make reparations to their victims, or take orders from a military chain of command. The most frightening part is that they are rarely defeated. When a conflict costs more than it is worth, these bandits are likely to melt away, joining the communities they terrorized or slipping across a border to regroup.

It is hard to remember, but in regions of desperate poverty and broken social structures, joining a militia is almost like finding a job. Fighters have food, comrades, and a common pursuit. As long as they are productive, clearing arable land or providing protection, for example, they can help themselves to anything of value. That could mean crops or cash or daughters.

Political will governs the number, nationality, and nature of Blue Helmets in a conflict zone. But it is also the single most important factor in determining how dangerous a peace operation will be. Without genuine support from the host country, peace operations will deploy with a significantly diminished capacity. Frankly, I'm not sure how to overcome this.

UNACCEPTABLE DEMANDS

I was surprised and discouraged when some of our most reliable troop contributors sought special treatment in exchange for maintaining or expanding their strength, especially in the most dangerous missions. I was shocked when nations, regardless of their boot print, tried to leverage their contributions to obtain a senior military position. An African state hinted that it would reduce its support if a favored general was not offered a senior post. An Asian state has Security Council aspirations, and U.S. President Donald Trump went further than any others, saying in 2017 that the United States will cut contributions to peacekeeping and other UN budgets if member states do not support American priorities.

Some don't want their troops sent on the most dangerous missions. Others will go to Darfur and South Sudan but don't want their soldiers doing foot patrols. Some say, okay, we'll do all of that, but we want a guarantee that our troops won't be in-country longer than a year. One government wanted to add a surcharge for every soldier sent into harm's way. These issues have grown more complex with the creation of hybrid missions in which regional groups seek to exert more control. Who can run peace operations this way?

I was disappointed in every government that tried to attach demands to their sovereign responsibility as a member of the United Nations. The UN is explicitly devoted to collective action to maintain peace and security. How would these governments explain their demands to the families whose survival depends on the Blue Helmets? There isn't much the Secretariat can do for these countries in any case. The Security Council alone decides if or when it will review its membership, and the General Assembly apportions the peacekeeping budget using an arcane measure akin to GDP. Without the political will of all member states, there is little the UN can do to make deployments safer.

What is the future of UN peace operations when so many countries lack the political will to participate? Peace operations will grow larger, more complex, and more numerous over time. This will strain UN peacekeeping operations and impose an even heavier burden on member states. If the United Nations is to prevent violence against civilians, political will must be renewed with a genuine sense of urgency and collaboration. By cooling the battle space, special political missions can advise ruling governments on human rights, law-making, and the rebuilding of broken societies.

Recent economic turmoil and lightning-fast pandemics have proven that "solidarity is self-interest," as Secretary-General Guterres has often said, and I wonder how so many governments and their people have failed to see the linkage between their own risks and responsibilities. I fear they have lost sight of the UN's bedrock philosophy that all nations are interconnected and have a moral responsibility to stop conflict, share the fruits of development, and invest in equality and human rights for all people, everywhere.

Nations also have a vested interest in doing the right thing. If the UN had been allowed to take a larger role earlier in the Syrian civil war, I believe Europe would not now be grappling with their own refugee crisis. In the twenty-first century, "somewhere else" just isn't as far away as it used to be.

Chapter Nine

SUDAN

War Criminals, Refugees, and a Cow Called Ban Ki-moo~~

No conflict had captured the world's compassion and consciousness like Omar al-Bashir's bloody, four-year assault on Darfur's virtually unarmed civilians. Many people marched for peace, others demanded military intervention. It was understood to be a religious and ethnic conflict, but I believe the hostilities were based on competition for natural resources. Two decades of failed rains had led to hard droughts that turned much of Sudan into a dustbowl. Most of Sudan's remaining arable land was in Darfur, on Sudan's western borders.

President al-Bashir had a reputation as an impatient man and a brutal leader who rarely concedes even obvious points and refuses to accept the global narrative of attacks against his own people. As a lifelong diplomat, I know the value of negotiation and compromise, but sometimes, I just can't be diplomatic. This was especially true when talking with Sudanese President Omar al-Bashir about his government's atrocities in Darfur.

We met for the first time on the sidelines of the January 2007 African Union summit to talk about deploying cargo for the new Darfur peacekeeping mission—a mission Khartoum was determined to delay forever. The meeting started out tense and quickly erupted in a torrent of words as al-Bashir raised his voice, clearly performing for his defense and foreign ministers at the end of the table. The Darfuris were terrorists, he said, and the rebels in South Sudan were nothing more than a gang of thieves stealing Sudan's oil-producing territory. I was shocked speechless and could only listen as al-Bashir raged against mounting pressure from the international community, including Security Council sanctions and a likely prosecution by the International Criminal Court. I was only twenty-nine days into my tenure, and I was blindsided. Nevertheless, I maintained my cool with a small, tight smile and perfect posture.

I was angry with President al-Bashir and disappointed in myself. The meeting did not get UN troops any closer to Darfur, where Sudanese soldiers and government-backed Arab Muslim militias—including the fearsome, horse-mounted Janjaweed—were still abducting, raping, slaughtering, and burning the African Christian Darfuris. That night I went alone to see President al-Bashir in his suite at the Addis Ababa Sheraton, the fanciest hotel in Ethiopia, and we had a surprisingly amicable conversation. Expanding the small African Union mission with UN peacekeepers and assets had been an explosive disagreement for Sudan and the United Nations for four years, but al-Bashir welcomed me into his sitting area and, without spectators to play to, we had a productive conversation about the delivery of helicopters and other materiel that needed to be in place before we could deploy peacekeepers.

This so-called heavy support package—including forward medical facilities, helicopter gunships, and crew-served weapons—is vital to any peace operation that is likely to involve heavy fighting and casualties. And the UN Department of Peacekeeping Operations expected this to be one of our most dangerous missions. The Sudanese president appeared to accept, or at least to consider, the peacekeeping package. As I walked across the Sheraton's grounds to my own hotel suite, I tried to make sense of it. President al-Bashir took pains to appear rational that night, but I doubted that he was giving in so easily. I knew his strategy was to play down the clock.

I had made the crisis in Darfur an early priority, and I was determined to make progress in any way possible. Certainly nothing would improve without our efforts. The Security Council had been trying since 2003 to pass a resolution authorizing the deployment of peacekeepers in Darfur. In 2004 al-Bashir allowed a small African Union force to deploy to Darfur, knowing there weren't nearly enough troops to interfere with his goal of largely depopulating Darfur's farmland. Between 2003 and 2007, land and air attacks, as well as subsequent starvation and contagious diseases, had killed three hundred thousand Darfuris. By mid-2007, months after I took office, the UN estimated that 2.5 million had been driven from their homes, and five million were forced to rely on foreign food aid. At the same time, hundreds of thousands of refugees had crossed invisible borders into Chad and the Central African Republic, a desperate and destabilizing tide that would soon lead to a peace operation there as well.

Sudan UN Ambassador Abdalmahmood Abdalhaleem Mohamad soon sent me a letter informing me that Khartoum would accept the heavy support package, effectively yielding to pressure to accept the UN-African Union Mission in Darfur (UNAMID). The letter was unambiguous, but I was sure President al-Bashir had little intention of accepting attack helicopters that would be used to control the skies over Darfur. Delay the helicopters, al-Bashir knew, and he could pause the whole peace operation. This could go on forever.

At the African Union summit the following morning, I let a few key leaders know that President al-Bashir appeared to soften his resistance. I chose a few presidents and prime ministers whose governments had some influence over Khartoum through business or political ties. I didn't want to pin him into a corner by telling the press we had an agreement, but I did want him to know that important people cared about the outcome, and they were watching. UNAMID was a $1.5 billion peace operation of unprecedented complexity, friction, and frustration, and it consumed much of my first year in office.[1]

MORE GENERAL THAN SECRETARY

But I did not have the luxury of focusing on only one conflict. During my first year in office, the United Nations launched five new special political missions and peace operations including the one in Sudan. Political missions focus on governance issues and conflict resolution to support the peace process before, during, and after conflict. These were civilian missions and are among the most dangerous in the UN system. The UN Mission in Nepal (UNMIN) was created on January 23, 2007, to monitor the disarmament of Maoist rebels who had fought the government for a decade.[2] The Office of the United Nations Special Coordinator for Lebanon (UNSCOL) coordinates the UN's many programs there.[3] I also created the United Nations Regional Centre for Preventive Diplomacy for Central Asia (UNRCCA), an ongoing mission to foster preventative diplomacy among five Central Asian nations and assist the UN operations in Afghanistan. In September, the Security Council established MINURCAT (the United Nations Mission in the Central African Republic and Chad), a small mission to help those countries cope with more than 230,000 refugees from Darfur.[4]

Sudan-related missions consumed unprecedented time, manpower, and money throughout my tenure. The cost of peacekeeping rocketed to $7 billion for the 2007 budget year, compared with a then-record $5 billion the year before. I think this is money well invested. Political missions can prevent or contain conflict by improving governance and resolving human rights issues. The civilian missions are dangerous, but they are important. It is far easier and less expensive to prevent hostilities than to end them, as we've seen in Syria and in other grinding conflicts.

But the tragedy in Darfur remained at the top of my list. The Sudanese government was ruthless, sickening, attacking civilians by air with military helicopters and by ground with the Janjaweed and other militias. All were paid and armed by Khartoum to sow terror on the ground. In the coming years, the al-Bashir government would repeat these steps to attack the predominantly black African Sudanese who lived in the country's south. Like Darfur, this would be a war fought between Arabs and black Africans. Darfur had rain, but South Sudan had oil. I didn't expect the southern front to be any less brutal.

DARFUR DELAYS

Despite a 2005 Security Council arms embargo, hostilities had taken a horrible toll in Darfur. The starkness of that hatred brought the crisis alive for many people who might not normally notice events in such a remote area with little strategic value. In June 2005, U.S. President George W. Bush got ahead of the United Nations and many in his own administration by calling the conflict in Darfur a genocide, a rarely used word that has, since World War II, carried an implicit military obligation.

But negotiations with the African Union were difficult. It was finally agreed that the African Union would provide most of the manpower and share the political efforts, but the United Nations would retain command and control over military operations, fund the mission through its peacekeeping account, and provide heavy support. The mission was primarily tasked with protecting civilians, facilitating the delivery of humanitarian assistance, and resolving the conflict. The African Union's peace operations with seven thousand troops were already on the ground, but they were spread way too thin to deter Khartoum's aerial bombardments and militias.

The Security Council finally created UNAMID on July 31, 2007, and at its height it was the largest peacekeeping mission in UN history. There was no way the United Nations could have handled UNAMID alone. The African Union was exactly the strong partner we needed, militarily and politically. I knew al-Bashir could valiantly stand up to the United Nations, an organization often seen as a Western fig leaf, but he couldn't ignore the weight of dozens of African leaders.

The mission was budgeted at $1.5 billion—more than $120 million a month—with an authorization of twenty-six thousand troops and civilians. UNAMID alone raised our overall helmet count by nearly one-third (to 127,000 from 89,400), but it was not nearly enough for peacekeepers to patrol an area almost as large as Germany. It would also be one of the UN's most challenging missions: Darfur had almost no paved roads, hardship conditions, a vast battlefield, and the ferocious resistance of government-aligned forces and the occasional rebel group. We had already learned that overcoming these conditions would be easier than gaining Khartoum's genuine permission for a mission. An autocrat as bold as al-Bashir could "consent" to a peace operation while impeding deployment by delaying visas, refusing to provide land for bases, imposing random restrictions on movement, halting equipment at the borders, and refusing the UN permission to import basic peacekeeping components.

PRESSURE FROM THE OVAL OFFICE

On January 16, 2007, two weeks into my tenure, I went to Washington for the secretary-general's customary first visit to the White House. This is a courtesy call and usually touches, briefly, on as many as a dozen topics. President Bush's passion was saved for Sudan. "I'm tired of getting blamed," President Bush said. He reminded me that he had already called the crisis a genocide and that the United States was the leading humanitarian donor. He was irritated that al-Bashir was allowed to dictate the process. "If it was up to me, I'd send in the military," the president said, "but I can't."

"Darfur will be my highest priority," I assured him.

"If the situation remains the same, we will implement Plan B, which is not a military option," President Bush told me, "but if wholesale slaughter continues, the pressure on the U.S. to act will increase." I assumed Plan B meant economic and travel sanctions. "Make it clear to President al-Bashir that he will be treated as a war criminal" if he continues his campaign in Darfur, President Bush added, with more vigor than he showed for the rest of the meeting. President Bush was frustrated. Very frustrated.

The carnage in Darfur had galvanized American human rights and religious groups into action. They raised money for relief, recruited celebrities to draw attention, and organized to demand government and multilateral action. The unimaginable level of persecution and its consequences motivated people to take action. I knew Darfur was a Western priority, and as my team and I left the White House, we agreed that it was heartening to hear the Americans give the UN such an emphatic mandate. Indeed, over the next year, the U.S. State Department and Congress gave us unrelenting encouragement—some would say pressure—to get UNAMID operational.

Soon after that meeting I spoke with European Union High Representative for Foreign Affairs Javier Solana, and former Malian President Alpha Oumar Konaré, chairperson of the African Union Commission. They, too, encouraged me to get peacekeepers into Darfur as quickly as possible. I used every carrot and stick at my disposal to move the process forward.

Few criticisms bothered me as much as the fallacy that al-Bashir was "calling the shots" on UNAMID in 2007 or in the UN Mission in South Sudan (UNMISS) in 2011.[5] When the Security Council creates a peacekeeping mission, it is implied but not mandatory for the United Nations to obtain the host country's consent. But it would be nearly impossible to deploy without it. A dictator had dozens of ways to thwart a peace operation he "approved," all of them within his sovereign rights. I, too, was frustrated. Very frustrated.

AL-BASHIR'S WORLD

On September 3, 2007, just a month after the Security Council created UNAMID, I made a whirlwind visit to Khartoum, Darfur, and the Southern Sudanese capital of Juba, now the capital of independent South Sudan. It was my second trip to the region since becoming secretary-general. I went directly to the Sudanese capital, where I was invited to an official dinner in President al-Bashir's residence, a large home whose formal living room is filled with somewhat heavy furnishings and photographs from every stage of his career.

I was accompanied by Jean-Marie Guéhenno, under secretary general for peacekeeping operations, and my special envoy for Darfur, Swedish diplomat Jan Eliasson, whom I appointed as deputy secretary-general during my second term. I was deeply apprehensive, expecting dinner to be as rancorous as our meeting in Addis Ababa, but it was a civil evening. When I returned to my hotel after dinner, President al-Bashir called asking me to return immediately to his residence. The president and I had a tête-à-tête in his library, and I strongly urged him to fully cooperate with the International Criminal Court (ICC). "Foreign governments don't understand this conflict and are asking the International Criminal Court to prosecute me for war crimes," he said, his voice rising with anger. "My government is completely justified, and I will not bow to the demands of foreigners."

I knew he would be angry and hoped to turn that emotion to the court's favor. "I understand a train is about to leave the station," I told him in a solemn voice. "If you surrender human rights violators to the ICC voluntarily, I may be able to stop the train. Otherwise this train may be heading toward your own self." Then I gave him a list of five names.

"I will not surrender my loyal ministers, who have been trying to protect the country from the Darfur militias," President al-Bashir thundered at me.

The ICC issued a warrant for al-Bashir's arrest on March 4, 2009, for war crimes and crimes against humanity committed in Darfur. This was later followed, on July 12, 2010, by a second indictment on several counts of genocide.[6] He had not transferred any of his ministers to the Hague, and I doubt now that it would have made any difference if he had. The ICC indictment made peace negotiations more complex for us because I and other UN officials required a waiver or understanding from the court to speak with President al-Bashir directly. More often, we spoke to members of his cabinet.

BLACK HATS AND BIG CATTLE

On September 4, 2007, I flew south to Juba, the capital of the breakaway South Sudan. I was hit with a wave of exhaustion. The south welcomed peacekeepers to stave off Khartoum's incursions, but its leaders had hoped for far more international assistance than they had received. I needn't have worried.

My protocol officers told me the government wanted to slaughter twenty-one cows in my honor. It was the twenty-one-gun salute given to a visiting head of state, Juba style. But I couldn't participate in this event, even though the meat was to be distributed among the poor. The optics were awful. I begged my hosts to let the animals go. Thankfully, they did. I had not expected that my first Sudan negotiation would be to save the lives of farm animals, but I was pleased to have passed this first test relatively quickly. Perhaps, I thought, it augured well for the rest of the trip.

As the UN motorcade moved from the airport to the center of town, I was startled to see thousands of people lining the road, holding signs and shouting “welcome, welcome, Ban Ki-moon!” The women wore wraps of brilliantly patterned cotton cloth and were making beautiful sounds, ululating like a blowing whistle. I felt humbled and moved by this reception, and I wanted to wave back, to show my appreciation. But my traveling security team would not allow me to open the tinted window, let alone lean out. I imagined this was how U.S. President-Elect President Dwight D. Eisenhower must have felt when he came to Korea during the war in December 1952. More than one million people went out to greet him. Remembering my own country’s rebirth, I resolved anew to use the United Nations’ resources to protect the people of South Sudan and help the country grow to be one of the most prosperous in Africa.

I spent the afternoon in meetings at the UN Mission in Sudan (UNMIS),[7] the first time I had visited Juba. Dinner that night was hosted by Sudan’s first vice president Salva Kiir, a hardened rebel at war with Khartoum to win independence for the country’s southern third. The commander of the Sudanese People’s Liberation Movement, Kiir joined Sudan’s government in a brokered attempt to unify the country. It was not a success. Even as a high official of the Sudanese government he still worked passionately—and violently—for South Sudan’s independence. The self-styled cowboy is a Dinka, a tall, heavily bearded man who stands out at UN summits because of his height and the black cowboy hat he never takes off. George Bush gave it to President Kiir during a White House visit, when the two became friends. He will tell you, confidently, it is his trademark. I will tell you, confidentially, that he is balding.

At dinner, Vice President Kiir gave me a white bull as a gift. I didn’t know quite what to say, but after rejecting twenty-one cows at the airport, I didn’t want to appear ungrateful. I accepted the bull with humility and assured him it would receive loving care from UNMIS peacekeepers. “All children born tonight will have the name Ban Ki-moon,” Kiir decreed over a dinner to celebrate my visit to South Sudan.

“Please don’t, Mr. Vice President,” I said. “I will only be here one night. I don’t want to be misunderstood as a man with that kind of ego.” That brought laughter from around the table. I and my entourage spent the night in the Spartan UNMIS base camp. I was well received, but the UN Associated Press reporter Edith Lederer said my traveling press corps was billeted in tiny rooms without air conditioning. She also confided that she and another woman had to shower very quickly in the men’s facilities because there was no women’s bathroom!

But now there was a bull, a beautiful white animal with tall curling horns. He became a ward of the Bangladesh Battalion, which named him Ban Ki-moo~~. Each time I visited Juba, I checked on my namesake to make sure he was happy and healthy. In fact, I have something of a menagerie. In addition to a bull, I have received or adopted several animals courtesy of my generous host countries. They include a baby tortoise, which took my name in the Galapagos, and in Kenya an abandoned lion cub, which I support financially. In Ulan Bator, President Tsakhiagiin Elbegdorj gave me an extremely rare Mongolian horse, which was brought back from near extinction. I named it *Enkhtaiwan*, meaning peace. When I visited Mongolia, I was able to watch through a telescope as my horse ran in the national park. She was a beautiful and powerful creature.

Although my 2007 visit to Juba was brief, I was shocked at how rudimentary the infrastructure was. Imagine a country of 240,000 square miles, with only four miles of paved roads. How could a country as large as this function without access to whole regions of its territory? I requested that key countries join in to help South Sudan. In March 2013, my own country, the Republic of Korea, sent the 280-person military engineering and medical corps called the Hanbit Contingent. China and Japan were among the others that heeded the call.

THE ABSTRACT MADE ALL TOO REAL

On September 6, I flew from Juba to Darfur. I was feeling much more anxious on this leg of the trip. I had researched, spoken, strategized, and worried about Darfur every day for so long that I felt like I knew the area intimately. But speeches, photographs, and statistics can never replace the experience of a place, the connection to its people. My group arrived at the El Fasher airstrip in northern Darfur, a chokingly hot and dusty area even by Sudan's standards. UNAMID was, at the time, the UN's largest peacekeeping mission and the very definition of a hardship post. We were met by the able and affable force commander Major General Martin Luther Agwai of Nigeria and Usman Mohammad Yusif Kabir, the Wali (governor) of Darfur.

I felt grateful for the compassionate presence of Jan Eliasson, my special envoy for Darfur, who served as the first ever UN under secretary general for humanitarian affairs in the early 1990s. We saw whole families sheltering in conditions so barren that they barely supported human life. The listless, displaced Darfuris were safe from Khartoum's militias here, but they were without even a tree for shade or room to sleep. This was years before peacekeeping missions were mandated to care for sheltering civilians, and we certainly didn't have the food, water, or sanitation to accommodate this many people. But we couldn't turn them out. It was a terrible problem with no clear answer.

Inside the base, General Agwai briefed our team from headquarters. Sudanese forces were escalating attacks on civilians and UNAMID troops, and as I had expected, there was simply no peace to keep or even enforce. The mission itself was not yet up to speed because Khartoum had repeatedly thrown obstacles in front of UN personnel, troops, aircraft, ammunition, and the like. Member states needed to contribute additional troops to the UNAMID.

It was a distressing presentation. Nonetheless, I was relieved that UNAMID officials did not seem to be disheartened, but positive and strong. One thing about the briefing bothered me deeply. When I walked into the room, a one-liter bottle of water had been left at every place. At least two dozen liters of water had been distributed to people attending a half-hour meeting. We were not on patrol. No one could drink a liter of water during a half-hour briefing. Indeed, by the end of the briefing, I knew that most of the bottles would be missing only a few sips, but all would be thrown away. As everyone well knew, Darfur was, at its root, a conflict over scarce water. This was not just waste. It was amoral.

In response to my questioning, a suddenly bashful UNAMID official said the mission would spend $2 million that year to import drinking water from Europe. The waste made me so angry that I couldn't think of what to say. "You can share the water," I told him a moment later. "Use cups." The water bottles of UNAMID inspired an economy for my own office at UN headquarters. For the remaining nine years of my tenure as secretary-general, visitors to the thirty-eighth floor received 350-ml bottles of water instead of liters. I never heard a complaint.

There were many issues to defuse in El Fasher. Even though we could protect the Darfuris from Khartoum's forces, we could not always protect them from each other. There were reports of theft, assault, rape, and violent clashes. Some of this demanded basic civilian policing, and I wanted to meet with the heads of different factions and try to build harmony among the suffering people. Representatives of three different groups had agreed to meet with me, but before we could sit down we were loudly interrupted by a fourth group demanding to be heard. They pounded on the walls of the Quonset hut, and I thought the whole structure was going to come down. We felt threatened, and security swiftly took me away to a better secured part of the base until the situation could be righted.

That afternoon, my team and I set off—admittedly against the advice of General Agwai, my own security team, and even Wali Kabir—for a camp for Darfuris who had to flee their homes. This camp, too, was extremely tense, although I didn't notice any animosity toward the UN or UNAMID. As our convoy rolled toward the al Salaam camp, population forty-five thousand, we came upon thousands of Darfuris lining the narrow road. We had driven right into a demonstration. The crowd was chanting something I couldn't understand, but I understood from the picket signs that they were waiting for the lawyer turned rebel leader Abdul Wahid al-Nur, whom I knew had been spending most of his time in Paris. I saw a lot of picket signs and a surprising number of weapons. It was a frightening moment, even after I realized they were not protesting against us!

In a moment, we were surrounded. I was instantly aware that so many people could easily flip over our vehicle. We were trapped. Our convoy stopped, unable to go forward or backward. I was desperate to diffuse the situation. That's when I noticed the water pump on a slight rise about twenty yards from the road. Despite the crush of people, I somehow opened the car door and eased out into and then through the crowd. It took at least five minutes to press my way onto clear ground. Free of the crowd, I ran up the hill even before security caught up. Everyone watched, some with fear and others with appetite, but I knew that UNICEF had been here, and I hoped the pump was now working.

"Keep it simple," I told myself. Long sentences would not work here as they did in New York. "Ladies and gentlemen," I said through the loudspeaker handed to me by a UNAMID soldier. I was sure that a few people could translate for the others. If the pump worked, words would be unnecessary. "I am here to bring you water! You will go back to your homes!" I said, straining just a little to move the handle up and down. The pump quickly loosened up in my hand, but I was acutely aware it might not work. I continued to pump the handle with a confidence I did not feel. Suddenly there was a gurgle and a snort and then a burst of precious water. I realized I had been holding my breath and exhaled, deeply relieved. Then I heard the chanting again. This time it was "Welcome, Welcome, Ban Ki-moon!"

THE BREAKTHROUGH

I had to pass through Khartoum on my way back to New York. Although he was surely not pleased with my travels, President al-Bashir invited me to a late dinner that night. Foreign Minister Ali Karti was there, and I was accompanied by my deputy chief of staff Kim Won-soo. There was another guest that night, Mark Siljander, a retired Republican congressman and former U.S. Alternative Representative to the UN. The congressman asked the president to pray with him to the Christian God, even though he knew President al-Bashir was a Muslim. He bowed his head as Siljander prayed aloud, passionately, for peace in Sudan.

That night Siljander convinced President al-Bashir to work closely with the United Nations. We spoke calmly about UNAMID's need for the helicopters, hospitals, and heavy weapons. It was quite an interesting evening. I almost held my breath at times, waiting for the president to grow angry, but he never did. Al-Bashir was acting as a person that night, not a dictator, and much of the conversation was thoughtful and respectful. Of course, President al-Bashir did not agree on the spot, but a few months later he did accept the UN's proposal for a heavy support package.

THE YOUNGEST NATION

The people of South Sudan celebrated their independence on July 9, 2011. Five days later, the General Assembly admitted the Republic of South Sudan as the one-hundred-ninety-third member state of the United Nations. I flew to Juba to attend the formal ceremony, hoping the militia leaders would turn to the business of building their new country rather than continue to tear down the people and their prospects.

Independence Day was an ecstatic event, beginning just after midnight with an all-night explosion of pride and joy. By dawn, people began filling the stands of the Juba football soccer stadium and pressing together in nearby Freedom Square. Some three hundred thousand people were there that day. Young men climbed trees for a view of the festivities, and joyous citizens screamed, danced, and wept as the flag was hoisted and a band played the newly composed national anthem. This was one of the proudest days of my diplomatic life. The United Nations, our partners, and I had worked so hard to help create the world's newest country, ending the devastating twenty-two-year civil war with Khartoum that had killed more than

1.4 million people. The Sudanese oil reserves, most of which were located in South Sudan, propelled and sustained the conflict. With independence, and al-Bashir's presence, I felt hope that the war was finished.

So many world leaders attended the ceremony that a special dais had to be built to accommodate as many VIPs as possible. Dozens of African leaders sat in tight rows in the full sun. Foreign Secretary William Hague represented the United Kingdom, and UN Ambassador Susan Rice represented the United States. Bitter rivals Salva Kiir and Omar al-Bashir entered together to thunderous applause. I was as surprised by this reception as I was to see the two leaders sitting together during the lengthy ceremony. The sun was absolutely scorching, and as I listened to General Assembly President Joseph Deiss speak, I wondered what the first signs of heat stroke might be. I marveled that so many people lived under these conditions.

Soon it was my turn to speak. "Both of you have made difficult decisions and compromises," I said. "Seeing both of you here today testifies to your common commitment to peace and partnership." Then I told the South Sudanese people to have hope despite political insecurity and deep poverty. "We must not underestimate South Sudan's remarkable potential, its resilient and talented people, abundant natural resources, huge areas of arable land, and the great Nile running through it. South Sudan could grow into a prosperous, productive nation capable of meeting the needs of its people." That is, I thought, if those leaders genuinely embrace each other.

The ceremony was moving, but also very long. I left in the middle of it to fly to Addis Ababa to catch my plane back to New York, but there was a traffic jam. At least thirty private planes were parked at the airstrip in one of the poorest countries in the world, and my plane was blocked. I briefly thought about asking world leaders to carpool when so many share a destination. Fortunately, we located the plane used by the head of UNAMID near the edge of the flock, and I took that one instead and arrived in Addis with no time to spare.

The political situation in South Sudan never did coalesce into a unified government. Factions were always rising and ruining, interfering with the stability of the world's newest country. Within a month of the Freedom Square celebration, three hundred people were killed in ethnic clashes in Jonglei State. Sudan and South Sudan were resurrecting their prolonged war. As in Darfur, the sides battled for natural resources—this time rich oil reserves—with an overlay of Khartoum's racist hatred of the black South Sudanese.

Shortly after that beautiful Independence celebration, President Kiir ordered his troops to seize oil fields in South Sudan, demanding that President al-Bashir agree to negotiate Juba's share of the heavy tariffs levied on oil exports. President al-Bashir quickly threatened a military response. I telephoned President Kiir and asked him to withdraw, and in response he addressed the South Sudan Parliament: "Secretary-General Ban Ki-moon asked me to withdraw from the oil fields, but he is not my commander," the president said. It was a warning to the international community that he would not brook interference.

By this point, rebel factions, too, were back at war, and tens of thousands of people were again running from their homes. I saw President Kiir again at the 2012 African Union summit and asked him for a moment. I think he knew what was coming because his shoulders drooped while his face hardened. "Mr. President," I said, "you are no longer a factional leader. You are president of a sovereign nation. Your country is just born. If I were you, I would focus on your domestic situations, making your society healthy, instead of feuding." I was surprised to hear my voice growing louder. "You should be concentrating on political stability and development."

I have always felt a special affinity for South Sudan, and I was angry and frustrated that President Kiir's lust for money and power had killed thousands and displaced more than a million people, just when it appeared their lives would improve. President Kiir was very uncomfortable. He didn't answer me, and I couldn't tell whether he was chastened or pensive. Either way, I thought, my message was getting through. It was beyond UN norms for the secretary-general to talk to a head of state in such a blunt way, but I knew I had to because there was so much bloodshed and instability.

VIOLENCE ERUPTS AND PEACEKEEPING ADAPTS

Perhaps my words were not forceful enough. Tensions between President Kiir and his former Vice President Riek Machar exploded in a wave of violence that quickly consumed Juba and then engulfed a country already fissured by civil wars. By May 27, 2014, nearly one hundred thousand South Sudanese were sheltering inside UNMISS bases. The Blue Helmets and so many civilians were a rich target for both the South Sudanese rebels and the nascent national army composed of the Sudan People's Liberation Army soldiers. I tried not to take it personally, but the whole UN system had supported Juba through its long struggle for independence. Kiir and the rebel leaders were backsliding to the gun instead of progressing to the negotiating table. Once again, ethnic conflict was out of control.

That same day, the Security Council, sensitive to criticism, renewed the UNMISS mandate putting the protection of civilians at its core. For years, most missions were permitted to shoot only in self-defense, but not to protect local populations. Stories of peacekeepers “allowing” harm to come to civilians almost destroyed our credibility. Updating the rules of engagement finally met the needs of individual conflicts, but it was also a recognition that in armed conflicts thousands of civilians have nowhere else to go.

The United Nations had made South Sudan's independence possible with peacekeeping, election monitoring, and early investments in education and infrastructure. But we failed to keep—or, more realistically, to enforce—the peace in this newborn nation. The promises of peace and development had been sidelined by tribal and ethnic conflicts and power politics infected by greed. As time goes by, I grow even more disappointed with militants who, a decade before, had presented themselves as leaders of their people.

President Salva Kiir and Vice President Riek Machar have twice eagerly renewed the conflict that's already forced six million people to rely on food aid and driven four million from their homes. By the time I left office, more than one hundred thousand desperate South Sudanese were still sheltering in UN compounds—often bringing their own rivalries with them. The country remains lacerated by militias controlled by Machar and Kiir.

I worked as hard as I could to bring the Sudanese people stability and relief, and I know that many others can say the same. I wonder what else could have been done to end this pointless conflict. Certainly, the African Union and the League of Arab States could have increased the pressure on Kiir and Machar to overcome their hatred and greed for the good of their young nation. Now, in 2021, it feels like Kiir and Machar have been married and divorced three times, and no amount of international pressure will compel them to remain together.

"JUST FALL, THAT'S ALL"

In December of 2018, by then a private citizen, I watched the people of Sudan rise like a wave against the dictator who had so utterly failed his people and his land. Mobilized by shortages and poverty, the Sudanese took to the streets to demand economic and political reforms. Hundreds of thousands of demonstrators turned out in cities and then towns throughout the country. Civil society was decimated under al-Bashir's rule, and the rebellion was, in part, launched by an ad hoc alliance of doctors, lawyers, and other professionals. But it was Sudan's women and the country's millions of young people who propelled the leaderless uprising across Sudan's rural villages and teeming cities. They sang in protest. They danced. At first, they chanted "No to high prices, no to corruption." As the people gathered strength and determination, their demands became more political: "Just fall, that's all."

I was disappointed that the international community had not raced to Sudan's aid. In April 2019, when the song-filled surge of change lapped against the government's own walls, Sudan's generals announced they had taken power in a nonviolent coup. They claimed to be a transitional government that would bring democracy to the country, and they told the people to disburse. But the Sudanese remained defiant. They continued to protest the high cost of such a poor quality of life and demand new civil and political human rights.

One of the enduring images of the demonstrations is the "Woman in White," a charismatic twenty-two-year-old Sudanese student and protester who climbed onto a car roof and led thousands of people in a call-and-response of protest outside the military headquarters. Clad in Sudan's once-fashionable *thoub*—a white cotton headscarf, shirt, and skirt—Alaa Salah gleamed against the dusty twilight. I watched the news on Korean TV and was moved by her determination and the joyous response from the tightly packed crowd. I silently implored the new leadership to let the Sudanese people rediscover their dignity, freedom, and purpose. The following day, when the junta's commanding general was said to be replaced by Khartoum's fearsome chief of intelligence, the Sudanese people did not blink. They stayed in the streets, often protected by the soldiers who had been ordered to disperse them. Millions of demonstrators throughout Sudan celebrated their victory, but it was too soon to say whether they had really won.

The Sovereignty Council, a civilian-military ruling coalition, appeared to seek legitimacy. The council announced in February 2020 that it might send al-Bashir for prosecution by the International Criminal Court. This was a welcome sign, and I hoped they meant it. Hearing the news, I thought about the meeting when I had strongly warned al-Bashir about possible humiliation by the ICC. Perhaps he regretted not listening to my advice, but it was too late.

The council chose Abdalla Hamdok, an economist and former official with the UN Economic Commission for Africa, as prime minister. He was a sturdy choice, and I hoped he had the wisdom and connections to lead

Sudan out of the desperate postwar economic crisis that once again had put the country on the verge of collapse.

By 2020, the UN Security Council had begun drawing down the joint UN-AU Mission in Darfur, to be replaced by a political and peace-building mission with far fewer police and troops. I am not confident that UNAMID's work is complete. Nonetheless, the shift to nation-building felt like a landmark, a triumphant accomplishment for the UN Department of Peacekeeping Operations. It is a rare victory when a peace operation ends, as evidenced by so many missions that are at least thirty and often sixty years old.

I hope peacekeepers will never need to return to South Sudan. President Salva Kiir and Vice President Riek Machar pledged to end their brutal struggle to rule the world's youngest country. The former warlords jointly announced a new cabinet in March 2020, which is very good news—if it lasts. I have my doubts. The two have reconciled and ruptured many times, and I feared this rapprochement might collapse as the others had.

Leaders in Khartoum and Juba must understand that they are responsible for creating the peace and security that will allow their exhausted people to recover and rebuild. Their countries are permanently intertwined, separate yet codependent. This means taking concrete steps to build legitimate governments that respect human rights, invest in development, and pursue peace at home and with neighboring states. If these conditions prevail, Sudan may be the only genuine success of the painful Arab Spring.

Chapter Ten

GAZA

Conveyor Belt Diplomacy

To my dismay, Hamas militants heightened their attacks on southern Israel on November 4, 2008, violating the final five weeks of a fragile cease-fire with volleys of homemade Qassem rockets. Islamic militia fired more than two hundred projectiles toward Israeli towns in only two days despite a near-global condemnation of this provocation. The rockets were rickety; they packed a relatively weak payload and had such a weak guidance system that they rarely hit a target. Nevertheless, they were effective tools of terror. By the end of December, Israelis living close to Gaza's northern border had begun to spend almost as much time in their bomb shelters as they did above ground.

I watched sadly, knowing that Israel would not hesitate to enter the Palestinian enclave and certain of what would happen when they got there. More than 1.5 million Gazans—hundreds of them working for the UN relief agency—were sealed inside a war zone, and the inevitable human toll would be brutal. Sure enough, Israeli tanks lined up around the tall, reinforced walls that would not protect Gaza from a ground war. Israel had already halted the electrical supply to the territory and shut down many water mains. Israel controlled the borders and refused to allow entry to journalists, human rights experts, and aid workers, drastically reducing outside witnesses to the incursion.

My political advisors and Middle East experts agreed that the situation was grim and would grow worse. B. Lynn Pascoe, under secretary general for political affairs, worked with me to organize and monitor the situation. I immediately began consulting with regional and international leaders, including President Hosni Mubarak of Egypt, Secretary General of the League of Arab States Amr Moussa, EU High Representative Javier Solana, and Israeli Prime Minister Ehud Olmert. I strongly appealed to the leaders to influence the parties so that the situation would not escalate. I urged Prime Minister Olmert to refrain from taking any military action. He and President Abbas had been engaging in negotiations to reach an agreement for a durable peace, but I was seriously concerned that these negotiations might be spoiled.

Personally, I was also concerned with my own son Woo-hyun's engagement ceremony to his fiancée Jay-young Yoo, who had just arrived in New York from Korea. This special day would be the first time for us to meet. I proceeded with the ceremony, but I was preoccupied with the situation in the Middle East.

Israel's Operation Cast Lead began with a bombing campaign the night of December 27, 2008. I watched armaments light the night sky and I felt a wave of fear for the people living below.

I began the next day, December 28, talking to President Bashar al-Assad of Syria and to Iranian Foreign Minister Manouchehr Mottaki, urging them to use their influence over Hamas to stop further provocations. I called an urgent meeting with my senior advisers, including Karen Abu Zayed, commissioner general of UNRWA, and the UN ambassadors of Egypt, Palestine, Libya, Syria, and the League of Arab States—all of whom would have some influence on Hamas. I also consulted with U.S. Ambassador Zalmay Khalilzad and asked the United States to use its influence with the Israeli government to keep the situation from further escalation. The next day, December 29, I addressed the UN press corps, publicly urging regional leaders to calm the situation.

The bombing intensified into a ground invasion on January 3, 2009. Hundreds of Israeli soldiers poured into Gaza in an operation Tel Aviv said would last until Hamas stopped firing rockets, the Rafah tunnels—a system of underground smuggling routes to circumvent the Israeli blockade of Gaza—were sealed, and a kidnapped Israeli soldier, Corporal Gilad Shalit, was returned home. I don't think their timing was by chance. U.S. President George W. Bush was leaving office on January 20, and the Israelis did not yet know whether Barak Obama would be as loyal. I urged the United States and other key countries to intercede in an attempt to lessen or end the siege.

On January 6, 2009, amid heavier shelling of towns near Gaza's northern wall, the Israeli army escalated its assault, firing two shells that exploded just outside the UN-run al Fakhura Elementary School, where thirteen hundred people from the nearby Jabaliya neighborhood had sought refuge. Israel claimed that it was returning fire but later acknowledged that this was a mistake. At least forty-eight people, including children, died in the attack, which was described in detail by the UNRWA office and the few local journalists inside the territory. Witnesses described shells falling on the outside of school property. One school guard heard the explosions and ran into the streets to find dead bodies "cut into pieces" and wounded people lying everywhere.

As I followed the horror, I wondered how many children were traumatized that day, as I had been at the same age during my family's desperate flight from North Korea's army. The lump in my throat was bigger than the knot in my stomach. Two days later, on January 8, the Security Council, acting after long private consultations and escalating public outrage, finally passed a resolution calling for both sides to respect an immediate, durable cease-fire.[1] Although the Americans had helped draft the legally binding two-page document, the outgoing Bush administration abstained after pressure from the Israelis. Meanwhile, Hamas continued to fire at Israeli targets under the cover of UN schools, clinics, and other buildings, effectively daring the army to kill Palestinian civilians when they returned fire—and they did. This was not a new tactic, but I hold both the Hamas fighters and the Israeli army responsible for this egregious lack of humanity.

PAYING IN BLOOD

My outrage peaked every time I read a report, but that didn't begin to express my overpowering emotion. I was angry and insulted by the reflexive violence that both sides were inflicting on each other—and on us. The United Nations *chose* to remain in Gaza through the latest round of combat. We *chose* to care for the Palestinian people who were otherwise alone. We *chose* to take the only moral path, not race for an early exit. UN operations are protected under international law, but Hamas has not signed any treaties. Instead, it treated the United Nations as a target and our people as accessories to cover violence.

I was deeply grateful for our local staff, most of whom continued to work despite imminent danger and fear for their families. In fact, many of them slept at their posts for days at a time. They were reluctant to abandon their neighbors, but I think they were also loyal to the UN Relief and Works Agency (UNRWA), which provided nearly all of the public services in Gaza, including medical care, education, humanitarian assistance, and the refugee camps that housed tens of thousands of Palestinians. Not only did we provide these services but the UN also trained and employed most of Gaza's teachers, social workers, medical staff, administrators, warehouse workers, and community leaders. UNRWA was the largest employer in the territory, and these were the only jobs in many areas.

Israel, among others, repeatedly criticized the UN for working with Hamas. I explained that this was impossible to avoid because the Islamist government ruled the enclave. Hamas was elected to power in January 25, 2006, in an election widely viewed as coercive. Many young and some older Gazans actively supported Hamas, but everyone lived under its rule. UNRWA director of Gaza Operations John Ging and Under Secretary General for Humanitarian Affairs John Holmes appeared not to sleep throughout the ordeal. Holmes monitored the intensifying human tragedy from New York, providing daily updates and coordinating with international contributors. John Ging barely left the UNRWA office during the siege and was in constant contact with employees and reporters, making difficult decisions with literal life and death consequences. He was remarkably effective with international journalists, vividly describing human rights violations, destruction, hardship, and fear. He was so meticulous with facts, and so quotably angered and saddened, that it was impossible to remain unmoved. Without his compassion and endurance, journalists trying to cover the crisis from outside would not have had such a clear picture of the carnage. His willingness to call out both parties won him immediate credibility. As the crisis endured, he was plainly in pain for the Gazans under siege, drawing criticism from the United States and Israel.

Many people could not be accounted for. Just halfway through the war, at least forty thousand Palestinians were displaced, many of them children. The families were mostly sheltering in deteriorating conditions inside UNRWA schools. The number of civilian dead and wounded was escalating rapidly, the scale of trauma unbearable. The UN was trying to care for and protect hundreds of thousands of unarmed civilians from high-tech weapons and age-old hatreds—and we were losing. By the end of the twenty-two-day war, 1,418 Palestinians were dead and 112,943 were injured according to the UN office for emergency relief. Among them, 339 children were killed, and 1,812 were injured.[2]

The invasion decimated Gaza, and its ruins were cataloged by a panel of independent investigators.[3] The Israeli invasion and militia's response damaged or destroyed almost four thousand homes, eighty-five schools, twelve miles of water pipes, eleven wells, and sewage networks and pumping stations throughout the territory. Provoked or not, the Israeli army and air force also damaged or destroyed one hundred and seven UN buildings, including schools.[4] The UN Office for the Coordination of Humanitarian Affairs estimated that Gaza's reconstruction would run to $2 billion.

Israel also suffered losses: ten people, including four soldiers, were killed during the war.[5] Residents of Sderot and nearby towns also experienced prolonged fear as air raid sirens blared several times a day. At least five hundred Israelis were injured. Every one of these was a tragedy, but it was hard for me to be evenhanded.

CONVEYER BELT DIPLOMACY

I had been relentlessly working the phones since December 27, urging both sides to abandon violence. Both sides were under international pressure to moderate their aggressions, especially to spare civilians, but neither party responded to condemnations. Israeli Prime Minister Olmert took my calls, probably with receding enthusiasm, but I was prevented from talking directly with Hamas because the United States, the European Union, and many other nations classified Hamas as a terrorist organization. The Palestinian National Authority, which controls only the West Bank, has long been the acknowledged government of both territories. However, its relationship with Hamas's de facto leaders was ice cold, and there wasn't much President Abbas could do.

The United States could usually be called upon to play a role, but the Bush administration was packing up, and no one seemed to be paying attention. The Obama administration didn't take office until January 20, and it was consumed by the financial crisis. With the vacuum of U.S. leadership, it fell to French President Nicolas Sarkozy to fly to the region. He arrived on January 6, 2009, confident that he could compel the leaders to observe a cease-fire. Unfortunately, neither side was interested, and he returned to Paris without a deal.

Then it was my turn. By the time I landed in Cairo, on Wednesday, January 14, 2009, I was motivated, not intimidated, by the pressure to succeed. I didn't know it then, but I would stay in the region for seven days, an unusually long trip for a secretary-general. It was a week of what I call "conveyer belt diplomacy." The pace of meetings never let up; I visited seven countries and attended two international conferences, met at least twenty-three world leaders, three monarchs, and dozens of ministers. If not for the planes and helicopter loaned to me by the governments of Qatar, Kuwait, and Jordan, I could not have made this work. I spent the first day visiting leaders of the two countries that could talk to Tel Aviv: Egyptian President Hosni Mubarak and King Abdullah of Jordan. These nations had signed peace treaties with Israel in 1979 and 1994, respectively, but their relations were not warm enough for Israel to accept their demands.

Eager to bring peace to their neighbors, both promised to try hard, and I was buoyed to know that we had allies in the region. But Israel had not yielded to their appeals in the past, and Hamas seemed to take orders only from Iran. Tehran has long denied Israel's "existence" and financed proxy militant groups to attack it. In addition to Hamas, Iran continues to support Lebanon's Hezbollah with money and military assistance, and it provides a safe harbor for their leaders.

By Thursday morning, January 15, the rockets continued to fall and weapons were still flooding into the territory through tunnels bored deep below the Egyptian border. The use of human shields by Hamas and disproportional force by Israel were outrageous to me, and shocking. The combatants were dug in for a long fight. By now, the situation was so grim that I was running out of ideas and, frankly, hope. I was getting nowhere with the cease-fire, and I needed to swap my strategy for an inventive alternative, a real out-of-the-box solution.

In my meeting with President Mubarak the day before, an idea came up to propose a unilateral cease-fire to Israel—a novel idea. It would require one of these tenacious combatants to gamble that if it laid down its arms its enemy would as well. I thought a cease-fire agreed upon by both sides would be very difficult. As the more powerful combatant, I knew Israel would have to take the first step. "If Israel first announces a cease-fire, I will make sure that Hamas responds," President Mubarak promised. I was receptive to any plan that would stop the fighting long enough to get food and medical supplies into Gaza.

FIRING ON THE UN, BUT HITTING GAZA

As I landed outside Tel Aviv early Thursday morning, I learned that the Israeli Defense Forces had just shelled the UN's main warehouse, the central supply point for all of Gaza's humanitarian aid. Within minutes the attack had incinerated thousands of tons of food, medicine, blankets, soap, and clothing. None of our staff was killed in the explosion, but I felt a moment of plummeting horror. UNRWA had learned from experience to clearly mark all UN buildings in the Gaza Strip and to give GPS coordinates to the Israeli Army. Israel cannot deny that its soldiers knew this was a UN compound, and they knew what was inside.

I assumed that the artillery was a response to a Hamas rocket fired from our shadows, but I quickly learned the truth. There had been no shooter; the attack was just a "grave mistake" by the Israelis. I appreciated the Israeli government taking immediate responsibility for such a terrible loss, but I was disturbed that officials could not explain why they had struck the warehouse and adjacent UNRWA headquarters. Information was coming in quickly from UNRWA staff. Three shells had hit the warehouse, immediately filling it with a noxious smoke that burst into leaping flames. Our people battled the blaze, but it burned out of control until every bag of rice, bottle of disinfectant, and package of diapers was destroyed. Israel had fired white phosphorus, a World War I–era chemical weapon that ignites in oxygen and cannot be extinguished by water alone. There was not enough sand or loose dirt near our Gaza City compound to smother the flames, so the damage was complete. The depot and its precious freight would burn for a day and smolder for a week.

I met as scheduled with Israeli officials. Defense Minister Ehud Barak immediately apologized again for the morning's attack. Nonetheless, I angrily demanded a full investigation. Then he told me that the military operation had achieved its objectives. And there it was—if one side were to stop fighting, the other might follow.

That afternoon, January 15, I met with Prime Minister Ehud Olmert. We had a tense conversation in which I demanded that he halt the Israeli army's attacks on UN facilities as well as on nonmilitary targets. Only after we covered this familiar ground did I discuss the phased cease-fire, urging him to declare one unilaterally. I assured him that I would do my best to make sure Hamas followed suit. "I'm willing to consider a cease-fire," the prime minister said after a long pause, "but I am skeptical that Hamas will do the same."

"Israel is a strong country with a regular army. If they continue to fight, you would certainly have the right to counterattack," I told him. Personally, I doubted that the cease-fire would backfire. The war was already three weeks old, and both sides had suffered deep political and civilian losses. "I have a way to impress this upon Hamas," I said. I would go to Damascus.

FOUR WORLD CAPITALS IN TWENTY-TWO HOURS

On January 16, 2009—a Friday, meaning a half-day of work for Muslims and Jews—diplomacy took me to four capital cities. I ate breakfast with Likud leader Benjamin Netanyahu in Jerusalem, spent hours in Ramallah with Palestinian President Abbas and his senior advisors, flew to Ankara to seek the assistance of Prime Minister Recep Tayyip Erdoğan and President Abdullah Gül, and slept—briefly—in Beirut. If four countries in a single day was not a world record, I thought, I'd like to meet the man or woman who had visited five.

Saturday was no less demanding. I met with Lebanese President Michel Suleiman, Prime Minister Fouad Siniora, and Nabih Berri, longtime Speaker of the Parliament. Speaker Berri invited me to address the 128-member Parliament the following day, January 17, telling me that I was only the second foreigner to be so honored. Lebanon was a major player in the region: home of Hezbollah, host to the UN peacekeeping mission on the Israeli border and, above all, a society destabilized by religious frictions. It was vital to ensure that Hezbollah—the powerful Lebanese militia and political party supported by Iran and Syria—did not reopen a second front on Israel's northern border. They were noncommittal, as I had expected.

By Saturday night, I was beyond exhausted. Each of the meetings was intense, and all sides forcefully defended their positions. I thought I would be desperate for sleep that night, but at 10:30 p.m. I joined my senior advisors to watch Prime Minister Olmert's press conference. He spoke about the war, of course, and I listened closely even though his words could not be any plainer. The prime minister concluded by announcing that Israel would observe a unilateral cease-fire at 2 a.m. Troops would immediately begin withdrawing from the shattered territory. At the end of his remarks, Prime Minister Olmert recognized my contribution. I was overcome with relief and, yes, felt a little bit of pride as I realized that Israel had committed to the plan. I quickly called Defense Minister Barak, urging him to observe the cease-fire without fail.

Despite the hour, I phoned Syrian Foreign Minister Walid Muallem, whom I knew would have just watched the speech as well. I told him I would go to Damascus the following morning to meet with President Bashar al-Assad. This was an extraordinary step, even by a secretary-general, but events were moving quickly now, and we needed Syria's support. At 11:30 p.m. I convened my traveling press corps, expressing relief that Israel had committed to pausing its attack and telling them I would be leaving in the morning for Syria.

ASSAD STEPS UP

Early the next day, buzzing from too little sleep, I flew to Damascus with my advisors Robert Serry, a Dutch diplomat and my special coordinator for Middle East peace; Special Coordinator for Lebanon Michael Williams of the United Kingdom; and Under Secretary-General Pascoe. I was received by Walid Muallem, foreign minister of Syria, with whom I had been working closely. Riding together in the car, he told me that the representatives of Syria, Turkey, and Hamas were scheduled to meet that day in Damascus to discuss the situation, and he would do his best to help find a solution to the conflict. When I told him about my intention to visit Gaza, he promised that he would tell Hamas to assure my security.

I had met President al-Assad once before, in April 2007, when he was already a political pariah. The Syrian leader had become isolated, disrespected, and even detested by many governments who were outraged by his personal support for Hamas and Hezbollah. The leaders of both movements live openly in Syria under President al-Assad's protection. The two militias are so destabilizing that accommodating them had earned the president scant respect in the Arab world and alienated the West. The president received me in his office at 9 a.m., and I discussed the situation in a very frank way. "Now is the time when you should show some leadership," I told the Syrian president, the same thing I had told him in 2007. "It is time for you to play a constructive role. If you do that, I will make sure that you will be respected and supported by others." I also promised to talk to the United States about improving their diplomatic relations and returning the U.S. ambassador to Damascus.

"How can I play a constructive role?" he asked—disingenuously, I thought.

"Tell Hamas to immediately stop fighting and agree to a cease-fire with the Israeli government, which has already announced a unilateral cease-fire." I was disappointed when President al-Assad told me that he did not control Hamas because it completely contradicted what Minister Muallem had told me just an hour earlier from the airport. "Mr. President, Hamas is headquartered in your country. You are hosting them. Just tell them to accept the deal." The Syrian leader insisted that the West should engage Hamas in a broader framework with the international community. He said he would do his best, and I left with little hope.

After the conversation with President al-Assad, I flew the short distance to Sharm El Sheikh, the Egyptian resort on the Red Sea. President Mubarak, who wanted to play a prominent role in resolving the crisis, had already arranged a summit of Arab and European countries to discuss Gaza's reconstruction. Among the participants were French President Nicolas Sarkozy, UK Prime Minister Gordon Brown, EU President and Czech Prime Minister Mirek Topolánek, EU Commissioner for External Relations Benita Ferrero-Waldner, Chancellor Angela Merkel of Germany, Spanish Prime Minister José Luis Rodríguez Zapatero, King Abdullah II of Jordan, Turkish President Abdullah Gül, Italian Prime Minister Silvio Berlusconi, Palestinian President Mahmoud Abbas, and Arab League Secretary General Amr Moussa.

During the meeting, one of my aides discretely handed me a six-word note from Syria's ambassador to Cairo, Yousef Ahmed: "*Hamas will accept the cease-fire.*" As distressed and angry as I was, I was surprised by the depth of my relief. After a moment to let my pulse slow down, I announced the news. All of the leaders immediately relaxed, slumping in their seats, closing their eyes, and speaking in momentary relief or gratitude. The fire had gone out in the room; the cease-fire made our talk unnecessary. Presidents Mubarak and Sarkozy looked delighted with the news. In fact, they also looked triumphant, each man certain that he had played an important role.

Then the group decided to have a joint press conference. In fact, it was scheduled by President Mubarak as the host. All twelve leaders—who never missed an opportunity to speak—made remarks. It became a bit lengthy, and the reporters were getting impatient because they had such big news to break. With little of substance left to discuss, I immediately left for Kuwait for the long-planned Arab League Economic Summit and the inauguration of the new $20 million UN office, generously funded by Emir Sheikh Sabah al-Ahmad al-Jaber al-Sabah. The UN House was equipped with all the modern facilities, including measures to protect against terrorist attacks. The next day the emir hosted the summit meeting. Gaza dominated the regional conference, and in every public remark and private conversation, I urged the seventeen Arab leaders present to support the cease-fire and, even more important now, to support reconstruction.

As I flew back to Israel Tuesday morning, the cease-fire appeared to be holding. I wondered how much of this life-saving calm could be attributed to the inauguration of President Barack Obama in the United States. I knew how important it was for Prime Minister Olmert to have a strong relationship with the new U.S. president. I had crisscrossed the region this week on an urgent mission of peace, but I knew this relationship couldn't be discounted.

My thoughts and emotions were unusually scattered, no doubt from lack of sleep. I was proud that I had used my office and diplomatic creativity to convince Hamas, Israel, and their allies to stop hostilities long enough to let people breathe, regroup, and start the long process of rebuilding. I was deeply relieved that the week's labors were successful. I was very tired, but I knew I had to do one more thing before I left the region. I thanked Prime Minister Olmert for his decisive leadership and informed him that I would like to visit the Gaza Strip immediately.

He was surprised and tried to persuade me not to go. With the Israeli military withdrawing, he said, he could not be responsible for my safety. "Mr. Secretary-General, we can make sure that nobody could ever touch even a single hair of you if we have our troops stationed inside Gaza. But with our troops pulling out, we cannot guarantee your safety and security." He paused and found a sheet of paper for me on his desk. "We are known for our intelligence-gathering, Mr. Secretary-General. I hope you will consider this before you go." Mossad, Israel's almost mythic intelligence agency, had recently intercepted Hamas's plans to attack "high value targets" such as Tony Blair.

According to this note, the head of Hamas's military wing had threatened to "eliminate a European dog" only six months before, meaning former British Prime Minister Tony Blair, who had spent time in the region as an envoy of the diplomatic initiative of the Quartet: the UN, the United States, the EU, and Russia. So warned, Tony Blair had canceled his trip, but I would not. "Mr. Prime Minister," I said. "I am not a European dog. I am the Secretary-General of the United Nations. I have to see the destruction for myself, and I need to be with our courageous UNRWA staff." Indeed, they had been through an almost unbearable endurance test of their physical and emotional strength, bravery, and professional commitment. I was proud of them.

My senior staff and I stepped outside President Olmert's office building to discuss the trip privately. It was a brisk and bright morning, but I knew the temperature would fall as it got dark. If we were going to drive the short distance to the Erez Crossing, especially with a dozen media vehicles in our convoy, we would have to leave now. I gathered with my senior advisors, including Under Secretary General Pascoe and Special Coordinator of the Middle East Peace Process Robert Serry. Both of them said the trip might not justify the risk. In fact, the idea was not popular with anyone. Within minutes, the chief of my security detail, Captain Robby Robinson, received a call from Israeli intelligence. Kim Won-soo, my deputy chief of staff, was warned by Korean Ambassador Ma Young-sam that the trip was too dangerous. Even UNRWA officials in Gaza were deeply apprehensive.

I had to make a quick decision. I called UNRWA Chief Karen Abu Zayd, who had been in Gaza for most of the war. I suggested a precaution. "Just listen to me carefully," I told her. "I know that you must have arranged my meetings. How many?"

"Three," she said.

"Don't mention them. I am going to visit number three on the schedule first. Push the number one appointment to number two, and push back number two to the end." She immediately understood, and we proceeded.

ENTERING THE ENCLAVE

When I crossed the Erez checkpoint that afternoon, my last day in the region, scores of Hamas supporters were waiting for me. They were angry, hitting the convoy with their hands and shouting. From time to time I felt a cluster of thuds against the side of the armored car. "They are throwing their shoes at us," one of our Gazan staff told me. I knew it was one of the most disrespectful gestures in the Arab world. As we wound deeper into Gaza, we also saw Hamas supporters cheering and chanting slogans, celebrating their "victory" over Israel. Green and white banners were everywhere.

So was the destruction. The war had been here, and clearly there were no winners. Two- and three-story buildings, often occupied, exploded into a gray-brown debris field strewn with scraps of clothing, broken pieces of furniture, and the countless small belongings that make a home. Other buildings were stripped open, walls blown out, revealing the intimate spaces that until that moment belonged only to a family.

Adults were shouting and sobbing in their fury and heartache. I found it impossible not to feel it too. How many children had died here? I shivered as I thought of bodies beneath the towering piles of concrete. It was a sensation that rocked me back to postwar Korea sixty years ago. Now that the fighting had stopped, shell-shocked Palestinians, mostly women, wandered over the rubble or sat down on the remains of their former homes. Many of them were sobbing or wailing. A few children raced over the sharp concrete, and others—maybe as young as six or seven—carried their infant sisters and brothers. Some were still wearing their pajamas. Even inside a steel-reinforced SUV with double-paned glass, I could hear the grief rising from the pile.

I wondered how long it would take to rebuild these homes and thousands more. Who would pay for that? The United Nations would soon issue an emergency relief appeal totaling $2 billion, but that would not be enough. Which nations would step up with direct aid? I hoped Saudi Arabia, which always contributed to rebuilding in areas controlled by predominantly Shia Hezbollah, would also make generous contributions here in their effort to counter Iran's influence in the region.

After a fitful drive, my entourage finally arrived UNRWA's Gaza City compound, or what was left of it. As I toured the warehouse, parts of which were still smoldering five days after Israel's strike, I felt my anger cresting with an unfamiliar intensity. UNRWA staff and I gazed at the scorched piles of humanitarian aid—rice, cooking oil, pulses, aspirin, insulin, rehydration salts, blankets, and so on—tons upon tons of food, medicine, and cargo that were literally the difference between life and death for hundreds of thousands of displaced families, more than 80 percent of whom live below the poverty line. The northern third of the territory, in particular, had sustained heavy damage. The UN was the sole source of food and other basic needs in many areas. Although a UN building was targeted, I still considered the bombing to be a direct attack on the civilians of Gaza. I was nearly speechless as I took in the scale of destruction and utterly unnecessary waste.

The chilly air had a slightly garlicky phosphorus tang, and many charred surfaces were coated with a visible rime of residue. The whole scene felt toxic. I didn't want to be there, but that was all the more reason to stay. The rest of the world needed to see what Gaza had endured for twenty-two days, and my visit had brought dozens of journalists who would share these images. The Israeli government had denied the media entry to the gated enclave for three weeks. I was determined that the world should see what had happened to Gaza, and I felt it was my duty to bring in as many international reporters and camerapeople as possible. I knew we needed independent witnesses to what had happened.

Many of these reporters, both Israeli and international, were disturbed by destruction in the warehouse, a concern that was reflected in their questions. The crowd of UNRWA refugees was large, and the warehouse echoed with workers. I had to shout over the sound, gulping in the poisoned air for more than half an hour. "This is an outrageous and totally unacceptable attack against the United Nations," I said. While speaking, I became aware of small spots moving through my vision. I didn't realize that I was standing on cement that had been sprayed by the phosphorus. "I have seen only a fraction of the damage." I was thinking of the scale of destruction and the excruciating pain and fear I know the Palestinians endured. "This is shocking . . . and alarming . . . these are heartbreaking scenes . . . and I am deeply aggrieved by what I have seen today." Overcome, I handed the microphone to the nearest staff member and slipped into the car.

SDEROT

When I left Gaza, I drove less than an hour to visit the Israeli town of Sderot, located less than one mile from Gaza's northern border. The population of twenty-two thousand had absorbed hundreds of Hamas rockets in the previous month, and I spoke quietly with many of the families who had stayed here despite the hostilities. They were defiant and wanted me to know that they would not abandon their homes. This time I stood in front of a shed filled with twisted lengths of metal recovered from the Qassem rockets.

"You live every day with fear of rockets falling from the sky," I told the Israelis. I pointed out that the civilians just to their south live with war as well. "All people wish for much the same thing, the chance to live an ordinary life, free from war, free from fear. Palestinians must be able to live a normal life just as Israelis are entitled to do," I said. "Political events may end the rockets for a little while but in the longer term will only serve to feed desperation and radicalism among Palestinians. And desperation only strengthens Hamas. This is in no one's interest."

By the next morning, I had lost my voice and could barely whisper to my advisors. I am sure it was the phosphorus. By the time I got back to New York, I still could not talk. Having heard my greetings, the presidents of the General Assembly and the Security Council allowed my deputy and under secretaries-general to deliver the reports on my behalf. My spokesperson, Michèle Montas, also spoke for me. Five years of injections were required to keep my vocal cords from freezing up. I am still grateful to the UN doctors and nurses who treated me regularly every two to three weeks for many years.

I am troubled and heartbroken that I could not end this war more quickly. I certainly tried every measure I was allowed to take in the early days and gave every particle of my strength and strategy once I touched down in Egypt. It is my purpose and my role as secretary-general to bring everyone aboard, building support for novel solutions such as the phased cease-fire. But even a moral voice can do little if the parties—political leaders, armies, or the people themselves—believe they have something to gain by conflict.

These so-called benefits are dangerous illusions, and I have and will continue to impress this upon leaders wherever conflict is brewing or already raging.

RECOGNITION

The situation in the Middle East grew even more dangerous by the end of my term. The Palestinians and the Israelis and their allies showed little interest in breaking the decades-old impasse. As a private citizen, I no longer have political responsibilities, but I have something almost as powerful: my voice.

The United States stirred up new territorial bitterness in 2017 by moving the U.S. Embassy to Jerusalem, which undermined the Arab's insistence that East Jerusalem is the capital of Palestine. In 2018, the Trump administration pulled out of UNRWA in order to pressure Palestinian leaders to loosen their demands. I find this abuse of humanitarian assistance to be among the most cynical and indefensible of political actions. And in January 2020, President Trump introduced another initiative to marginalize the Palestinians. Standing beside the smiling Israeli Prime Minister Benjamin Netanyahu, the president announced his own so-called Middle East peace plan, which effectively kills the two-state solution by allowing Israel to keep the settlements it illegally built in the West Bank. "The deal of the century" also confers on the Palestinians only limited sovereignty, and even then, only after security concerns are met.

The Palestinians were not consulted, but the Israeli government, with few exceptions, was delighted by what was effectively a green light from the United States for an irreparable land grab for one-third of the West Bank. Miraculously, it was the United Arab Emirates that had delayed implementation of this disastrous endeavor. On September 15, 2020, the White House announced the Abraham Accords, in which the UAE agreed to diplomatic recognition of a state that, theoretically, is at war with most of the Arab world. Bahrain soon followed. Most of the Gulf countries have quiet trade agreements with Israel, but full recognition was, indeed, a momentous development. It had been twenty-five years since Jordan established relations with Israel and forty years since Egypt paved the way.

I do not know why the UAE and Bahrain agreed to recognize Israel, nor do I know which states will follow. But I expect we will see a pattern that runs through Riyad. Saudi Arabia's de facto leader, Mohammed bin Salman, has excellent relations with the Trump White House, but as one of Islam's holiest sites, it cannot publicly recognize the Jewish State. I have no doubt that bin

Salman encouraged, or perhaps ordered, the detente by states within Saudi Arabia's sphere.

Washington's involvement came at a time of eroding solidarity among the leaders of the world. Multilateralism is under threat. The once solid League of Arab States and the Gulf Cooperation Council are largely divided among themselves. The European Union is also in disarray and has not played a prominent role in the region. I doubt that President Trump had any aspiration to play the honest broker. The president may have been more interested in garnering diplomatic victories in his pursuit of a second term. I am concerned that his decision to move the U.S. Embassy to Jerusalem will capsize many Security Council and General Assembly resolutions urging the Israelis and Palestinians to "live side by side in peace and security."

Moreover, the Israeli government has merely "suspended" its intention to annex the West bank, a plan to which Palestine and all the Arab countries are strongly against. Nonetheless, UAE leaders said they had won Israel's assurance that it would not annex Palestinian land as the Trump plan permitted. I expect the exchange of ambassadors by Israel and the two nation-states will deflate some of the animosity in the region.

I have stated publicly that the Israelis have legitimate security concerns, but the Palestinians also have inviolable rights to self-determination. Until they are able to decide their own future, Palestinians are among the weakest group in the world. But this widely held view is almost inconsequential on the ground. All the world leaders, international think tanks, multinational organizations, and private individuals can propose ideas and create incentives, but it is up to the people and, particularly, their elected leaders, to make peace work. I still believe that Middle East peace is possible. I don't know what shape it will take, but I will work to make it real.

The Israelis and the Palestinians must do the hardest work of all, and there is no way that only one of them can make the effort successful. Wisdom says that even a sheet of paper is lighter when carried by two hands.

Chapter Eleven

ARAB SPRING

Season of Discontent

As the Arab Spring crept into its deadly winter, I felt whiplashed by events and emotions. In all my years of diplomacy, I've never felt so much dizzying hope, crushing sorrow, and even horror in the span of a single year. The democracy movement was ignited, literally, on December 17, 2010, when Tunisian police seized the cart of an unpermitted produce vendor. Poor and desperate and once again humiliated by police officers, twenty-six-year-old Mohamed Bouazizi set himself on fire outside a government office. The ghastly story replayed again and again, one man's final, desperate scream against the hopelessness of a corrupt political system.

This was not really global news, a single suicide in a small town very far away. News and social media were seizing on the sensational act itself, not on the political protest that inspired it. Bouazizi's death resonated with me. I had regularly spoken of the frustrations of young people, so often unable to find the education or work they required to achieve their own goals. As I left the office that night, bundled up for another night of diplomatic holiday receptions, the man in Tunisia was in my thoughts. On that brisk December evening, I could not have known that this one action would unleash an unprecedented wave of protests throughout the region.

The path to self-determination was not clearly marked. The bravery of human rights advocates quickly backfired in several countries. Despite economic and political concessions, Bahrain's royal family crushed dissenters with the help of Saudi Arabian troops; Yemen's government deployed soldiers and militias to put down the rebellion with tanks, guns, knives, and clubs; Oman arrested and tortured scores of protesters; and a half-dozen nations passed or enforced laws further restricting civil rights. Even more frightening, some protests toppled regimes without a clear succession, creating power vacuums quickly filled by well-armed forces with little respect for human life let alone human rights. Syria, Libya, and Yemen spiraled into brutal civil wars. Extremists, notably the Islamic State, plunged Syria and much of Iraq into a horrifying abyss of terror. And in Libya, a self-proclaimed government with Western support tried to take control but failed.

KINDLING

Tunisians were the first protesters, and they inspired others. I cut short a trip to Los Angeles to coordinate our response to the unprecedented demonstrations. I called on the Tunisian government to work on resolving the long-standing social and economic needs of the people that were among the protesters' chief concerns. With its culture of political moderation, Tunisia could serve as a model for encouraging dialogue with the protesters without any more violence. Tunisian forces killed eleven demonstrators in early January.[1] It was clear that the country needed the prompt restoration of the rule of law to move forward.

As the month wore on, people in Cairo and Sana'a began their own demonstrations, but these regimes quickly arrested, attacked, and even killed the dissidents. After only four weeks of mostly peaceful dissent in Tunisia, Zine El Abidine Ben Ali stepped down and fled to Saudi Arabia. The date was January 14, 2011, the same day that unrest was reported in neighboring Libya. As our attention turned to nascent protests in Zawiya, a restive seaside town in northern Libya, young Egyptians were already simmering. By early January 2011, gruesome pictures had been circulating of the body of an Egyptian activist police had dragged out of an internet cafe and tortured and killed in June 2010. Khaled Mohamed Saeed, only twenty-eight, was the latest example of police brutality and arbitrary power. An Egyptian Google marketing executive living in Dubai began a Facebook page in protest, "We are all Khaled Saeed."

COMBUSTION

One social media post immediately splintered into dozens, then hundreds. Wael Ghonim—only thirteen months older than Saeed—urged fellow

Egyptians to mass in Tahrir Square on January 25, 2011, for a "day of rage" to protest police brutality, unemployment, and corruption. It was the beginning of the revolution; protestors stayed for months. Tunisia continued to smolder, and the United Nations braced for new rebellions in Egypt and, possibly, Libya in late January. We did not know what to expect, but violence seemed like a strong possibility. It was hard to imagine Egyptian dictator Hosni Mubarak or Libyan strongman Muammar Gaddafi stepping down voluntarily.

Throughout this tumultuous period, the Secretariat was ably served by Undersecretary General for Political Affairs Lynn Pascoe, who briefed me every morning and, often, throughout the day. I had worked with him in the early 1990s when I was a political minister of the Korean Embassy in Washington, D.C. and he was the principal deputy assistant secretary of state for Asian and Pacific Affairs. By now the UN situation room was devoting most of its resources to the region, and I relied on Pascoe's judgment in many matters.

Protesters posed the most serious challenge yet to Egypt's ruler of thirty years, from the very beginning, they demanded that Hosni Mubarak leave office. Police tear-gassed dissidents and arrested hundreds. The regime attempted to contain the protests by cutting off cell phone service and internet access, but supporters around the world were eager to disseminate information. As unrest spread from Alexandria to Aswan, protesters skirmished with the police, sometimes instigating violence themselves. If threatened, I was all but certain that President Mubarak would command the army to use the tanks that had been driven up to the very edges of Tahrir Square. He ordered tear gas, beatings, and mass arrests. Security forces killed at least one hundred demonstrators in the space of only five days.

People, including journalists from around world, were pouring into Tahrir Square in those early days. And they kept coming! The people were unified and determined, and the mood in the square was upbeat. We had never seen anything like it. By the end of January, most of the Egyptian police and army rebelled, refusing to arrest or attack the dissidents. It was a remarkable defection by the security forces that had, in large part, driven the protesters to Tahrir Square in the first place. By the first week of February, President Mubarak had fired his cabinet and promised not to run for reelection later that year. That did not appease the demonstrators, who refused to stand down until the despot left office.

The rest of the world was finally tuning into events in the Maghreb, and thousands of Egyptian protesters weaponized Facebook and Twitter against the Mubarak regime. As the uprising spread, dissidents from around the country posted pictures and short videos of protests and the military's response. The government cut off communications, but protesters continued to raise money, look for missing comrades, solicit donations of food and supplies, lobby for international support, and cheer on demonstrators in other cities and countries. I watched with a mixture of astonishment and foreboding as hundreds of thousands of young Egyptians protested with one voice. I publicly called on President Mubarak to hold transparent and orderly elections and to ensure the Egyptian people's right to freedom of assembly and speech. U.S. President Barack Obama and other Western leaders were already pressuring the Egyptian strongman to deliver a concrete plan to transition to democracy, or even to step down.

Egypt was a complicated situation, and even the experts were getting tangled up. In early February, President Obama dispatched former U.S. Ambassador to Egypt Frank Wisner for a private meeting with the Egyptian leader. I assumed he had delivered the president's message to step down. But on February 5, Wisner told foreign and defense ministers at the annual Munich Security Conference that President Mubarak was Washington's strategic partner and that it was "critical" that he stay in power to maintain Egypt's stability. Those remarks were the opposite of U.S. policy, and the Obama administration had to repeatedly disavow Ambassador Wisner's remarks. Secretary of State Hillary Clinton publicly criticized him, saying those were his "personal views," not the administration's.

I had a lot of respect for Wisner, a former undersecretary of state for political affairs, and I regret that this happened. Four years earlier, Secretary of State Condoleezza Rice recommended him to me for the post of under secretary general for political affairs. When I discussed it with him, Wisner told me "I'm too old, and can be of only limited service." Anyone else would have jumped on it. I thought Wisner was a decent man.

A few days earlier, on February 2, I was in London discussing the Egyptian situation with British Prime Minister David Cameron. We decided to have a joint press conference, live, just in front of 10 Downing Street.[2] "An unbearable situation is happening," I told the cameras. "Any attack against the peaceful demonstrators is unacceptable, and I strongly condemn it." I couldn't remember how many times I had simply condemned political violence. I was so frustrated that I finally broke with UN tradition and spoke my true feelings: "President Mubarak should step down *now*!" Asked for clarification, I said it again: "*Now*!"

President Mubarak did, in fact, step down on February 11, less than two weeks later. I think it must have been a difficult decision for him after being in power for so long, but I also wondered if he really still wanted to be president. He was out of touch with his people and incredulous that so many Egyptians wanted him replaced. More than a million citizens were protesting now, and they would not go home because only one of their demands had been met. The movement was spreading like wildfire, and I did everything in my power to support peaceful protesters and blunt violent responses by panicking capitals.

Personally, I felt some degree of sympathy for President Mubarak; he had helped me and the United Nations facilitate peace processes in the region, in particular between Israel and Palestine. He was also the first Middle Eastern or African leader to publicly back my candidacy for the post of secretary-general. His March 2006 public statement supporting my candidacy spread immediately across the Middle East and Africa.

RAGE FUELS PROTESTS

My heart swung between elation and dread. I had been in touch with regional leaders, including Arab League Secretary General Amr Moussa throughout the early months of the Arab Spring, but my entreaties for calm were not successful. My regular meetings with the full Security Council and with just the five permanent members did little to bridge the hardening gap between the three Western states and Russia and China.

By mid-February, Libya's protests were spreading from Zawiya up the coast to the regional capital of Benghazi. Protesters were fueled by a long-simmering rage over lack of housing and government corruption, stoked by local rap and rock musicians, and emboldened by the protests in Tunisia and Egypt. But unlike those countries, the protesters in Libya quickly resorted to violent provocation of the police and military forces. On February 18, the port city Benghazi exploded with the rage of thousands of demonstrators. The day before, the military had killed fourteen protesters, ending three days of tense but largely peaceful protests. As a funeral cortege moved through the city, demonstrators threw rocks at security forces, who answered with bullets. Two policemen were hanged in response. By February 20, at least 230 protesters had been killed, but there was no agreement after that on the number of civilian casualties, nor on who had caused them.

The government's violent response galvanized the Libyans, tens of thousands quickly joining the protest movement spreading across the country. In

New York, I was transfixed by the sight of so many people reaching out to claim their rightful freedoms. I redoubled my diplomatic efforts to keep the momentum peaceful and moving in the right direction, but the secretary-general is no match for a despot determined to remain in power.

"*YOU* ARE THE TERRORISTS"

The mercurial Libyan dictator Muammar Gaddafi was growing more paranoid and, I thought, more unhinged. We spoke over the phone twice at the beginning of the February uprising. Gaddafi strongly urged me to visit to see the "reality" on the ground, but I knew there was nothing to be gained by going. He was calling dissidents "rats" and insisting that most of the demonstrators were drug addicts and mercenaries paid for by neighboring countries. I was taken aback that he didn't seem to be paying serious attention to the uprising.

I had known Gaddafi for more than five years. Although he took power in a coup, he once appeared to have the interests of Libya at heart. But I must say, I didn't recognize the brutal and narcissistic ruler he became. President Gaddafi had long antagonized world leaders, but I can't imagine how he could ever be ruder than he was at the Arab League summit in Doha in March 2009.

Qatar's Sheikh Khalifa bin Hamad Al Thani delayed the meeting by an hour hoping that Gaddafi would soon arrive. Exasperated, he began to deliver his remarks. As the emir of Qatar was reading his opening statement, Muammar Gaddafi entered with his entourage. All the journalists flocked to him, and the emir had to pause the meeting because of this deliberate disruption. When Sheikh al Thani finally finished his opening statement, Arab League Secretary General Amr Moussa spoke, followed by me. At that moment, Gaddafi raised his hand. "My brother, did you have anything to say? There is a speakers list, why don't you wait?" Qatar's leader said.

Gaddafi was incensed. "I am the Imam of Imams! The Leader of Leaders! I am the King of Kings! What do you mean by 'speakers list'?" Then he pointed to Saudi King Abdullah and said, "I know you are a friend of the United States and you are a collaborator. My status as such does not allow me sit with lower people like you." And then, to everyone's amazement, he turned and left.

"Did it bother you," I asked King Abdullah during a meeting recess, "when Gaddafi accused you of being too close to the Americans?"

The King gave me a tight smile. "I did not know what he said. Had I heard what he said, I would have responded." Ignoring or, more charitably, *overlooking* strange behavior seemed to be an international strategy for coping with the Leader of Leaders.

Gaddafi shocked me again two months later during his first and last visit to the United Nations. It was the memorable 2009 General Assembly General Debate, and the Libyan dictator spoke and shouted for an exhausting one hundred minutes—seven times longer than the fifteen-minute allotment most other world leaders observed. The speech was so intense that his English translator collapsed and another quickly stepped in. Gaddafi had drawn a plum place on the schedule: third speaker on the first day, right after the hugely popular President Obama. When the American president left the podium, many world leaders followed him for a few minutes of traditional chat and handshaking. This left the General Assembly chamber with swathes of empty—and highly visible—blue chairs. The Libyan refused to speak until the presidents and prime ministers had returned to their seats. Five minutes . . . ten minutes . . . fifteen minutes.

Upon begging by the General Assembly president, Gaddafi finally took the podium—with seismic effect. He chastised the world body for having no power and complained about the West's long mistreatment of Libya. He demanded that the United Nations do more to help Africa. He singled out Western leaders by name for bullying, double standards, and warmongering. And then there was Israel. It was terrible, but I had already escaped. I am supposed to be on the podium when presidents and prime ministers speak, but I had Deputy Secretary General Asha-Rose Migiro sit in my place. And then it got worse.

The remaining heads of state jerked back to attention when Gaddafi ripped up a copy of the UN Charter right there on the podium and tossed it behind him. Libya's former foreign minister Ali Treki happened to be General Assembly president that year and was seated next to Migiro behind the podium. Treki leaned forward and caught the Charter like a baseball player. The lack of respect for 192 nations was disgraceful.

In July 2009, Italian Prime Minister Silvio Berlusconi invited Gaddafi to the Group of 8 Summit in L'Aquila, Italy, where international terrorism was among the many topics of discussion. The Libyan was now referring to himself as the "Guide of the Revolution," and he pointed his finger at each leader of the G3—Obama, Sarkozy, and Cameron—and said, "*you* are the terrorists."

He accompanied each accusation with a chopping gesture of beheading. To my surprise, no one responded. The G8 leaders just ignored him.

ALL NECESSARY MEASURES

I will never forget my visit to Sirte that autumn. Our meeting was strange, and I remember it very clearly. The King of Kings received me in one of the luxurious tents he favored because it reminded him of his Bedouin roots. A madness was already setting in, which was evident from the layers of security outside the tent and the plastic surgery that had already disfigured Gaddafi's face. While I was talking, the dictator swatted obsessively at flies and demanded to be called the King of Kings of Africa. Gaddafi clearly felt contempt for the United Nations and for his own people.

As uprisings spread, I hoped he would trust me enough to listen to reason. When we spoke in mid-February 2011, I demanded that Gaddafi halt the military's bloody response to civilian protests. I warned him that Western nations were considering the use of force. But my message was ignored. The dictator deployed tanks and even airplanes to break up the increasingly fractious demonstrations. In New York and Geneva, the UN was stuck. While the world waited, the General Assembly, the Security Council, and the Human Rights Council tried to draft language for approval by multiple member states. It was especially difficult for the Human Rights Council because Libya then was a member.

I followed my conscience and committed to the protesters who were so effectively taking their demands to the streets and the internet. Defying the will of regional powers, I spoke out publicly, privately, and repeatedly, urging governments to heed their citizens' aspirations for essential human rights instead of violently dispersing them. But I alone did not carry the force of law. Those who did—the Security Council's five permanent members—were at an impasse over their response to the deepening crisis in Libya.

Unilateral arms embargoes were just one step in the overall effort to protect civilians, and they were not enough to counteract the government's weapons stockpiles and call to foreign mercenaries. London, Paris, and Washington argued that the Security Council had a duty to intervene in Libya under the untested principle "responsibility to protect." R2P was adopted at the 2005 World Summit as a tool to prevent genocide—and this was starting to come close.

Council members laboriously drafted a resolution under Chapter VII of the UN Charter, which authorizes "all necessary measures"—a euphemism understood by all to mean the use of force. Despite R2P, Moscow and Beijing would not consider military intervention in what they argued was a domestic matter. The Security Council finally passed landmark Resolution 1970 on February 26, 2011, imposing an arms embargo, travel ban, and freeze of Libyan assets. Three weeks later the Council passed with five abstentions Resolution 1973, creating a no-fly zone over Libya.

In the beginning, the Arab Spring was exhilarating, and it exemplified the United Nations' bedrock truth of self-determination. The Tunisian and Egyptian presidents had stepped down, and Gaddafi was in hiding somewhere in the country. I rejoiced in every incremental victory: In Saudi Arabia, women won a constitutional right to vote and stand for election; Algeria ended a two-decade-long state of emergency; the *ancien régime*—dictators in Tunis, Libya, Egypt, and Yemen—had been stripped of their power. Even the monarchies that held a tight grip on their kingdoms began to loosen their fists—at first.

For every success, there was a setback. In the Gulf states, demonstrations were crushed. Throughout the region, moderately free speech, always exercised judiciously, was no longer tolerated. And income inequality and ethnic and religious tensions still had a tight grip on most people in the region. I watched with mounting alarm as the backlash to the Arab Spring ultimately claimed countless lives, displaced millions, and set fires that continue to burn.

THE IMPASSIONED ENVOYS

On February 21, 2011, a staffer hurried into my office with a terse news dispatch filed from Libya's UN Mission, just a block from headquarters. Ibrahim Dabbashi, Libya's very able deputy ambassador to the UN, had defected. In fact, more than a dozen senior Libyan diplomats around the world had coordinated their renunciation of Gaddafi's regime. "We are sure that what is going on now in Libya are crimes against humanity and crimes of war," Dabbashi told reporters. "We find it is impossible to stay silent. . . . We have to transfer the voice of the Libyan people to the world." Soon enough the remarkable statement was on television.

I was astounded. Diplomats hardly ever turn on the governments they represent. But here was a good man, abandoning his bloodthirsty regime.

I liked him, and now I respected him immensely. I was delighted when he stayed on to serve as Libyan ambassador after Gaddafi's fall. The regime suffered a surge of defections and rejections. The next day, February 22, the Arab League expelled the country.[3]

Libya UN Ambassador Abdurrahman Mohamed Shalgham had not resigned with the others. But when he addressed a formal Security Council meeting only three days later, I saw immediately that he, too, had turned on Tripoli. I was at the top of the horseshoe-shaped table for what would be an emotional discussion of the deteriorating situation in Libya. I demanded that council governments put aside their own interests and consider the lives of hundreds of thousands of Libyans. Toward the end of a public Security Council meeting, ambassadors from countries under discussion are allowed to speak, always defending their government and "explaining" the situation on the ground. But that did not happened on this day.

When he began to speak, Libyan Ambassador Shalgham, who had looked unwell during the two-hour meeting, burst into tears. "Please, United Nations, save Libya!" Ambassador Shalgham shouted. He pleaded with the Security Council to authorize a no-fly zone to prevent mercenaries and the Libyan air force from crushing civilians. "No to bloodshed! No to killing of innocents! We want a decisive, a rapid, and a courageous resolution from you." The historic event was carried live on television.

Shalgham had known Gaddafi since childhood, and I understood that this was a righteous but overwhelming betrayal of his "brother Gaddafi." As Ambassador Shalgham sobbed into a handkerchief, a score of diplomats huddled around him, patting his shoulder, shaking his hand, kissing his cheeks, and embracing him. The meeting was adjourned while the representatives of more than a dozen countries rushed to comfort and congratulate him. I passed through the group and shook Ambassador Shalgham's hand in both of mine, embraced him briefly, and offered reassurances. It was quite moving.

I didn't think it was possible to see this kind of emotional scene at the UN. It was the most incredible moment of diplomatic history I had ever witnessed. "We have witnessed an extraordinary scene in the UN Security Council; a truly historic moment. The Libyan ambassador delivered an impassioned plea for our help," I said to the scores of journalists who had crowded at the microphone set up outside the council door. Earlier that same day, in Geneva, the Human Rights Council voted to suspend Libya, which was, somewhat embarrassingly, a member.

"ENOUGH!"

I urged the Security Council to take decisive action as its fifteen members continued difficult negotiations about enforcement under R2P. This was the first time the principle had been put to the test militarily, and it was one of the most important, and divisive, principles of the previous decade. Western countries finally convinced Russia and China to abstain rather than veto by promising that there would be no attempt to oust Gaddafi. Historic Resolution 1973 was adopted without enthusiasm on March 17, with five of the fifteen council members—China, Russia, Brazil, Germany, and India—abstaining.[4]

Two days later, in Paris, I attended an international meeting on Libya convened by French President Nicolas Sarkozy. Speaker after speaker said, over and over, that their country supported the Libyan people but could no longer accept the Gaddafi regime. Sitting just in front of President Sarkozy, I felt a bit bored as the same speech was delivered repeatedly. I was jogged to attention when the president roared, "*Absolument pas*!" Absolutely not! Everybody was startled. I immediately learned that the president had flatly objected to the advice of his diplomatic advisor, former UN Ambassador Jean-David Levitte, to extend the meeting time because there were still many speakers on the list. President Sarkozy announced that he would give the floor only to heads of state and government.

President Sarkozy soon erupted again. "*Ça suffit*!" "That's enough!" he shouted, to everyone's surprise. He said the remaining dignitaries could submit their written statements, and he abruptly adjourned the meeting. It was just a few minutes before 6 P.M., and the president asked me to join him for a joint press conference outside. I was briefly intercepted by other leaders, so President Sarkozy proceeded alone and announced to the world that, at that very moment, NATO and the French Air Force had entered Libyan airspace to carry out the Security Council resolution. It was a dramatic event, which he seemed to have carefully choreographed. At the urging of the French president—who perhaps thought a potent display of force would bump up his popularity—war planes were at that moment overflying armored units south of Benghazi and other areas to destroy Libya's air defense capabilities. The Arab Spring was spreading east, and it was almost too much to absorb.

While the Security Council and I were consumed by Libya, a dozen teenagers in Dara'a, a small city in Syria's southeast region, were arrested and tortured for scrawling antigovernment graffiti that might have been inspired by the Arab Spring. As in Egypt, the arrest triggered peaceful demonstrations. But the Syrian people were the last to challenge their regime, and by then President Bashar al-Assad was prepared. The protest was quickly and brutally broken up, and few outside Dara'a took note.

At the same time, in the Persian Gulf, as many as ten thousand Shia Bahrainis gathered in Pearl Square to demand economic opportunity, political representation, and full human rights from the Khalifa monarchy. Most dangerous, the resistance called for the royal family to abdicate or adopt a constitutional monarchy. The protests were not large, but neither is Bahrain. The response was immediate: On March 16, 2011, as many as two thousand troops from the Gulf Cooperation Council attacked demonstrators, backed by helicopters and armored vehicles. About one hundred dissidents were killed, and hundreds more were detained and tortured. In addition, thousands were fired from their jobs because of their political activity.

THE COOLING GROUND

I had been eager to visit North Africa and landed in Cairo on March 20. Libya was still raging next door, but here the eye of the storm had passed. The military junta led by Field Marshall Mohamed Tantawi had promised to return power to a civilian government that was to be elected within the next six months. But I felt uncomfortable with the way these military people received me. Normally the secretary-general was met immediately, but I was told to wait. They were the ones that needed international support, and this was neither polite nor strategic.

General Tantawi appeared calm, not tough but gentle, kind, and soft-spoken. I was almost surprised to have such a good impression of him. I conveyed my firm message to him and to former Vice President Omar Suleiman that this military administration must be handed over to civilians as quickly as possible. He assured me he didn't have any intention of remaining in politics and would return to the barracks.

Outside, in Tahrir Square, the demonstrators were still vigilant, still protesting, but the atmosphere was not so tense. I looked forward to addressing them. I knew this speech would be carried throughout the Arabic-speaking world, and it was carefully written to offer courage and hope to those seeking democracy and equality. It was a joyful, exciting day. "*Kullena masreyeen*," I said. "Today, we are all Egyptians." It was a deliberate reference to the Facebook postings that started the Cairo protests, as well as a nod to John F.

Kennedy, whose landmark 1963 "Ich bin ein Berliner" speech denounced Communism.

"This is Egypt's time," I told the hundreds of thousands before me and unknown millions watching on television. "You have the courage to stand for justice, to demand your rights and reclaim your dignity, to come together in the name of the Egyptian people to build a better future for all, young and old, women and men, Muslims and Copts, from the Delta to the upper Nile." I paused for the unexpected applause. "My hope is that an Egypt reborn can help produce a Middle East reborn—a Middle East with dignity and justice for all, a Middle East that is prosperous and at peace."

Wherever I went in the region, I urged leaders and society to listen to the generation of young men and women who were deeply concerned about their futures. Many received little education, but even those who did were unable to find suitable jobs or enough income to marry and start families of their own. Two-thirds of the Arab region's population is below the age of thirty, a demographic that could, like the American baby boomer generation, shape the economy and culture for decades to come.

Emboldened by the Maghreb, dissidents began protesting in Bahrain, Saudi Arabia, Iraq, Jordan, the West Bank, Iran, Djibouti, Sudan, Kuwait, Morocco, Mauritania, and Yemen. Some voluntarily abandoned their demonstrations, but rulers often quickly quashed the gatherings, some more brutally than others. Developments were happening so fast that diplomats in New York kept in close touch with their capitals but also trained an eye on television and social media. I marveled at this grassroots demand for human rights, dignity, and accountability. It was startling to see such widespread hope and activism, often undertaken at great personal cost. I was determined to aid these protesters with all the tools the United Nations could offer.

Two days after NATO's operation ended its Libya mission, on October 31, 2011, I visited Tripoli for just a few hours to meet with UN staff and the self-proclaimed government of the National Transitional Council (NTC). I told the NTC that it was vital for them to secure Gaddafi's enormous stockpile of weapons, from bullets to artillery to surface-to-air missiles that could shoot down a passenger plane. Libyan weapons had already been trafficked to other African conflicts, and it was important that we lock down this lethal bazaar.

As chaos swirled around Libya's restive areas and government targets, Gaddafi went into hiding. Two months later the despot was pulled from a drainpipe near his hometown of Sirte and killed, but it was not clear by whom—angry Libyans, civilians aligned with the NTC, or his own bodyguards? Regardless, the Russians felt that they had been duped by the Americans and Europeans, who had promised not to use the R2P precedent as a cover for regime change. Moscow said it would not consider authorizing any future military action under the R2P principle. This position would quickly have dire consequences when the Syrian people rose against their government.

THE ARAB WINTER

We knew that the Arab Spring would bring trouble to Syria. Bashar al-Assad brooked no dissent, no challenge to his absolute rule. Damascus had one of the worst human rights records of all UN members, and I was concerned that protests would end in brutality. There was no way of knowing in 2011, however, that peaceful demonstrations would lead to a civil war that is still blazing a decade later, creating an unprecedented human rights catastrophe. Religious extremists flooded into Syria, and neighboring countries took sides. Hundreds of thousands of Syrians have been killed, half the population displaced, and the economy utterly destroyed. Conditions were just right for the sadistic Islamic State and the Levant, which would soon roar into the chaos and terrorize civilians with gruesome killings, sexual enslavement, and forced conversions.

Again, the United Nations was deadlocked, with two permanent members of the Security Council refusing to look beyond their national interests to save the country. The United States, France, and the United Kingdom were afraid of further Middle East destabilization and particularly concerned for allies Turkey, Jordan, and Israel. But Russia blocked every draft resolution, regardless of the escalating violence. Beijing again refused to intervene in domestic affairs—a consequence of its position on Tibet. And Moscow, which had since the beginning supported the al-Assad regime militarily and politically, was also protecting its Tartus naval base, Russia's only overseas port and, strategically, one that is not frozen solid for six months each year.

Broadly speaking, the Western governments supported the Syrian opposition, a position that grew more complicated as militants and then religious extremists joined the fight. But Moscow and Beijing were unyielding in their refusal to consider the R2P doctrine, citing the example in Libya. Tehran was equally intractable, aiding the Syrian regime with logistical, technical, and financial support, as well as military training. Iran had forged a strong relationship with both Bashar al-Assad and his father, Hafez al-Assad, who had ruled Syria with an iron fist for nearly three decades. Although Tehran had particular clout with the Syrian government, its leaders were determined not to use it.

I had a tense conversation with Iranian Foreign Minister Ali Akbar Salehi on July 8, 2012, on the sidelines of the Tokyo conference on Afghanistan. Iran could play an important role in de-escalating the civil war, I said, and it was crucial that Tehran engage with the Syrian peace process unfolding in Geneva. With more than fifteen thousand casualties at the time, I asked him to convey to Assad that the first international priority is to stop the violence.

"Iran's position is clear and has not changed," Salehi said, acknowledging what he called Damascus's deficiencies, shortcomings, and mistakes. Nonetheless, the foreign minister said that Tehran would not push for elections because that would usurp the rights of the Syrian people. Iran "supports President Assad as a person because he is the main pillar of the tent and without him the tent would fall," Salehi told me. He warned that Assad's ouster could destabilize the region, particularly Lebanon, which would be "susceptible to agitation."

Tehran's support had made al-Assad defiant, even arrogant. I told Minister Salehi, anger creeping into my voice, "Given the scale of destruction, President Assad has lost his moral credibility and legitimacy." As I turned away I was angry, overwhelmed by the futility of seeking Iran's help but glad I had spoken my mind. I knew the battle for Syria was more complex than the fate of a single man.

A BURNING IN THE LUNGS

On August 21, 2013, an evil, evil wind blew through eastern Ghouta, a Damascus suburb that already had enough troubles without poison gas. Well before dawn, Syrian soldiers launched a bank of eight to twelve rockets into rebel-held areas. These were off-the-shelf Russian armaments, but their warheads were custom-made to hold up to sixty liters of the powerful chemical weapon sarin. As the colorless, odorless nerve agent misted silently across populated areas, few people were awake to raise the alarm. There was no warning before the painful and frightening loss of control. Sarin kills by paralyzing muscles, technically suffocating victims when their lungs can no longer draw air. The attack killed as many as fifteen hundred civilians and injured five thousand—a great number of them children. Pictures of the victims, glassy-eyed, twitching, and gasping for breath, were unbearable. There were so many bodies that they had to be laid outside on sheets with as much respect as their neighbors could muster. It was the deadliest use of poison gas since the Iran-Iraq War in the 1980s.

Damascus denied that it had used sarin and suggested that the rebels had delivered the poison gas to trick the international community. But the Syrian military was known to have stockpiled the weapon, and it was widely suspected of deploying the gas on other areas that had aligned against the Syrian Ba'athist regime. In fact, an international team of UN chemical weapons experts were already in-country to investigate suspected sarin attacks, and they immediately requested permission to visit Ghouta. The government initially gave its approval, but Bashar al-Assad seemed to be taking a page from Saddam Hussein's old playbook: delay and equivocate. Almost as soon as I announced that the team would visit Ghouta, Damascus began to back off from its commitment. They would not agree on modalities for the inspection, stymieing our efforts to get the team into Ghouta. Furious, I demanded that the government and rebels observe a cease-fire to let the inspectors work. Between August 26 and 29, the combatants refrained from hostilities for about five hours each day, allowing the team to interview survivors and gather samples from victims, livestock, and the soil.

A RED-HOT WARNING

On August 28, 2013, I was in a car heading to Schiphol Airport for a flight from Amsterdam to Vienna. I had just participated in a historic centennial celebration of the Peace Palace with King Willem-Alexander of the Netherlands, and my wife and I were going to participate in a ceremony the next day when the mayor of Vienna awarded me the Commemorative Medal of Freedom. President Obama called me urgently that day. The call was just seventeen minutes long, and it was disturbing. "Let me be very direct," President Obama said after we exchanged a few pleasantries. "I would strongly urge you to get the UN team out of Syria."

UN chemical weapons experts had just been deployed to Ghouta, and they were making good progress. The inspectors were to leave in two days, a Saturday. Nonetheless, the president insisted the team leave by Friday morning or even Thursday night. "If they remain in Syria, it risks becoming a problem for the personal safety of the UN team because Friday morning presses against some of our assessments in terms of what may happen on the ground," he told me. "After all, you are not going to designate who used the chemical weapons. We know who did it."

"With due respect," I said, "I would really appreciate it if you could take some more patience. Of course, we were not mandated to say who did it, but at least we can confirm chemical weapons were used." I reminded President Obama of the possibility that withdrawing UN inspectors early would remind everyone of the 2003 U.S.-led war in Iraq, which had damaged U.S. credibility and integrity. But President Obama pressed hard, rejecting my concerns about the political implications. "If you go ahead bombing, you will not have legitimacy," I persisted. "If you wait just a couple of days, we can give you at least a half of legitimacy."

Urging me again to extract the team early, the president added, "I don't expect you to agree publicly. Just pack and leave!" He raised his voice as if he were ordering his own people.

With my voice calm but firm, I said, "Mr. President, with due respect, let's keep in touch." My wife had listened to my side of the conversation and was very anxious about what was going on between her husband and the U.S. president. I did not order the team home. But I was not surprised that the Obama administration was considering military action, and I shared his concern about further destabilizing the civilian population.

I was expecting force any day now, but the attack never came. I learned that the British Parliament boycotted Prime Minister David Cameron's proposal for the UK to participate in bombing Syria. In addition, the U.S. Congress had asked the administration to get its approval before launching military strikes. The lawmakers were reluctant to agree, and President Obama gave up the plan to bomb Syria.

THREE NEGOTIATORS, NO SPARK

The fighting in Syria had been raging for a year when a window for negotiation cracked open in March 2012. I was determined to make the most of this brief opportunity with as much diplomatic power as I could muster. I needed an esteemed special envoy, the best of the best, to negotiate a political path out of the Syrian mire. I needed someone patient and creative, a negotiator who understood the long roots of the conflict, a senior statesman with moral authority and personal relationships. I needed Kofi Annan, my immediate predecessor as UN secretary-general. We knew at the time that this was a monumental undertaking with only a slim chance of early success, but Annan gracefully accepted: "Mr. Secretary General," he said, "it is a request to which I cannot say 'No.'"

As the joint special envoy of the United Nations and the League of Arab States, he was charged with developing a peace plan and bringing everyone on board. The priority was to stop the attacks against civilians, and then frame a durable cease-fire and peace that Damascus and other governments could genuinely support. He would have to be both statesman and salesman. We both knew we were racing against a merciless clock, the timekeeper of atrocity. At this point, more than fifty-five hundred Syrians had already been killed and two hundred seventy thousand had been driven from their homes.

Many local and regional authorities in rebel-held areas had been executed or exiled by the end of 2011, and I was deeply concerned that organized crime, foreign fighters, and even neighboring armies would infiltrate these voids. Religious extremists, who took root in the region during Iraq's 2004 civil war, would surely take advantage of—or take part in—the wartime chaos. Damascus had tolerated and protected Hamas and Hezbollah leadership for years, and those groups would almost surely support the regime.

Bashar al-Assad, like his father, had crushed demonstrations and other perceived threats with swift and nauseating force. We knew Assad had stockpiled the most fearsome weapons of war, including such lethal chemicals as sarin gas. Those were the threats we anticipated. Frankly, we were not prepared for the Islamic State, which unleashed a shockingly sadistic new Islamist terrorism.

As soon as events began sliding into a new chaotic situation, I called President al-Assad to tell him privately that the UN and scores of other organizations demand that he respect human rights. Each time I called al-Assad he assured me that he would do his best not to harm the people and would guarantee their freedom of speech and assembly. But he repeatedly lied to me. Whatever he promised was false by the following day. After six telephone calls, I decided not to deal with him anymore.

Many years later, Special Envoy Lakhdar Brahimi—who succeeded Kofi Annan as joint envoy—told me an interesting story about how Assad had behaved. In the beginning of the Syrian crisis, King Abdullah of Saudi Arabia telephoned President Assad almost daily, and each time Assad assured the king that he would do his best. Then Assad would ask for financial support, which King Abdullah provided almost every time. The Saudi king also lost confidence in the strongman and joined the coalition aiding the legitimate rebels.

Kofi Annan had served as under secretary general for peacekeeping operations in the past, and he had a vision for using Blue Helmets to help end the conflict and bring about peace. I fully supported him in this effort. The UN Supervision Mission in Syria (UNSMIS) was an unarmed military observer mission with three hundred troops. We were able to deploy almost immediately. However, the cessation of hostilities did not hold, and the violence became even worse by the second week of May 2012. This made it impossible for the mission to function, and its operations were suspended the following month. In my report to the Security Council on July 6, I offered several options to keep a presence on the ground. The council extended the mission until August 10 but said it would extend it no further without significant progress. The team was on the ground less than four months.

Former Secretary-General Annan had been working extensively with the Syrian government, the League of Arab States, and P5—in particular, with the Russians and the Americans. They appeared to have negotiated a way out of this humanitarian crisis, but Syria was not negotiating in good faith. On March 25, Assad ordered the destruction of rebel-held Houla, a small city only twenty-five miles from Damascus. At least 115 people were killed, many of them children. The attack was planned even as the government negotiated with Annan on a six-point agreement.

Only two days after the Houla massacre, the Syrian government agreed in informal talks to halt all hostilities, permit the safe distribution of humanitarian aid, stop the use of troops and heavy artillery in civilian areas, release political prisoners and other arbitrary detainees, honor the safe passage of journalists, appoint a representative for peace talks, and guarantee citizens' freedom of association and demonstrations. But the situation was growing more desperate despite our efforts. On June 30, 2012, I met in Geneva for informal talks with foreign ministers of the P5, the Arab League, the European Union, Turkey, Iraq, Kuwait, and Qatar—known as the Action Group for Syria. Chaired by Annan, the meeting produced a plan to establish "a transitional governing body with full executive functions." I was only mildly optimistic.

Within six weeks, it was clear that Damascus had no intention of honoring the terms to which it had agreed. Fighting between government forces and the Free Syrian Army intensified even while they participated in peace talks, and on August 12, 2012, only four months after establishing UNSMIS, the Security Council dissolved the military monitoring mission because of escalating violence. Outraged and frustrated with Syria's intransigence and with divisions among the P5, Annan resigned on August 2, 2012. Announcing his decision to reporters, the former secretary-general said, "Let me say that the world is full of crazy people like me, so don't be surprised if someone else decides to take it on."

Fortunately, the United Nations had a deep bench of skilled envoys. In the next five years, the former secretary-general was succeeded by no less than three equally seasoned diplomats: former Algerian Foreign Minister Lakhdar Brahimi, followed by versatile longtime UN political hand Staffan de Mistura of Italy, and then Geir Pedersen, former special coordinator for Lebanon. They fared no better.

At the beginning of the process, then Secretary of State Hillary Clinton urged me to split the envoy's roles, with the Arab League overseeing the political process and the UN focusing on humanitarian affairs. I didn't take her advice because the UN and the AU had learned the hard way in Darfur that splitting the negotiator's role can be, at the very least, inefficient and create unnecessary struggles for power. The United Nations itself had limited influence in Geneva because the influential governments wanted to negotiate themselves. I threw myself into alleviating the suffering, mobilizing tens of billions of dollars to deliver relief to Syrians trapped in their own country or forced to escape to refugee camps in neighboring countries.

On January 22, 2014, forty nations and the Arab League met for a UN conference in the same set of rooms to discuss the same Syrian bonfire. As I flew across the Atlantic, I knew that the atmosphere was not conducive to negotiation, let alone meaningful compromise. Brahimi had reported little progress since Geneva I, but I was still hopeful that this larger conference could cobble together a breakthrough to end the fighting and put the country on the path to a stable transitional government.

Most of the countries were adamant that I not invite Syria's ultimate political and military supporter, Iran. But I could not imagine a durable solution that did not include the regime's powerful enabler. I discussed this matter with U.S. Secretary of State John Kerry, who said it was my conference so it was up to me. But he also told me to make sure that the Iranians were committed to creating peace, not extending the civil war. The other members of the Security Council were more or less positive as well. Finally, I telephoned Iranian Foreign Minister Mohammad Javad Zarif and told him that I would invite him only if Iran would support the objectives of the Geneva

II conference. He agreed, and on January 19, I personally announced to the press that I would invite Tehran.

I was immediately overwhelmed by telephone calls from Secretary Kerry and Saudi Arabian Foreign Minister Prince Saud bin Faisal. Secretary Kerry called three times a day to urge me to cancel the Iranian invitation. The Saudi foreign minister angrily threatened that all the Arab countries would boycott the conference. I tried to make sure that the Iranian government would abide by the Geneva Action Group communiqué, to which Foreign Minister Zarif was noncommittal, saying that he could not attend the conference with preconditions. It was a total about-face, and I canceled the invitation. This was one of the most embarrassing and agonizing moments of my entire diplomatic life. I had never encountered such a blatant threat from member states.

I understood that Syria was a geostrategic prize: Tehran, Moscow, Hezbollah, militant Salafists, Sunni rebels, and, nominally, Iraq were pro-Assad. The United States, NATO countries, Turkey, Israel, the Kurds, and later Saudi Arabia backed the Syrian rebels, all while trying not to empower the Islamic State and other militant groups operating in the region. Each of these parties fueled the civil war for their own political and military purposes.

The United Nations has been a valuable forum for international discussion, and the organization's moral authority and global heft cannot be dismissed. However, I think we were most effective in bringing a measure of relief to the Syrian people. The London Conference, which concluded on February 4, 2016, raised $12 billion—a global record for pledges in a single day. The United Nations estimated that some four hundred thousand civilians had died in five years of hostilities, and the horrors the living were enduring were unimaginable.[5] I convened four pledging conferences, three times in Kuwait, with Sheikh Sabah al-Ahmed Al-Jaber Al-Sabah of Kuwait, whose work I recognized by awarding him the UN Humanitarian Certificate of Appreciation.[6] I will always remember how faithfully committed the emir of Kuwait has been in helping the Syrian refugees despite his country's own difficulty with neighboring Iraq. The Kuwaiti emir cohosted the fourth Pledging Conference in London with UK Prime Minister David Cameron.

It was agonizing to follow the fighting on maps and easily predict where the carnage would spread next. Foreign countries were still pouring resources into the war, prolonging the horror. The rest of the international community did not have the tools to prevent the barbarous war crimes, which we knew would be committed by both sides. I was already losing sleep over the violence, and it was getting worse by the day. By November 2015, the

Arab League, Western nations, Lebanon, Japan, and many other countries had formed an advisory committee. The International Syria Support Group (ISSG) issued a number of political statements demanding a complete and immediate cessation of hostilities, but they were shouting into the wind.

Insurgents advanced on Aleppo in late July 2012, and fighting grew even more intense. The UN situation room updated us as often as once or twice a day, and the under secretaries generals for humanitarian affairs, political affairs, and peacekeeping analyzed the toll. I grew to dread these briefings. Satellite photos of before and after illustrated how quickly and completely the conflict had destroyed homes, buildings, agriculture, and infrastructure. By 2015, it was clear that it would be impossible to rebuild the ancient city. Aleppo had become a synonym for hell.

THE ARAB FUTURE

The Arab Spring did not live up to its rich promise, but the seeds of self-determination have been planted, and in some places, they have taken root. In 2018, Sudan experienced a Spring-like rebellion, a nearly yearlong protest that gathered power and numbers as it spread across the country. At this time, Sudan now has a civilian leader and the new Constitution contains no references to Sharia Law.

Young Algerians took to the streets in 2019 to demand the resignation of Abdelaziz Bouteflika, Algeria's putative civilian leader for more than thirty years. His declining health should have long ago disqualified him from office. Elections were held that December, but they were marred by boycotts and protests, in part because all five candidates were members of Bouteflika's regime.

At the start of this decade, millions of people throughout the Arab world—and hundreds of millions more who cheered for them—thought they could demand the peace and dignity that is their human right. But not all of those people were able to move the warlords, kleptocrats, and dynastic rulers who benefit from their oppression. I'm encouraged, however, to see that electronic insurrections, such as those in Sudan and Egypt, have supplemented street protests to such an important extent—even in countries where literacy, income, and internet access fall far below international norms. Social media has kept the quest for justice and equality alive by stoking the sympathy and support of people tens of thousands of miles away, and their outpouring of support is a positive development.

The Arab Spring still haunts me. The Islamic State has been driven from most of Iraq, but many of those fighters have regrouped in Syria. Militias are still supported by foreign governments that are playing out their own Great Game in the region without heed for the excruciating human costs. I'm sorry to say that the two-year democratization movement did not change the world as much as the stunning collapse of Communism did in 1988. The Arab Spring had the same potential to remake North Africa and the Middle East as the former did Central Asia and Eastern Europe. The people in the region took this once-in-a-century opportunity to change their leaders and even their style of governance, but they were not able to overcome the violence and chaos with which they were met. There is a saying: "If God passes in front of you, you must firmly grasp God's coattails." The Arab people ultimately were unable to do that.

All human beings yearn to live in security, with self-determination and equality, and they always will—regardless of their region or religion. That gives me hope. We must remember that the seasons rotate, but they are eternal.

Chapter Twelve

IRAN

The Importance of Promises

In 1974, as a young diplomat, I was loaned to our embassy in Tehran for about a month and a half to help the more than two hundred Korean athletes who were taking part in the Fourth Asian Games. It was hard not to be impressed by Iran's long history and culture, and I felt a special affection for Iran. They were improving the standard of living in the country and the cities, and the shah was one of the most important leaders in the region. Iran also had good relations with the United States.

That was not the Iran I knew, however, when I became secretary-general of the United Nations. During my tenure, Iran was in violation of so many UN ideals and resolutions that I was exhausted and disappointed just thinking about it. This ancient and beautiful culture now destabilizes the Middle East and the Gulf by fomenting bloody conflicts, brutally constricting the aspirations of its citizens, and pursuing a single-minded effort to, as its leaders publicly phrase it, "obliterate" the state of Israel. Even more troubling, the country is quite likely closer than ever to attaining nuclear weapons. Iranian officials have repeatedly denied this, but their efforts to keep the enrichment program a secret and stonewalling nuclear inspectors indicate otherwise. Iran's long-standing mendacity regarding its nuclear program was revealed dramatically on the margins of the G20 summit in Pittsburgh in September 2009 when U.S. President Obama, UK Prime Minister Brown, and French President Sarkozy publicly revealed compelling evidence of Iran's covert nuclear enrichment facilities outside Qom.[1]

The UN Security Council has condemned aspects of Iran's nuclear program six times since 2006. In addition to unilateral sanctions from some countries, in 2006 the Security Council imposed increasingly painful multilateral sanctions against the regime to cut off its ability to develop the necessary nuclear technology. Within a decade, senior Iranian officials were banned from international travel, countries were forbidden to buy Iranian oil, and Tehran was excluded from global systems regulating aspects of the internet and international banking. The cumulative effect of these restrictions was to send Iran's economy into a dangerous slide, with inflation briefly swelled to 40 percent in 2013.[2] Youth unemployment, an important leading indicator, doubled, soaring to 30 percent in only four years.[3] A decade of escalation left the Iranian rial in freefall, trading at about 135,000 to the U.S. dollar compared to 9,041 in 2007.

Despite this mounting hardship, Iran continued to defy the International Atomic Energy Agency (IAEA), which is empowered by both the Non-Proliferation Treaty (NPT) and Security Council resolutions to inspect all nuclear-related facilities, including civilian and military sites. Iran has signed on to several important arms control pacts, including the NPT, but the government remains opaque. As secretary-general, I felt it was my duty to work with anyone, anywhere, to prevent these circumstances from fraying further into potentially devastating collisions. But despite the peace and security consequences of a nuclear-armed and unpredictable Iran, there was surprisingly little room for the United Nations to play a part.

VISITING TEHRAN

The Iranian ambassador to the UN, Mohammad Khazaee, came to my office in early summer 2012 looking unusually pleased. He conveyed an official invitation on behalf of the Non-Aligned Movement (NAM) for me to speak at their August 2012 summit and urged me to favorably consider it. I was intrigued but replied ambivalently. However, the more I thought about it, the more compelling the trip became. The NAM remarks would directly address two-thirds of the UN's membership, but it would also give me cover to meet face-to-face with Iran's supreme leader, Ali Khamenei. I had been invited many times, but I knew a state visit would be perceived by many UN member states as rewarding Tehran for its bad behavior. Yet with Tehran at the center of so many regional problems, I felt a strong sense of duty as secretary-general to engage the Iranian leadership directly. It was far easier for me to justify a trip to the NAM summit than to undertake a stand-alone state visit to Iran.

Given Tehran's increasingly bellicose rhetoric, I instructed my chief of staff, Susana Malcorra, to accept the invitation confidentially lest I become a political target. I hoped that a face-to-face meeting with the supreme leader, the country's true decision-maker, could bring more cooperation with the United Nations and lenience for Iranian demonstrators who were being persecuted for holding peaceful political protests. I doubted I could make much of a political difference with only one visit, but I knew that establishing trust was a crucial first step.

I had met many times with the mercurial president, Mahmoud Ahmadinejad, and found the conversations extremely frustrating. He was emotional, theatrical, and committed to inaccurate and inflammatory ideas. He remained defiant about international efforts to rein in Iran's nuclear program, which was starting to make rapid progress on uranium enrichment that could lead to either a peaceful energy source or a devastating weapon. We spoke privately in Bonn, on the sidelines of the climate change conference in May 2012, just three months before my visit to Tehran. President Ahmadinejad was ominously ambiguous about his country's nuclear aspirations, and I was not sure how to evaluate his words, which were neither reassuring nor convincing. The president was adamant that Tehran "was not trying to get such threats . . . but had to deal with others that had such weapons"—a threat directed at the United States and, surely, at Israel.

I hoped I could be effective in the short time I would have with Iran's senior officials. I knew the broader Iranian leadership was comfortable with me since my days as Korean foreign minister, and I was certain they appreciated dealing with someone from an Asian culture. They trusted me to keep our conversations confidential, to treat officials with respect, and not to cause embarrassment. My approach was often successful, and I was able to help win the release of two dozen Iran-Western dual nationals held in Iranian prisons.

Iran is a beautiful and fascinating place, but I had no illusions; resolving its international problems would require a balance of patience, urgency, authority, and creativity. It was important for me to sit down with the supreme leader face-to-face, and the less international attention to the meeting the better. Unfortunately, Iranian First Vice President Mohammad Reza Rahimi prematurely told journalists that the UN secretary-general was going to participate in the Non-Aligned summit. Tehran wanted my brief visit to be as formal as possible, and now this looked like a state visit. This was certainly not my intention, and it made me uncomfortable to think that so many others would interpret it that way.

I was, of course, pilloried by the international media, especially those sympathetic to Jewish and Israeli positions. Many news outlets tried to amplify the pressure by criticizing me through editorials and articles. I had already advised the United States and Israel about the trip, but they were furious that my visit would "legitimize" the Iranian regime. Israeli Prime Minister Benjamin Netanyahu and U.S. Secretary of State Hillary Clinton both said they wanted to see Iran isolated, not embraced. They were unmoved when I assured them that I would deliver the same messages they themselves would to the NAM and the Iranian leaders.

On August 10 and 11, I again received telephone calls from Mr. Netanyahu and Secretary of State Mrs. Clinton, respectively. Prime Minister Netanyahu was angry with me and opposed my visit using undiplomatic language such as "shocked," "bad judgment," "big mistake," "wrong decision," and "annihilation of Israel." He was never an amicable person, but it was unacceptable for him to speak so rudely to a secretary-general. Our conversations left me feeling bitter.

"Has any leader from the West met him?" I asked. I then invoked a metaphor that often encouraged me: Just lying under a tree waiting until the apple drops into your mouth—it will never happen. You have to shake the tree! He then argued that I could issue a strong statement. To this I gently advised him, "I can issue a hundred statements, but they won't be as effective as my visit." I also underscored to those criticizing my trip that I was sandwiching the NAM summit in between visits to the United Arab Emirates and Saudi Arabia, Iran's fiercest Arab adversaries, demonstrating my interest in hearing regional perspectives on Iran's behavior.

PERSONAL DIPLOMACY

Whenever possible, you have to meet face-to-face. Skilled ambassadors are the anchors of diplomacy, and Iran's envoys are among the toughest I have encountered. But envoys are ultimately an additional layer between the principals. A secure telephone is still the standard tool for direct conversations, but I often find video conferencing is better. In every one of my positions, I have found there is simply no substitute for personal diplomacy. Communiqués, public statements, and even Security Council censures are one-sided and, if they are even read, can leave as little impression as words upon water.

I arrived in Tehran on August 29, 2012, and met Supreme Leader Ayatollah Ali Khamenei. He does not travel outside the country, and we had not met. In fact, we had never even spoken. I was the first UN secretary-general to meet the Iranian leader, and leaders from the Western world had not met him either. The supreme leader welcomed me into his office. I heard that he had lost his right arm in a terrorist attack, but nonetheless we had a long handshake and a traditional Persian greeting.

I was struck by his genuine warmth and welcome to me and my team, which included UN Under Secretary General for Political Affairs Ambassador Jeffrey Feltman, a former U.S. State Department official who had served as the assistant secretary of state for the Middle East and ambassador to Lebanon. He was capable and thoughtful, and I often relied on his counsel. As we were settling into the office, I wondered how this career U.S. foreign service officer felt about meeting the man considered to be an enemy of the United States. I also wondered if the Iranian, who had never met a U.S. official, had any reservations.

Iran's leader and I discussed many subjects, including the country's fractious relations with its neighbors. One of the world's largest sponsors of terrorism, in 2012 Iran was undermining the safety and security in Lebanon, Israel, the Palestinian territories, Iraq, Saudi Arabia, Pakistan, and Afghanistan. The specter of a nuclear-armed Iran could only make the region less trustful, I said. Iran's leader listened closely but did not say anything that would indicate a change of mind or heart. Neither did First Vice President Mohammad Reza Rahimi, UN Ambassador Mohammad Khazaee, or other Iranian officials who attended the meeting.

The most important issue I wanted to discuss with the supreme leader was the need for his country to take action that would begin to reverse the decades of hostility and profound mistrust between Iran and the United States. Khamenei's deep antipathy to the United States was the dominant theme in his presentation. As long as Iran continued on its current path, I responded, there would be no chance of easing the crippling sanctions connected to the country's race for uranium enrichment. Moreover, threats against Israel would make any improvement unlikely. I also emphasized that Iran is mistaken if it truly believes that the United States is the only problem; multiple Security Council resolutions adopted unanimously demonstrated that Iran's nuclear ambitions trouble the world.

I raised several other issues: Tehran, as the NAM chair, should play a more moderate role to promote greater integration with the international community; Iran must play a more constructive role in the Syrian situation; the government must fully cooperate and implement Security Council resolutions pertaining to Iran's nuclear issues to earn confidence and trust; and Iran must fully cooperate with the IAEA inspections and conclude outstanding agreements. I told the supreme leader that Iran seemed to focus only on the United States. I suggested to Ayatollah Khamenei that he use the United Nations as a back channel to Washington. A familiar role for the UN was to facilitate communications between nations that cannot meet because of political pressure or because they lack diplomatic relations. I offered my service as an informal liaison to the United States.

I was visibly surprised when the supreme leader said that such a channel would not be necessary because he was already in touch with President Barack Obama—and they had traded letters! It was hard for me to believe that the U.S. government, which so strongly objected to my visit to Iran even for an international gathering like the NAM summit, had been secretly communicating with Tehran behind the scenes! The Iranian leader said that Washington had initiated the exchange and that he had responded. However, the supreme leader added, he had no intention of answering President Obama's second letter because the president had made negative remarks against Iran only a few days earlier. Even today, I wish I knew what they had said through such closely guarded correspondence.

The revelation reminded me of President Bill Clinton's letter to the North Korean leader Kim Jong-il in 2001, when Pyongyang's nuclear program was one of the most frightening issues of the day. Although the contents were never revealed, the South Korean government believed that, without prior consultation, the American president had offered economic aid and thawed relations in exchange for dismantling the nuclear program. If this secret contact between the United States and Iran was disclosed to the public, American allies, including the Koreans, would have been shocked. That said, political strategies have changed over the past twenty years. In 2019, President Trump boasted that he had received "a beautiful letter from Kim Jong-un of North Korea," a development that left people surprised, if not exactly hopeful.

Relations with Washington and the American people were only one of the areas where I felt Tehran must carefully assess its steps. It is tempting to focus on a single issue, but we didn't have that luxury. Another important issue

I raised was about the denial of Holocaust. I strongly advised the Iranian leaders to stop denying the historical fact of the Holocaust, but the supreme leader defended Ahmadinejad's statements as being "reasonable."He stated that these were the machinations of the U.S. and Israeli governments, but I strongly countered that the Holocaust is a historical fact that nobody can deny. If Iranians continued to deny such facts, I emphasized, nobody will trust that Iran's nuclear development is for "peaceful purpose."

I strongly urged him to respect universal human rights, and I urged him to release two opposition leaders—Mir-Hossein Mousavi and Mehdi Karroubi, who were in house arrest—and human rights activist Nasrin Sotoudeh who was in prison. He said that this is a judiciary issue, and he did not have the authority to do so. But he went on to say that he might be able to favorably consider releasing them "only because of you."

I was deeply concerned about Tehran's crackdown on free speech, assembly, and the independent media. In addition, security forces were using unacceptably violent tactics to prevent or disburse the waves of demonstrators peacefully protesting human rights abuses. The enduring hostilities between Saudi Arabia and Iran also filled me with dread. The supreme leader listened politely during our conversation, sometimes asking questions or nodding. But I was not sure how much I had influenced him toward changing any of Iran's most dangerous trajectories.

AN AUDIENCE OF 119 +IRAN

I addressed the 120-member Non-Aligned Movement summit on August 30, 2012. Today the NAM is ill defined, and it is difficult to know what its membership collectively stands for. In the Cold War era, this bloc of nations considered themselves independent of the United States and the Soviet Union, and they frequently voted together in the UN General Assembly and on committees as a countervailing force against whichever superpower was trying to dominate the process.

From the podium of the Summit Convention Center, I spoke about "the powerful yearning for freedom within nations—the freedom to participate, to make one's voice heard, and the freedom to choose one's government." I decried the gathering conflict in Syria, denounced the pursuit of nuclear weapons, and explicitly affirmed Israel's right to exist. I also criticized the Iranian president's frequent remarks denying the historical facts of the Holocaust. These issues were relevant to the world leaders before me, but I hoped that a single government would hear these words. I have since learned that President Ahmadinejad took off his translation earpiece several times during my speech, which disappointed me greatly. I wanted him to hear that what I said to the world was very much what I had been saying to him and other Iranian leaders in private and in public.

My speech was well received, particularly by the West.[4] I was pleasantly surprised when the most critical editorial writers of the *New York Post* posted an editorial September 2, 2012, under the title "UN Secretary General Speaks Truth to Tehran at the International Conference." They praised my activities and admitted that "we were among those who urged Ban not to set foot in Tehran . . . but "admiringly, we stand corrected." Now it can be told: I came uncomfortably close to delivering improvised remarks when my carefully revised speech disappeared. I can hold my own in press conferences, but I did not relish offering impromptu remarks to hundreds of world leaders, ministers, and diplomats.

An Iranian delegation came to the hotel to pick up my team and take us to the Summit Convention Center. Under Secretary General Feltman was holding the speech I had marked up with pink highlighter, and we had planned to go over a few more points while driving together to the venue. But without warning, Mohammad Khazaee, Iran's UN ambassador, insisted he ride with me as a show of respect for a visiting leader. Feltman was diverted to a second car, with the only copy of my speech! I was momentarily concerned but mostly irritated that we wouldn't have those last minutes to improve my remarks. While following my motorcade, Feltman's car suddenly turned off from our convoy. Our Iranian hosts seemed to have deliberately planned to separate us.

When I arrived at the auditorium, I was immediately escorted to the VIP lounge, where I engaged with world leaders. I did not know what was happening, but I was concerned when I could not find my political advisor and my speech. When it was time to enter the assembly room, I stepped to one side of the crowd and scanned the horizon of the vast chamber. No Jeffrey Feltman. We entered the hall from different doors, and he raced over, visibly flustered and out of breath. "I was surprised when the car was suddenly cut off from the convoy," he explained to me later. "I tried to tell the driver to stay with the other cars, but he acted as though he didn't speak any English or understand me pointing. That's when I got nervous too."

I was grateful that he had returned in time with my speech. To this day I wonder why Tehran wanted to undermine my remarks or, at least, put me

Very few Koreans had personal cameras when I was young, so all the families would go to photography studios to have their portraits taken. From left, my sister Jong-ran, my brother Ki-hoon (deceased), myself, and Ki-ho, the youngest. My younger brother Ki-sang is standing at the back. My youngest sister, Kyung-Hee, had not yet been born. Few Korean students wear school uniforms anymore. *Courtesy of Ban Ki-moon*

I joined the Korean Boy Scouts at 16. It was very popular in the 1950s and 60s. We went camping and were involved with nature. Scouting stressed the importance of observation, a valuable skill for a diplomat. But it also spoke of a moral re-armament, of holding on to values and qualities and living in honesty and generosity. As the Honorary President of the Korean Scout Network I spoke the National Scout Jamboree in West Virginia in 2017. There were sixty thousand scouts—boys, girls and adults. More than ever before the world needs a new generation of thinkers and doers that are globally engaged and sustainability-minded. *Courtesy of Ban Ki-moon.*

(*above*) My life's trajectory began in 1962 with a visit to the White House when I was 18 years old. I was selected to join the American Red Cross's Operation VISTA, a program that brought me and other young adults to the United States from some 40 countries. Our group was invited to the White House and I was electrified by President John F. Kennedy's remarks. I knew I wanted to help my country recover and grow peaceful and prosperous. But after President Kennedy told us that good work has no borders, no nationality, I wanted to be an international civil servant. I was grateful to the world for saving my country and my family. *Courtesy of Ban Ki-moon*

(*right*) By the time I went to college, all young Korean men were required to serve in the armed forces, usually after their education. But I chose to serve after my sophomore year because classes were so often cancelled during the student strikes of the early 1960s, and I didn't want to waste any time! If I'd waited until I finished my officer training program, I could have entered military with a higher rank, but here I am, Private First Class Ban Ki-moon of the Korean Army. *Courtesy of Ban Ki-moon.*

Taking the oath of the UN Secretary-General on December 14, 2006, one of the proudest days of my life. My whole life had prepared me for this job, and I was happy that I would truly repay the world's nations for saving my family and my country. *UNPhoto/Mark Garten*

My team and I travelled to King George Island, Antarctica on November 9, 2007, where we saw for ourselves the tragic consequences of the climate crisis. The visit stoked my passion to abate damage caused by humans' over-consumption, waste, and heavily polluting energy. *UN Photo/Eskinder Debebe*

This photo was taken on December 12, 2015, just moments after the world's nations accepted responsibility to save the planet from the ravages of climate change. With the Paris Climate Agreement, governments committed themselves to lowering carbon emissions and embracing clean energy. It took years to reach an unanimous agreement. This would not have been possible without the ceaseless efforts of Earth's allies in government, science, academia, advocacy, civil society and the media. This electrifying moment—shared with Executive Director of the UN Climate Change Framework Christiana Figueres, French Foreign Minister and President of the COP21 Laurent Fabius, and French President François Hollande—was one of the most gratifying of my life, and I display this picture in my office. *UN Photo/Mark Garten*

One of my great privileges as Secretary General was visiting more than a dozen UN peace missions around the world. These men and women, civilian and military, work to end the hostilities that threaten every aspect of life in a conflict region. The peacekeepers of MONUC (United Nations Mission in the Democratic Republic of Congo) served in what was, in 2007, the United Nations' most complex, dangerous, and expensive mission. *UN Photo/Eskinder Debebe*

No one could have possibly been prepared for the horror in Haiti. A massive earthquake on January 12, 2010 shook Port-au-Prince to its foundations and convulsed the United Nations at its core. We lost 102 staff members and peacekeepers in the 27-second temblor. I visited the rubble of the capital only four days later, when staff with shovels and bloody hands were still trying to recover the bodies of their friends and coworkers. The sight of our headquarters was too much to bear and I lost my composure when a Haitian staff member handed me the concrete-covered UN flag. At least 200,000 Haitians were also killed in the earthquake, and hundreds of thousands more perished soon afterward in unsafe and unsanitary conditions. *UN Photo/Marco Dormino*

On January 15, 2009, the Israeli Army shelled the United Nations' Gaza headquarters and warehouse during Operation Cast Lead. This indiscriminate bombing destroyed thousands of tons of emergency relief supplies and it felt like a deliberate attack on the United Nations as well as the Gazan people. Some shells carried white phosphorus, an extremely toxic WWI-era chemical weapon that cannot be extinguished with water. I gave a press conference five days after the attack while the warehouse was still smoldering and the air was filled with poison, but I didn't understand until later why I immediately grew dizzy and my vision began to blur. Israel's Prime Minister Ehud Olmert and Defense Minister Ehud Barak apologized for what they called a "grave mistake," but loss of desperately needed food, medicine, blankets and other goods was an incalculable hardship to civilians displaced by Hamas's mortars and Israel's response. *UN Photo/Eskinder Debebe*

In a crisis, I could telephone ten capitals in a day. Even in ordinary times, these calls are all business—there's never small talk about family. Both sides have note-takers and experts on the line, and the subjects are generally agreed in advance. Less scripted were the calls I would receive at all hours of the day and night from presidents and prime ministers reacting to news or calling with updates on a simmering situation. I always picked up the call. They wouldn't reach out if it wasn't important. *UN Photo/Mark Garten*

I am still haunted by the emotions that stirred me during my November 18, 2003, visit to the Auschwitz-Birkenau concentration camp in Poland. As I walked around the grounds, it was impossible not to feel the murder of six million Jews and other minorities—one million in this camp alone. I also felt the weight of the genocides committed since World War II and shivered to know these crimes against humanity are still happening. The United Nations was created just after the war to bring peace and human rights to far corners of the world, and ensure this never happens again. Tragically, the organization has often failed. I remain deeply distressed that we have not been able to protect so many vulnerable populations. *UN Photo/Evan Schneider*

By mid-February 2011, the Arab Spring turned deadly in Libya, with most of the indiscriminate violence committed by Muammar Gaddafi's air and ground assaults on rebel areas. But the Security Council's five permanent members were deadlocked over whether to authorize the use of force. As violence raged, Libyan diplomats around the world were in agony, reluctant to break with their government but keenly aware of their responsibility to the people. On February 24, 2011, the Libya's UN Ambassador Abdurrahman Mohamed Shalgham burst into tears during his remarks to the UN Security Council. "Please United Nations, save Libya!," he sobbed. I could not have imagined such raw emotion in this solemn chamber, nor the compassionate hugs and handshakes that followed. *UN Photo/Evan Schneider*

Pope Francis has been one of my greatest allies in building global support for the UN's ambitious development and climate change agreements. The Pope, truly a gentle and loving man, framed the fight against poverty and environmental destruction as imperatives for humanity. He told world leaders, religious figures and even non-Catholics that sustainable development represented the deepest ethical and religious values. Pope Francis's 2015 encyclical *Laudato Si* calls on all people to take care of the Earth, "our common home." I visited him at the Vatican on April 28, 2015, one of our many meetings. *UN Photo/Eskinder Debebe*

Nelson Mandela inspired me with his life-long dignity, devotion to human rights, and determination to bring stability to post-Apartheid South Africa. Soon-Taek and I had the honor of visiting Mandela at his home in Pretoria on February 24, 2009, and we discussed his legacy of patience and persistence. This was two years after he founded The Elders, a small group of former world leaders who could use their influence to avert a looming crisis and encourage equality and development. I joined The Elders when I left the United Nations, and I am proud to serve as the group's vice chair.

I was boarding the last shuttle home from Washington when long-shot Presidential candidate Barack Obama waved me to the seat across the aisle. We spoke about North Korea for most of the flight, and he explained his position on the United Nations. I was impressed but, in mid-2007 I did not expect he would win the nomination against Democratic rival Hillary Clinton. *UN Photo/Evan Schneiderman*

I flew to West Africa in the winter of 2014 as the Ebola virus was sweeping across Liberia, Sierra Leone, and Guinea. People didn't understand the deadly virus in the early days, but we knew it was highly contagious and often fatal. This was the first time I saw people bumping elbows instead of shaking hands. My office established an unprecedented health mission that combined the strengths of the World Health Organization, peacekeeping UN aid agencies, and we were able to stem the epidemic. I would not have guessed that these same fears and precautions would return to us only six years later as the Covid-19 coronavirus. *UN Photo/Evan Schneider*

My mother Shin Hyun-soon and I embraced at a welcome ceremony held by county officials in my hometown, Eumseong, in North Chungcheong Province, Republic of Korea. I know I inherited from her my strength and capacity for hard work. She died in 2019 at the age of 100. *UN Photo/Evan Schneider*

When I arrived in the United States in 1962, at age 18, I was so intimidated I could not remember a single word of English. But I was met at the San Francisco airport by Libba Patterson, a suburban California homemaker who welcomed me into the family like her fourth child. Over the next five days, the Pattersons patiently helped me polish my English and introduced me to waffles, ping-pong, and American slang. The family also took me to the astonishing Pacific Ocean, where I watched the waves and marveled at nature's power. I stayed in touch with my "American mom" for nearly 60 years and was deeply moved when she came to the United Nations for my swearing-in as Secretary General. *UN Photo/Mark Garten*

I worked well with Chinese Premier Xi Jinping, who succeeded Hu Jintao just two years into my term as Secretary General. I encouraged him to play a larger role in global issues, as befits a rapidly developing nation of vast size, population, and potential. China sent soldiers to UN peace missions and contributed billions of dollars to development and public health efforts. China already is a global power. I hope Beijing commits to support the positive aspects of engagement. *UN Photo/Mark Garten*

Former U.S. President Bill Clinton has always supported the United Nations, and he quickly accepted my request that he serve as the UN Special Envoy to Haiti. Remarkably, I appointed him six months before the January 2010 earthquake, and he was with us from the beginning of the crisis. We travelled to Haiti together in March to look at the early phase of reconstruction. President Clinton raised millions of dollars for reconstruction directly and through the Clinton Foundation. *UN Photo/Eskinder Debebe*

My wife and I travelled from Zurich to Davos for the annual World Economic Forum aboard a Swiss military helicopter—a short flight but very cold and very loud. I travelled extensively as Secretary-General, making 559 official visits to 154 countries in ten years. My staff estimated I had flown far enough to travel to the moon and back six times.

I make it a point when travelling to visit camps for those uprooted by conflict or environmental degradation. My family and I fled our village to escape North Korean soldiers when I was only six, and my heart goes out to the children, in particular, who have experienced the terror of leaving everything behind. I want to comfort and encourage them. I want them to know that their world should not be limited to a thin shelter in a teeming camp. In August 2010, I visited this camp for hundreds of Pakistani families escaping unprecedented floods. *UN Photo/Eskinder Debebe*

Amy Robach (left), ABC News anchor, took a selfie with me and Malala Yousafzai, education advocate and cofounder of the Malala Fund, during the event to mark 500 Days of Action for the Millennium Development Goals. The MDGs and successor, the Sustainable Development Goals, were enthusiastically embraced by governments, NGOs, and civil society. These efforts also caught the imaginations of world leaders and the media by forging a roadmap out of entrenched poverty, one tailored to each country and its particular social, economic, and political issues. *UN Photo/Mark Garten*

Sport is one of the most underestimated peacebuilding tools. A fair match can build confidence and respect while providing a non-violent alternative to greater hostilities. Football, or soccer, from the World Cup to children's pick-up games, creates a unity that endures beyond religion, ethnicity and class. That's why I chair the International Olympic Commitee's Ethics Commision and worked to bring together South Korean and North Korean atheletes to march under the Korean Peninsula flag at the 2018 PyeongChang Winter Olympics. I played a brief match against Ugandan President Yoweri Museveni on May 30, 2010, the day that honors victims of war. He is a formidable competitor. *UN Photo/Evan Schneider*

It is impossible to overestimate the importance of a water well in parched agricultural and pastoral regions such as Oromia, Ethiopia. Water means hygiene, health, livelihood and life itself and is one of the most important objectives of the Sustainable Development Goals. I visited this health station on January 31, 2016. *UN Photo/Eskinder Debebe*

I visited the flattened Philippine island Leyte on December 21, 2013, just a month after super-typhoon Haiyan killed an unprecedented six thousand people and displaced fourteen million. The UN's first donors' conference raised pledges of $400 million, but my heart was still heavy to see such total devastation. *UN Photo/Evan Schneider*

Kuwaiti Emir Sheikh Sabah Al-Ahmad Al-Jaber Al-Sabah passionately supported the United Nations and its work. He was known around the UN as "the dean of Arab diplomacy," and I valued his advice on regional security and sustainability. Here we are meeting at one of the five donors' conferences he organized for Syrians displaced by recent conflicts. Emir al-Sabah's death in September 2020 was a terrible loss to the international community. *UN Photo/EskinderDebebe*

I first met Joe Biden in 2008, when he was on the Senate Foreign Relations Committee and I was already Secretary General. He has always been a friend of the United Nations, and I am confident his natural warmth and strong foreign policy team will return the United States to its role as an indispensable nation. The Biden Administration has rejoined many international agreements after a four-year lapse. With his forty-seven years of public service, most of it relating to foreign affairs, I take comfort in knowing he will pursue North Korea's complete denuclearization instead of "love letters." *UN Photo/Mark Garten*

Former Secretaries-General Kofi Annan (left) and I paid a courtesy call on Secretary-General António Guterres on October 13, 2017, the first time three UN leaders have been together. Kofi Annan was an outstanding diplomat and his death, just ten months after this picture was taken, is a terrible loss. Our role has never been clear cut, but every Secretary General has gently countered powerful member states to maintain his independence and pressed UN bodies to serve the organization's founding principles. The job requires strength, compassion, energy and conviction and I look forward to the day when we will welcome the first female Secretary General to our small circle. *UN Photo/Mark Garten*

off balance. Perhaps the Iranian leadership knew how critical I would be in front of a very powerful audience of its equals.

DESTRUCTIVE, DESTABILIZING, AND UNREPENTANT

Iran's campaign to delegitimize Israel is clearly meant to underscore Iran's "revolutionary" and "resistance" credibility and to build domestic support for funding for militant groups. These inflammatory declarations also provoke U.S. hostility, and Iranian leaders use this to justify their own domestic and regional policies. I thought that Iran's high-profile rhetorical opposition to Israel's existence would ultimately gain Iran some support in the Middle East by championing the one issue—Palestinian rights—on which many of the region's peoples and governments agree. This long campaign predates the Obama administration and escalated under President Donald Trump.

For decades Tehran has openly armed and funded Hezbollah, Palestinian Islamic Jihad, and Hamas, the Islamist military and political movements that share Iran's goal of expanding Palestine from the Jordan border to the coast of the Mediterranean. This jarring image—a map without Israel—appears on buttons, cigarette lighters, posters, and even in textbooks. I find this illustrated goal of anti-Semites and regional militants quite chilling. I visited the region many times during my tenure, urging leaders and officials to use their influence to end the recurring violence kindled by Hamas's provocations and Israel's overwhelming and disproportionate military response. But Hamas listened only to Tehran and Damascus, and Israel listened to no one.

HARD-FOUGHT AND SHORT-LIVED

Western governments, often joined by Russia and China, had been trying to negotiate Iran's enrichment and other capabilities for a decade, but until 2013 there was more animosity than progress. Despite quiet support from countries in the region, a deal remained out of reach. I took every opportunity to counsel Iranian leaders that antagonism and provocation would win no friends nor concessions anywhere. I encouraged the leadership to look back to the Iran I had known and to reawaken in Ambassador Khazaee the sense of possibility.

Hassan Rouhani, a moderate, was elected in June 2013 to succeed the hardliner President Ahmadinejad. President Rouhani was thought to be far more receptive to a deal than his predecessor, and many of those who had been watching Iran with dread began to feel an unfamiliar optimism. Three months into Rouhani's presidency, as he was concluding his trip to New York for the UN General Assembly, he received a phone call from President Barack Obama—the first time Washington and Tehran had direct talks at the summit level since the 1979 hostage-taking at the U.S. Embassy. The call generated cautious optimism: oil prices relaxed slightly, international experts declared this was a step forward in a dangerous relationship, and even in denuclearization circles there was a brief updraft of hope.

I don't know what they talked about, but I am sure the most important part of the call was the dialing. Personal diplomacy may not resolve a nuclear impasse, but it can buy time, reduce tensions, build trust, and even create goodwill—factors that contribute to a successful negotiation. Just two months later, slightly before dawn on November 24, 2013, EU High Representative for Foreign Affairs Catherine Ashton, on behalf of the "P5+Germany," U.S. Secretary of State John Kerry, and Iranian Foreign Minister Javad Zarif reached an agreement to severely limit Iran's nuclear production in exchange for a phased lifting of sanctions.

The Joint Plan of Action was the first breakthrough on the Iranian nuclear issue in nearly a decade. It called on Iran to pause its nuclear development program, significantly reduce its stockpile of 20 percent enriched uranium, and submit to more aggressive IAEA inspections. In exchange, the Security Council, the European Union, and the United States would relax and lift Iranian sanctions. Tehran would soon be allowed to access the global banking system, a prerequisite for international trade. After ten years of ruinous sanctions and often acrimonious arbitration, Iran could once again sell oil on the open market and invest the revenue in oil and gas production as well as social subsidies. Some $4 billion in Tehran's deposits and commodities would soon be unfrozen,[6] and foreign investment would again flow into Iranian manufacturing and energy sectors. However, the next two six-month deadlines passed without progress.

I thought I could be helpful to the negotiation as an honest broker, but I was quietly advised by one of the permanent members not to get involved. I never did get an explanation. Maybe it was concern about my engagements with nuclear North Korea. Maybe they were uncomfortable with my continued somewhat strained relationship with Tehran. Or maybe it was just that I was independent. Nevertheless, I made sure that all parties knew that I supported a comprehensive peace and security plan and that the United Nations was prepared to play any role requested.

Iran's foreign ministers negotiated throughout the process. Manouchehr Mottaki, Ali Akbar Salehi, and Javad Zarif were excellent diplomats. I knew Zarif best because he had been Iran's UN ambassador for the first half-year of my tenure as secretary-general. The P5, EU, Germany, and Iran met in Lausanne and then Vienna and worked out the final stages of the new Joint Comprehensive Plan of Action (JCPOA), finalizing it on July 14, 2015. This agreement codified the earlier accord. and as important, it included a road map for IAEA inspections of military sites. President Obama announced the Iran deal in a live 7 a.m. address to the nation, saying the JCPOA meets "every single one of our bottom lines," emphasizing that all of Iran's roads to a nuclear weapon were now cut off. "Today, after two years of negotiations, the United States, together with our international partners, has achieved something that decades of animosity has not," he said. "Because of this deal, we will, for the first time, be in a position to verify all of these commitments. That means this deal is not built on trust; it is built on verification."[7]

THE UNITED STATES EXITS

Four days later the Security Council unanimously passed Resolution 2231, which adopted the framework of JCPOA and urged participants to negotiate the details.[8] Understanding the unique legitimacy of the United Nations, the UN was given important monitoring and reporting responsibilities under 2231. Would the Iranians honor their obligations? For that matter, would the Americans? As I came to dread, it was Washington that first walked away from the deal.

Iran was compliant with the terms of the agreement, and the IAEA reported only minor violations in the first years of inspections. Even without this cautious assessment, the JCPOA was always endangered. The agreement was never popular with American conservatives, who believed it would at best slow Tehran's development of a nuclear weapon, but not prevent it. Israel, Saudi Arabia, and the United Arab Emirates publicly expressed frustration that Iran's regional behavior was not addressed. But there was another, insurmountable flaw: It was negotiated by the Obama administration, and President Donald Trump could not allow it to stand. He had repeatedly promised to rescue Americans from "the worst deal ever," one he said had made Americans an international joke. As other governments watched with dread, my only surprise was that it took seventeen months for Washington to pull the plug.

As late as November 2016, barely six weeks before I left office, I still held the faintest hope for success. The foreign ministers sat down once again to narrow the smallest and most vexing gaps between their positions. By this time Secretary of State Clinton had left office, and her successor, John Kerry, had met with high-ranking Iranian negotiators eighteen times in eleven cities. This would have been unthinkable not long ago, when the United States was boycotting Iran for fomenting terrorism.

I was deeply concerned that Washington would not certify Iran's compliance with IAEA inspections. Decertification is the first step toward withdrawal, and I knew the Iranians would receive this as a punitive act; in return they would blow past limits in the agreement. As worrying as this was to me, this would send the wrong message to other nations trying to build trust and draft an agreement with the United States. North Korea, for example.

I met with U.S. Ambassador Nikki Haley in October 2017. I told this to Ambassador Haley during our October meeting, urging her not to let Washington make the mistake of leaving Iran uncontrolled. "A nuclear Iran will be much more difficult to handle than nuclear North Korea," I told her. "The Iranian nuclear issue has made the Middle East even more complex."

I didn't have to remind Ambassador Haley that in 1994 the Clinton administration had negotiated with Pyongyang for the freeze of its covert nuclear program in exchange for two proliferation-resistant light water nuclear reactors. That agreement, the so-called Geneva Agreed Framework, was canceled by President George W. Bush shortly after he took office in 2001. The North had a covert program to develop nuclear weapons, which betrayed the agreement, and cancellation left North Korea without any legal or political sanctions until Pyongyang tested its first nuclear weapon on October 9, 2006. Ambassador Haley told me that she would immediately share my views with President Trump, possibly by the next day.

To my great relief, the president did not decertify Iran's compliance the following month; however, on May 8, 2018, he did. This effectively killed the accord that so many nations had agreed was the best—or even the only—way to contain Iran's nuclear program. The United States almost immediately restored painful unilateral sanctions, and Iran's barely recovering economy swooned again. "U.S. hypocrisy knows no bounds," Iranian Foreign Minister Zarif tweeted.[9] As someone who worked for so many years in constructive and positive partnership with the United States, I could not understand the logic behind President Trump's decision. The once-solid word of the United States was now provisional; America had become an unreliable negotiator.

There was no guarantee that Iran would have honored its commitment to abandon prohibited enrichment and expansion for fifteen years. Certainly, I had my doubts. But for President Trump to destroy the JCPOA all but gave Iran permission to restart enrichment as well as research and development. Nor does destroying the JCPOA help address Iran's regional behavior that so alarms Iran's critics and neighbors. Sure enough, in November 2019, the head of the Iranian nuclear program, former Foreign Minister Ali Akbar Salehi, announced that Iran was producing about eleven pounds of low-enriched uranium each day, compared to one pound while the JCPOA was in force. In addition, its stockpile of low-enriched uranium is estimated at five hundred pounds, a dramatic increase from the three hundred pounds permitted under the JCPOA. What is done is done, and we must all accept the consequences.

Tehran has hostile relations with many countries. If the Iranian nuclear program is in fact weapons-oriented, Tehran has the potential to destabilize the world far beyond the Middle East. The prospect of a weapon has long exacerbated animosity in Israel, leading to widespread fears of preemptive strikes on Iranian facilities. I fear it could also lead Saudi Arabia and Egypt to develop weapons of their own. The region is fragile enough without adding more weapons of mass destruction—especially in the hands of a country as ambitious and bombastic as present-day Iran.

The JCPOA's collapse could have wide-ranging or even catastrophic implications. The IAEA reported on February 19, 2020, that Iran had built its stockpile of enriched uranium to five times the limit set in the 2015 agreement. Tehran still has to take many steps to build and deliver a nuclear weapon, but it appears ever more likely. The international community must negotiate in good faith and honesty. They have no alternative but to honor the terms they accept. Iran must approach the negotiating table with an open mind, a clear heart, and the wisdom of its ancient civilization. In this instance, it's not too melodramatic to say that the Earth's fate depends on it.

ENGAGING AS AN ELDER

Even though I am now a private citizen, Iranian issues continue to trouble my mind. Iran is regarded as one of the world's rogue states. When I joined The Elders, I knew I wanted to engage the Iranians, particularly Foreign Minister Mohammad Javad Zarif. The nuclear issue was and is likely to remain a top geopolitical concern. The Elders, unlike national positions or even that of the

United Nations, is largely beyond politics, and members engage with sitting world leaders in the service of development, human rights, and peace.

On September 22, 2019, former Irish President Mary Robinson, chair of The Elders, and I, now deputy chair, met with Minister Zarif in New York while attending the UN Climate Action Summit. President Robinson is a tough negotiator and a trusted friend. She proposed that I lead a delegation of The Elders to Iran in January 2020, joined by former Algerian Foreign Minister Lakhdar Brahimi, a lifelong expert in Middle East issues. Minister Zarif welcomed our visit, and I was thrilled that I would have an opportunity to help Iran play a more constructive role in the region. Unfortunately, the visit was delayed, first by the U.S. assassination of General Qasem Soleimani, commander of the Islamic Revolutionary Guard Corps, and then again by the coronavirus pandemic.

Will Iran ever choose peace in the region over belligerence? A lot depends on its leadership and on the leadership of its neighbors. Proxy wars such as the staggeringly indiscriminate war in Yemen only prolong animosity. Tehran's likely pursuit of nuclear weapons and its quest for regional dominance understandably inflames distrust among its neighbors and around the world. Personally, I don't believe Iran needs these weapons; no country needs nuclear weapons. As we have seen, the distrust and destruction outlast the conflict.

Chapter Thirteen

MYANMAR

Cyclone Nargis Opens the Hermit Nation

On April 27, 2008, a storm brooded off the coasts of India, Bangladesh, and Myanmar, all of which braced for an unprecedented impact. Despite winds of one hundred miles per hour, the storm just hung there, gathering strength. It wasn't clear when the storm would start moving, or where it would make landfall. Cyclone Nargis was not yet on the world's radar, but in New York the UN Crisis and Operations Center was already updating me hourly. By the time cable news mentioned it, headquarters was drawing up evacuation plans.

I was preparing for a Middle East meeting later that afternoon, but my usual tight focus wandered back to South Asia. How many of our staff were in danger? Most of them were involved in humanitarian relief, refugee assistance, and similar aid programs—how many of them would be willing to leave their posts when they were most needed? UN Undersecretary General for Humanitarian Affairs John Holmes, a British diplomat with unique compassion and commitment, had directed the staff to build up existing stockpiles of food and emergency supplies throughout the region. I was filled with gratitude for these brave women and men, but I knew that the supplies on hand would not be enough.

Holmes, my chief of staff Vijay Nambiar, and I watched in disbelief as Nargis grew stronger by the hour. Myanmar's UN Ambassador Kyaw Tint Swe stayed in touch throughout the day and night. Being at nature's mercy, and watching and waiting, is one of the most frustrating times for a diplomat. The United Nations cannot make a cyclone change course with quick-thinking diplomacy or by passing a General Assembly resolution. Our staff in the field were sending regular updates, but communications grew spotty as the storm slammed into the country's southwest coast with 130 mph (215 km/h) winds and a thick rain that didn't fall so much as blow parallel to the ground. The cyclone made landfall on the evening of May 2, with winds strong enough to knock down wood and thatch homes, tear loose electrical lines, and snap the tops off ancient trees.

The storm lasted two agonizing days. We learned later that this was the second deadliest storm ever recorded, only Typhoon Nina, which battered the Philippines in 1975, was worse. When the sky dried and the air was again calm, the devastation was even worse than we feared. The cyclone and resulting storm surge, pushing floodwaters twenty-five miles up the Irrawaddy Delta, smashed hundreds of villages and flooded thousands of rice paddies. This would quickly exacerbate Myanmar's food insecurity.

AIDING MILLIONS YOU CANNOT REACH

Cyclone Nargis created such an acute humanitarian disaster that Myanmar's isolated military regime was forced to open its borders for the first time in decades and accept foreign emergency assistance. Myanmar (formerly Burma) had been isolated from most of the world since the 1962 coup d'état froze foreign relations, nationalized businesses, and crushed dissent.

The military government, headquartered in its newly built inland capital Naypyidaw, consistently underestimated the storm's toll. Destruction of the coastal areas was so complete that it was difficult to quantify, and within a week the government had stopped counting. We began to receive reports that much of the southern and eastern third of the country was without drinking water, food, fuel, communications, sanitation, electricity, transportation, medical care, and shelter. Many humanitarian relief workers were in the region but had evacuated to safer ground nearby, and they reported that they were unable to get back into the country. UN agencies estimated that Cyclone Nargis killed about 140,000 people in Myanmar and destroyed the homes of some 800,000. Another 2.4 million were affected by tainted water, hunger, and lack of medical care.[1] Crucial infrastructure from electricity to roads was knocked out. The destruction reminded me of the aftermath of the 2004 tsunami in Southeast Asia. As Korea's minister for foreign affairs and trade, I had worked intensely on that recovery effort, attending the international donor conference organized by ASEAN in Indonesia in January 2005 and then flying to Sri Lanka to see the tsunami-stricken disaster areas for myself.

I knew Naypyidaw's deep suspicion of foreign interference would complicate emergency assistance. Myanmar's rulers had shunned contact with the outside world except for neighboring Thailand and trading partner China, and they refused to accept any other foreign assistance for three full days after the disaster. To worsen matters, on May 7 French Foreign Minister Bernard Kouchner urged the Security Council to authorize the delivery of emergency assistance by force, arguing that Myanmar's refusal to accept help justified global intervention because they were manifestly unwilling to fulfill their responsibility to protect Myanmar's citizens.

The international community bears a responsibility to support a state in meeting its responsibility to protect its own population, but the international community also bears a responsibility to intervene when a state is unwilling or unable to dispense its responsibility to protect (R2P). After the international community's spectacular failures in the 1990s to stem genocide and ethnic cleansing in Rwanda, Srebrenica, and Kosovo, the R2P principle was adopted at the UN in 2005. Reserved for the most egregious cases of mass atrocity crimes, it was incendiary, inappropriate, and counterproductive for Kouchner to invoke it in relation to Myanmar.

However, our fears were confirmed two days later. The World Food Program (WFP) won permission to land two cargo planes of aid, only to have the military government impound the emergency supplies so it could distribute the high-energy biscuits, water purification tablets, and medicine itself. I was furious that politics was impeding life-saving efforts for hundreds of thousands of storm victims in desperate need. I was shocked when the government in Naypyidaw made the unprecedented demand that it alone would choose the countries from which it would accept bilateral assistance. And Western governments and aid groups needlessly antagonized the generals when they insisted on calling the country by its pre-junta name (Burma). This was disastrous.

Politicizing the relief effort would slow the arrival of desperately needed aid and gave the regime control over where or whether it was distributed—both inherently immoral. Tens of millions of dollar worth of emergency assistance from the WFP, the World Health Organization, the UN Office for the Coordination of Humanitarian Affairs, the Food and Agriculture Organization, Red Cross organizations, and many other international aid groups were already positioned in the region. They just couldn't go forward those last few miles to reach the people in need!

At the same time, the government refused to delay the May 10 constitutional referendum that reserved Parliamentary seats for military officers, a change that would perpetuate the army's influence even in a civilian government. The election's timing and initiative drew sharp criticism from around the world. Nonetheless, the referendum was held behind the usual curtain of secrecy and passed by an overwhelming majority. Millions of survivors in Myanmar's coastal regions could not possibly have cast ballots, and various UN agencies had repeatedly called out the regime's human rights record. I agreed but felt strongly that it was more important to get aid workers into the country than to stand on principles.

The amount of relief available to Myanmar after the storm was a testament to the generosity of the governments, groups, and people who immediately contributed to disaster relief despite the deep distrust of the government. The UK's Department for International Development sent twenty cargo planes filled with tarps, blankets, and more nonfood assistance in the first month alone. The largest single donor to the emergency recovery effort, London initially contributed more than 45 million pounds (USD $88 million in 2008) in cash, plus valuable air and sea assistance.[2] President George W. Bush had long been one of the generals' most passionate critics, but the United States was among the first nations to respond. Washington sent $75 million worth of aid within a month, mostly related to the food and health sectors. The U.S. Department of Defense also established an air bridge to move cargo from Thailand to Myanmar.

The United Nations worked closely with the Association of Southeast Asian Nations (ASEAN). Myanmar's neighbors helped negotiate with Naypyidaw to receive humanitarian assistance and, as important, the group agreed to cohost a donors' conference for emergency relief on May 25. But UN agencies were still unable to distribute 90 percent of the aid needed, and some reported that relief supplies had been impounded by the government. Within a day it was clear that Myanmar's military rulers were prepared to risk hundreds of thousands of lives in order to maintain the isolation that fed their power.

While all eyes were looking east to the Bay of Bengal, I was in my office on the Secretariat's thirty-eighth floor, increasingly impatient to speak with Myanmar's head of state, Senior General Than Shwe. My staff had been trying to reach him or his deputies since Nargis made landfall, but communications were impossible. The problem may have been technical or it could have been his unwillingness to engage with outside organizations. I think it was the latter. The government continued to delay the visa process, leaving aid workers and support staff stranded in the region.

Unable to speak directly and privately with the leadership, I was forced to openly engage the regime with a press conference. I opened the May 12 briefing for reporters by again appealing directly to the capital in language that was calibrated to sound forceful but not bullying: "I want to register my deep concern—and immense frustration—at the unacceptably slow response to this grave humanitarian crisis," I told reporters in New York. "This is not about politics, it is about saving people's lives. I therefore call, in the most strenuous terms, on the government of Myanmar to put its people's lives first. It must do all that it can to prevent the disaster from becoming even more serious." The UN office in Yangon rounded out the picture, showing a large area plunged into deep water and darkness.

Although the regime had made some initial moves to ease access restrictions, Emergency Relief Coordinator Holmes said that the UN agencies had been able to reach less than a third of the more than one million people at risk of starvation and infectious diseases. Holmes told reporters that the government needed to set up major logistics operations to deliver supplies to the most affected areas, a complex undertaking requiring the specialized expertise of international relief agencies. "Myanmar just can't handle this emergency alone."

I knew I needed to talk to the generals in person by visiting Myanmar. Every day that food and medicine was not distributed was prolonging a hardship we could not imagine. I privately promised Ambassador Kyaw Tint Swe that I would not embarrass the government, nor would I try to visit the prominent political prisoner Daw Aung San Suu Kyi. I told him I would not even mention the "P-word," which stood for politics. One week later I received an invitation from Naypyidaw. It was the first of my five visits to Myanmar.

STEPPING ASHORE

A Thai airline whisked me to Yangon from Bangkok the morning of May 22, the first time in forty-four years that a UN secretary-general has visited Myanmar. More than one hundred reporters were waiting for my arrival. I went first to the two-thousand-year-old Shwedagon pagoda, Myanmar's holiest site. I was pleased that Prime Minister Thein Sein accompanied me, a gesture of respect. I removed my shoes and socks, as was tradition, and offered flowers to the statues within. "The United Nations and the whole international community stand ready to help you overcome this tragedy," I said silently, offering flowers to the statue of Buddha. "I have come to demonstrate my solidarity and bring a message of hope."

Then my team and I boarded a helicopter to see the Irrawaddy Delta, where whole villages and towns had been blown flat and flooded and miles of brown sludge blanketed the rice paddies. I stared out the windows, unable to look away from the rudimentary buildings collapsed into murky water. It was a terrible sight. I feared the "second wave" of disaster that would endanger many survivors—cholera and dehydrating disease spread by putrid conditions.

That afternoon Myanmar's ministers of National Planning, Economic Development, and Health were waiting for me when I landed at the Kyondah Refugee Center. Here I met many people who were displaced by the storm, and my heart sank with sadness. I encouraged them and told them to have hope, to have strong courage. I assured them that the UN would help. The human cost was evident. I was moved to meet a baby who was born just that day. He looked healthy. But I also met a listless nineteen-day-old girl whose face was already sunburned red. The little girl had experienced so much chaos in only three weeks. I wondered how many other infants and children would fail to thrive because their homes, families, and communities were upended by the waters.

Prime Minister Thein Sein and I met again later that afternoon to discuss the cyclone and the humanitarian disaster it created. I thought it was a good meeting; he seemed quite reasonable and tactical. He became my main contact in the government and was especially helpful after he became president in the 2010 elections. I still have deep appreciation for his leadership.

The following day, May 23, I took a special aircraft provided by the Myanmar government and flew 203 miles (327 km) from Yangon to Naypyidaw. I knew I was going to a place few outsiders were permitted to see and was energized with anticipation. No one could help the Nargis victims except the generals, and I was hopeful that my presence, as well as my words, would convince them to let the world help them. With a very modest presence on the ground, aid workers were proceeding slowly, stocking distribution centers, and delivering limited assistance. I pressed that advantage throughout my visit.

At long last my team and I were escorted across the modern campus and led across a huge room hung with Ikat tapestries and scenes of the country's monasteries. Senior General Than Shwe received me. He was flanked by second-in-command, General Maung Aye, and the highest members of the regime, the State Peace and Development Council. I was accompanied by my chief of staff, Vijay Nambiar, John Holmes, and Communications Director Michael Meyer, as well as Bishow Parajuli, the UN Resident Coordinator.

Than Shwe, a stocky man in military fatigues, greeted me brusquely and got right down to business. "We cannot accept any assistance delivered by foreign naval vessels," he said. "It is a matter of national sovereignty." I reminded him that the Indonesian government had initially said the same thing after the tsunami, but they ultimately received assistance from U.S., Chinese, and Indian military ships, not to mention scores of international aid groups, NGOs, and direct government contributions. I insisted there be no political consideration in a humanitarian emergency.

"That won't be necessary, the relief operation is already over," Than Shwe said. "We have the situation under control."

"But people are still in need," I said in alarm. "We flew over the Irrawaddy Delta yesterday and saw miles upon miles of destruction." I persisted, urging the senior general to immediately import six months' worth of food staples and medical supplies. I told him that the world wanted to help his people, but his government had an obligation to facilitate our work.

The general appeared unmoved. "We will not open our borders for every international aid worker," he said, citing security concerns. But I pushed hard, very hard, and after more than an hour, I noticed the generals nodding slowly. Then Than Shwe abruptly reversed himself, saying he would accept aid from any source and would issue "all" aid workers of any nationality visas and access to afflicted areas.

This was a surprising breakthrough, but it was fragile and, frankly, not entirely unexpected. Surely it was not an accident that the government was promising to cooperate fully with the international community just two days before scores of donor nations gathered in a pledging conference to raise millions of dollars in aid. I knew relief organizations would be wary and the donors skittish. I needed to reinforce the general's decision before he changed his mind again. I was all too aware that in recent weeks mere verbal agreements with the government meant little.

The traveling press corps and Myanmar's own media were just outside. So I opened the door, took a deep breath, and announced to a couple of dozen news organizations, including Myanmar's media, CNN, BBC, CBC, and Asian media, that the government had agreed to accept "all aid workers" and emergency assistance. The press began to shout questions in several languages, but I couldn't say much more. As I expected, this was urgent news, and it quickly circled the globe. It was also a form of insurance: Myanmar's rulers would have a much harder time reversing themselves when the decision had been widely reported and universally welcomed.

I'm sure the senior general was not pleased by that, but when I returned to the sitting room, Than Shwe agreed to my request to speak privately. It was unexpectedly cordial. In fact, the general looked quite at home in this ornate sitting room, which complemented his pressed military uniform with rows of decorations. I was startled when the senior general told me he wanted to be remembered as the General Park Chung-hee of Myanmar. Park, like Than Shwe a four-star general, led the 1961 coup that made him the Korean leader until his assassination in 1979. Although he was a dictator, General Park is remembered with respect for expanding and upgrading Korea's manufacturing industry and overseeing my country's transition from deep poverty to export-oriented industrialization. He also normalized relations with Japan, Korea's former occupying power.

I told Myanmar's leader that General Park was not an isolationist. He welcomed foreign dignitaries, world leaders, and press interviews. "Even I, Secretary-General of the United Nations, had a difficult time meeting you," I told him. I also said that refusing to engage with leaders that were trying to help and refusing international assistance was damaging his reputation. "If you want to be like Park Chung-hee, you must change your leadership style. You must open your doors to the world!" The general relaxed the most onerous rules the next day, but it was only temporary.

PRINCIPLES AND PROXIMITY

Many nations shared my wariness. Fifty-one countries, aid agencies, and NGOs sent representatives to the donors' conference to raise money for Myanmar, raising just under half of the $187 million goal. Many diplomats told me privately that their governments wanted to be more generous with assistance, but they were taking a cautious approach due to the mercurial leadership. Most thanked me for exerting gentle pressure where their own governments could not. The situation was especially fraught for ASEAN, which in three years' time would be chaired by Myanmar. Member states were concerned that the country's ruling generals would damage ASEAN's credibility. Worse, no one wanted an unstable country in the region. As one

Asian diplomat put it, "We don't have the luxury of distance, we have the challenge of proximity."

Despite the senior general's promise to accept foreign aid and aid workers, donors had another problem I could not address: human rights. Protests in 1988 had led to a vicious military crackdown that killed as many as ten thousand students, Buddhist monks, and other demonstrators. Since then the military government has harassed and imprisoned thousands of non-Buddhists, journalists, and others on fraudulent charges. In addition, the generals have fomented ethnic conflicts and seized land.

The jailed political prisoner Daw Aung San Suu Kyi, at the time a charismatic democracy advocate, embodied the victims of the totalitarian government. As the daughter of Burma's foremost "national hero," Bogyoke Aung San, she was widely admired for her tenacity and stubborn resolve. Who would imagine that less than a decade later, on assuming state power, she would direct these very qualities perversely against the country's own beleaguered minorities—the Rohingya Muslims. Aung San Suu Kyi's house arrest was to be completed the following day, and many predicted that the generals would not free her. They didn't. Than Shwe added a year to her sentence in punishment for receiving an unapproved guest, an American citizen, John Yettaw, who had recently swum all the way across Lake Inya to "save" her.

The chaos and hardship imposed by Cyclone Nargis was too high a price for any person to rightly pay. But I hoped my actions helped turn the coastal devastation into an opportunity by being able to reach out proactively to General Than Shwe and Prime Minister Thein Sein. My access was only possible because I focused the UN position on the tragedy and the global response rather than discussing widely held concerns about human rights and economic reform. The West was filled with suspicion and frustration, but most of the East was willing to provide cautious support and encouragement.

A SMALL WIND BLOWS

My second trip to Myanmar in July 2009 was controversial and only partially successful. General Than Shwe denied my request to visit Aung San Suu Kyi. Commentators said I looked "weak," but I didn't care about that because the success or failure of the trip hinged on more than the visit. I did meet with Myanmar's registered political parties and several ethnic groups half-heartedly negotiating a cease-fire agreement with the government.

Meanwhile, my special advisor on Myanmar, Ibrahim Gambari, who had previously served as undersecretary general for political affairs under Kofi Annan and briefly in my tenure as well, was becoming problematic. The Myanmar government did not want to deal with him, complaining that this longtime UN political expert kept a "double standard" on human rights. Other nations had also begun to doubt his judgment, saying that he was too trusting of the regime. I had to consider how to handle this issue.

In December 2010, I transferred Gambari, a former Nigerian foreign minister, to Darfur as my special representative in the United Nations-African Union Mission in Darfur (UNAMID). In New York my chief of staff, Vijay Nambiar, became my special advisor on Myanmar. An able diplomat, Nambiar was already well known to all the parties, and I knew they would welcome this change. The United Nations' diplomacy and emergency aid was beginning to work in Myanmar. The supply line to the coastal areas was nearly unimpeded, and people were finally getting the aid they needed—three weeks after the disaster. Surprisingly, this cooperation traveled as far as New York, with Myanmar's diplomats beginning to participate in a few of the General Assembly committees.

THE LADY

The Western world lionized democracy advocate Aung San Suu Kyi, whom the generals arrested in 1989 for her political activities. The government convicted her on a variety of dubious charges and kept her confined ay home for the next twenty-one years. She was beautiful and tragic—a silent symbol of political oppression around the world. In 1991 she was awarded the Nobel Peace Prize "for her nonviolent struggle for democracy and human rights." Aung San Suu Kyi was internationally known simply as the Lady.

I continued to condemn the military government's widespread human rights violations. Chief among these were the regime's attacks on ethnic minorities, institutionalized poverty, brutal attacks on free speech and, of course, the Lady's detention. President George W. Bush was deeply concerned about the junta's abuses, often raising the issue with me in private and offering political support. What I didn't realize at first was that the Lady's biggest advocate in Washington might not have been the president, but his wife, First Lady Laura Bush. We privately discussed Aung San Suu Kyi and the authorities' crackdown on free speech, including the treatment of Buddhist monks critical of the military.

I began to wonder what would happen when Aung San Suu Kyi was finally released and would have to become the leader we thought her to be. Could she hold onto her democratic positions? What kind of leadership would she demonstrate? Until this point, the Lady enjoyed unconditional, whole-hearted support—not for her deeds or statements but for what she symbolized. Once she entered the political world, I knew she would have to prove her leadership by vision and action. I told my senior advisors that I was skeptical. The military released Aung San Suu Kyi on November 13, 2010. Human rights advocates around the world celebrated her freedom, a few of us warily.

Meanwhile, in the elections held three days earlier, the former prime minister, General Thein Sein became president. Although a nominee of the army, Thein Sein quickly introduced wide-ranging political and economic reforms and, more important, launched the first truly comprehensive peace process by engaging with the country's different armed ethnic groups with the declared aim of building a "democratic and federal Myanmar." During the extensive and productive meeting I had with President Thein Sein at the 2012 ASEAN Summit in Phnom Penh, he assured me that his government would continue down this democratic path.

The National League for Democracy had boycotted the 2010 Parliamentary election, but when released from detention, Aung San Suu Kyi agreed to contest the 2012 by-election and enter Parliament as the main opposition leader. These changes were welcomed around the world, and economic sanctions were slowly lifted. By then Western powers were competing to take credit, and in November 2011, Hillary Clinton, the U.S. secretary of state, was the first to visit Myanmar, quickly followed by British Prime Minister David Cameron. President Barak Obama himself finally visited, one year after Clinton. Each one pressured President Thein Sein to address the country's human rights problems, specifically freedom of speech and the persecution of religious and ethnic minorities, such as the Rohingya. "Mr. Secretary-General," an aide said around this time. "They are all trying to take credit for our work. You should also speak out and visit the country now."

"This is a natural tendency" I said. "Let's wait. They have more powerful resources to influence the government, so let them do it. They can augment our efforts by pressuring Myanmar to make agreements, make contracts, and create incentives to encourage Naypyidaw to do the right thing." They would learn soon enough, I thought, that the UN secretary-general's job was supposed to be thankless. We were a shadow power, unacknowledged by those who took credit for success.

After all the visits by powerful countries, I was invited to address a joint session of Myanmar's Parliament on April 30, 2012, the first foreign leader ever invited to do so. I was deeply moved by the honor, which I accepted as a gesture of gratitude for the UN system's life-saving interventions in 2008 and our continued encouragements to civilian rule. "The dramatic changes sweeping Myanmar have inspired the world, and we know that your ambitions for the future reach higher still," I said from a podium on the vast wooden stage. "We know that Myanmar can meet the challenges of reconciliation, democracy, and development, but it will take your full determination and your common leadership and partnership."[3]

Aung San Suu Kyi, who had chosen to delay her inauguration as a parliamentarian, was not in the room. She refused to take her seat because of a dispute over the wording of the oath of office, in which representatives swear to defend the Constitution, including articles that her party described as undemocratic. Chief among these is reserving one-quarter of the legislature's seats for the military. Reporters asked me what I thought about her not joining the Parliament. For the third time during the Myanmar crisis, I used the media to underscore a point meant for a single individual. I told the press that, in my experience with the democratic process, individuals are more effective when they work from the inside rather than from the outside. "A real leader demonstrates flexibility for the greater cause of the people," I said. The next morning Aung San Suu Kyi took her seat, an action I admired and respected.

My wife Soon-taek and I drove past scores of journalists to visit Aung San Suu Kyi in her large and somewhat rundown home on the shore of Yangon's Inya Lake. We all sat together, speaking casually and admiring the lakefront view, and then Myanmar's leader and I had a private meeting. I delivered UN promises to help with electoral management and mobilizing official development assistance, and I requested full support for the UN country team and the human rights office in Myanmar.

Aung San Suu Kyi expressed her deep concern that President Thein Sein would not be able to carry out reforms unless the Constitution was revised because the chief military commander had full power to annul any decisions made by the president. She was worried that he was a good man but not strong enough to stand up to the regime.

This was my most successful visit; I was welcomed by the Myanmar government and the people. Wherever I went, in Shan State and at the airport, there were a few hundreds of people welcoming my delegation.

"INCENDIARY"

At our last meeting, August 30, 2016, I was in Naypyidaw to participate in the Twenty-First Century Panglong Conference, the first step in a peace process to resolve seventy years of ethnic conflict. During the previous three years and more, the UN had participated as an Observer in the "peace talks" at the specific invitation of the government and the armed ethnic groups. We had helped to negotiate a preliminary cease-fire agreement and the first elements of a political resolution to the civil war that continued to afflict the country.

My conversations with the Lady were encouraging, but I'm sorry to say that I have since grown disappointed in her human rights record. The Buddhist government's treatment of the Rohingyas continues to appall me—and many others as well. At least 120,000 have been herded into squalid refugee camps in Rakhine State, and 650,000 have been driven into the sea or forced into neighboring countries in a sustained campaign of arson, rape, and murder.

Privately, I expressed my extreme concerns to Aung San Suu Kyi, who was, by now, the de facto leader of Myanmar with the title State Counsellor. It was a long talk, maybe even an argument. It started with a question of nomenclature, specifically, what to call this persecuted group. The government calls them "Bengalis," which implies they have only just emigrated, whereas some families have been in the country for several generations. Officials also use "Muslims in Rakhine State," further complicating the situation by unnecessarily linking them to the Islamic world. It is the long-standing policy of the UN to call places and people what they call themselves. In this case, Rohingya. During my previous visit, I received a letter from the minister in charge protesting my use of this nomenclature in a press conference. The international "Call Me Rohingya" movement was fully underway by now, putting pressure on Naypyidaw to extend security and full citizenship to the stateless group.

Aung San Suu Kyi struck a defensive position throughout our meeting and insisted that the UN was not being impartial. The name Rohingya, she told me, is "incendiary." I told the community leaders at the Panglong

Conference that the only path to peace is to secure a common future of hope and dignity. At the press conference that followed, I again sharply criticized the government and called for an end to violence against the country's dozen ethnic minorities. Standing before dozens of reporters, I advocated full citizenship and benefits for the Rohingya.

In her 2016 address to the UN General Assembly, State Counsellor Aung San Suu Kyi reaffirmed Myanmar's faith in "fundamental human rights, in the dignity and worth of the human person." She also declared that she personally "stood firm against the forces of prejudice and intolerance." By now these just felt like words. The Lady's inability or refusal to end the attacks on the Rohingya has disappointed me deeply.

Aung San Suu Kyi defended her government's policy, telling me that the international community did not have a "fair view" of what is happening in ethnically mixed Rakhine State. She agreed to partner with former Secretary-General Annan, who by then had founded the Kofi Annan Foundation, to make recommendations to improve their quality of life. His commission strongly urged closing the internally displaced persons camps and extending the benefits of citizenship.

The State Counsellor theoretically accepted the recommendations—just days before the military staged another brutal crackdown in the region. As the world viewed the deteriorating conditions of the Rohingyas with increasing alarm, the UN high commissioner for human rights and former peacekeeper Zeid Ra'ad Al Hussein condemned the attacks, describing them in 2017 as "a textbook case of ethnic cleansing." Others went so far as to call it genocide.

THE FACE OF THE REGIME

Today the Lady is under fire by international human rights groups, student unions, and many governments for failing to protect the Rohingya and other minorities, pointing out that her silence and recent defense of the attacks is a betrayal of the values for which she once stood. The Nobel Prize Committee was under pressure to revoke her Peace Prize, and in late 2018 Amnesty International stripped her of its highest award, the Ambassador of Conscience. A dozen more international citations and awards have been withdrawn.

Aung San Suu Kyi startled her remaining supporters on December 11, 2019, when she defended her government before the International Court of Justice, which hears disputes between nations and issues advisory opinions. The Gambia, on behalf of the Organization of Islamic Cooperation, has launched a suit against Myanmar for violating the Genocide Convention of 1948 in its attacks on the Rohingya minority. "Mr. President, it cannot be ruled out that disproportionate force was used by members of the Defense Services in some cases in disregard of international humanitarian law, or that they did not distinguish clearly enough between fighters and civilians. There may also have been failures to prevent civilians from looting or destroying property after fighting or in abandoned villages," the State Counsellor said. She also clarified her government's use of the phrase "clearance operation," a military term that is associated with ethnic cleansing. "In the Myanmar language, 'nae myay shin lin yeh'—literally 'clearing of locality'—simply means to clear an area of insurgents or terrorists," she said. "If war crimes have been committed, they will be prosecuted within our military justice system."

Her public defense of the government's actions drew immediate international condemnation. I expected that she would have some difficulties as the leader of a country whose military was so active in policy-making. However, if I were her, I would have spoken out and used my political clout even though it was likely to have been challenged by the generals. The Rohingya exodus is a humanitarian nightmare that can only be resolved through political means, and I continued to appeal to the Myanmar authorities to show compassion.

After I retired, on July 10, 2019, I traveled to Bangladesh, where the government had built a refugee camp for 1.1 million Rohingyas displaced by brutal attacks. The Cox's Bazar Camp was rugged and difficult terrain, spread across a mountainous region, but this mattered less to these families than safety. I flew over the sprawling area accompanied by Foreign Minister Abdul Momen, who explained what his country was doing to mitigate these unbearable circumstances. Mothers, wrapped in colorful cloth, moved slowly across the sloping area, often surrounded by their children. My heart dropped to see so many people trying to bathe in a dirty red-clay river. From the air, I saw shelters provided by UN agencies and other humanitarian organizations, their logos vibrant in the sun. I was again humbled and grateful to so many generous people and organizations—including WHO, UNICEF, the UN Population Fund, and the UN High Commissioner for Refugees—who were helping the Rohingya refugees. But this is not sustainable. Myanmar must allow the Rohingya to return to their homes safely and freely. I have been working closely with UNHCR's Korea office to mobilize global support for Rohingya refugees.

I watched the February 1, 2020 coup d'etat with sadness and alarm, hoping the new regime will respect the rights of the Rohingyas and all the other Myanmarese.

Tens of thousands have turned out in recent weeks to protest the new rulers. I am somewhat startled to see the people have once again turned to Daw Aung San Suu Kyi in this time of political turmoil. The leader of the democratically elected NLD, who was immediately detained by the junta on meritless charges, is still a guiding light for demonstrators. They are carrying her picture on signs and wearing her face on t-shirts. Some placards demand her freedom. Other signs link her fate to that of the nation: "Please save our leader–future–hope."

Aung San Suu Kyi is, at this time, under house arrest. But when she is able, she must reclaim her legitimacy by once again standing up for peace and the democratic rule of law. She is too important a symbol to her county to defend a new military regime.

On a trip to Copenhagen on June 18, 2018, I visited Rysensteen High School with Her Royal Crown Princess Mary of Denmark and several senior officials eager to showcase the quality of Danish education. Upon entering the school, I was pleasantly surprised to see nearly a dozen portraits of esteemed leaders, including U.S. President Abraham Lincoln, Albert Einstein, Nelson Mandela, myself—and Aung San Suu Kyi.

I hope these students and educators—who had once found her so inspiring—may again celebrate this strong and graceful woman for positive contributions to her country.

Chapter Fourteen

SRI LANKA

Access and Inaction

Sri Lanka had plunged into a sustained civil war decades before I became secretary-general. As early as the 1980s, this teardrop-shaped island off the coast of India was wracked by a violent uprising and a merciless response. When the shooting finally stopped, in mid-2009, more than one hundred thousand civilians were dead and eight hundred thousand had been displaced—often more than once—as the war engulfed cities, towns, and villages. At least forty thousand combatants were killed over the duration of this civil war.

For two decades, insurgents from the small Tamil minority had waged a rebellion against the government, claiming much of the island's north and east coasts as its own. Well-armed but still at a disadvantage against the Sri Lankan military, the Liberation Tigers of Tamil Eelam (LTTE) resorted to terrorism, suicide bombings in public buildings, and firefights with Sri Lankan police and soldiers. The government in Colombo responded with overwhelming and often indiscriminate force. Neither the rebels nor the government spared civilians in Colombo and the contested regions. The conflict created one of the world's highest rates of disappearances, suicide bombings, extrajudicial killings, and torture.

THE BOOMING SILENCE

Despite this ongoing horror, the Security Council had not once put Sri Lanka on their agenda, and the Secretariat had not dispatched much more manpower than a country team to look after bedrock development initiatives. The Security Council was too riven by its members' own domestic politics to take any action. The independent Human Rights Council in Geneva had repeatedly criticized combatants, but that hardly seemed to matter half the world away.

By mid-2007, the LTTE had breached a succession of cease-fires and launched another volley of violence. President Mahinda Rajapaksa abruptly escalated his government's strategic objective from negotiation to annihilation. Despite my strong public statements and private conversations, the government waged indiscriminate ground and aerial attacks on LTTE's positions. The insurgents fought back, but hundreds of thousands of civilians and rebels were pushed into a cul-de-sac in the LTTE stronghold in the Vanni, on Sri Lanka's northwestern coast. The LTTE continued to fight, conscripting child soldiers and using civilians as human shields. Colombo sent attack helicopters to strafe the region and soldiers to fight whomever was left. During a pause in fighting, civilians were told to move to an area designated as a safe harbor. But it wasn't.

We knew this, of course. Regional news covered the civil war for years, and we periodically received worrying reports from the UN country team. Nonetheless, a divided Security Council declined to take up the matter: China was opposed to intervening in domestic affairs, and elected member India was reluctant to jeopardize its efforts to shore up influence in the region. As I waded through the UN dossier on Sri Lanka, I was shocked by the brutality on the ground and sickened over the inability of the UN to stem these hostilities or reach the people most in need.

The United Nations had more than sixty years of experience protecting and caring for noncombatants trapped by conflict, but Sri Lanka was among the world's most devastating civil wars. The randomness of violence made it impossible for international organizations to stockpile and distribute emergency assistance because civilians were always on the run. The Rajapaksa government ominously informed the United Nations in September 2008 that it could no longer "guarantee the safety" of our personnel. This is a diplomatic term of art for the government's expulsion of our international staff, a step that is almost always an augur of atrocities to come.

The Security Council remained detached despite numerous UN reports and discussions inside the Human Rights Council in Geneva. The council had passed no resolution regarding Sri Lanka since 1955 when it approved the country for UN membership. This body simply took no action. Sri Lanka, a small and desperately poor island-state, was not considered sufficiently strategic for members to devote time or attention to it.

Individual council members encouraged me to persuade the Sri Lankan government to avoid large-scale humanitarian disaster. I did my best, adding UN political engagement to unilateral efforts by India, China, Japan, the European Union, and the United States. I suggested a sequence of visits by various under secretaries general as well as my chief of staff, Vijay Nambiar. Colombo received these officials, but it rejected most of our substantive initiatives. UN Resident Coordinator Neil Buhne, who headed our office in the capital, routinely informed his foreign ministry counterparts about the deteriorating humanitarian situation, but he, too, made little progress.

A large percent of the LTTE's money and weapons came from the sizable Tamil diaspora. Cutting off these funding networks would quickly hobble the militants, but there was no reliable way to do that without Security Council sanctions. Colombo began to reach out bilaterally to key governments, urging them to use economic, diplomatic, and legal tools to halt the flow of support to the Tamil militants. International cooperation was slow to come and didn't ramp up significantly until the post-September 11 era, when countering Muslim extremism became a global priority. On March 13, 2009, UN High Commissioner for Human Rights Navanethem Pillay harshly criticized both sides by name: "Certain actions being undertaken by the Sri Lankan military and by the LTTE may constitute violations of international human rights and humanitarian law," she said.[1]

By April, LTTE fighters were confined to a no-fire zone, and the government announced a two-day humanitarian cease-fire. People lay dying and wounded, and there was a desperate lack of food and water. I argued with the Sri Lankan president to extend the pause so civilians could leave, but this appeal, like so many others, was not honored. During my May 5 phone call to President Rajapaksa, he seemed so agitated by the UN's position that he kept shouting at me as if he were speaking to his subordinates. It was inappropriate and one of my most embarrassing engagements with any world leader.

CONQUERING WITH CARNAGE

On May 13, 2009, after widespread bloodshed and four private "informal" discussions, the Security Council finally issued a low-level press statement expressing concern for the worsening humanitarian crisis in the Vanni area.[2]

Later that day I told the Geneva press corps that I planned to go to Sri Lanka to make an assessment of the areas of heaviest fighting.

On May 18, Sri Lanka's Department of Defense unexpectedly announced the end of the recent hostilities and declared victory in the twenty-six-year civil war.[3] Conflict between the government and the LTTE had "officially" ended. Colombo broke the LTTE, the clearest victory yet against a terrorist organization. But this win was terribly hard on the Sri Lankan people.

Three days later, on May 22, I landed in Colombo for a two-day visit that had been scheduled earlier in the month.[4] I knew the timing of this visit was awkward, but I was determined to go while my heart was painful. Sure enough, the immediate visit was criticized as looking like an endorsement of the government's actions, but I was not there to congratulate the Rajapaksa government. That afternoon I took a helicopter over the conflict areas in the north to see the vast devastation in the "no-fire zone" established in nearby Mullaitivu in the war's final days. Civilians had been trapped here in the barest circumstances during the worst of the fighting. I also visited overflowing internally displaced persons (IDP) sites at the Manik Farm camp, home to an almost unimaginable 220,000 displaced people. Confronted by squalor and tragedy, I mourned humankind's sometimes insatiable cruelty.

I later flew to Kandy to meet President Mahinda Rajapaksa and Foreign Minister Rohitha Bogollagama. They greeted me warmly and said I was the first to visit postconflict Sri Lanka. Nambiar, my chief of staff, had arrived a few days earlier to prepare for my visit. I told President Rajapaksa that it was critical to begin the hard work of relief, rehabilitation, resettlement, and reconciliation. Immediately would not be soon enough. Colombo would also have to guarantee and provide the United Nations and other aid agencies with immediate and unimpeded access to populations in need. Millions of displaced civilians waited to be resettled—a massive financial and logistical undertaking requiring security, investment, and jobs.

President Rajapaksa resisted holding a genuine dialogue with the LTTE, which was the only way to begin the necessary accommodation and reconciliation that could finally bring his country peace. I told him clearly that an accountability process was a necessary prerequisite for any political process. I also warned him that without reconciliation violence was likely to return. These steps must go forward in parallel, I told him, and I again emphasized that they must begin now.

I was pleased that President Rajapaksa agreed, even saying that rebuilding the shattered LTTE areas was an opportunity to invest in long-term sustainable development. The president promised to expedite infrastructure construction and job creation. I deeply hoped he meant it. However, the president's advisors, especially his brothers Defense Minister Gotabaya and senior advisor Basil, were fiercely opposed to this, and they frequently shouted. The Rajapaksa brothers were never far from power, having served for years as ministers of several departments, as parlimentarians, and as presidential advisors. Plainly embarrassed by such vehement opposition by his own close advisors, President Rajapaksa called in the rest of his cabinet, one by one, and asking their views in front of me. "The United Nations Secretary-General is here to help us, and I think we need to listen to his advice. Can you agree with my decision to establish an accountability panel?" One by one, the advisors reluctantly concurred, including Defense Minister Gotabaya.

President Rajapaksa and I finally agreed to address the aspirations and grievances of all communities and to work toward a lasting political solution fundamental to long-term development. Finally, the president told me the government would accept accountability for its wartime actions. At the end of my visit, Sri Lanka and the United Nations issued a joint statement that addressed the UN's most pressing concerns and offered a broad road map to reconciliation.[5]

Throughout my long diplomatic career, I have found that personal friendship is sometimes more effective than the formal relationship. Looking back, I think our relationship helped President Rajapaksa eventually accept the UN position. I had known him since my time as foreign minister of Korea. When his country was severely hit by a tsunami in 2004, I had visited his devastated hometown of Hambantota together with the Korean prime minister and a disaster relief team. Later, when he paid an official visit to Korea as prime minister, I accompanied him to many events.

Two weeks later, I told reporters that Colombo must stop gloating about vanquishing the LTTE. "I would like to take this opportunity to warn against the risk of triumphalism in the wake of victory, after this military conflict," I said. "This will hinder the ongoing efforts by the Sri Lankan government, its people, and the international community to heal the wounds. It is very important at this time to unite and heal the wounds."

By March 2010 it was clear that Colombo was not going to accept responsibility as it had agreed to do in May of 2009. The UN Panel of Experts on Accountability in Sri Lanka was soon established,[6] and I appointed Marzuki Darusman of Indonesia as its chair with investigators South African human rights advocate Yasmin Sooka and Steven R. Ratner, an American lawyer.

Two months later Colombo established its own "Lessons Learned and Reconciliation Commission," but it did not focus on actual accountability and provided no judicial follow-up. The Human Rights Council responded by demanding that the government take steps toward accountability.

The UN panel released its report on April 25, 2011, revealing a very different version of the final stages of the war than that described by the Sri Lankan government.[7] The panel found "credible allegations" indicating that war crimes and crimes against humanity were committed by the Sri Lankan military and the separatist militia. I was painfully aware that the UN as a whole could have done a lot more to protect human rights and prevent atrocities, and I understood why the UN was criticized in the media and in some capitals. I accepted this blame and grew even more determined to discover how this lapse had happened and to ensure that it is never repeated.

In June 2012, I established an internal panel to review UN actions during the final stages of the conflict and appointed an experienced former UN senior official, Charles Petrie, of the United Kingdom, to lead it. The panel report on November 14, 2012, described a "systemic failure" across the United Nations at headquarters and in the field. The review panel's 128-page report concluded that the whole UN system—me, the Secretariat, the Security Council, relief agencies, and the country team—had failed to call sufficient global attention to the bloodiest phase of the civil war. It also found that the UN had failed to respond to early warnings, "to the detriment of hundreds of thousands." The panel specifically criticized the Security Council for failing to call a single formal meeting during the final months of the civil war. These findings were very hard for me to read. The UN team on the ground had not done their jobs properly, a lapse that would have profound implications for our work across the world. The whole UN system needed to learn the appropriate lessons from the assessment, and we would have to work very hard to win the confidence of people caught in conflict who look to the UN for help.

RECOMMITTING TO RIGHT AND WRONG

I resolved to improve the way UN agencies carry out their missions, particularly with regard to protecting human rights. I asked Deputy Secretary General Jan Eliasson to identify our shortcomings and issue recommendations. Eliasson was internationally respected, a high-powered and effective diplomat who had served as president of the General Assembly from September

2006 through September 2007. The most notable outcome from the UN panel's recommendations was the creation of Human Rights Up Front (HRUF), my initiative to strengthen the capacity of the UN to detect and prevent serious human rights abuses wherever they occur. This would become one of the most important elements of my decade-long effort to expand human rights protections around the world.

Concerns about Colombo's ability to take a hard look at its actions and draft a plan to bring about the promised improvements continued for a long time. UN High Commissioner for Human Rights Prince Zeid bin Ra'ad of Jordan urged an end to impunity and said "we hope that, given the signals the president himself and Foreign Minister Mangala Samaraweera have sent, there is an openness, an acceptance that the past must be reckoned with." Because the government and rebel forces have committed crimes, both must face credible justice, Mr. Zeid said at the Human Rights Council in September 2015. He suggested creating a hybrid Sri Lankan court with international lawyers, prosecutors, investigators, and justices. Several member states advocated for an international inquiry, noting that Sri Lanka was unable to conduct a satisfactory examination and is not a party to the International Criminal Court.

In March 2014 the Human Rights Council adopted the report and asked the Office of the High Commissioner for Human Rights to conduct an investigation into human rights in the final stages of the war.[8] The three lead investigators, including Martti Ahtisaari, released their own twenty-page report September 28, 2015.[9] It was clear to all that the UN had failed to prevent or mitigate the escalating bloodshed in Sri Lanka. The human rights violations committed by Colombo and the LTTE were well documented. Many UN agencies, funds, and programs were on the ground, and our country staff was fully aware of what was happening. I don't know how much of a difference the United Nations as a whole could have made during the last desperate months of Sri Lanka's civil war. But I do know we should have tried harder to protect human rights and to prevent atrocities. Somehow a generation's worth of conflict that killed more than one hundred thousand civilians had passed without even a Security Council resolution. The UN was widely criticized, and I grew determined to find out how this lapse happened and to ensure that it would never be repeated.

The Rajapaksa brothers continue to rule Sri Lanka, as their family has since 1945. In November 2019, Gotabaya was elected president and appointed his older brother Mahinda prime minister. All three have served as ministers, prime ministers, and presidents since 1970 and have taken seats in the Parliament. That's fifty years!

FOR THE FUTURE OF TODAY'S YOUTH

Despite my long frustration with the government, I still have hope for Sri Lanka's future. My wife and I traveled to Sri Lanka in August 2016, just four months before I left the United Nations. I had been asked to address the conference "Reconciliation and Coexistence: Role of Youth" and explore the ways young Sri Lankans can repair decades of damage and start anew to rebuild their nation. These young adults will be the first generation responsible for stabilizing and strengthening their country's postconflict future. I asked them, "Why should young people be sent off to fight wars but be prevented from building peace?" I urged them to participate in the process because of their natural openness to new ideas and a willingness to listen. I noted that the goals for Sri Lanka's postwar development include many priority areas for young people, such as a quality education, empowering women and girls, and ensuring decent work for all. "I call on young people to lead the way," I said.[10]

They were born and lived the early stages of their lives in conflict, terror, and displacement, and they had suffered the deprivations, fear, and injustice of a civil war. I could not help but think of my own childhood, spent in fear during the brutal war that devastated the Korean Peninsula.

I believe that a subsequent generation of young adults will be the most successful in unifying hearts and minds. This is what gives me hope for my country, for Sri Lanka, and for so many other societies struggling to recover from the scourge of war.

Chapter Fifteen

HAITI

From Earthquake to Heartbreak

"Something terrible has happened," UN spokesman Martin Nesirky told me. "It's very serious, but it's too soon to know how bad." I had just returned to the residence from a two-day retreat with senior advisors, but I had heard about the Port-au-Prince earthquake immediately after it happened at 6 P.M. Tuesday evening, January 12, 2010. Within the hour we had learned that the five-story United Nations headquarters building—which would have been nearly full at 5 P.M.—had collapsed in the magnitude 7.0 quake. It would be impossible to know more before sunrise.

The UN had more than 9,057 international staff in Haiti at the time, including 8,500 peacekeepers from forty-seven countries serving in the UN Stabilization Mission for Haiti (MINUSTAH).[1] The peacekeeping mission was created by the Security Council in 2004 to assist in Haiti's restoration of law and order after a coup; it was specifically tasked with supporting the country's hapless civilian police against the armed gangs that controlled the sprawling Cité Soleil slum. The criminal gangs were destabilizing the country and much of the region, thriving on international drug-running and a kidnapping economy that preyed on the general population. But the mission was not beloved by the Haitians, who often thought the peacekeepers stirred up violence instead of quelling it. This perception sharpened when people noticed that the peacekeepers were not assisting with rescue and emergency repairs. In fact, they were assigned to patrol the increasingly dangerous tent camps for crime and assault, problems that grew as time wore on and many Haitians grew angrier and more frustrated.

Our headquarters was in the seventy-five-room Christopher Hotel, a solid breeze-block building that was pancaked, one floor dropping down on the next, trapping scores of UN staff. These heroic people were doing difficult jobs, and at that hour I knew many would be talking on the phone, chatting in the hallways, completing paperwork, and engaging in the administrative life of civilian and military deployment. I'm sure several staff members on the swing shift were just waking up in their shared bedrooms on the Christopher's upper floors. It was too much to absorb; I had to sit down.

I spent much of the night on the telephone. First, I summoned my senior advisors for an early morning emergency meeting. As news of the disaster spread, the phone rang with offers of aid and support from capitals around the world. I monitored the situation from my residence, apprehension growing with each update from Port-au-Prince and the UN command center in New York. Later that evening I spoke with UN Ambassador Susan Rice and former U.S. President Bill Clinton, whom I had appointed as the UN secretary-general's special envoy for Haiti only six months earlier. Talking to these trusted partners did not lessen the shock or the horror.

The questions rushed at me all night: How many dead? How much emergency assistance would Haiti immediately require? What would aftershocks do to the rescue efforts? And, of course, what was the fate of thousands of UN peacekeepers and staff?

REALITY EXCEEDS OUR IMAGINATION

By dawn Wednesday morning, MINUSTAH was sending photos and information via email from the part of the Toussaint Louverture Airport that was still standing, but these updates only hinted at the scope of the destruction. Information was incomplete because we could not receive reports from some of the hardest-hit areas. It would be days before we could assess, or even quantify, the damage because it was impossible for anyone to get around. Satellite photographs showed the scale of the destruction, and helicopters identified the hardest hit neighborhoods. But the human toll required human intelligence.

I convened an urgent 7:50 A.M. Haiti crisis management meeting with my senior advisors: Deputy Secretary General Asha-Rose Migiro, UN Development Program Administrator Helen Clark, Under Secretary General for Peacekeeping Operations Alain Le Roy, Undersecretary General for Humanitarian Affairs John Holmes, Chief of Staff Vijay Nambiar, and Deputy Chief of Staff Kim Won-soo. It was clear that no one had slept more than an hour or two, but each was focused on his or her brief, and we quickly forged an early course of action.

The Department of Peacekeeping and Office for the Coordination of Humanitarian Affairs had worked through the night prioritizing what Haiti would likely need most and how to get it there. This would be a global effort: The World Food Program in Rome, UNICEF in New York, the UN High Commissioner for Refugees (UNHCR) in Geneva, and the World Bank in Washington all swung into action to plan, execute, and fund emergency relief. Capitals around the world were making the same calculations.

John Holmes and Alain Le Roy presented a rough plan to me later that morning. Even at this most preliminary stage, we knew that Haiti would require tens of millions of dollars for massive airlifts of food, medicine, tarps, and other emergency supplies. Haiti had been on our radar for years, and humanitarian experts and aid officials had been well aware of Haitians' dire existence for more than two decades. A massive earthquake could only add to the misery. I was confident that donors would not turn their backs on Haiti.

The UN aid operation would be one of the most complex, requiring logistical creativity and cooperation. The airport and seaport were both partially destroyed, and there was no way to deliver aid throughout the rubbled city. The epicenter of the earthquake was just sixteen miles west of Port-au-Prince, and the capital city had been shaken down into the wreckage-choked ground. But that was all we knew. Television cameras had not yet arrived. Our satellite communications were nonresponsive. Email was erratic. Many of our surviving colleagues in Port-au-Prince who would be coordinating aid delivery and distribution were overpowered with shock and grief by the events of the last twenty hours. For most of the night, it was impossible to know exactly what was happening just two hours off the coast of Miami. But we could picture it.

At four UN compounds around Port-au-Prince, able-bodied staff had worked through the night with ladders, flashlights, and shovels to find their coworkers. Many of the survivors, unharmed but surely overwhelmed, joined the search and helped move the injured to safety. These men and women also found the crushed or suffocated bodies of their colleagues. Imagining the scene, I too felt airless and overwhelmed. The United Nations lost 102 people in a matter of minutes, by far the single largest loss of life for the organization in peace, war, terrorist attacks, or previous natural disasters. I resisted the early news that my two most senior representatives were among the dead. We felt like the earthquake had rocked us almost as hard as it did the people who needed our help. More than a quarter-million Haitians were killed in the same quake. The tragedy linked the United Nations and Haiti in a bond of grief, however short-lived.

THE LONGEST DAYS

Thirteen long hours after the earthquake, UN headquarters in New York was the closest most of the world could get to Port-au-Prince. We were deluged by international journalists eager for an assessment of the damage and news of our emergency response. The UN communications office buzzed, verifying information as quickly as it was available. My former spokesperson, Michèle Montas, a prominent Haitian journalist who had recently returned home, sent regular updates through her tears.

At 10:30 A.M., UN Security Council President Li Baodong, China's permanent representative, opened a scheduled meeting with a moment of standing silence. My thoughts were racing and unsorted. I tried to focus my compassion, but a swirl of questions constantly intruded. By noon we had initial damage assessments: At least two million survivors would need shelter, food, water, and electricity. The dead—estimates ranged from thirty thousand to fifty-five thousand—would need to be quickly buried. I stood before the cameras again and issued an emergency appeal for urgent humanitarian assistance: tents and tarps, generators, medicine, medical personnel, dump trucks, cranes, backhoes, water purification units, and, of course, money. Television news had begun showing pictures of unfathomable devastation, and even the reporters were subdued by the scale of the disaster.

I spent most of my time from Wednesday morning until I left to visit Port-au-Prince on Sunday, January 17, with our humanitarian response coordinators who briefed me several times a day. I updated the press, addressed the General Assembly, and beseeched nearly two dozen governments to contribute funds, deliver cargo, and share technical expertise. Each one promised specific assistance. The one world leader I could not reach was René Préval, the president of Haiti.

U.S. President Barack Obama immediately took my call the morning after the earthquake and extended his and Michelle Obama's condolences.

He said the U.S. military was already preparing to send supplies by sea, air, and overland through the Dominican Republic. The first U.S. military and cargo ships would soon be off the coast. It took hours and hours to return all the calls I received from capitals. Even the poorest nations offered financial and technical support. Every leader I spoke to in those first days expressed horror and offered condolences for the United Nations' heavy losses.

We needed vast expertise. The living required immediate road clearance, medical support, potable water and mobile filtration systems, food, tarps and tents, and myriad other supplies. We also needed heavy machinery and refrigerated trucks and seasoned mortuary personnel who knew how to safely handle the volume of bodies that follow a natural disaster. Governments, aid groups, and even individuals had been promising emergency assistance all morning. The problem was logistics. The airport and seaport were destroyed, making it almost impossible to land supplies or to evacuate the wounded.

General Assembly President Ali Abdussalam Treki of Libya convened a rare emergency session late Wednesday afternoon. By this time, darkness was falling again in Port-au-Prince. "We are still struggling to learn the full extent of the devastation from yesterday's earthquake, but you have all seen the images on television—collapsed hospitals and schools, public buildings in ruins," I said. "Tens of thousands of people are in the streets, without shelter. Uncounted numbers remain trapped in the rubble. Casualties cannot yet be estimated, but they are certain to be heavy. Of Haiti's nine million people, initial reports suggest that roughly a third may be affected by the disaster." I told member states I had authorized an initial $10 million in emergency UN funds and called on them to contribute generously. This was our best estimate of what needed to be spent immediately on the hundreds of thousands of Haitians who might be homeless or injured. We were committed to stabilizing the population and caring for the sick. It was imperative to prevent the "second wave" of mortality that could come from diseases such as dysentery.

My office continued to call every contact number we had for Haitian officials in an effort to reach President Préval. It was impossible; the quake had knocked out communications, and by the middle of the first afternoon I began to fear the worst. I did not know how the UN could function in Haiti without a government to reassure the people and ease our operations. I finally reached the president late Thursday. It was rare for contact to take this long in disasters of this magnitude, but from our brief call, I knew he would not be a proactive partner in the relief effort. To my dismay and concern, President Préval was clearly in shock and unprepared for the crisis ahead. I assured him that the international community had rallied to help his people.

NO NEWS, DWINDLING HOPE

UN headquarters still had no word on the fate of dozens of staff members, including my Special Representative, the veteran Tunisian diplomat Hédi Annabi, and Deputy Special Representative Luiz Carlos da Costa of Brazil. I had known Annabi for nine years and admired him greatly. He was a gifted and creative diplomat whose candid assessments and suggestions were usually spot on. It was likely that Annabi had been in his office at the Christopher Hotel, but I clung to hope while the operation remained classified as search and rescue. More people could still be pulled from the rubble alive. I named Edmond Mulet, the assistant secretary general for peacekeeping operations, as my interim representative for MINUSTAH. A Guatemalan diplomat, he had served as my first special representative to Haiti and would later serve as my chief of staff. My heart and energy went out to the Haitian people in their time of desperate fear and need, but part of me also felt the need to take care of our UN family first. I knew this was a natural instinct, and I resolved to find enough compassion and strength for everyone.

Thursday morning brought the first good news. The United States was setting up a mobile airport control tower so cargo planes filled with relief could land in Port-au-Prince. I was proud to see my own country, Korea, and China and Japan competing to send in the first excavation packages, which included military engineering units. U.S. Secretary of State Hillary Clinton was the first foreign dignitary to land, meeting Haitian leaders at the airport.

MAGNITUDE 7

On Sunday, January 17, I flew to Port-au-Prince. It was a very long day and among the saddest days I had ever endured. I had no words for the destruction I saw below. Nearly all the buildings, including several UN facilities, were shaken flat. Even the Parliament building sustained gaping damage. I imagined that I could feel the capital's collective stress and pain while we were still in the air. Before our plane landed at Port-au-Prince, I instructed my UN staff to drink as much water as possible. "Do not expect water and food all day long. Do not even carry water. Show our solidarity with the Haitian people."

Upon arrival at the airport, I met with President René Préval, but he seemed lost. He had not even sent a message of hope to the Haitian people, and I strongly urged him to do so. "Mr. President, why don't you use the UN radio and reassure the nation. Tell them what you are doing; tell them help is on the way. Tell them to be strong." But he seemed so shaken that he didn't know what to do. In fact, he was terrified. He was panicked. It had been five days, and he still didn't know what to say or what to do for his own country! Help was finally arriving from around the world, and we would need strong partners in the Haitian government. I was very concerned.

The security situation was deteriorating with every day and night that people could not find their loved ones or were sleeping in the streets. It was important to show the Haitian people that the United Nations would not abandon them. I insisted on meeting the Haitian people and hearing their voices. I wanted to see the situation from the ground as well as from the air. So I went for a walk through Port-au-Prince. Shockingly, the Presidential Palace and other official buildings were in ruins. Whole blocks—whole neighborhoods!—had been leveled. Everywhere we went, I heard the sounds of crying and yelling.

After I spoke to the president, I wanted to be with our surviving staff at the Christopher Hotel site. The Haitian sun beat down mercilessly on a field of smashed concrete and twisted metal. UN staffers were trying not to cry, and some were succeeding. They had already been through the kind of disaster no one can be prepared for, and everyone knew colleagues who were still missing. By now workers had recovered the bodies of Hédi Annabi and Luiz Carlos da Costa, and they would fly home with me that night.

I was trying hard to keep my breath under control as I took in this scene. A Haitian staff member handed me the UN flag that had flown over the MINUSTAH building. The blue and white fabric—ripped and grimy with concrete dust—was folded into the triangle of tribute to our fallen. I didn't know the man's name, but his eyes were red and puffy and one hand was crudely bandaged. His whole body radiated fatigue and pain. I wasn't expecting this moment. I felt a punch of sadness and horror as I took the flag, which so perfectly symbolized our losses. I was overcome and, momentarily, speechless. Finally, I thanked him and told the staff to be strong. Our missing colleagues would want us to continue our work for the Haitian people, I said reflexively, aware that my voice was shaking and too low for most of them to hear over the sound of the search parties.

There were thousands of Haitians, young people, out in the sun because there was no other place for them to go. People were just wandering around, not knowing what to do. I wondered why they weren't clearing roads so machinery and trucks could get through. But they couldn't; these people seemed to be in shock too. They surrounded me, shouting for help. I knew they didn't mean me any harm, but so many people crowded near me, all talking or yelling in Creole and gesturing emphatically, and it left me feeling frightened. It became difficult to move in such a large, unruly crowd, and my security team wanted to take me back to the airport. But I wasn't ready to go. I watched a group of boys digging at a collapsed building, shouting to someone inside. I wanted to stay, but we had to keep moving.

When I returned to the airport late that afternoon, I was wrung out from an unbearably emotional day. And then I saw the two caskets carrying the bodies of SRSG Hédi Annabi and DSRSG da Costa. The caskets were draped with UN flags, ready to be loaded into the plane's cargo bay. For the second time that day, the greatest grief overwhelmed me. My breath caught on a swallowed cry, and my knees shook. But I remained upright. I think I said a few remarks of praise and solace. I barely remember the flight home, and I fell into a deep but brief sleep as we drove back to the residence from the airport.

The following morning, I immediately told Helen Clark, the administrator of the UN Development Program, that the Haitians were dazed and would struggle to undertake relief efforts on their own. We decided to initiate the Cash for Work Program, paying $5 per person per day to do whatever they could do without machinery: clear the street of rocks or pebbles; move trash or whatever they could lift.[2] Tens of thousands of people were willing to help, and they did as much as they could by hand. The country needed heavy cranes, but we still didn't have them.

During these initial days, UN member states contributed money and equipment, soldiers and civilians, technical experts and aid workers. Over the next few weeks, my representative Edmond Mulet and his deputy Tony Banbury worked heroically to expand and organize our presence on the ground. SRSG Mulet was particularly devoted to the country's reconstruction, and he was loved and respected by the Haitian people. When I visited Haiti, many Haitians praised him for his compassion and leadership.

Caribbean and Latin American nations sent army units to restore critical infrastructure and assist in the distribution of aid. People saw this and were grateful, or at least supportive. With humanitarian support handled by international troops, UN peacekeepers were assigned to the overcrowded makeshift camps to prevent the soaring incidents of rapes and robberies. Of course, they could not prevent every assault. Unfortunately, many Haitians saw them only in the camps and assumed they were not addressing the country's acute needs. Inevitably, this tension flared into open hostility. By the time cholera came to Haiti in October 2010, the Haitians were willing to believe that the peacekeepers were responsible.

THE WORLD PITCHES IN

The UN donor's conference for Haiti on March 31, 2010, was organized by the United Nations with President Clinton, and it raised pledges of $9.9 billion in a single day—by far the largest single mobilization of international assistance in UN history.[3] In my time as secretary-general, I've led or participated in conferences for Syria, Afghanistan, Palestine, Lebanon, and several other countries in crisis, but I have never seen such a successful conference or stronger support. The meeting was held at UN headquarters, with Special Envoy Bill Clinton to my left and Secretary of State Hillary Clinton to my right—typical positions for my chief diplomatic representative and a representative for the convening country. "Usually they sit together," I said to laughter, "but not today." Although I did not mention it publicly, I knew Haiti was special to them; the Clintons had visited as newlyweds in 1975.

The international community was especially generous to Haiti, in part because of the scale of utter destruction and the UN's history of military, political, and humanitarian engagement. But Haiti also benefited from this being the first financial pledging conference of its kind in a while. Governments were not yet suffering from donors' fatigue.

Meanwhile, the Haitian diaspora mobilized resources small and large to powerful and still unheralded effect. Hundreds of thousands of Haitians living abroad contributed money and services, undertook fund-raising and political and humanitarian efforts, and returned to share in the heavy lifting. Haitian businesses kept charity bowls by the cash register, and athletes and actors who had never even been to Haiti made six-figure contributions. It was impossible to keep track of it all.

Haiti also struck a nerve with Hollywood. Scores of entertainment and sports stars prominently pledged money for emergency relief or targeted reconstruction and urged their fans to do the same. Haitian singer and music producer Wyclef Jean advocated tirelessly for his country's rescue and reconstruction, leveraging his musical connections for two superstar events. His Hope for Haiti Now telethon raised $61 million in two hours, and a fundraising song featuring many of the same artists played everywhere that winter from car radios to international sporting events.

I lost track of the celebrities who visited Haiti that winter and spring: Matt Damon, Susan Sarandon, Demi Moore, John Travolta, Julio Iglesias, and UNICEF goodwill ambassadors Lionel Messi and Shakira. The popular Colombian singer spoke of her many visits to Haiti over the years. Even Michelle Obama came to Haiti on a trip of support and compassion. But no celebrity seemed able to match the determination of American movie star Sean Penn, who landed in Port-au-Prince days after the earthquake and stayed for two years. He slept in a tent next to the homeless sheltering in the Pétionville camp, joining his Haitian neighbors to clear rubble and carry supplies. I was introduced to Penn and I saw him sweating, running here and there. Not only did he raise awareness of the situation in Haiti, but he also contributed personally to the relief effort.

I am even more grateful to the countless medical professionals who closed their own practices to come to Haiti. Nurses quit their jobs. Laborers and logistics experts traveled at their own expense. This crisis touched more people, more deeply, than many other unimaginable disasters. For example, we didn't see teachers going to Lebanon or Afghanistan on their summer breaks, but they came to Haiti.

After an initial period of emergency rescue and aid operations, the UN expanded its focus to Haiti's mid- and long-term reconstruction. President Clinton worked his connections to mobilize corporate donations. He even brought many business leaders to Haiti to drum up investment and jobs. Several of them, in turn, encouraged other corporate leaders to do the same. In March 2009, President Clinton and I visited factories and schools, met workers and students, and encouraged them all to work hard and stay in Haiti while the international community was sending in continuous support.

At the same time, I grew even more disappointed with Haiti's political leaders who were divided and fighting among themselves. President Préval, and later his successor President Michel Martelly, was not able to get parliamentary support for his initiatives, and in-fighting stalled rebuilding projects for an unconscionably long time. I was furious that the lawmakers could not unite to rebuild their country but instead seemed to be living in different worlds. I knew that only a very long-term commitment and a torrent of resources would bring a measure of stability to Haiti again.

THE GREAT UNDOING

But stability never came to Haiti. Instead, a ravaging cholera epidemic took hold and still flares up periodically. In October 2010, only ten months after the earthquake, several people in the northern countryside contracted the highly contagious disease. The seemingly isolated cholera cases raised no alarms for UN field staff or the peacekeeping base nearby. But the bacteria—spread by infected water and human waste—got into a small tributary that feeds the Artibonite River, which thousands used for drinking, washing, and bathing.

Aid workers reported that cholera quickly roared into a deadly epidemic of breathtaking size and speed. It sluiced through tent cities erected for survivors of the January earthquake, and then it spread beyond to the worn-down population. The disease's strength was compounded by Haiti's broken infrastructure, overcrowding, and a paucity of health care. In six years, cholera killed more than 9,000 and sickened 750,000 people in the capital and beyond.[4] It was the world's largest outbreak of cholera, and Haiti's first in more than a century.

This disaster forever destroyed the United Nations' reputation in Haiti. I am sickened that the country has not fully recovered. The Haitians believed UN peacekeepers brought the disease to their country, singling out the newly arrived battalion from Nepal, which had just left a similar strain behind them. In response to the growing outrage, I appointed an independent panel of scientists, each of whom had a specialty in cholera. Chairman Alejandro Cravioto (Brazil), Claudio E. Lanata (Peru), Daniele Lantagne (USA) and Balakrish Nair of the National Institute of Cholera and Enteric Diseases in India did not fully exonerate the United Nations but found that "a confluence of circumstances" contributed to the outbreak.[5] However, other investigations traced the source of the cholera epidemic directly to MINUSTAH, and specifically to the Nepalese peacekeepers, whose barracks had damaged pipes that leaked sewage into the tributary.

Given the disparities, I ordered another investigation. That report, released on August 8, 2016, found no doubt that the Nepalese peacekeepers—specifically, a sanitation contractor—allowed fecal waste to contaminate the waters. WHO also urged the UN to accept legal responsibility. UN officials, including me, were still not convinced, but there was no denying the desperation of their situation. It was vital to commit to long-term development projects to improve sanitation, sewage, and health care systems. I ordered UN agencies to commit all available medical and engineering resources to support sanitation construction in hard-hit areas. UN staff also worked with Haitian health experts to orchestrate massive distributions of emergency kits, including soap and water purification tablets.

THE LAWYERS COME KNOCKING

I was incredulous—no, shocked—when, in October 2013, a class action on behalf of five named plaintiffs and a potential class of thousands of Haitian cholera victims was filed against the United Nations and me as its secretary-general in the U.S. District Court for the Southern District of New York. The lawsuit sought $2.2 billion for Haiti's government to eradicate cholera, punitive damages, and unspecified actual and compensatory damages for the class, which were later estimated to be $40 billion according to the September 2016 Report on the situation by UN Human Rights Rapporteur Philip Alston.

The legal challenge lasted five years as lawyers for the plaintiffs demanded that the United Nations pay reparations. The UN disputed that we had brought cholera to Haiti and claimed diplomatic immunity under the Vienna Convention, which establishes our diplomatic privileges and immunity. I thought this lawsuit was fraudulent from the beginning, and I was incensed every time I thought about this attempt to extort money from the United Nations. The effort required a substantial amount of financial investment and a knowledge of the U.S. legal system, and it was difficult to believe that this route was in the best interests of the Haitian people.

The law firms and organizations representing the survivors in the suit against the United Nations are based in the United States and Haiti. One of the senior lawyers had a history of bringing class action lawsuits. I thought they were after a big fee and media coverage. I was advised to say as little as possible when questioned by diplomats or the press. Nonetheless, my heart bled for the Haitian people who have been whipped by catastrophe and criminal political leaders throughout the country's history. I felt we had not done enough to stem the epidemic or care for the sick.

It was a huge relief when District Court Judge J. Paul Oetken decided that the court had no jurisdiction over the case and dismissed it. The date was January 9, 2015, exactly five years after the earthquake struck.[6] I made another of my six visits to Haiti in July 2014. I felt it was a necessary pilgrimage to meet affected families, one of the most difficult journeys I made as secretary-general. I heard stories of families splintered, breadwinners lost, orphans suffering, and children, partners, and parents gone forever. As a husband, father, and grandfather, I felt tremendous heartache at the pain so many families have had to endure. I will never forget it.

The lawsuits and the lingering cholera crisis were draining, not just for me but for much of the UN's staff. Of course, an appeal was inevitable. Thankfully, on August 18, 2016, a federal Court of Appeals judge upheld the United Nations' absolute immunity in U.S. courts, citing a "lack of subject-matter jurisdiction." I was too relieved for words.

REGRET AND RECOVERY

With my term as secretary-general drawing to an end, I wanted to address the cholera tragedy fully, publicly, and honestly. Our delayed and insufficient early response had made the tragedy worse. Although I had made some remarks the day the lawsuit was settled, these words weren't enough for me. I had to set the record straight before my tenure as secretary-general ended.

It was important to reinforce the commitment of member states and the UN itself and to ensure that an epidemic such as this one never happens again. The Haitians needed to hear it too. So did governments and people. "We simply did not do enough with regard to the cholera outbreak and its spread in Haiti," I told the General Assembly on December 1, 2016, an apology I delivered in English, French, and Creole. "We are profoundly sorry for our role."

In December 2016, I announced a two-track approach to eradicate the cholera bacteria in Haiti and assist those directly affected by the epidemic. Track 1 is a significant long-term effort to address unsanitary living conditions so waterborne diseases, such as cholera, will not flourish. This effort was already underway. In the last year of my term, we made great progress in prevention, vaccinating more than one million people and nearly tripling the number of rapid-response health teams that could contain new outbreaks.

Track 2, to directly aid those affected by cholera, was more complex. This requires identification of the victims, a frequently impossible undertaking after a natural disaster such as the earthquake. Many Haitians were already left undocumented because most records were destroyed in the earthquake or in subsequent hurricanes. As important, any effort to provide a meaningful benefit to family members and others affected by the outbreak will depend on reliable and sufficient funding. The likely price tag for these efforts is about $400 million, to be financed by voluntary contributions to a special fund established for this purpose. I am sorry to say that this sum has overwhelmed the UN's most reliable contributors. Member states have contributed only a fraction of that amount, and much of it is earmarked for specific development initiatives. Many developing nations have said they cannot afford to pay more than the assessments. Several ambassadors told me that their governments do not want to pay UN debts stemming from our own negligence. I disputed that position in the most strenuous terms, but there is still nothing I can do about it.

The cholera epidemic continues to poison the Haitian people's relationship with the United Nations. I hope member states and other contributors remember that we have a moral responsibility to commit to these programs for the sake of the Haitian people and the UN organization itself. The cholera epidemic in Haiti remains a blemish on UN peacekeeping and on the organization worldwide. I know I will continue to regret our role.

My hope is for the United Nations to become more aware of the threats facing the people we are trying to help. We must take more decisive action when even one of those challenges is detected.

PART III

Human Rights and Development

Supporting Our People and Our Planet

Chapter Sixteen

HUMAN RIGHTS

Born Free and Equal

On January 2, 2007, my first day at work as UN secretary-general, I arrived early, filled with anticipation. I was deeply touched to find hundreds of staff members gathered in the United Nations lobby, as is the custom, to welcome the new secretary-general. I bowed to them and silently vowed to do my best for the organization and its staff. Soon-taek and I made our way to the small meditation room off the lobby to offer our silent tribute to Dag Hammarskjöld and all UN staff who sacrificed their lives for UN ideals. As I stood there, I thought about how the world was likely to grow even more tumultuous over the next five years, and I hoped events would spare our committed men and women.

The staff waited for us in the lobby, joined by dozens of journalists from around the world, all there to record the first day of the eighth UN secretary-general. I made some introductory remarks, but they were lost amid the commotion that immediately followed. Reporters began shouting questions about Saddam Hussein, the Iraqi dictator who had been executed only three days earlier. Was the execution legitimate? Would it bring stability to Iraq? A civil war? Does the United Nations support a global moratorium on capital punishment? I said:

> Saddam Hussein was responsible for committing heinous crimes and unspeakable atrocities against the Iraqi people." The issue of capital punishment is for each and every member state to decide. While I am firmly against impunity,

> I also hope that the members of the international community should pay due regard to all aspects of international humanitarian laws. During my entire tenure, I will try my best to help member states and the international community strengthen the rule of law.[1]

Although factually correct, this was not received favorably by the media.

By the time the elevator reached my thirty-eighth floor office, the press office was already doing damage control. I learned quickly that the secretary-general does not just wade into an issue as divisive as the global abolition of the death penalty. The backlash was immediate and oddly personal. Human rights groups said my remarks legitimized Saddam's trial and set back UN efforts to abolish capital punishment. The press unfavorably compared my measured remarks to the passion shown by human rights officials. The headline on a *New York Times* editorial a few days later called me a "status quo secretary-general" and mischaracterized my remarks.[2]

I was shocked. My personal view is that the death penalty has absolutely no place in the twenty-first century, and I had already committed to using my pulpit to work toward its abolition. On January 11, I made another statement in my first official press conference:

> I believe life is precious and must be respected and protected. Every human being has the right to live in dignity. I recognize there is a trend in international law and domestic practice to phase out the death penalty. I encourage that trend as member states are debating this issue.

The press often does not cover what happens after a postmortem, but after this statement most stopped criticizing my position.

The Universal Declaration of Human Rights enshrines "the right to life, liberty, and the security of the person." Yet there have been few issues before the United Nations as consistently divisive as a global moratorium on capital punishment. At that time, the UN had no official position on abolishing the death penalty, deferring to member states to make their own laws.

It was not until December 18, 2007, that the General Assembly passed a resolution introduced by the Italian government urging states to respect international standards by abolishing the death penalty and to progressively reduce the number of offenses punishable by death.[3] Similar resolutions were adopted five times while I was secretary-general, with as many as 117 states in support.

Nearly fifty countries continued with executions during my tenure as secretary-general, all making it clear that they vigorously opposed international pressure to change their penal codes. These holdouts have dug into their already entrenched positions: I would often reach out to Washington, D.C., Beijing, Riyadh, and other capitals to stay an imminent execution, and I'm sorry to say that they rarely did.

I continue to work on abolishment of the death penalty. I've been working with NGOs such as the International Commission Against the Death Penalty led by former UN High Commissioner for Human Rights Navathem Pillay.

THE RESPONSIBILITY TO PROTECT

We all knew my speech about the humanitarian doctrine called the Responsibility to Protect would be one of the most important I would deliver during my first term as Secretary General. R2P, as it is known, wasn't a new idea then, but by the summer of 2008, it was just starting to gain traction beyond human rights NGOs. The R2P doctrine—that sovereign states have a duty of care to protect their populations from atrocities, and that the international community at large shares this responsibility—had never been fully defined and its legal underpinning was still the subject of many debates. Even though it existed in only the broadest brush strokes, R2P was already complex and controversial.

German Foreign Minister Frank-Walter Steinmeier, later the President of Germany, invited me to give the keynote speech[4] at a day-long conference about R2P issues called Responsible Sovereignty: International Cooperation for a Changed World," convened in Berlin on July 15, 2008.

R2P was still a novelty when I came into office, but it was not new. Former UN Secretary General Kofi Annan introduced what was then an "emerging norm" in the wide-ranging resolution adopted by consensus on the United Nations' sixtieth anniversary. Annan played a pivotal role in winning its acceptance, and it is one of the singular accomplishments of his tenure.

The Responsibility to Protect holds that nations have the duty to use political, legal, economic, and military means to abate bloodshed, all in accordance with the UN Charter and Security Council resolutions. Some governments accepted R2P as an important legal response to preventable massacres such as those in Rwanda and the former Yugoslavia. But others were wary of what they saw as a proposal, imposed by the West, that could violate their sovereignty.

The principle rests on three pillars: a country's own responsibility to protect its people; the international community's responsibility to help states meet this obligation; and, finally, the duty to step in when mass atrocities are looming or already occurring.

I don't think we should dismiss, though, how genuinely revolutionary it was for states to agree that they can't do whatever they please inside their own borders. This recognition upended centuries of history while advancing the protection of human rights.

The United Nations had a powerful ally in Edward Luck, a Columbia University professor of international relations and an early advocate of the principles that became R2P. In 2008 I appointed Luck as my special adviser on the responsibility to protect, and he worked mightily to dispel the concern among member states that it was a new code for humanitarian intervention.

It was, from the beginning, a tough sell. A number of states showed their resistance in the UN budget committee, effectively strangling the effort by refusing to fund it. Ed Luck continued to advance R2P without a salary, office, staff, or mandate. He worked closely with my Special Adviser on the Prevention of Genocide Francis Deng, a South Sudanese professor and scholar who, with his colleagues at the Brookings Institute had developed the outline of R2P a decade earlier.[5]

My team and I laid out a comprehensive vision of R2P in a landmark report to the General Assembly on January 12, 2009, "Implementing the Responsibility to Protect."[6] This was the first time anyone had conceptualized in detail what R2P means, how to apply it and who ultimately bears the responsibility to protect civilians. The UN model became the blueprint going forward. I felt proud to take concrete action on one of my campaign pledges.

Then came Libya. Muammar Gaddafi was the test case for R2P when, in the aftermath of the Arab Spring, he barraged his own citizens with attack helicopters and soldiers. Upon my urging, the Security Council on March 17, 2011 authorized NATO to enforce a no-fly zone over Libya.[7] Gaddafi was killed while on the run, and Russia, furious, accused the United States and Europeans in the Security Council of pursuing a regime change in violation of their private reassurances. Russia vowed to veto future humanitarian interventions invoking R2P.

The immediate ramifications were tragic: The Security Council was impotent just when it needed a similar response to Syria. I lobbied them intensely in private conversations and even in public to dissuade them, but I could not convince them to relent.

SUFFERING FOR WHOM YOU LOVE

I had no experience with sexual minorities until my fifties when I was serving as Korea's ambassador to Austria. In 1998, the ambassador of a European country invited my wife and me and several other couples to dinner in his residence, where I noticed many pictures of him and a male counselor in the embassy. These were personal pictures, small framed memories of vacations and the like. During the dinner I became aware that their relationship was as close as many married couples. The men seemed very comfortable with each other. It was the first positive example of homosexuality I'd ever seen.

This was all new to me. Growing up, I had no thoughts about gay rights. Homosexuality was taboo in Asian society. Korea, in particular, was a very conservative country. Also, I had been educated in Confucianism, which teaches rectitude. Now that I look back, I think gay children were often hidden away by their parents. I know now, of course, that even in Korea there were people with different sexual orientations, but they lived in the shadows. Lesbian, gay, bisexual, transgender, and intersex people did not talk about themselves publicly, and there were no positive depictions in the media.

Discrimination, violence, and fear grew even more virulent worldwide in the 1980s and 1990s when AIDS began afflicting gay men. It was around this time that I had begun thinking about gay rights and how much their fight mirrored women's demands for inclusivity, equality, and opportunity. These are the cornerstones of the United Nations, and they are essential to my own values. I knew it would take a long time to change the attitudes in many member states, but I believed the UN must embody its own ideals.

Shortly after I became secretary-general in 2007, I learned that many married same-sex couples were denied UN benefits granted to married heterosexual couples. At some duty stations, these benefits could be significant, including housing, living, and educational subsidies. Some months into my tenure, the UN human rights office suggested I meet with a group of staff members who were unhappy with the disparities.

Before the meeting began, I asked the group to stand with me for the photograph that everyone wants to take with the UN secretary-general.

I was genuinely surprised when they refused—most were still closeted at work! I prevailed, telling them it was for my own records and would not be published.

"I take human rights seriously, everyone's rights, and I am committed to the UN being the best workplace for lesbians, gays, and transgender people," I told them. "Do not be discouraged." Many of them were reassured. In fact, it gave some staff members the courage to come out. As the year was ending, I was pleasantly surprised to receive a calendar featuring the photograph. That experience stiffened my resolve to harmonize UN benefits. My aides urged me not to take on such a divisive fight, arguing that many countries would consider this meddling in their own societies. But I was determined to address this. In fact, I was surprised no previous secretary-general had done so.

As I looked into issues relating to lesbians, gays, bisexuals, transgender, and intersex individuals (LGBTI), I realized just how many opportunities had fallen through our fingers. So many people were at risk of terrible personal violence just because of whom they love. Nonetheless, I knew many countries were not yet receptive to a plea on behalf of people who were seen as somehow outside nature. Almost one-third of members states had outlawed homosexuality, including five that imposed the death penalty for specific sex acts. In many of these cultures, from Russia to Uganda to Colombia, violence and harassment of sexual minorities was all but encouraged.

In May 2010, I paid an official visit to Malawi. At that time, there was a serious case involving a gay couple sentenced to fourteen years of hard labor "for knowing each other as husband and wife." When I met President Bingu wa Mutharika, I appealed to him to pardon the young men. He listened carefully and said, "I do not agree with your position. But since you raised this issue as UN secretary-general, I will try to think about it."

We stepped outside to take questions during a joint press conference, and the president immediately announced his pardon of Steven Monjeza and Tiwonge Chimbalanga, effective immediately.[8] He did not tell me in advance that he had made up his mind, and I was as surprised as others. I hoped my intervention would spare other same-sex couples.

Then I proceeded to Uganda and met President Yoweri Museveni. When I raised the LGBTI issue, he said he did not agree with me, nor would Uganda's conservative culture. Sexuality of all kinds was taboo, and even public displays of affection between heterosexual couples were frowned upon. The president had, in fact, recently explained the same thing to U.S. Secretary of

State Hillary Clinton. "I told her, 'Madam Secretary, you may kiss publicly with President Clinton, but if I do that with my wife, I will lose my presidency,'" President Museveni recalled.

For this reason, I was concerned about bringing a discussion of gay and transgender rights to the UN Human Rights Council, the logical place for it. Many HRC member states are so religiously or culturally conservative that they, too, openly criminalize or demonize sexual minorities. The human rights body had already passed several resolutions that upheld "traditional norms" and "families." But I continued to press for the inclusion of sexual minorities in all UN human rights work.

Latin singer Ricky Martin was among the entertainers and celebrities who came to the United Nations on December 11, 2012, to participate in an International Human Rights Day forum on gay leadership that felt more like a celebration than a summit meeting. Scores of LGBTI staff attended, as did global advocates, openly gay ambassadors, and those who support their efforts.[9] It was a brave stand for the diplomats; in 2011, seventy-five nations had outlawed homosexuality.

The following year UN High Commissioner for Human Rights Navi Pillay created UN Free & Equal, an unprecedented public outreach program crafted to counter homophobia and transphobia around the world.[10] Hundreds of celebrities, politicians, religious leaders, and other prominent figures have participated in local campaigns to promote empathy, acceptance, and visibility of gay and transgender people. Unlike so much of the United Nations' work, which is based on legal or structural frameworks, UN Free & Equal translates universal values into personal stories.

Meanwhile a dozen UN agencies and programs with staff in the field had, over several months, drafted a joint statement calling on all nations to protect LGBTI individuals from violence and discrimination and to repeal punitive laws. The 2015 document was signed by the agencies overseeing the UN's work for refugees, women, health, food, drugs and organized crime prevention, population, culture, labor, and AIDS, and it was a significant step toward legitimizing sexual minorities.

Throughout my service as secretary-general, I tried to build global support by speaking out often and passionately about gay and transgender rights. I stressed the global tragedy of the hundreds murdered, thousands attacked, and millions of LGBTI people who live under a shadow. I used every opportunity to seek compassion and acceptance, even embarrassing world leaders if necessary. At the 2014 Winter Olympic Games in Sochi, I criticized Moscow's ban on openly gay athletes and those with HIV/AIDS to participate in the Olympic Games. I had failed to move the government with private conversations, so one day before the Winter Olympics were to begin, I addressed the controversy in my remarks to the International Olympic Committee Session. Despite Russia's embarrassment, I knew the time was right to speak out; in many Western cities, people were blocking the Olympic torch in protest.

My remarks were received by Moscow with embarrassment, even though President Putin had officially lifted the ban on participation by gay athletes. Back in New York, Russian Ambassador Vitaly Churkin almost shouted at me for "destroying" the joyful atmosphere of the Olympic Games. Then, to my amazement, he threatened me. "How will you manage your relations with the P5?" he asked. I thought he must have been badly scolded by his government and was giving all his anger to me. "What do you mean by that?" I pushed back, and it stopped there.

Advocates for gay and transgender issues came to recognize me as an ally. On June 26, 2015, in San Francisco, I was awarded the Harvey Milk Medal for my "unparalleled and unequivocal support" of LGBT issues, and specifically for the UN Free & Equal campaign. Milk, an openly gay lawmaker, was already a touchstone of homosexual pride when he was assassinated for his politics in 1978. I proudly accepted this honor in his name in front of the largest rainbow flag I'd ever seen. In a remarkable, breath-taking coincidence, the U.S. Supreme Court that morning upheld the right of lesbians and gay men to marry. It was a great day for the community, and many people were overjoyed by the Supreme Court decision.

I was surprised to learn, however, that my advocacy was deeply unpopular in Korea. The spouse of a close advisor, herself a career ambassador, told me she had seen a demonstration with placards condemning my support for homosexuals. By then I was thought to be a potential candidate in Korea's upcoming presidential election, and many of my confidantes told me to step away from the issue. But I could not.

Sometimes it seemed that the harder hearts were winning. Robert Mugabe, president of Zimbabwe, mocked the UN-wide commitment to sexual equality in his remarks at the seventieth General Assembly. Veering from his prepared remarks, the president said in his imperious voice, "We reject attempts to prescribe new rights that are contrary to our values, norms, traditions, and beliefs. 'We are not gays.' "[11] The line drew gasps and mild, scattered applause. Nonetheless, on June 30, 2016, the Human Rights Council created a special rapporteur to investigate violence and discrimination based on sexual orientation and gender identity.[12] Designating a human rights expert for LGBTI issues was a remarkable accomplishment, one that surprised many observers given the composition of the Human Rights Council.

What happened next was truly unprecedented—and disturbing. A significant number of member states, led by Russia and several African and Middle East countries, presented a draft resolution that would have annulled my administrative decision to recognize these families, regardless of the position of their own governments. I owe much of the credit for this to the U.S. government's diplomatic interventions led by UN Ambassador Samantha Power. The outcome has validated the time and political capital I invested. I hope homophobic and transphobic governments, communities, and individuals will come to believe that it is wrong to hate, discriminate, and attack people based on whom they love. I will continue to encourage them to open their eyes and their minds, much as I did so long ago.

As secretary-general, I held a number of priorities for my tenure, all in support of my ultimate goal: advancing human rights for all people regardless of their race, sex, religion, economic, or personal particulars. More than fifty years in civil service created my signal belief that the highest accomplishment of the United Nations is to ensure that dignity and equality remain attainable, sustainable, and nonnegotiable.

Chapter Seventeen

WOMEN

Expanding Opportunity Inside the UN and Around the World

My mother, Shin Hyun-soon, was one of the strongest women I've ever known. She lived an inspiring life, passing at the age of one hundred on June 17, 2019. She was not educated, but she was a life force throughout the tumult of my childhood. She gave birth to my younger sister while we ran from North Korean and Chinese soldiers, a traumatic birth that caused her pain for the rest of her life. Just three days after giving birth, she had to walk miles on a snowy road.

This image has remained a vivid memory for me throughout my life. Even as a small boy, I instinctively recognized that this was wrong. As I grew older, I came to understand that inequality and injustice had to be corrected so women could contribute fully in their communities.

A LIFELONG FEMINIST

When I was a middle school student, I won a prize from the education superintendent of my province for the essay I wrote commemorating UN Human Rights Day, which is celebrated around the world on December 10. As I remember, it started this way: " 'A girl again!' the father screamed and ran out of the house in disappointment." His wife had just given birth to a girl, the family's fourth, but he had been anxiously waiting for a boy. This happened frequently from the 1950s to the 1970s. It was common for Korean women to continue giving birth until they had a boy. But I was surrounded by strong women who had survived the war and maintained their families, and my respect for them was absolute.

Decades later and throughout my career in the Korean Ministry of Foreign Affairs, I looked for and promoted women with the same skills and qualities as our most accomplished men. There were no women in the senior level at that time, and this was not a popular reform effort. Nonetheless, in July 2005 I appointed Kang Kyung-wha director general for international organizations, making her the first and only senior woman in the entire ministry. She served as an assistant secretary-general at the UN during my time, and she later became the Korean foreign minister. Gender advocates praised my efforts to hire and promote women, but I didn't feel I deserved special merit for honoring equality—it should have been the norm.

My tenure at the United Nations was filled with opportunities to empower women within the organization and around the world. In December 2006, while I was studying the United Nations in preparation for leading it, I found plenty of room for the organization to improve gender parity. The ratio improved dramatically during my time in office and beyond, but further improvement remains vital. To this day the United Nations must hire more women who bring fresh perspectives and energy. It is especially important that more women work in field offices to show local and national government officials that women can be extremely effective in positions of responsibility. I know that example will fuel the ambition of girls around the world.

When I studied the records, I came across the memorable British diplomat Margaret Anstee, who over her forty-year career with the United Nations racked up a series of "firsts" for women. She delivered disaster relief in Bangladesh and helped four crumbling Soviet Republics plan aid for the children of Chernobyl. She took on several other difficult assignments, traveling through a world that had just survived World War II. Kurt Waldheim, the UN's fourth secretary-general, chose Anstee as the first-ever female UN under secretary-general, and she ran the UN office against organized crime in Vienna. In 1992 Perez de Cuellar appointed her to lead the successful political mission in Angola. My predecessor, Kofi Annan, appointed a significant number of women, but there was room for more. In the first few months of my tenure, I selected my predecessor's former chief of staff, Alicia Bárcena of Mexico, to serve as the under secretary general for management. I asked Michèle Montas, a deeply respected Haitian journalist, who had been working with the UN radio service, to be my spokesperson—one of the most visible positions in the United Nations. I tapped former New Zealand Prime

Minister Helen Clark to be the first female Administrator of the UN Development Program, and chose Tanzanian Foreign Minister Asha-Rose Migiro as my deputy secretary-general.

I wanted member states and career UN staff to see that I was serious about appointing women to important, visible, and challenging senior positions in the Secretariat, peacekeeping, and the field. But I was frustrated to find that the problem was baked into the UN itself by a bureaucracy that favored male candidates. When there was a vacancy, senior staff would form a selection committee and give me three finalists, and at first only men were recommended. After we filled several jobs this way, I knew the organization would never achieve the gender empowerment we urged member states to practice. I asked why there were no female finalists. There are female candidates, I was told, but they were not up to the standards. Finally, I asked them to let me interview the female candidate who failed "best." I soon met many qualified women and appointed them to the ranks of senior management.

That sent a strong message to my senior male advisors. At first they complained that I was meddling, but I said it was my prerogative. I instructed them to include at least one woman in each group of three final candidates, and the number of new female hires grew over time. In fact, sometimes the whole selection committee was composed of women! But the quality of UN appointments never suffered. In all, I appointed or promoted more than 150 women within the UN's senior management around the world.

UPGRADING OUR EFFORT

I established a new agency, UN Women, in 2010 to improve coordination between UN agencies, NGOs, the public, and women around the world. This would be a prominent agency with an ambitious agenda promoting women's rights, gender equality, reproductive health, literacy, and other important issues facing females of all ages in every region of the world. I knew I needed a powerful executive director, someone who commanded the respect of the advocates she would be working with and had the political and professional authority to confidently and even aggressively engage world leaders.

I believed that Michelle Bachelet, whose term as the president of Chile had just ended, would be a good fit for this position. I mentioned the new agency to her at a conference in Spain and was delighted by her enthusiasm. Bachelet even agreed to meet with the search committee. Several other prominent women let us know of their interest in the position, including

Kim Campbell, Canada's trailblazing female former prime minister whose political leadership and strong reputation would make her a good fit for the United Nations as well. In the end, Michelle Bachelet accepted the role.

Under Executive Director Bachelet's leadership, the office embedded gender concerns into all UN initiatives and provided information and perspective to diplomats and leaders about important steps needed to improve women's lives. It is no coincidence that every peace operation authorized by the Security Council now includes a specific mandate to protect girls and women. Bachelet went on to serve another term as the president of Chile and then returned to the UN as the high commissioner for human rights.

UN Women provides essential support, encouragement, and representation to NGOs and advocacy groups who are increasing vital resources for legal reform, education, and information gathering, not to mention the delivery of services. Civil society had long demanded a larger, more coherent, and well-respected UN focal point to represent their concerns, and I passionately agreed with them.

On July 2, 2010, the General Assembly approved creation of the United Nations Entity for Gender Equality and the Empowerment of Women, commonly called UN Women. This approval had taken longer than it should have because some member states were concerned that this office would focus on practices they found socially unacceptable, such as reproductive autonomy or full political rights. This high-level UN department was created by merging four narrowly tasked offices—the Division for the Advancement of Women, the International Research and Training Institute for the Advancement of Women (INSTRAW), the Office of the Special Adviser on Gender Issues and Advancement of Women, and the UN Development Fund for Women (UNIFEM)—into one efficient entity that coordinates women's issues across the UN. But the heads of the existing four offices were against combining power. To my consternation, most of their governments agreed and lobbied other countries to reject UN Women for these reasons.

I met first with the member states that objected to or only weakly supported the UN Women office, explaining the need for a stronger and more effective women's superagency. Then I went to the four heads of the women's offices and told them to pull together for the good of the UN and their constituents. I did not believe that their offices were devalued by the creation of UN Women, and I convinced them that they would have nearly the same responsibilities in the new department. Singapore's Noeleen Heyzer had been leading the UNIFEM for thirteen years, and I was impressed with her skillful lobbying. Once the UN Women was established, I appointed Heyzer as executive secretary of the Economic and Social Commission for Asia and the Pacific (ESCAP).

However, the whole situation irritated me. It was still early in my tenure, but I had made it clear during my campaign that the United Nations must seek new ways to encourage women's participation and power within the organization and around the world. I admit that I had not expected so much political opposition.

WOMEN'S RIGHTS ARE HUMAN RIGHTS

In 1995, member states unanimously accepted the Beijing Declaration and Platform for Action, a landmark twelve-point agenda that calls for women's full civil, political, economic, educational, and reproductive rights.[1] It also calls for special protection of girls and the right of all women to live without the fear or fact of gender-based violence. Implementation has been slow, as slow as snails.

Much of human rights work involves breaking down walls—the walls of silence, of complicity, of ignorance. There was no better place to do that than at the United Nations and no better way than to lead by example. To truly help women in developing countries, the United Nations needed to target our limited resources and maximize delivery of aid and expertise. I thought often about my mother's young life and how hard every day must have been. This forged my unshakable belief that development initiatives must focus first on women.

I put women's and girls' health and equality at the center of the Sustainable Development Goals (SDG), knowing that no society can prosper if half of its people are unable to contribute or benefit. The 2015 SDGs are a package of seventeen goals meant to eradicate the extreme poverty afflicting 10 percent of the global population by 2030. More than 730 million people live on less than $1.90 a day.[2] The initiative builds on the 2000 Millennium Development Goals and takes a broad, systemic look at development and holds governments to a timeline to improve sanitation, education, nutrition, and access to health care. Several Sustainable Development Goals explicitly address women's urgent needs, such as access to reproductive health services and equal access to education and legal protections.

Historically, women have suffered disproportionately in the poorest societies where they are often marginalized, disenfranchised, and abused. I was initially disheartened that some member states still could not accept the reality and centrality of women's and girls' basic human rights. Until governments prioritize women's health and civil rights, I told them, progress would be elusive and equality would remain a dream for the future instead of a reality today. No single issue ties together the security, prosperity, and progress of our world more than women's health. Initiatives to make childbirth safer are intuitive and compassionate, but some world leaders didn't seem to fully recognize the risks of reproduction, even in their own countries.

I launched Every Woman Every Child (EWEC) in June 2010 with $40 billion in pledges to reduce maternal and child mortality by sixteen million and prevent an estimated thirty-three million unwanted pregnancies over the next five years. I thought of my mother's lifelong pain at losing two pregnancies and vowed to put the United Nations global infrastructure to work to make this tragedy a rare exception rather than a fatalistic risk. It is indefensible in the twenty-first century that a woman still has to risk her life to bring a new life into the world. This truth motivated me and so many others before me to reduce infant and maternal mortality in the developing world. As I often told diplomats and world leaders, there is no reason a woman giving birth in South Sudan or Afghanistan should be any less safe than a woman in Sweden or Australia. When my own three children were born, I was grateful to know that Soon-taek was in a hospital with skilled attendants. I can't imagine how my father weathered his wife's eight pregnancies, three of them during Japan's colonialism.

It is unacceptable that some 300,000 women still die during pregnancy and childbirth every year. This figure is shocking. Sexual assault, fistula injuries, early marriage, and slavery are equally unacceptable. Women-focused NGOs now have a foot in the door, and they have grown to be effective advocates and information sources. The United Nations could not have made these gains without the NGOs and other organizations that share their strength with us, including research and anecdotal information from program areas, an existing network to deliver medication or services, political goodwill, and the best practices for working in remote areas with little infrastructure.

Media have always been important in the struggle to legitimize "women's" concerns; they are an unparalleled source of information and images. I participated in several events organized by *The Guardian* newspaper in 2014 related to their series on female genital mutilation. Local media, radio, and other communication sources also reinforced the message that women are equals and must be treated with respect. My own advocacy took various forms, but the message was consistent. I spoke about women's issues in bilateral conversations with world leaders and from every podium in the UN and around the world: the General Assembly, World Bank, World Health Organization, regional summits, and countless international conferences. The media has quoted me hundreds of times on the importance of equal rights, education, investment, ending violence, and spacing children.

I am grateful to Soon-taek for her determination and support, particularly during my first term. My mother-in-law, who lost her husband during the Korean War, taught me about passion and will, but my wife has shown me the power of patience. It was Soon-taek who encouraged me to be more generous and understanding about women's lives. She pointed out that men have ruled the planet throughout our history, and now women are beginning to raise their voices. "Why are men so narrow-minded?" she asked. "We are men's mothers, wives, and daughters. Women are trying to elevate our status to equal men's."

PEACEKEEPERS, NOT PREDATORS

In the Security Council, change was already underway. In 2000, the council unanimously passed Resolution 1325, which explicitly calls for protection of women during conflict and recognizes their role as peacemakers, not just victims.[3] This becomes more vital all the time because combatants have grown even more sadistic. Women and girls from Afghanistan to Syria to Mali and beyond are increasingly likely to endure sexual torture and violence by soldiers and rebel combatants. Even more repulsive, we learned that some of our own UN peacekeeping troops were also to blame.

Our Blue Helmets are brave enough to confront Congolese militias high on home brew and fear, and they are strong enough to build a camp in the dense Sudanese darkness. They have restored order to Sierra Leone and provided security for political negotiations in East Timor and Afghanistan. In 1950, a coalition of twenty-one countries brought peace to my own country, Korea. But the troops are not infallible. Hundreds of women and children have learned this the hardest way imaginable—suffering sexual abuse at the hands of peacekeepers sent to protect them.

Sexual abuse is the most intimate of violations, and I was sickened that some peacekeepers could behave with such brutality toward the people we were there to protect. Most allegations have been made by local civilians seeking protection inside UN base camps: women and even children who felt that they must trade sex for safety. There is no condition under which this can be considered consensual, and I couldn't understand how superior officers either didn't know or didn't care.

After repeated unbearable complaints from civilians about the peacekeepers in the Central African Republic, I took an unprecedented step, demanding the resignation of Senegalese General Babacar Gaye, head of the United Nations Multidimensional Integrated Stabilization Mission in the Central African Republic (MINUSCA). The decision to fire my special representative and the force commander, a respected veteran of many UN missions, was controversial but warranted. Senior political and military officers in every mission now learn that the UN's zero-tolerance policy is serious, enforceable, and will rise up the chain of command. I was determined to end the impunity.

In 2015, three dozen sexual assault complaints against peacekeepers were reported from only two missions: MINUSCA and the United Nations Organization Stabilization Mission in the Democratic Republic of Congo (MONUSCO). Many of these troops did not receive ethics training, but that cannot be the whole problem. I could not put into words how anguished, angered, and ashamed I was by these reports from Africa. Each accusation of sexual exploitation or abuse stained the UN's global reputation, blotted out our successes in the field, compromised local respect and cooperation, and sometimes even wiped away nearly four thousand noble sacrifices.

The United Nations was, admittedly, slow to address the horror we ourselves imposed on people who had already been through an earthly hell. Complaints were filed, but there was no uniform reporting procedure, and the Department of Peacekeeping Operations frequently did not know about the allegations. Rules were made and directives issued, but they were rarely followed by any action. Initially, few of us at UN headquarters understood the problem—it was not the bad-apple peacekeeper but the system itself.

In 2010, I appointed Margot Wallstrom, a former vice president of the European Commission, as my special representative on sexual violence in conflict. Wallstrom understood the field and the UN system, and she did remarkable work. With her help, I felt that we were finally able to get a grip on the problem. We put mandatory ethics training programs in place, and I notified the Security Council that superior officers would be held accountable if their troops did not receive that education before deploying with UN peacekeeping.

We also learned how important it is to deploy more women as troops, uniformed police, and, especially, officers. Female commanders can shape their mission's treatment of sex offenders, and the very presence of women in the ranks will tame some of the poisonous excess testosterone among troops. I recommitted myself to appointing women to more visible and important positions, and on March 8, 2010, I promoted Ann-Marie Orler of Sweden to be the Department of Peacekeeping Operations police advisor. A veteran police officer with a legal degree and a specialty in human rights, Orler has led the organization's effort to recruit more women civilian police for missions.

In May 2014, I appointed Major General Kristin Lund of Norway to command the UN Force in Cyprus (UNFICYP), the first woman in UN peacekeeping to head a military mission. Several male officials expressed reservations about a female general's ability to lead multinational forces despite Lund's obvious competence. As I expected, she was a fine Force Commander. In fact, Secretary-General Guterres appointed Lund to be the chief of staff of the UN Truce Supervision Organization (UNTSO) in Jerusalem, and my special representative in Cyprus, Lisa Buttenheim, became the deputy of the Department of Field Support.

The gender ratio in peacekeeping is still at odds with so much the United Nations is trying to project and accomplish as regions emerge from conflict. During my decade in office, female troops more than doubled, from 1,400 in 2007 to 3,200 in 2016.[4] Even with 5,200 women in 2019, peacekeeping and member states can and must do better than roughly 5 percent. India raised the bar for all troop contributing countries in 2007, providing the United Nation's first all-female Formed Police Unit (FPU) for service in Liberia, which was just beginning to recover from a violent two-decade power struggle. The FPU's unwavering performance and professionalism inspired self-confidence in Liberian girls, many of whom were victims of sexual trauma, and they now comprise 17 percent of the country's security sector.

Contributing nations are beginning to send women to peacekeeping missions in other nontraditional roles. Rwanda sent us two newly minted female pilots, and they were desperately needed on the South Sudan mission. They have been flying helicopters for military operations, traversing supply routes for one of the most dangerous UN missions.

WHERE ARE THE FEMALE LEADERS?

With the United Nations on track to achieving goals of gender parity and greater inclusion, I began reaching out to the world's political leaders. I first looked at the statistics. I would ask world leaders: "How many female ministers are there in your government? How many women parliamentarians are in your country?" I even spoke publicly in the General Assembly, urging the leaders to clear the social and legal obstacles to women's political participation. This is vital; for every success in Rwanda and Spain, a dozen countries are falling short.

This problem is by no means limited to developing or religiously conservative nations. How often has German Chancellor Angela Merkel been the only woman in the G7 group photo? In dozens of countries, women are literally invisible. Many stay home with children and might earn money with low-paying piecework. Others cloak themselves from hair to shoes for a trip to the local market. This portends a marginalized future for those girls who aspire to be integrated into their communities. The message is getting out, but not quickly enough. Privately, I pointed out to King Abdullah of Saudi Arabia that there was not a single woman in his government. He soon appointed thirty-two women to Sharia courts. I called out several Gulf leaders about the scarcity of women in their governments, and I discussed this situation with more than a dozen South Pacific and Caribbean leaders. No leaders accused me of interfering with domestic affairs because they knew I was right.

Member states have also begun to send more female ambassadors to the United Nations. When I began my term in 2007, I counted only eleven, but when I made my farewell speech, the General Assembly had more than forty female ambassadors. That's still about one in five, but I am heartened to see so many women as foreign ministers and delegates with specialized expertise in everything from development to disarmament.

I was surprised and humbled in 2017 when the Asia Initiatives, the woman-centered NGO led by Geeta Mehta, established an award in my name: Ban Ki-moon Award for Women's Empowerment. Soon-taek and I have been delighted to attend the three award ceremonies. In 2017 the group honored the American feminist, author, and political activist Gloria Steinem and Yue Sai Kan, the powerful Chinese television host and producer. In 2018 they honored children's book author and global health advocate Chelsea Clinton and Susan Blaustein, the founder of Women Strong International and cofounder and director of Columbia University's Millennium Cities Initiative. In 2019 the honors went to Cecile Richards, a cofounder of Supermajority; Kathy Matsui, vice chair of Goldman Sachs Japan; and Madhura Swaminathan, chair of MS Swaminathan Research Foundation of Chennai India. I was deeply honored to award Dame Jane Goodall, renowned primatologist, anthropologist, and UN Messenger of Peace as the 2020 recipient.

TYRANNY OF THE TYPEWRITER

I had not realized there is a symbol for the sexism women still encounter at nearly every level of employment—the typewriter. I had the privilege of meeting the intrepid UN official who blazed a trail for women starting in the 1950s, Dame Margaret Anstee in June 2016, in Birmingham, England. She told me that her mother would not let her learn to type because in Great Britain in the 1940s a secretary was about as high as a woman could rise. Dame Anstee quickly showed the world that clever and fearless women could succeed outside the office. She gave me a copy of her 2003 autobiography, *Never Learn to Type*, and when she celebrated her ninetieth birthday, I was surprised to learn that the typewriter was the theme. I sent her a birthday card and received a lovely reply. I still keep her letter in my file.

Over a lunch in 2010, I asked former U.S. Secretary of State Condoleezza Rice if she planned to write a memoir and whether she would have an assistant. "No," she said, "I can type very well." When she was young, her father urged her to learn to type because the best job an African American girl was likely to find in 1960s Denver was secretarial.

"Well, Dr. Rice," I joked, "you have indeed become a great secretary—Secretary of State of the United States!" Her memoir, *No Higher Honor*, is in one of my book collections.

There was no question that my daughters, born in the computer generation, would learn to type. Today it is expected that everyone from chief executives to part-time workers can research and produce their own words, charts, and images. It would surprise Dame Anstee's generation that the keyboard has become another form of empowerment. That's the world I want to create, one in which girls overcome limitations to become strong and capable women. I want to see them as healthy mothers and skilled workers respected by men as equals.

Personally, I expected that my successor would be a woman. There were thirteen candidates in the running for the UN secretary-general's post, seven of them women. Only a few women have contested for the job in the history of the UN, so the mere number of candidates is something to celebrate. These are women of high-caliber, including world leaders and strong UN officials. But 2016 would not be the year. Susana Malcorra, my former chief of staff and head of the Department of Field Support, was one of the candidates, and she said that in the United Nations "there is not a glass ceiling but a steel ceiling."

Former Portuguese Prime Minister Antonio Guterres was elected the ninth UN secretary-general, and his commitment to recruiting and promoting women is evident.

I have traveled widely as a diplomat and now as a private citizen and closely observed the dignity deficit between the sexes. An evolution is taking place, but too many countries are backsliding. We still need more male and female voices to demand, sing, and shout for equality—in the industrialized world as well as in the developing nations.

Chapter Eighteen

THE SUSTAINABLE DEVELOPMENT GOALS

Toward Dignity for All

"When women were going into labor, they would look at their rubber shoes," my mother told me when I was a young boy. "They would sigh deeply and worry whether they would ever be able to wear those shoes again." I did not understand then what my mother meant. The brutality of childbirth was one thing women could count on in the developing world, including Korea in the 1950s. Hundreds of millions of women contemplated severe injury or death as they labored to create a new life. These women were giving birth at home, attended only by a village woman whose expertise came from surviving a few births of her own. No medicine. No medical care. No hope if something went very wrong, which frequently happened in regions with staggering poverty. This is still the case for forty-four million women giving birth each year around the world.

And what about that baby? It might be stunted at birth, born to an injured mother, or given away because the family could not afford to care for it. A boy might be put to work before he reached his teens. A girl could be forced into an early marriage. Instead of learning, these young people would grow up without the skills to better their own lives or their families' lives. That child needs good food to grow, sanitation to stay healthy, education to advance, a safe environment in which to thrive, and the prospect of decent work when he or she is older.

Today, at least 734 million people around the world live in abject poverty, most of them children who think it's normal to go to bed hungry. Regardless of where on the globe you live, it is impossible to create a life of vigor and dignity on less than $1.90 per day. Scarcities are often the root cause of armed conflict. Poverty can suffocate communities with inequality, hunger, and poor health. The only way to solve any of these problems was to make great progress on all of them.

SURPASSING THE STATUS QUO

In September 2000, world leaders adopted the Millennium Declaration Development Goals at a special summit organized to celebrate the dawn of the new era.

The MDGs were an audacious set of eight goals and twenty-one incremental targets to reduce extreme poverty and hunger, empower women, emphasize primary education, and combat HIV/AIDS, malaria, and other diseases. The declaration asserted the fundamental values of freedom, equality, solidarity, tolerance, and shared responsibility. The MDGs were a success. Among indicators that had dropped by at least half: extreme poverty, child mortality, and new HIV infections.

During this time, many countries had achieved gender parity in primary schools; maternal mortality had plunged by 40 percent since 1990; two billion people gained access to improved sanitation; more than twelve million people with HIV/AIDS received antiretroviral treatments; and official development assistance from developed nations increased 66 percent, to $135.2 billion, between 2000 and 2014. In 2010, five years before the target date, the World Bank proudly announced that the number one goal had been achieved. In reality, this benchmark was owing to China's strong measures to lift almost four hundred million people out of poverty.

I was determined to bring similar successes to many other countries with gaping needs. Hundreds of millions of the world's citizen's were still suffering from poverty entrenched for generations. I knew this cycle must be broken for their futures to be more promising than the past. There was never a question—not even for a minute—that the MDGs would continue in some form after the mandate expired in 2015. Member states encouraged me to come up with a plan by 2013 so the transition would be seamless.

A battery of world leaders and prominent individuals shared their insight into development priorities and realities. With five years of hard work, we crafted the Sustainable Development Goals (SDGs), a seventeen-item to-do list to challenge climate change and poverty while enhancing human rights and global cooperation. If these goals are met by 2030, extreme poverty would end; damage from climate change would be reduced; and human rights, health care, and development would be expanded to hundreds of millions of people around the world.

GLOBAL PROBLEMS, GLOBAL SOLUTIONS

The Sustainable Development Goals are the very essence of collective action, the bedrock principle of the United Nations. Both the MDGs and the SDGs were far-reaching, audacious, ambitious, extensive, and required faith in the generosity and commitment of every government. I convened an MDG Advocacy Group of eminent people whose support of the goals had been outstanding. I wanted a more inclusive process than had been the norm, and the advocacy group members would be able to build that kind of support. I chose President Paul Kagame of Rwanda, which had experienced remarkable gains, and Prime Minister Jose Luis Rodriguez Zapatero of Spain to cochair the group. I was delighted that so many luminaries in health, the environment, education, and women's rights were among those eager to be involved.

The Advocacy Group had its first meeting in Madrid in July 2010, but there was a complication. A petition was circulating against Kagame's visit and it called on Spain's elected leaders not to meet with him because of allegations of war crimes against Tutsi-dominated army. Zapatero declined to meet with the Rwandan leader. This posed a terrible problem— the cochairs could not be in the same room.

President Kagame had already arrived in Madrid and I spoke to him about the situation. I was afraid he would leave Spain before the meeting, and I vividly remember how angry and humiliated he looked. President Kagame was devoted to the MDGs, however, and he agreed to stay. I proposed that President Kagame preside over the first meeting with Foreign Minister Miguel Ángel Moratinos attending on behalf of the Spanish prime minister. Then Prime Minister Zapatero would chair the next meeting of the group in his office without President Kagame being present. I was grateful to the Rwandan president for accepting this novel arrangement with grace. I shudder to think of everyone's embarrassment if this situation had not been defused.

With that resolved, I turned to the MDG advocates, including Nobel Peace laureates Muhammad Yunus and environmentalist Wangari Maathai of Kenya; Sir Bob Geldorf of Live Aid fame; Graca Machel, the former first lady of both Mozambique and South Africa, and longtime champion of African women and girls; the former Mexican Health Minister Julio Frenk, Dean of Harvard University's School of Public Health; and philanthropist Bill Gates. Queen Sheika Mozah Bint Nasser of Qatar, Columbia University professor Jeffrey Sachs, Ambassador Dho Young-Shim of Korea, Ted Turner, American philanthropist Ray Chambers, and some others were also very effective advocates. "When it comes to raising public awareness and mobilizing political will, we need eloquent voices, inspiring leadership, and creative minds," I told them. "That is why I have called upon you."

I could now focus my attention on a successor vision beyond the 2015 deadline of the MDGs. I established the high-level Global Sustainability Panel, cochaired by presidents Tarja Halonen of Finland and Jacob Zuma of South Africa, in August 2010. The twenty-two panel members included Ali Babacan, deputy prime minister of Turkey; former Korean Prime Minister Han Seung-soo, who also served as General Assembly president in 2001–2002; former Prime Minister Yukio Hatoyama of Japan; and U.S. Ambassador to the United Nations Susan Rice, among others.

I was especially enthusiastic when Harlem Brundtland, the former prime minister of Norway, agreed to lead another panel looking at environmental degradation. The Brundtland Commission released "Resilient People, Resilient Planet: A Future Worth Choosing" in January of 2012. It made a convincing case for pursuing low-carbon prosperity, and I was eager to work with her. She has devoted herself to development issues for more than thirty years, even coining the phrase "sustainable development" in her landmark 1987 report to the United Nations.[1] That assessment laid out a philosophy of sustainable development in which improvements are made to meet the needs of the present without compromising the ability of future generations to do the same. I read that work long before I came to the United Nations, and it influenced my thinking.

I have known Brundtland—a former director general for the World Health Organization—for many years, and I most recently worked with her as a member of The Elders. She raised many provocative insights, which moved the discussion along, although I found the drafting experience closer to herding cats. I was grateful for her ability to focus the meetings on ambitious but attainable goals.

In August 2012, I established yet another powerful panel. President Susilo Bambang Yudhoyono of Indonesia, Liberian President Ellen Sirleaf Johnson, and Prime Minister David Cameron of the United Kingdom cochaired the twenty-seven-member Panel of Eminent Persons, leaders who would concentrate on the post-2030 development agenda. This was a vital undertaking that would expand our planning for the years beyond expiration of the Sustainable Development Goals. The panel thought big and suggested five recommendations to transform governments, development, and people. This "revolution of transparency" stressed the need to use data collected for the public benefit. In fact, all the advocacy panel members were steeped in the complexities of development, and I knew I could count on them for fresh ideas.

At the same time, I worked closely with officials throughout the UN system of agencies, funds, and programs. Wu Hongbo, the under secretary general of the Department of the Economic and Social Affairs (DESA), and Helen Clark, administrator of the UN Development Program (UNDP) were particularly important allies. Their priorities, experience, and access to data gave me a global overview of where development was heading and where it needed to improve. I was committed to maintaining the MDG momentum, but I also wanted to address a new set of concerns and realities, including environmental degradation and responsible consumption.

FINDING CLARITY IN RIO

The first SDG conference was held June 20–22, 2012, in Brazil, the country that had hosted the first Earth Summit in Rio de Janeiro exactly twenty years earlier. Officially titled the UN Conference on Sustainable Development, this meeting was known the world over as Rio+20. The meetings were an extended session of brainstorming, advocacy, and diplomacy meant to clarified the key issues and priorities in drafting the SDGs. Delegates from nearly all 193 UN member states landed in the seaside resort to negotiate the political declaration that would underpin the future Sustainable Development Goals. We would have more than a week to hammer out the language before world leaders arrived for the summit. I knew from experience that no one would have time to sneak in a swim.

Thousands of SDG delegates and advocates traveled from their hotels to the conference center and back, often at peak hours. The number of attendees grew by as much as half when the heads of state, heads of government, economic and foreign ministers, politicians, and all of their entourages arrived. I didn't let myself think about the carbon footprint of so many airplanes. I also banished my unspoken suggestion that even the highest-ranking officials should carpool. For me, Rio was the culmination of a two-year immersion in humankind's impact on the environment and the need to draw still more from the earth while taking less. It could be done—but we needed to make sustainable development a global priority.

Prime Minister David Cameron of the United Kingdom—ambitious, dynamic, and bracingly forthright—led the preliminary negotiations. British politics had given him plenty of experience with fractious delegations, personalities, and issues. He was tireless, pushing hard to get member states to accept not just the goals but the deadlines to meet them. As usual, little progress was made that first week. Fortunately, Brazilian envoys are well respected for their subtle diplomatic skills, and Foreign Minister Antonio de Aguiar Patriota was one of the best. As chairman of the Rio+20 conference, I am sure he needed all his diplomatic skills as we hammered out these complicated matters.

As the days melted away and the summit loomed, I took off my suit jacket and plunged into the discussions. I consulted with one group, then another, and then another. One day I made thirteen different speeches! That was a record for my ten years in office. The material was familiar to me, and I delivered most of my remarks off the record and off the cuff. I didn't have time to eat and for many stretches barely slept, but I finally wore everybody down. Country by country, bloc by bloc, region by region, day by day, we inched toward an agreement on the language.

It's always that way. Negotiations go down to the wire. Always. No matter how much time is allotted, no matter how anodyne the subject, people will find it necessary to debate a point until it's time to come together or pull the plug. This was the moment. Delegations will almost always join the group rather than capsize an agreement. As I raced off to make yet another last-minute appeal or give a television interview, I was grateful for that instinct. The world literally hung in the balance, but the mood in Rio was curiously festive.

Hundreds of groups from around the world converged on Rio for the People's Summit, bringing their own visions and urgencies. During the two-week drafting sessions, tens of thousands of activists for scores of issues demonstrated peacefully—even joyously. I saw the pictures every day and read many of their manifestos shortly afterward. There were many original ideas, unexpected solutions! I imagined exchanging my suit for a baseball cap and jeans and spending a day surrounded by so much crackling energy. I hoped their leaders would help craft a vision of the world that reflected their own.

My aides cleaned up and circulated the final draft of Rio's political statement, "The Future We Want," just as the leaders began arriving. The forty-nine-page document is a nonbinding agreement, but it put presidents and prime ministers on record, affirming their commitment to ending unconscionable poverty by 2030. It also gave the United Nations the authority to draft a new set of fifteen-year global goals and targets.

I wanted the SDGs to be written so clearly and concisely that the language left no room to hide. By this time, I already knew which governments weren't genuinely willing to invest in global improvements, overcome the marginalization of minorities, empower women and girls, root out corruption at the highest levels, increase their official development assistance, or share in low-cost new money- and energy-saving technologies. I wanted all citizens to share equally in the success of this ambitious program, not just those in developing countries. The second set of goals would be more complex and more specific. Twelve years after adoption of the MDGs, all the delegations understood the overarching and interlocking principles as well as the importance of deliberate action.

I am proud of our accomplishments at Rio+20 and other climate-related activities at the UN. And Rio also delivered two concrete accomplishments that stand to this day: Sustainable Energy for All, an initiative to provide greater access to cleaner energy around the world; and the Zero Hunger Challenge, developed with Brazilian agronomist Graziano da Silva to provide 100 percent of the people with access to the food they need 100 percent of the time.

TARGETS AND TIMELINES

No longer did world leaders merely aspire to the eventual betterment of their citizens, they recommitted themselves to a concrete timetable to make it happen. The SDGs are ultimately a social contract between the world's governments and their citizens that would improve millions of lives over the next fifteen years. Each of the seventeen goals is, ultimately, an ambition. Each one is a complex, long-term puzzle that must be solved in tandem with the others, which requires coordinating timing, reliable funding, and priorities. To keep governments on track, we developed a list of 169 targets to evaluate their progress.

The planet's people were not shy about sharing their opinions. In 2012, an unprecedented nine million people took the UN's online survey "My World," explaining what kind of future they wanted. When we compiled the answers, we were shocked to find six thousand pages of opinions and suggestions representing every nation, ideology, and socioeconomic strata on the planet.[2] Department of Economic and Social Affairs (DESA) Under Secretary General Wu Hongbo and Korea's UN Ambassador Kim Sook tried to read them all. Ambassador Kim was particularly invested in the process and had long been committed to sustainable development. He served in 2011–2012 as cochair of the Preparatory Committee for Rio+20 with Ambassador John Ashe of Antigua and Barbuda, and their efforts made our successes possible.

The hardworking UN staff, in particular the director of DESA, Under-Secretary General Wu, and Ambassador Kim ultimately winnowed down these six thousand pages to a slim and readable thirty pages. They spent many nights categorizing the hundreds of ideas suggested by the world's people. But that was not the end of it. When we circulated that thirty-page document to member states at the first meeting, the comments and additions swelled the synopsis to three hundred pages!

Nonetheless, ordinary people from 193 countries had spoken, and their priorities were clear: poverty, education, health care, gender empowerment, the environment, and honest government. I came to think of their priorities as our to-do list:

- Abate poverty and economic imbalance by expanding the economy and creating new jobs, especially for young adults.
- Provide quality education.
- Hold government responsible for the corruption that bankrupts even resource-rich countries.
- Empower girls to learn and women to lead.
- Adopt sustainable energy practices.
- Mitigate the climate chaos that is disrupting farming, grazing, fishing, habitation, and the availability of food, energy, and land.
- Share heavily subsidized technology, innovation, and opportunity with nations or regions in need.

Slowly but surely, the Sustainable Development Goals, a monumental undertaking, were starting to come into focus, and so was my team.

The principled and talented Amina J. Mohammed, former environment minister of Nigeria, led the Secretariat on this issue. I had known her even before she had an official position. I would often see her at meetings devoted to health and women's well-being, and each time her pointed remarks drew my attention. Mohammad was my sturdy link to member states. I'm glad she has continued rallying for the SDGs as deputy secretary-general in my successor's administration. I also benefited from the energy and experience of my senior advisor, Robert Orr, now dean of the Maryland University; and Jeffrey Sachs, the well-known economist who had spent decades grappling with the problem of poverty, advised us at every step.

I was fortunate to have the brilliant Swiss diplomat Thomas Gass serving on my team, and I asked him to take the lead producing a first draft of the SDGs. His intense labors, polished by many others, was published in December 2014, and it set out six elements: ending poverty and tackling inequalities; improving people's lives and well-being; ensuring inclusive economic transformation; promoting just, safe, and peaceful societies; protecting the planet; and building partnerships.[3]

Although all nations agreed in principle, the SDG details could not have been more divisive. My biggest challenge was to convince every government to take responsibility for its role in this global endeavor. In the developing world, that means creating civil, political, and economic rights for all citizens, regardless of gender, race, status, or religion. Although most of the developed nations concurred with the SDG components, many were wary of their cost. I expected that. But these leaders were also taken aback by the SDGs' radical universality: unlike the MDGs, we did not draw a line between the developing world and the developed world. These goals would apply to even the poorest citizens of the richest countries, which have an obligation to improve the quality of life for all their people, not just those who can already afford it. When the United States, the world's most developed nation, can't provide health care to thirty million people, that is an injustice.

The industrialized nations wanted the SDGs to emphasize good governance, justice, equal rights, and strong institutions. But the powerful Group of 77, which was actually composed of 134 developing nations, anticipated these repeated criticisms and would not accept the SDGs as discussed. Its members said repeatedly that they were tired of demands that place all the improvement on their shoulders. Without transparency, the richer nations said, they cannot justify contributing hundreds of millions of dollars a year. Governments have a right to know how their money is spent, so they could decide if this was the best use of their resources. There was a lot of back-and-forth on this point. I wasn't sure how it would be resolved. At first, almost every government had reservations about at least one of the SDGs. I expected that too.

A goal of responsible production and consumption (Goal 12) was proposed, and it was a very good idea because it was absolutely right. Overconsumption is filling landfills and choking the sea with plastic and other discards. Some Western governments needed to be reminded that they are part of a larger, interconnected ecosystem.

Several nations were concerned about the gender equality language (Goal 5). Fifteen predominantly Muslim countries—including Iran, Afghanistan, Pakistan, Saudi Arabia, and Yemen—have constitutions based in part on Sharia law, an Islamic code that can deal harshly with women. Others said they agreed with the SDGs but did not have the resources to provide universal health care (Goal 3), education (Goal 4), water and sanitation systems (Goal 6), clean energy (Goal 7), and modern infrastructure (Goal 9).

Good health and well-being (Goal 3) also posed problems. This goal addresses access to medical care, maternal and infant mortality, and recognizes women's right to sexual and reproductive health care. Catholic and Muslim nations, in particular, were concerned that this would guarantee the right to an abortion. And finally, I'm all too aware that the first sixteen goals can't happen without Goal 17: creating partnerships. This remains the UN's best strategy to optimize resources, knowledge, and technology.

A UN promise of this size cannot be kept without the vital contribution of our partners: NGOs, policy experts, academics, international and multinational organizations, celebrities, religious institutions, corporations, indigenous leaders, and so many more. The media is one of our most important, but somewhat unpredictable, allies. There is no better way to disseminate relevant information or encouragement to even the farthest villages and most isolated societies. It can make stars of key players, whip up popular support that can influence most governments, and present a variety of views—all in the local languages. But I knew we couldn't count on reliable support. The media also bite, get it wrong, disseminate negative analyses, and even vilify those with radical suggestions.

ONE THING ON WHICH ECONOMISTS AGREE

Eradicating poverty won't be cheap. In fact, it will take several generations for the total cost and the full benefits to be realized. Economists from the World Bank to graduate schools have been studying the MDGs and SDGs for more than a decade, and their estimates diverge wildly. I fear the unknowable price, not to mention the number of zeros, will probably shake the confidence of many governments that like assured outcomes and exact timetables.

The truth is there are no high or low estimates on such a vast undertaking. Analyses swing wildly, and few seem to evaluate apples to apples. An early UN report put the cost of SDG Goal 1—lifting 734 million people out of poverty—at $11 trillion over fifteen years. Another UN report, in 2014, estimated the investment in infrastructure alone could cost $7 trillion a year if a region is to create and keep jobs and growth.[4] These sums are enormous and hard to grasp, but they shouldn't frighten us. If there is political will, we can do anything. I always tell that to world leaders, and they always say they agree with me. But I won't believe that until they are able to enact laws, revise constitutions, invest in clinics and schools, and make meaningful efforts to develop clean energy.

Benefits to the developing world are myriad. But what do the richer nations receive by achieving the SDGs? Perhaps a potential payoff in the long term. The World Resources Institute, a U.S.-based coalition of development-minded big business and finance, estimated in 2017 that achieving only four sectors of the goals—food and agriculture, cities, energy and materials, and health and well-being—could generate as much as $12 trillion in new business by the expiration of the SDGs in 2030. Another $17 trillion could be saved by reducing carbon emissions and limiting the consumption of water, energy, and other resources.

The Global Commission on Adaptation, which I cochaired with Bill Gates and Kristalina Geogieva, managing director of the IMF, presented an ambitious report to the UN Climate Action Summit on September 23, 2019. As part of meeting the climate crisis, they emphasized investing wisely in adaptation in five major areas: effective early warning systems, climate resilient infrastructure, dry highland agriculture, mangrove reforestation, and water resources. They predict that $1.9 trillion invested incrementally in infrastructure until the end of 2030 will provide an effective benefit of more than $7 trillion.[5]

The MDGs and SDGs are closer in spirit to the broad "human development" approach pioneered in the 1990s by economic experts Amartya Sen and Mahbub ul Haq than to the economy-based World Bank model. The new approach radically reshapes the way we define and measure poverty by supplementing GDP statistics with social data such as adult literacy, child mortality, gender equality, mobile phone subscriptions, carbon dioxide emissions, and access to the internet, electricity, and improved sanitation. Both measures are important, but the quality of life for all people—not just those in the official economic sector—is a more accurate gauge of development than a ten-thousand-foot snapshot of a country's economy.

The Sustainable Development Goals take a holistic approach to bettering lives. It would almost be impossible to fully achieve one goal without making progress on them all. However, if I had to pick the most important of the seventeen planks, I would choose Goal 4: education. Learning pulled me up out of desperate poverty. Education improved every aspect of my life and made it possible for me to achieve my dream of international civil service. Every child should experience the pleasure of reading and the thrill of learning. U.S. President John F. Kennedy opened my eyes to compassion in 1962 when I was only eighteen. Ever since then I have carried inside of me a moral obligation to help the world's most vulnerable people. We all share this idea. Fortunately, Seoul was an enthusiastic participant. The Republic of Korea advanced from a war-whipped agrarian economy in the 1950s to a thriving industrialized nation in only three decades. With gratitude to the United Nations for its irreplaceable assistance, my country has generously contributed funding, technology, and expertise to development efforts around the world.

Ultimately, the MDGs and SDGs are ambitious and far-reaching. I have no illusions about how many member states accepted the most important outcome statements because they are political documents expressing intention, not a legally binding treaty. Many member states found this voluntary pledge more digestible, and despite some reservations, they adopted it by consensus at the 2012 Sustainable Development Summit in Rio. What matters most is that every government remains engaged and puts its resources into its people and their future. Leaders know what is expected of them, and I hope they will follow through on their commitments to realize their people's dreams. I anticipate, and even expect, that we can expand on Secretary-General Annan's success and create lasting improvements for generations to come.

HOPE IS A GLOWING LANTERN

I have attended countless sessions of the General Assembly, including the annual General Debate of world leaders every September. I have seen the adoption of complex resolutions and attended events celebrating sexual minorities and African women that instill pride and embody optimism. But the spontaneous excitement of more than 150 world leaders on September

25, 2015, when General Assembly President Mogens Lykketoft brought down the gavel adopting the 2030 Agenda for the Sustainable Development Goals was unique. This august audience burst into a standing ovation that lasted nearly two minutes. I felt exhaustion and exhilaration, even though I had no doubt about the outcome. All the presidents and prime ministers felt joy and even personal triumph in their support of dignity and development for all the world's people—especially for their own citizens. No one talked about divisive politics on this day. No nation abstained. It was a rare moment when the United Nations was truly united.

I give much of the credit to Pope Francis who has consistently expressed the Catholic Church's support for the SDGs. I was honored when His Holiness agreed to speak to the world leaders just before the vote. "A selfish and boundless thirst for power and material prosperity leads both to the misuse of available natural resources and to the exclusion of the weak and the disadvantaged," he admonished world leaders. Speaking in Spanish, the Catholic leader made an interfaith and even humanist appeal for governments and individuals to cultivate their conscience and compassion. His remarks were met with an unprecedented sixty-seven-second standing ovation.

Many leaders from the developing and developed worlds spoke about what the MDGs meant for their country or the world and welcomed the SDGs to carry on this work. All of the presidents and prime ministers who spoke that day made concrete pledges of support. Nobel Prize laureate Malala Yousafzi addressed the dignitaries from a balcony above the General Assembly hall. "Education is hope," the eighteen-year-old Pakistani girl proclaimed. "Education is peace."[6] She called upon the leaders to ensure that all children are given free, high-quality primary and secondary schooling. To emphasize the point, 193 young people representing every UN member state stood behind her, each holding a glowing blue cube. "Each lantern we hold represents the hope we have for our future because of the commitments you have made to the global goals," she said. It was a dramatic moment that impressed many world leaders, some of whom were smiling or nodding in agreement.

THE SUSTAINABLE FUTURE

I have left the UN but not the fight. I am on the boards of more than a dozen advocacy groups and think tanks, most of them directly involved with climate change or some facet of development. But my engagements are tempered by growing concerns. The global economy has weakened dramatically, and many sovereign nations and their investments are losing value. Commerce is in flux, and international trade is constrained or dropping. In many developed countries, corporations are failing, which reduces the tax base to fund SDG-related commitments.

And now Covid has swept the globe, amplifying these and many other problems. The virus has actually reversed development, in some areas erasing years worth of progress. Hopefully, governments will learn from the pandemic and invest in resilience as well as relief.

I am also deeply worried about the international turn toward authoritarianism, which is upending democracies, jeopardizing citizens' well-being, and reversing economic and social gains. In many nations, this has exacerbated antipathy for society's most vulnerable—the poor, minorities, women, and immigrants—that exist in every country, however prosperous. This is a dangerous trend, and we must use all of our tools to champion democracy and equality.

But I also have hope. Building the Sustainable Development Goals has been something of a crusade for me and for tens of thousands of individuals across the planet. Millions more are demonstrating in larger numbers. With this kind of bottom-up support, I am increasingly confident that the SDGs are too big to ignore and too important to shirk. And by any measure, developed societies fare better than those in poverty.

I hope the United Nations remains unified and that the world's leaders continue to embrace their obligations to their own people. I have faith that the light of those glowing blue lanterns will someday reach even into the darkest corners.

Chapter Nineteen

CLIMATE CRISIS

Do or Die

The Solomon Islands are a romantic South Pacific paradise of swaying palm trees and pale sand beaches, licked by an angry tide. But this beautiful crescent of tiny islands and atolls is no longer a carefree vacation spot; it's the coming attraction for a disaster movie of warming oceans and dissolving shorelines.

My wife and I visited the Solomon Islands and Kiribati—both small islands and developing states—in September 2011 on a tour of the world's most fragile environments on the frontline of man-made environmental peril. This archipelago and hundreds nearby are sinking into the waves, threatening more than half a million people with the choice of relocation or extinction. The fear casts a shadow over everyday life. When we checked into our hotel in the capital, Honiara, Solomon Islands, we were warned that the Pacific is as dangerous as it is beautiful. The hotel underscored the message by giving us not bathrobes but life jackets. In nearby Kiribati, the houses are built on stilts and parents are petrified that their families could be swept away by rough seas. The highest point is only about three meters (9.8 feet) above sea level and is frequently submerged by high tides. We were shocked to see waves lapping at our car wheels as we drove along the main road.

There are thousands of islands in similar danger, not to mention coastlines from Miami to Macau. Many elderly people told me that during their lifetime they saw many distant islands disappear. And it is not just islands. From the Sahara to Siberia, global warming has unleashed encroaching deserts, set uncontrollable wildfires, thawed permafrost, and launched deadly typhoons. So many habitats are shrinking that species are becoming extinct at a rapid pace, and people are developing new illnesses by interacting with wild animals.

Greta Thunberg and the Rainforest Foundation are doing their best. Donald Trump and Jair Bolsonaro did their worst. And you and I and everyone we know are already living with the consequences. The climate crisis is no longer just scientific degrees and parts-per-million. Now it has faces, names, and dreams.

WEATHER OF MASS DESTRUCTION

My proudest accomplishment in ten years of public service at the United Nations is the international accord to slow the global havoc of man-made global warming. I championed what would become the 2015 Paris Climate Agreement long before anyone thought the world's governments could agree to limit greenhouse gas emissions. As a young boy in Korea, I spent hours hiking through the countryside. This was right after the war and nature was all we had. I used to hike all day, delighted to come upon one of the many small streams that ran through the grasses and rocks. I would kneel beside the stream and scoop the cold clear water into my mouth. Would my grandchildren be able to do the same?

I hadn't focused on climate change until I set my sights on election as the eighth secretary-general of the United Nations. I knew about the looming crisis, but I admit it was only one of dozens of issues in my portfolio. It quickly occurred to me that every UN goal—from ending extreme poverty and armed conflict to producing food and finding drinkable water—was largely dependent on a stable climate with centuries of similar temperatures and rainfall.

It was impossible to overlook the thinning majesty of the polar ice caps, increasingly violent weather, destruction of species and their environs, the thirty million acres of land yielding to advancing deserts, or the billions of dollars drought siphons out of countries' "economic development first" policies every year. The Northern Hemisphere suffers through hotter summers and colder winters as the Southern Hemisphere experiences desiccated crops and rising seas. Climate change is the ultimate threat to international peace and security. This was not a common view in 2006, but I nevertheless explained to every diplomat and government minister that climate change would be on the top of my agenda if I were elected secretary-general.

As soon as I set up my transition office, I set out to make good on that promise. I turned to Bob Orr, a senior advisor to Kofi Annan who had been briefing me during my transition. Bob is a soft-spoken American with a background in academia and international affairs, and I deeply admired his quick mind and his ability to see a problem realistically and in full. I asked him candidly about the viability of a climate campaign.

"Climate is a serious issue that needs to be tackled," he said. "But it will be a very steep uphill climb." That was not encouraging, but at least he did not say "zero." I decided right then that it was worth spending political capital on the single issue that would affect many of our children and every one of our grandchildren.

This was also the quintessential global problem requiring a global solution.

THE TURBULENT FORECAST

Curbing carbon dioxide emissions was, in fact, downright unpopular among member states; few were willing to forgo immediate economic growth to tackle what they perceived as an abstract future threat. In fact, many developing countries in the process of rapid industrialization, including Korea, saw the dark smoke coming from the factories as a blessing for their prosperity. Indeed, the process to limit those emissions was all but dead. The last big agreement on climate change was the Kyoto Protocol of 1997. It was clearly insufficient because key developed countries such as the United States were never a party to that protocol, and key developing countries such as China and India were not bound to produce emissions cuts under the agreement. Without curbing these major emitters, the planet would continue to cook.

Although not overtly a political issue, climate change was deeply mired in the strategic considerations of member states, especially the large powers. They would not easily accept an agreement with economic implications. Even the developing countries, which on the surface could only gain, had reservations because these and scores of smaller states refused to hamper their own development while others had burned their way to prosperity.

It was a Gordian knot, but I decided to try to untangle it using the best tools in my arsenal: passion, compassion, and perseverance. I spoke about some aspect of climate change practically everywhere I went, from one-hundred-watt radio stations in Central Africa to security forums in Central Asia.

I gave at least one hundred statements and speeches on climate change in my first two years in office, and I had countless private conversations with world leaders. I did not shy away from raising climate change, even with known skeptics.

SPEAKING TREES TO POWER

I raised climate change at one of my first and probably most important meetings with U.S. President George W. Bush on January 16, 2007. Nearly all of my aides advised me not to confront climate in my first meeting with such an important leader. They were concerned that my relationship with the president would have a rocky start and would remain difficult. But I decided to speak up after Yvo de Boer, who headed the Secretariat of the UN Framework Convention on Climate Change (UNFCCC), flew from its headquarters in Bonn to New York to ask me to broach the subject. Orr, who negotiated the agenda with the White House staff, simply wrote "UN Priorities."

In my meeting in the Oval Office, I raised a number of expected issues, including U.S.-UN relations, Darfur, and many troubled areas. Only then did I tell the president of the United States that the climate issue was quite serious and required immediate attention. To my surprise, he responded defensively. He said that the United States could not do more than its fair share of lowering emissions. He also pointed the finger at China and India. "The U.S. is spending billions of dollars on technology to address climate change that we will share with the rest of the world," President Bush told me. "I'm not sure there will ever be international agreement on how to tackle this issue." Although it was not a great discussion, it was an important start with a key country.

When I briefed reporters in the White House after the meeting, they all focused on the climate issue. They knew this was a flashpoint, and I suppose this is exactly why my aides did not want me to speak about climate. They didn't want it to drown out all the areas of cooperation between the United States and the UN or leave the impression that I had a contentious discussion with President Bush. But some in the press praised me for my strong stance and courage in raising the issue with Washington—and with a man whose family has long been involved in the oil industry.

I wanted to invite President Bush to a summit meeting of world leaders. He did not agree at first, but I told him that we needed him there for any effort to be meaningful. I certainly did not want another climate agreement that excluded the major powers and emitters. So I pressed the reluctant president, personally handing him an invitation during our second meeting on July 17, 2007. "Mr. President," I told him, "you are the first head of state to whom I am delivering an invitation in person. The success of the summit will depend on your participation."

"You're trying to subpoena me!" he joked. At that moment, Secretary of State Condoleezza Rice said, "You made the sale, Mr. Secretary-General. That means 'Yes!' " Eighty world leaders came to New York on September 24, 2007, for an unprecedented discussion on climate change. But President Bush refused to speak in the General Assembly during the one-day summit, and it was a total embarrassment for me.

I consulted with Secretary Rice, and she advised me to convene an informal working dinner with a small group of heads of state and government. Despite my embarrassment, I did indeed invite around thirty world leaders, representing every continent, to an informal UN dinner. I was careful to invite many leaders of the thirty-eight designated small island developing states (SIDS). These nations—including Cuba, Fiji, and the Seychelles—occupied a special moral stature in the climate talks: each was losing inches or acres to the rising seas, and their citizens were already grappling with the painful adaptations we would all soon face.

Not surprising, the dinner—with its softer contours of food and conversation—was the more productive of the two events. I made the opening statement; the U.S. president would normally follow me because he is the leader of the host country, but I knew he had a reputation for impatience. I told him that we'd let a few other presidents and prime ministers speak, and he could address the room when he'd listened to their perspectives. And sure enough, after the U.S. president spoke, he asked my forgiveness for leaving the dinner early. As soon as President Bush left the room, Italian Prime Minister Silvio Berlusconi followed, then French President Nicolas Sarkozy. I was more disappointed than angry or even surprised. The only leaders who kept their seats until the end were German Chancellor Angela Merkel and most of the Asian, African, and island nations. But my plan had worked, President Bush had listened to candid and passionate perspectives from people he respected.

I called attention to climate change wherever I traveled as secretary-general and often chose to visit fragile environments to underscore their peril. From the Polar Ice Rim to Antarctica, to the shrinking Aral Sea, to Lake Chad and the Amazon River basin, and beyond I saw the damage, and I spoke about it. I also went to see climate solutions, such as geothermal plants, solar panel factories, desalination plants, research labs, and other innovations around the world. I saw green cities and met with the indigenous peoples who feel a special guardianship for the earth, including those in the Galápagos Islands. I thought their timeless traditions deserved attention and support. Finally, I made allies within the business community, particularly in the insurance industry, which has a strong financial interest in reducing the severity of natural disasters and their corresponding liability.

DIFFUSING THE STORM

The Bali Conference of Parties—formally the Conference of the Parties, or COP to the UN Framework Convention on Climate Change, or the UNFCCC, and informally COP13—opened December 3, 2007. This was the thirteenth time nations had met to consider the climate crisis and attempted to forge agreements to meet it. We had not gotten very far, but I was determined to energize the process. I emphasized that climate is the defining issue of our time, and I passionately urged delegates to compromise and seek creative solutions to their differences. As with most conferences with a sweeping mandate, two weeks of negotiations led to a two-day summit. I knew we would need every hour of those two weeks to reach a draft on which leaders could agree.

At first, the negotiation seemed to be moving relatively well. Australia's new Prime Minister Kevin Rudd hand-delivered to me the documents ratifying the Kyoto Protocol. After a series of meetings with leaders, I left the conference to pay an official visit to nearby Timor-Leste, which had recently won independence from Indonesia through the United Nations and still had a strong UN presence in its territory. The COP negotiations were not moving, and many of the delegates were already exhausted. There were no breakthroughs until the very end of the conference.

The next day, in Timor-Leste, I received an urgent call from Bob Orr to say that the talks in Bali were stalled. I couldn't let that happen. I immediately flew back to Bali and joined Indonesian President Susilo Bambang Yudhoyono—a former UN peacekeeper—in a joint appeal to the delegates to return to work. The atmosphere was very tense. But when we walked into the conference hall, the delegates stood up and gave us huge applause. I was reassured because this showed that they desperately wanted a climate agreement. I made another strong speech calling for delegates to "do your homework for humanity!" But the work had only begun.

At first, delegates were deadlocked, and countries refused to accept terms that would limit their economic growth. Industrialized nations, most passionately the United States, were generally unwilling to sign any agreement that would slap what they viewed as onerous environmental regulations on manufacturing, farming, and other sectors. It was clear that the developed and developing worlds would play by different rules, and the industrial nations wanted to make sure that they were not disadvantaged compared to relatively poor nations with rich potential, such as India and China. They advocated lenient emissions targets.

Developing nations also rejected limits to their economic potential. Dozens of governments pointed out that richer nations had burned their way to prosperity, and they needed the same opportunities for growth. Furthermore, world leaders said, their countries cannot adopt cleaner practices without financing, training, and shared technology. Developing nations had more skin in the game: their naturally warmer climates meant that they would feel the changes most severely, particularly in agricultural areas. Islands and coastal regions were already enduring wild weather swings and flooding.

Delegates pressed Yvo de Boer, executive director of the UNFCCC, with such difficult questions that he finally left the stage. The United States was the big holdout, and everyone wanted action from Washington. At one point, the U.S. delegation was booed! Frustrated delegates were already leaving Bali, openly booking their departure flights from the middle of the conference. Then a miracle happened. U.S. Under Secretary of State for Democracy and Global Affairs Paula Dobriansky, who had served in five Democratic and Republican administrations, electrified the session when she announced that the United States would join the consensus. India and other major economies reaffirmed their commitment, and these victories gave the delegates a shot of oxygen. With Washington's support, the Bali Roadmap was quickly adopted, paving the way to an eventual climate change agreement.

I had often wondered why Washington was willing to change its position 180 degrees, but I didn't learned why until a year later. My wife and I were invited to a farewell luncheon by President Bush on January 6, 2009, just two weeks before he left office. I was surprised and honored to find that President Bush had invited only us. Our White House lunch for four was quite enjoyable, and toward the end the president volunteered that Dobriansky had called him from the Bali Conference, asking for final instructions. The president said he thought about me at that moment and told her to "do what

Ban wants." I was grateful to him for finally accepting responsibility to work with other nations to address the impact of global climate change.

My first meeting in the Oval Office and the UN's continued engagement with the United States had paid off in a way I never could have expected. President Bush translated his respect and trust in me into support for emissions targets. I knew we were a long way from an agreement, but this was living proof that the United States could be brought on board through delicate personal diplomacy. I now knew my approach could work. When the historic Paris Climate Agreement was finally adopted on December 12, 2015, in an interview with the *New York Times* I specifically thanked President Bush for his help in getting us to this point.

PLANTING AND PAVING

The Bali Roadmap was the first step in negotiating a complex new climate agreement, beginning with reductions in dangerous emissions. I set up an expert climate team within my office, which was highly unusual. Normally such a team would be relegated to development or another department. Orr led my initial team followed by Hungarian climate expert Janos Pasztor. It soon evolved to include experts in green business, economics, diplomacy, and more.

We decided to focus on small, incremental victories that would accumulate into momentum. We started with forests. Working with the prime minister of Norway, Jens Stoltenberg, we set up a new deforestation initiative called Reducing Emissions from Deforestation and Forest Degradation (REDD). Many similar initiatives were developed by the time of the Paris Conference in 2015. Each was a brick in the wall of protection for our planet Earth. I also led by example, in my enthusiasm I reduced our heavy carbon footprint by distributing smaller bottles of water and lowering energy consumption by changing temperature settings.

It will not surprise UN critics to learn that one of our biggest wastes was paper. Many official documents—and there could be more than a dozen every day—are translated into six official languages (French, Chinese, English, Russian, Spanish, and Arabic). Reports and meeting minutes can easily run to two dozen pages, and we published a number of those on an average day. The UN Department of Management told me that the UN used enough paper every day to make a stack as high as my thirty-eighth floor offices! I cannot guess how much paper we saved by improving our websites and making the www.UN.org portal much easier to use, and I always printed on both sides of the paper.

I did fly frequently, creating a lightning rod for climate deniers, who ask how a diplomat can be a leader on this issue when jetting around the world in airplanes that consume tons of energy, run on toxic fuel, and emit long plumes of carbon. I asked myself similar questions, even as I offset these emissions by addressing the climate crisis on all my travels. Even in such places as the Democratic Republic of the Congo, where war, strife, and political turmoil were the top issues on the agenda, I discussed climate as the root of so many national problems. Swathes of the famously verdant country were becoming deforested, and Kinshasa would need to be part of a global climate accord if it were ever to see a safe and sustainable future. I was shocked and dismayed to see that President Joseph Kabila seemed to be unaware of deforestation and its impact on his country, surely one of the most verdant places in the world.

There were many encouraging developments as well. President Obama's election was a boost for the anti-emissions movement. During the campaign he promised to change Washington's approach to the environment and even spoke about his trust in former vice president and climate champion Al Gore. President Obama showed a willingness to negotiate and to lead. He took part in the climate summit I convened in September 2009 in New York along with more than one hundred other leaders. They were just speaking without making commitments, but these remarks put their positions on the record. All in all this was the biggest climate gathering of leaders to that date. This time, when I convened an informal summit-level dinner, no one left early, not even President Obama.

CLOUDS AND SUN IN COPENHAGEN

The Bali success was followed by COP14 in Poznań, Poland, and COP15 in Copenhagen. The December 2009 summit in Copenhagen was widely viewed as a failure. We began a vigorous campaign to "Seal the Deal"—the slogan the UN climate and communications offices had crafted to give governments a sense of obligation and inevitability. Unfortunately, we carried on using the slogan long past the point when it became obvious that a binding legal agreement to significantly cut carbon emissions was not going to happen. I'm sorry to say that the Danish climate team also made some errors. Traditionally, the host government of any conference does much more than provide a venue; they are responsible for political and diplomatic leadership to guide the process. In this case, I had high hopes for Denmark, which had long been a global leader on environmental and social issues.

Copenhagen's officials set out to save the conference with a political agreement, which does not obligate governments to take action but only expresses their intentions. This was a good idea in theory, but in practice it did not hold up because only a few countries were invited to draft it. This sent the wrong signal to conference participants who felt shut out. Hugo Chávez of Venezuela and many other leaders were not invited, and, naturally, their exclusion soured the negotiations. Worse, *The Guardian* published an already outdated version of the agreement. This leak angered most climate delegates because they learned what was happening in a newspaper before they had even been consulted. The representatives of developing countries felt insulted, and rightly so. I began to worry about these mounting errors.

Our Danish hosts had meant well. But by Friday night, December 16, our second-to-last full day, we realized that a legal agreement was unattainable. The atmosphere was almost toxic. I nonetheless urged leaders to "Seal the Deal," but I also gave a realistic account of the troubles, concerns, and high stakes. I remained in good standing by acknowledging their domestic pressures and politics. To solicit support from the developing states who were reluctant to join the consensus, the largest emitters sweetened the deal. The United States, led by Secretary of State Hillary Clinton, the European Union, and Japan pledged to mobilize $100 billion for developing countries by 2020, and thereafter to provide $100 billion every year. This hasn't happened.

The primary division centered on how ambitious we should be in setting targets, specifically how much global warming we as a world were willing to accept. I wanted our goal to be less than 1.5°C; past that point scientists say that we'll do irreparable damage to the planet with unforeseeable consequences. Islands and many coastal countries emphatically endorsed this position, but more developed nations—the biggest polluters—insisted on a ceiling of 2°C. This schism would complicate negotiations all the way to Paris. I marveled that so many nations—and the "haves," at that—could be so selfish. Now that we had U.S. support, we needed the so-called BRIC countries—Brazil, Russia, India, and China—and President Obama went so far as to "drop in" on an internal meeting of BRIC leaders. This nudged things forward, but Chinese Premier Wen Jiabao still refused to negotiate on the substance. In other words, he would talk but not engage.

Pressed by time, Danish Prime Minister Lars Rasmussen, who chaired the conference, President Obama, and I separately visited the Chinese premier's hotel. This was unusual. It was customary for a visiting foreign leader to pay a call on the host government's highest representative at a conference, but Premier Wen did not. Our visits were necessary to reach a breakthrough on the Copenhagen Accord. I was adamant that we needed every participating government to help, and especially Beijing because it was one of the planet's largest emitters and wielded so much influence in Asia and, increasingly, in Africa.

On the other hand, I was delighted that protestors demonstrated peacefully outside the venue, a concrete reminder that the people demanded strong and sustained climate action. But this was not the way to have a dialogue. I would later insist that we make more space for civil society and nongovernmental organizations at every climate conference. They are our allies and partners, and I have the greatest respect for their views and contributions. This view was not universal, but I hoped my successors would also feel that they deserved a seat at the table.

When informal negotiations began under the chairmanship of Prime Minister Rasmussen, key players crowded into one small, overheated room. Just as bad, the usual platters of sandwiches, crudités, and cookies were inadequate. Obviously, these heads of state were not worried about having a meal, but forty years of diplomatic experience had taught me that people are more collaborative when properly fed and hydrated. Even in this environment, President Obama distinguished himself with graceful engagement. He worked on the most recent draft of the political agreement on his own laptop which he carried around to show the language to other leaders. I knew U.S. support was vital in the long run and was overjoyed to see his spirited engagement. After agonizing negotiations, we concluded that there was no way to reach an agreement in Copenhagen. The atmosphere was very contentious. One of the Chinese delegates even became undiplomatic, challenging several heads of states and governments during the negotiation.

The room grew quiet in disappointment. Delegates lowered their voices as they realized they had failed. The final Copenhagen text does not include a target; it merely "recognizes" the scientific case for limiting atmospheric warming by less than 2°C, without advocating the lower target of 1.5°C. Some representatives of small developing states were even in tears. But most of the developed countries and China were dismissive of their cries. As soon as Prime Minister Rasmussen opened the conference plenary, he asked whether there was any opposition to the draft decision. Of course there was. Instead of agreeing or abstaining, many speakers took to the floor to object. This was not a diplomatic atmosphere; it was turning fractious and negative. Some speakers were even shouting and banging the tables. The room was noisy and filled with bad feelings. It was a chaotic situation.

Two days earlier, during the plenary session, a Sudanese representative made an analogy between the political agreement and the Holocaust, contending that the agreement was a "suicide pact" that could affect six million African people. This was absolutely unacceptable and very offensive to many. The toxic atmosphere was starting to poison everything. But it got worse still! During the same day, Venezuelan negotiator Claudia Salerno raised her nameplate to speak. When she was not called on, she started banging it and deeply cut herself. Finally given the floor, Salerno held up her bloody hand and raised the emotional temperature another 2 degrees. Finally, with no consensus, an overwhelmed Prime Minister Rasmussen ran off the podium after gaveling that there was no consensus. I was incredulous and left alone in this chaotic milieu. Yvo de Boer and I chose to stand our ground. Many angry and frustrated delegates—including UK Environment Minister Ed Miliband, U.S. Chief Negotiator Todd Stern, and the European Union's Benita Ferrero-Waldner—rushed to the podium, some pointing their fingers at me, shouting or protesting. I have never in my long diplomatic career been faced with such an awkward moment. Later, after all the dust had settled, I asked Bob Orr to make sure that my deep regret was delivered to the U.S. chief negotiator, and Stern later conveyed his deep apology.

I invited several key delegates from Cuba, Egypt, Nicaragua, Venezuela, and India, among others, to gather on the sideline after the plenary meeting was adjourned in chaos. "Please," I implored them. "You have to agree. This conference must have an outcome, and it is up to us to save it." They were very angry, but I deliberately asked for their ideas. I have learned that listening is important in diplomacy because sometimes people just need to be heard. By giving space to the delegates to air their solutions, they were less likely to focus on the fractiousness. This strategy paid off. The Egyptian negotiator complained that nations were being forced to opt out of an agreement that others had negotiated. I turned the tables by asking if they could agree to a text that countries would choose to opt into instead.

When the plenary session was reconvened, I made an impromptu passionate appeal for unity of the member states to at least "take note of the Copenhagen Accord." It was early morning of the following day when delegates finally accepted the "information paper," which carries far less weight than a resolution.

Even though Copenhagen was widely viewed as a failure because it did not Seal the Deal, in the end more than one hundred countries endorsed that document.

THE MOST FRAGILE PLACE ON EARTH

From Day 1, I began intensifying my climate diplomacy, visiting places that are most affected by rising seas and creeping deserts. I knew my trips would generate a lot of press and provoke wider public concern, which in many countries could influence policy. I visited Antarctica to demonstrate my commitment to addressing climate change. I wanted to see the melting and breaking glaciers that would raise the level of the sea. My visit would not have been possible without support from the Chilean government and its president at the time, Michelle Bachelet. She provided a Chilean air force plane that brought us to the Chilean air base in Antarctica on November 11, 2007. Standing on the Antarctic ice surrounded by global media, I spoke of the urgency of addressing climate change, pointing to the breaking glaciers.

One of the most memorable episodes during the trip was my visit to Korea's King Sejong Station. The research facility is a cluster of bright red buildings nestled on permafrost on the Barton peninsula of King George Island, one of many national research stations there. King Sejong Station monitors climate from the distant atmosphere to the cold deep waters. The temperature in early winter grazed −10°C (14°F), but I was too awed by the clear air and icy waters to feel the cold. Behind me there was laughter. The rest of the UN expedition had to wear so many layers of such heavy clothes that no one could move freely. My senior advisors were laughing at each other and walking like penguins! Soon-taek was so deeply swaddled in a thick red and blue ice suit that I could see only part of her face. But as we marveled at this most alien atmosphere, I saw that she, too, was smiling. It was a brief moment of levity surrounded by disappearing beauty.

The Korean scientists that evening provided an unexpected sashimi and scotch reception for our team. It was an extraordinarily memorable meal. Our hosts caught the fish in the nearby waters and served drinks with forty-thousand-year-old ice! I tried to imagine that but had nothing so ancient to compare to this melting ice cube. No one could resist this experience, not even the staffer who didn't normally drink.

RAINING PENNIES (JUST PENNIES) FROM HEAVEN

Despite, or maybe because of, the bitter taste of Copenhagen, the November-December 2010 UN climate conference in Cancún was efficient, effective, and without drama. Delegates established a novel funding mechanism. Donor countries would deposit contributions into the Green Climate Fund (GCF), which would select and fund projects to help developing countries adapt to political and environmental demands, such as converting from fossil fuels to clean energy, mitigating climate-caused degradation, developing and implementing policy, and other assistance. I was proud when Korea offered to provide a headquarters for the GCF in Songdo, Incheon. We spent 2014 and 2015, the two years leading up to Paris, carefully building the broad coalition that would be needed to deliver not just any agreement but a good one. This would require help not only from politicians but also the active and passionate support of business leaders, mayors, NGOs, and celebrities. Really, it was all about mobilizing the world's peoples. Pledges topped $10 billion, and it felt like an excellent start. I was confident that contributions would ramp up with international imperatives and demonstrable successes. The unanimous support for the GCF was a sign of good faith, but to be effective it needed capital. Delegates had set the ambitious target of $100 billion in contributions by 2020, annually authorizing the same amount for projects that aided the developing states. This was a promising starting point. As I and everyone else was aware, however, setting goals and winning pledges are not the same as cash in hand. I could only hope governments would follow through.

I led the effort to capitalize the fund, cajoling, reasoning, guilting, and just plain wearing governments down to make their contributions. President François Hollande and Chancellor Angela Merkel in 2014 announced that France and Germany would deposit $1 billion each into the GCF. Japanese Prime Minister Shinzo Abe promised $1.5 billion; British Prime Minister David Cameron, $1.15 billion; Canadian Prime Minister Stephen Harper, $70 million. Seoul added $100 million, as did Norway, Canada, and Sweden. Smaller contributors came from diverse nations, from Panama to Bulgaria and New Zealand.

Washington became problematic. The United States pledged $3 billion, and I had continually badgered President Obama to honor America's commitment. But he was hamstrung by U.S. budgets. In November 2014, at the G20 summit in Brisbane, Australia, he watched me approach. With something between a smile and a smirk and before I could open my mouth in greeting, he said, "I have your $3 billion." He knew me that well! He was able to transfer one-third of the money before the end of his term. I do not know when the remaining $2 billion will arrive, if ever. Obama's successor, Donald Trump, withdrew the United States from the Paris Climate Agreement and did not prioritize international assistance or adopt clean energy alternatives.

DUELING CLIMATE CONFERENCES

The 2014 climate conference in Lima would be a defining moment for the climate movement, and I began thinking about that summit well in advance. In December 2012, at the otherwise sleepy climate conference in Doha, Qatar, I told Bob Orr I wanted to shake things up. He suggested that I simply announce that it was my intent before the Lima conference to host a summit in New York, not just of national leaders but of all the other leaders we would need as well, from business to subnational governments to civil society. It surprised all the negotiators, but in the end they welcomed my announcement. We spent the whole next year organizing a summit that would do everything differently from previous summits.

Leaders would be invited, but there would be no negotiation. We would pack the UN with business and finance experts who could advise on the economic aspects. We developed major initiatives and catalyzed big announcements that would give governments confidence to make a deal a year later.

On September 21, two days before the opening of the Lima summit, a variety of organizations rallied in New York for the People's Climate March, a massive mobilization of more than three hundred thousand people down New York City's Fifth Avenue. It is highly unusual for a UN leader to engage in any sort of public demonstration, but I knew I belonged there, marching down the streets of New York with Mayor Bill de Blasio, French Foreign Minister Laurent Fabius—who later gaveled adoption of the historic Paris Climate Agreement—and former Vice President Al Gore, who won the 2007 Nobel Peace Prize for his passionate climate leadership and film, *An Inconvenient Truth*. It was thrilling to know hundreds of thousands more also marched for climate justice in cities around the world. Leonardo DiCaprio, whom I named a UN Messenger of Peace for his work to sound the climate alarm, marched as well. He would go on to produce a major film about climate change, *Before the Flood*, in which I am proud to have had a small part.

There was another bright spot. The New York Declaration on Forests was adopted by more than one hundred fifty partners, including countries, companies, and key concerned groups such as the indigenous peoples. They pledged to end natural forest loss by 2030, with an interim goal of a 50 percent reduction by 2020. This was a climate promise because deforestation is linked to carbon dioxide emissions, and it was another sign that major players cared about environmentally sustainable development. Mayors from more than two thousand cities—led by Michael Bloomberg, Climate Change Special Envoy and former New York City mayor—joined our Compact of Mayors to pledge climate action. Nearly one hundred of the world's megacities have pledged to meet the Paris Climate Agreement goals at the municipal level. This was a breakthrough because cities have a major impact on the green economy and the environment, and their cooperation could yield significant reductions in greenhouse gas emissions.

In Lima, the Global Alliance for Climate-Smart Agriculture, an alliance of 500 million farmers, was announced. So was a Climate Risk Investment Framework, which has attracted support from insurance industry bigwigs worth collectively $30 trillion. I felt swept along by the sheer force of the momentum we had created. Climate change had reached the tipping point; our action was unstoppable.

The 2014 conference in Lima was far more than a talkfest. The business and finance leaders, mayors, and civil society leaders came with concrete solutions and bold targets in key sectors. Thanks to the hard work of my climate change support team and the hundreds of meetings I had attended on climate with leaders from industry, we saw major breakthroughs. As we gathered material support, our biggest boost from the spiritual world came in the form of His Holiness Pope Francis. The Catholic Church has always used its non-voting observer status to lobby member states on social issues. It made sense to me when the Holy See began to advocate for climate action.

I see Pope Francis as a true visionary, a spiritual leader of the highest order who is also remarkably down to earth as he has repeatedly demonstrated through his humble service to the poor. I remember his quiet conviction in speaking to me about global warming. Although focused on the realm of Heaven, the value of life on Earth was never far from his mind. The Pope applied his enormous influence in the service of the Paris Climate Agreement on May 24, 2015, when he issued his encyclical on climate change, called *Laudato si* (On Care for Our Common Home). Its language is beautiful, and the Pope was clearly asking more than a billion Catholics to care about the environment—and he urged action. The Pope reinforced this message during his historic visit to the United Nations on September 25, 2015.

THE PULL OF THE POLES

On July 6, 2015, I visited the Arctic for the second time. Before going to Paris for the final negotiation, I wanted to send another strong message to the world while standing on the ice. We boarded a small science research ship going to the frontline at Svalbard, a Norwegian archipelago in the Arctic region. I remember staring intently at the breathtaking blue-green sea, which was topped by broken sheets of ice all the way to the horizon. It was both extraordinarily beautiful and deeply disturbing. I began to wonder if we were too late.

This polar visit was instructive but lacked the exhilaration of my 2008 trip. The icebergs had continued to thaw, leaving deep, slippery mud. Janos Pasztor's boots sank in, and I had to be especially careful not to slip. I had bruised a few ribs and it wasn't easy walking.

BEGGERS' BANQUET

It was time to tackle attitudes surrounding the production and consumption of food—one-third of which goes to waste on any given day. For a climate change luncheon on September 27, 2015, I asked former White House chef Sam Kass to make a vegetarian meal for thirty world leaders using food that would normally go to waste. Kass created an Instagram-worthy meal of "landfill salad" and a patty of "off-grade vegetables" on "spent grain bread." The humble and delicious meal of scraps was even more potent for being served on china to the most powerful people on Earth. There could be no better way to protest the nearly three trillion pounds of food discarded every year. The meal also stimulated talk between the leaders, some of whom had not been aware of this unconscionable waste.

THE FULL SUN SHINES ON PARIS

Tragically, terrorist attacks ripped through Paris on November 13–14, 2015, just weeks before it was to host scores of world leaders. All of France was reeling. President Hollande showed great leadership, and the French people united against the threat. They were resolved to stay the course and welcome the world to Paris to save the planet. I was moved by the way Parisians returned to their lives and, in an act of quiet condolence and defiance, drank a coffee with Mayor of Paris Anne Hidalgo at "À la bonne bière," where five people had been killed. There was nothing more Parisian, nothing that better symbolized the city's *joie du vivre*. I was also deeply respectful of the government, whose decision to maintain the conference underscored for me its determination to uphold the values of the United Nations—liberty, peace, and justice. I paid my respects by laying a wreath at the scene of the terror attacks.

I would later speak often of this example of how we have to respond to the terrorist threat: bravely, with no hesitation, and with a focus on our shared future. The people of Paris and the leaders of France demonstrated that together we are stronger than any violence, and that those who divide us are much weaker than those who unite us. On the eve of the Paris summit, I was invited by Mayor Hidalgo to meet hundreds of the world's mayors, including Mayor Park Won-soon of Seoul. Around one thousand mayors came from all over the world to lend their political support to the climate summit.

The Paris climate conference opened as planned with one hundred fifty leaders in attendance, and I delivered a strong appeal to all of them. I warned that we may never again have a political momentum like this. "You have the power to secure the well-being of this and succeeding generations," I said, urging the leaders to "instruct your negotiators to choose the path of compromise and consensus." They answered this call. All of the major players aligned themselves behind the agreement. The Alliance of Small Island States, which had been the "canary in a coal mine," warned us about the dangers of global warming long before the rest of the world had noticed. They were joined by the major emitters, including China, India, the United States, and every nation in between. Consensus was ours, but suddenly one country threatened to break it. I never would have anticipated that the lone holdout would be the delegate from Nicaragua.

I had enjoyed good relations with the Nicaraguan government. I had traveled to Managua for meetings with President Daniel Ortega and other senior officials the previous year and remember being impressed by how the former revolutionary had personally chauffeured me around. He was the first world leader I ever rode with who took the wheel himself. But the Nicaraguan president had not come to Paris; instead he sent Environmental Minister Paul Oquist Kelley, a large red-haired man with no aversion to conflict. President Hollande,

Chancellor Angela Merkel, U.S. Secretary of State John Kerry, and Laurent Fabius tried to convince Kelley to approve the delicately worded agreement.

The Nicaraguan delegate would not budge, claiming that the agreement might hurt developing countries. President Hollande suggested that we appeal to His Holiness Pope Francis. I agreed because Nicaragua is a Catholic country, but we could not get through to the Vatican. I tried many times to call President Ortega, but nobody picked up the phone. The extremely hopeful environment at the summit could collapse at any point, and I worried about a domino effect in which the break from consensus by one country might trigger more objections. The shadow of Copenhagen loomed. Minister Kelley suddenly wanted to meet alone in my office. He said Nicaragua would go along with the consensus with one condition: President Ortega wanted me to visit again before the end of the year. In that moment, I would have promised anything. Literally, the very future of our planet rested on it.

The stage was set with Fabius at the podium of the auditorium of the Parc des Expositions. As soon as Nicaragua agreed, I phoned Fabius's mobile with the good news, and he forcefully gaveled the agreement. President Hollande and I waited outside until the vast auditorium suddenly erupted, and then we raced inside. The chamber was filled with cheers, tears, hugs, and an applause that seemed never to end! Al Gore, seated in the VIP row, leaped to his feet and hollered with joy, and delegates danced at their seats and in the aisles. I have never shaken so many hands in so few minutes.

One of the most reproduced images from that day is of the final moment of the vote when Christiana Figueres, the current chief of the UN Framework Convention on Climate Change, I, President Francois Hollande, and President of the Conference Laurent Fabius spontaneously threw our clasped hands into the air, grinning in triumph. I am wearing the pale green tie Soon-taek had picked out for me. It was one of my most exciting days as UN secretary-general.

THE FINAL MILE

I decided to hold a marathon signing ceremony in New York on Earth Day, April 22, 2016. We hoped to set a climate record, but in fact we shattered every treaty event with an amazing 175 countries signing at once. I caught some of my climate experts high-fiving when certain milestones were reached. I wished I could join in the levity. I was determined that the treaty should become binding, or enter into force before the end of my term on December

31, 2016. To do so, it needed ratification by fifty-five countries representing 55 percent of the world's greenhouse gas emissions. The problem was that the countries signing on immediately were also the countries with the lowest emissions, and they did not go far toward the 55 percent requirement. As I watched the dial move incrementally, I began to worry.

This changed on September 3, 2016, just before the start of the G20 summit in Hangzhou, China. I was astounded and ecstatic when President Xi Jinping organized a special ceremony in Hangzhou in which he and President Obama personally deposited with me their instruments of ratification. The two countries alone accounted for 38 percent of global emissions. That sent a strong message to the world that those two largest emitters were committed. This event accelerated the ratification process like a vessel sailing with a fair wind.

On September 30, the European Union voted to fast-track the ratification process. I personally visited the EU Parliament and spoke passionately right before the measure passed. "In the name of humanity and for the sake of future generations, I encourage you to support the speedy ratification of the Paris Agreement." The measure passed by a large majority.

President Obama personally applauded me in a private conversation in Hangzhou: "You showed outstanding leadership," he said.

The Paris Agreement officially entered into force on November 4, 2016, less than two months before my retirement from the United Nations and exactly ten years after I had promised to make climate change a priority. This set a record for any major international agreement; the Paris Agreement entered into force in the shortest time ever in the history of the United Nations. I was almost dizzy by the rush of my emotions. I was overjoyed, proud, exhausted, hopeful, and filled with appreciation for all the nations that negotiated in good faith and ultimately signed onto the Paris Agreement.

WASHINGTON VERSUS THE WORLD

Only one nation—the indispensable United States—stepped back. Donald Trump's unilateral decision stunned us, but no one was surprised by the announcement on June 1, 2017. The president had repeatedly disparaged the United Nations, climate science, and multilateral agreements. Yet we couldn't quite see Trump—or anyone—withdrawing from the Paris Agreement. Surely, I thought, the climate crisis was evident, even to this administration.

Harvard University Professor Robert Stavins and I tried to preempt the U.S. departure by writing a joint op-ed for the *Boston Globe* on April 20, 2017, urging the United States to remain in the Paris Agreement. Far from being "a bad deal" for the United States, we wrote, it levels the playing field by including industrialized nations and large emerging economies as well. In addition, private industry broadly supports the agreement, including companies in oil, electricity, manufacturing, and others directly affected by it.

Climate advocates also had hope for the high-profile campaign called "We Are Still In," a declaration by a dozen of America's largest states, three hundred cities, five hundred universities, and nine hundred corporations that they will keep their own commitments to the principles of the Paris Agreement regardless of Washington's actions. A decade of UN climate studies showed with painful and frightening clarity why it was in America's interest to remain a party to the international agreement.

Trump said the accord put the United States at "a very, very big economic disadvantage," particularly against China. This is untrue. The Paris Agreement was a historic commitment. Backing out was a historic mistake. A remarkable 193 nations plus Palestine stood at a fork in the road in 2015 and said, "Let's take this first step together." But with one act, Donald Trump—unpredictable, unreliable, irresponsible and imperious—undercut the global accord.

But President Joe Biden is nearly his opposite. His Green New Deal, if implemented even in part, will be a major recalibration in Washington's attitude toward the climate crisis. I am heartened by his appointment of former Secretary of State John Kerry as the United States' first-ever environmental envoy. The choice to deploy such a respected diplomat to a high-level cabinet post indicates to me that Washington intends to play a leading role in future climate negotiations.

The United States is the world's second largest polluter after China, accounting for 14 percent of the planet's greenhouse gas emissions. It is clear to everyone—including Mr. Biden—that Washington's participation is vital to the success of the Paris Climate Agreement, not to mention to the health of the Earth itself.

THE CLIMATE WARRIOR

Climate crusader Greta Thunberg began her lonely vigil at age fifteen, and within a year she had galvanized young people around the world to skip school one day each week, a peaceful call to action known as "Fridays for the Future." These demonstrations have already spurred powerful long-term awareness of the climate emergency we face. I was surprised and impressed when she challenged world leaders to examine and defend their own records. This is a powerful example of youth leading the agenda and another reason we must encourage and prepare them to make their world a better place. Thunberg made me feel a little bit guilty, and I wondered what I might have said or done when I was her age.

Invited to the January 2019 World Economic Forum, Thunberg demanded immediate and meaningful action by the world's rich and powerful. "Your house is on fire!" she warned. Preternaturally articulate and single-minded, Thunberg was one of the most electrifying speakers at the September 23, 2019, UN Climate Action Summit, delivering her now famous "how dare you!" speech directly to startled presidents and prime ministers.

Several weeks later, at the otherwise disappointing COP25 meeting in Madrid, she criticized CEOs and politicians for hiding behind "clever accounting and creative PR"—a reference to the public relations effort to show an automobile manufacturer's concern about clean air or a social media company's commitment to privacy. Thunberg drew applause from delegates and even some laughter when she described the conference as a place for governments to share loopholes rather than solutions. Greta Thunberg is the opposite of a diplomat, but in some ways she is much more powerful. Her edge, energy, and age make her far more charismatic than one would expect from such an unsparing critic.

In fact, she has inspired me to be more forceful and a little less diplomatic in my own approach to the climate emergency. In January 2020, I made a keynote speech at the Brookings Institution in Washington, and the discussion turned to President Donald Trump.

"I can just tell you that President Trump is politically very shortsighted, scientifically wrong, and morally irresponsible," I said. "Even economically, it doesn't make any sense. He will stand on the wrong side of history." I could never have said that as secretary-general. It felt good to speak my mind now that I am, for almost the first time in my adult life, a private citizen. I am no longer speaking for the interests of 193 nations, or even just one, and I am no longer muted by the traditions of diplomacy.

Greta Thunberg and others like her are exactly what we need to rally climate action. She has started a green revolution, and that's something we cannot just be grateful for—it's a revolution we must join. I have said many times that nature has its own way, and it does not negotiate. It's up to us to find a way to live harmoniously on the Earth. On April 11, 2018, traveling as a private citizen, I met Pope Francis in the Vatican. It was my fifth audience with this very special man. He told me, "God always forgives, we human beings sometimes forgive, but Nature never forgives." What an inspiring and strong message!

My own grandchildren are not yet teenagers, and I do worry about the world they will inherit. I look forward to taking them hiking on the Korean hillside, where I hope they will develop my love of nature and respect for its power. And I know they will carry on with the important work of saving those cold, clear streams for their own grandchildren.

Chapter Twenty

GLOBAL HEALTH

Preventing, Containing, and Curing Together

Ebola stoked global fear as it roared across Sierra Leone, Liberia, and Guinea throughout the summer and autumn of 2014. I was filled with dread. We still didn't understand the disease, and it was highly contagious and fatal in half of its victims. The United Nations and its system of autonomous agencies such as the World Health Organization were on the frontline, and I worried that we could not mount a robust enough response.

Ebola is a terrible disease, killing its victims with uncontrollable vomiting, bleeding, and diarrhea. The disease was so feared that afflicted areas suffered panic, raids, and even attacks on medical personnel perceived to be spreading the disease. Nonetheless, there were frightened people to reassure and contributions to raise for a tenacious fight against the epidemic. Although I felt uneasy, I knew I had to go to West Africa. My staff vigorously objected to the visit. Soon-taek was not as dramatic, but she looked worried. "Be careful" is all she said.

I left for the region on December 17, 2014, to visit the three frontline countries as well as Ghana and Mali. I started the five-day journey at the United Nations' regional Ebola command center, the UN Mission for Ebola Emergency Response (UNMEER), which was headquartered in Ghana. Veteran political and peacekeeping official Tony Banbury served in Accra as my special representative and head of UNMEER, keeping in contact with regional governments on my behalf. The office opened during the thick of the epidemic in mid-September 2014. From the beginning, UNMEER approached the disease holistically: not just as a public health crisis but as a force affecting economics, transportation, national security, and human rights as well.

As a lifelong diplomat who travels between countries and cultures, I am accustomed to etiquette and its more demanding cousin, protocol. Both govern the intricacies of polite behavior in an official or political setting so the focus is on the business at hand and not on who goes through the door first. Ebola threw that through the window. It took me some time to get used to touching elbows; just a tap, one elbow atop the other. It was fast, hygienic, and it brought people together during these terrible times. From a public health viewpoint, handshakes and the intimate and awkward air-kiss (signature gestures of diplomacy) make no sense. I heard from UN staff throughout the region that people became closer and friendlier by bumping elbows, a momentary acknowledgment that strangers shared a common humanity and a common fear.

Even presidents were vulnerable. I was surprised when Ghanaian President John Dramani Mahama greeted me with an elbow. Ebola was not present in Ghana, but everyone was playing it extra safe. In fact, the president had taken some domestic political heat when he agreed to host UNMEER in Accra. I was deeply grateful to him. As for me, I agreed to follow strict health precautions for my entire trip, even when I was traveling far from Ebola territories. I took my body temperature often and carefully washed my hands in chlorinated water each time I entered or left a building. This protected me and everyone who would come across my path. The anxiety level was so high that I was sure most others were following the same safeguards.

After a light supper, feeling uncomfortable, I returned to my room. I realized I was starting to feel nervous about going to Sierra Leone, my first stop the next day. I was grateful for my robust health at age seventy, and I knew every precaution would be taken while we were in the "hot zone." But I began to investigate the disease in my mind that night: the heavy lungs, painful eyes, dehydration headache, high fever, wracking aches, and then the final decline. I imagined that the sick were also thirsty but were too weak to drink. Did they wonder why their families haven't visited?

I woke up early the next morning. Medical tents throughout the region were operating at or beyond their capacity. In Sierra Leone, I spoke to worried staff about the prospect of treating still more victims. Every one of these men and women said they would continue to treat the sick, even though they clearly had not slept or eaten properly for days. The unspoken threat, of course, was not exhaustion but contamination. The patients were also wrung out. Those who would survive had to build their strength before they could even sit up again. Others were deep in the throes of Ebola's torture—not quite lucid and curled in pain.

Outside the medical tents, I told survivors and their families that the United Nations supported them medically, financially, and even physically. I wanted these people to see me—a healthy stranger—unafraid of Ebola and unafraid of them. But my message was compromised by my costume: a surgical mask and face shield; a long-sleeved, waterproof gown and rubber boots; and two pairs of gloves. I felt like an astronaut. I was dressed for distance, not compassion. The clothing and other understandably strict precautions were recommended by the U.S. Centers for Disease Control and Prevention and accepted worldwide and copied as closely as possible when there weren't enough face shields and rubber boots to go around.

Some of the most courageous people I've ever met were working in the hospital tents. These were ordinary people who did not retreat from a lethal threat. These family members, medics, neighbors, and survivors donned paper masks and latex gloves and volunteered to help. I met Rebecca Johnson, an Ebola survivor who volunteered at the medical tent in Hastings, Sierra Leone. She told me she had been so sick that she needed help eating and even talking and had feared it was "the end of the world." When she had triumphed over the disease, she discovered that her community treated her like a pariah. So she came to the hospital and offered to help others. Her commitment moved me to do more to end the outbreak and confirmed my decision to break the stigma that clings to so many survivors.

On the day I visited Sierra Leone, we learned that Victor Willoughby, Sierra Leone's "father of medicine," had died. He was the eleventh doctor to succumb to Ebola in this country alone, a grave loss to a country with one of the lowest doctor-patient ratios in the world.

I traveled to West Africa as a vaccine was just making its way through an accelerated approval process. It was reserved for the bravest doctors and nurses who were willing to test a dose. This outbreak of Ebola had quickly spread from Guinea to Sierra Leone and to Liberia, desperately poor countries emerging from the destabilizing aftershocks of war. Cases were also reported in Mali and Nigeria, but the virus was weak enough to fight in those countries. In the Mano River region, Ebola left tens of thousands of survivors to face an uncertain future without family, a home, or even a community. It tore at my heart to learn that many of those who survived the disease recovered to find themselves ostracized rather than celebrated.

I believed the scale of each Ebola outbreak could have been blunted if the Millennium Development Goals to relieve extreme poverty had been more fully enacted. But without adequate water, sanitation, and health care, these tragedies were playing out across the region, often blasting past anyone's worst-case scenarios. At every turn, nature and fate conspired to make this outbreak Ebola's largest and most deadly.

PATIENT ZERO

In December 2013, in a small village in Guinea, an eighteen-month-old boy was bitten by bats. He is believed to be the "index patient" or "patient zero"—the victim that sparked the Ebola outbreak that within a year had sickened 28,600 people, killing 11,300, nearly 40 percent of the confirmed cases. The little boy passed the bat's disease to his extended family in the three days before he died. His village, Meliandou, is located in a remote forest that borders the triangle where Guinea meets Liberia and Sierra Leone. All three countries have been pounded by poverty and civil unrest, and refugees pass freely around Meliandou in their quest for someplace better. Ebola circulated quietly in this forest for months, infecting people who would be far away when the coughing began. At least 3,800 people became sick in Guinea alone, and 2,536 died.

By mid-August Ebola was loose in West Point, a Liberian slum of seventy thousand on the outskirts of the capital, Monrovia. Survivors described the sickness as spreading like waves in all directions through an overcrowded area with no sanitation or access to medical care and dwindling supplies of food. Despite severe criticism from the medical community and human rights advocates, including UN agencies, Monrovia ordered the army to quarantine West Point. The barbed wire and barricades complicated medical care and quickly led to shortages and panic. Equally frightening, this policy almost guaranteed that the healthy would become infected. I was chilled to see patients, doctors, and soldiers in a single photograph, knowing that the military was not there to help the medical efforts but to enforce containment. UN experts said Liberia's estimate of the damage—officially 4,800 deaths out of 10,600 infections—was too low because frightened undertakers and families disposed of bodies by piling corpses in mass graves or slipping them into the river.

Meanwhile Sierra Leone's Ebola epidemic was also spreading before our eyes. The surge was likely sparked by a widely respected spiritual healer who was well known even far away. Infected villagers traveled to see her, leaving a plume of Ebola virus behind them. Her traditional funeral was attended by hundreds, and contact tracing indicates it was the probable source of more than three hundred of Sierra Leone's fourteen thousand confirmed cases.

CREATING UNMEER

The UN Development Program's country offices were among the first responders, along with the Secretariat's office overseeing emergency response. At first, the World Health Organization was the lead agency, but our partners in the Ebola effort had long been frustrated by disorganization in WHO's West African offices and its tragically delayed response to the crisis. I deeply respected WHO Director General Margaret Chan, but I had to point out that we were wasting time and money and failing to help as many people as possible. World Bank President Jim Yong Kim, who served as WHO director in the early 2000s, was particularly critical of the organization's handling of the Ebola crisis.

The emergency had grown too complex for any one agency, and my Special Advisor on Ebola David Nabarro, my Chief of Staff Susana Malcorra, and others agreed that it was time for the whole UN system to contribute to the effort. We would need to mobilize the organization's financial, medical, political, and humanitarian expertise, as well as the logistics and operational capacities of the Department of Peacekeeping Operations. The Ebola epidemic was a war, and we would fight it with UNMEER, the first United Nations mission devoted to a health threat.

On September 18, 2014, with the epidemic near its peak, I made the case to the Security Council for an Ebola-specific mission to deploy expertise and equipment to infected areas. I stressed that the disease often destroyed communities where it raged, and not just medically. By September people were already afraid to leave their homes. "The virus is also taking an economic toll," I told the Security Council. "Inflation and food prices are rising. Transport and social services are being disrupted. The situation is especially tragic given the remarkable strides that Liberia and Sierra Leone have made in putting their brutal war and interwoven domestic conflicts behind them."

The next day, September 19, the council adopted by consensus Resolution 2177 (2014), determining that "the unprecedented extent of the Ebola outbreak in Africa constitutes a threat to international peace and security." The UNMEER resolution was sponsored by an unprecedented 130 nations. This was the first and to date only UN mission for a public health emergency. (I wished member states would seriously consider a similar response to the Covid-19 coronavirus.)

The UN Budget Committee (ACABQ) recommended that the General Assembly approve $50 million for the rest of 2014. President of the General Assembly, Sam Kutesa, Uganda's foreign minister, took an immediate action to approve the budget—a process that has always taken months or more. This was the fastest financial decision I had ever witnessed.

ENGAGING A MICROSCOPIC ENEMY

The United Nations and WHO were slow to recognize an ample resource—the UN Mission in Liberia. UNMIL provided transportation, security, and other support functions for health workers.[1] This was possible because UNMIL was predominantly a civilian police mission, having deployed after the country's calamitous decade of civil war. Troop contributing countries, UN bodies, and the host government would have to agree on whether or how to press peacekeepers into service if or when a serious public health crisis erupted in a country with UN peacekeepers.

The United States, the United Kingdom, and Germany were the primary early donors to the Ebola fund, contributing a combined $3.6 billion in cash and kind. Nevertheless, the mission was very thinly funded, and I remain sorry, even ashamed, that so few other countries felt the compassion and urgency that would have compelled them to give freely. As the crisis wore on, others did pledge support, but it was never enough for the comprehensive plan to locate and eradicate every case. Guinean President Alpha Condé complained often to me that the French government had not sent enough support, particularly in terms of soldiers.

U.S. President Obama announced on September 16, 2014, that the United States would deploy three thousand soldiers and $750 million in Liberia. The British provided 750 soldiers in Sierra Leone, and France sent four hundred soldiers with a treatment center into Guinea. I visited all three military bases and thanked them for their selfless contribution in the red zones.

I sometimes wonder whether the UN could have done more to arrest the Ebola virus before it engulfed swathes of Eastern Congo in 2017. The fabric of these societies was shredded. Generations-old traditions had shaped how people lived, how they connected, and, especially, how they died. Burial was one custom that needed to be abandoned immediately. In much of West Africa, traditional burials honor the deceased by washing and hugging him or her before dozens or more mourners nestle the body in its grave. But corpses were still contagious, and the virus passed quickly among the mourners. How do you tell frightened people in the midst of an epidemic that they cannot bury their dead with comforting rituals? Tony Banbury consulted an anthropologist about alternative burial customs, a brilliant idea that undoubtedly helped contain transmission. For example, many mourners were more inclined to accept a hasty and distant burial if the body bag enclosing their neighbor was carried with great gentleness and respect. Sometimes mourners accepted a tree trunk, a piece of metal, or some other object to substitute for the body—a practice that was also useful during war. These precautions helped quite a bit, but they were not enough to end the harrowing epidemic.

QUARANTINED

Coming home from the Ebola red zone was not quite as onerous as being near it. My entourage and I should have expected that after the thorough exams we had received at JFK Airport. Out of courtesy, I was let go with a simple temperature check and a few questions, but my delegation members had to go through thorough evaluations. They had to explain exactly where they went and how they felt and submit to exams.

I was in a light quarantine for twenty-one days—just in case. The CDC issued me and everyone in my team an "Ebola control phone," which called the CDC directly. I was to use it twice a day to report my temperature or any other symptoms, and I relaxed with time when I did not feel sick or contagious. Nonetheless, I worried about my health and washed my hands repeatedly. And, yes, when someone put out his or her hand to shake, I offered my elbow. I went to my office daily, but I was secretly happy to forgo the nightly receptions where it was more difficult to keep people from getting too close.

I was not allowed any physical contact with another person—including my family. After this painful week in West Africa, I was unable to embrace my wife. My granddaughters, still toddlers, were upset when I did not lift them up and kiss them, and they looked at me strangely when I only waved. Nor was I able to leave Manhattan—the same restriction the United States imposes on the UN ambassadors of North Korea and Iran. Once I forgot and went to New Jersey to play golf with friends. Before I even arrived, the Ebola phone rang and a recorded message informed me I was leaving the Manhattan perimeter. When I realized I was under watch by a satellite, I lost my appetite to play. At the time, I was deeply impressed by the power and capacity of the U.S. government to protect people from this kind of danger. Potential Ebola carriers in the United States were treated quite humanely with what they referred to as house arrest.

In North Korea, Foreign Minister Ri Su-yong was said to be confined in isolation for twenty-one days, even though Minister Ri was not anywhere near the Ebola zone during his recent African visit. Pyongyang, which did not have the medical infrastructure to treat Ebola virus or contain an outbreak, was the first country to seal its borders against anyone who had been near the afflicted area.

I could not have imagined then that only six years later the United States would so badly fumble its response to the coronavirus.

The United Nations, WHO, the World Bank, the CDC, and other affiliates and agencies did remarkable work in West Africa, averting what could have been a catastrophe many times larger. In particular, President Jim Yong Kim of the World Bank, a trained medical doctor and epidemiologist, toured the affected areas and provided much of UNMEER's $500 million budget.[2] I know the death toll could have been even higher, and maybe next time it will be. But I am also sure that the cost of the 2014 epidemic could have been far lower in every way.

An internal WHO report conducted after the Ebola crisis was scathingly critical of West Africa's operations. The main office was disorganized and poorly staffed, which was particularly problematic when it came to coordinating and communicating between frontline NGOs and headquarters. This cost us critical time and led to duplicating our efforts. The assessment also found that WHO coordinated the UN response "by the playbook," without accounting for the region's inadequate health facilities and free flows of contagious refugees. A 2018 study estimated the full cost of the West African Ebola outbreak in excess of $59 billion. The disease claimed at least 11,310 lives, evaporated a minimum of $15 billion in trade and investment, and took an unquantifiable toll on regional education, tourism, and development.

As a private citizen, I watched with utter sadness as authorities in Congo's North Kivu region coped with their own outbreak of the Ebola virus in August 2018. Medical teams operated hospital tents despite armed attacks and obvious dangers. They appeared to have stamped out the virus in early 2020, only to see it return when the region pivoted to fight Covid-19.

Like the Mano River region, Eastern Congo is sparsely populated, very poor, and traversed by refugees leaving poverty and conflict. But I am not as worried about Congo. Neighboring countries are aware of the threat and are alert for symptoms. At least one vaccine has since been approved for emergency use and others will be online soon. If necessary, the UN can reconstitute UNMEER, which was shut down when the crisis in Liberia, Sierra Leone, and Guinea ended.

THE INFLUENZAS

Throughout 2007, and sporadically during my tenure, avian and swine influenzas broke out around the globe, renewing fears about the devastating potential of deadly respiratory pandemics. These escalating infectious diseases were the kind of emergency that showed how indispensable the United Nations can and should be: across the system and around the world, UN experts were coordinating international efforts to aid the sick, protect the healthy, monitor farm conditions, surveil new cases, contain outbreaks, disseminate warnings, appeal for funding, track medical research, and—perhaps most important—provide a podium from which to address each region, in its own language, about the local impact and precautions to be taken.

In Southeast Asia, poultry farmers were forced to kill and dispose of tens of millions of chickens that might have been exposed to the virus. Most of the initial human infections were also coming from here, likely because of the crowded living conditions and preference for buying birds freshly killed in local markets. An unrelated outbreak of swine flu began in the spring of 2009 at a Mexican pig farm, sickening thousands before the strain was discovered and confirmed. The two influenzas caused severe coughing and fevers, but I thought the signature symptom was fear. Eating habits around the world seemed to change as Asian poultry and Mexican pork were suddenly off the menu. Airlines reported a spike in cancellations as governments issued travel warnings. In North America, schools closed throughout a region when a case was confirmed—or even suspected.

In retrospect, I realize that the United Nations might even have fanned some of the alarm. The Geneva-based World Health Organization raised the H1N1 swine flu alert level from Phase 3, to Phase 4, to Phase 5 in only three days in late April 2009. And it did so with disconcerting zeal. "The declaration of Phase 5 is a strong signal that a pandemic is imminent and that the time to finalize the organization, communication, and implementation of the planned mitigation measures is short," the WHO warned. Phase 5 indicates the disease is transmitted between humans. Indeed, by the end of my tenure, the WHO had confirmed 452 avian flu deaths and more than 130 cases of swine flu. But it wasn't just the numbers that scared people, I think it was the words: transmission, pandemic, mutation, saliva, threat, cull. I urged calm at every opportunity, but it wasn't easy to be heard over the din of schools closing, government warnings, public panic, and breathless media reports.

I could not have imagined that in 2020 a new coronavirus would kill millions of people around the world in less than a year.

MALARIA

I've often marveled that anything as tiny as a mosquito could bring so much grief and pain to hundreds of millions of people. More than 429,000 people died of malaria in 2015 alone; this was the same year that I announced malaria-related deaths had reached an all-time low. In fact, the WHO had found a 29 percent reduction in cases since 2010. This is a most pernicious disease, and one that seems to target young children. Malaria often doesn't go away; it just lies dormant, ready to erupt again with bone-rattling fevers and terrible headaches. It was hard enough on UN officers, and I pitied the young children who had recurring bouts.

Nearly half of the world's population is at risk of contracting malaria, a mosquito-borne disease the WHO has vowed to eradicate since 1955. I was struck to see a display poster for Malaria eradication printed by the League of Nations! Malaria has been a life-threatening concern since the end of World War I. We have taken some small steps, but not enough effort has been dedicated to combating new infections. The most distressing thought for me is that we know how to defeat the mosquito population but still haven't done it.

We need to go town-by-town building proper sanitation and drainage systems to replace the buckets and gullies that line so many roads. We could make rainy seasons less deadly by removing the filthy standing water where a hellish stew of childhood diseases and stubborn viruses incubate. Waste and water management are among the tent poles of the Sustainable Development Goals, a timeline of socioeconomic steps necessary to eradicate the most severe poverty by 2030. The seventeen-plank SDGs follow the Millennium Development Goals, which in 2000 launched the first detailed commitments by governments to expand access to health care, education, and sanitation, among other necessary improvements.

Malaria is just a small piece of a large and complex process, yet the World Bank finds the African economy slows 1.3 percent each year because of the disease, which also has a crippling effect on development. UN Special Envoy for Malaria Ray Chambers told me that lost productivity alone costs the continent around $30 billion a year! I believe we could conquer malaria for good and it would cost less than $30 billion a year. At the moment all we have are bed nets treated with insecticides—a temporary measure that can be an extremely effective barrier against the bite of an infected mosquito—but bed nets are no substitute for a solution.

During the G8 summit held in Tōyako, Hokkaido, Japan, in July 2008, I urged the G8 leaders to contribute at least $1 billion to provide insecticide-treated bed nets to protect the children. I was grateful to Prime Minister Yasuo Fukuda, who chaired this session of the G8, for ably mobilizing political support for my appeal. But I worry that the assistance—or investment—may be too little and too late. During my last year in office, the WHO reported that malaria was still endemic in seventy-six countries, and sixty-one of those countries had at least one drug-resistant strain. I have participated in the African Leaders Malaria Alliance (ALMA) meetings on the sidelines of the annual African Union summit held in Addis Ababa, Ethiopia. I am always moved by the strong commitment shown by the African leaders to protect their citizens, particularly young children.

THE PERSISTENT SCOURGE

Global health officials beat polio back to only three countries by the end of my term, an extraordinary achievement that has saved countless lives. The World Health Organization had begun the millennium pleading for "mop up money," but two multinational wars in Muslim nations had put religious leaders on edge.[3] In northern Nigeria, many religious and political leaders declared in 2003 that the polio vaccine was a Western plot to inhibit the

Muslim population. Some Islamic leaders ordered their congregants to reject the vaccine outright, saying it would make the little boys sterile and the little girls infertile. To prevent such false beliefs, I sent personal letters to the presidents or prime ministers and the highest religious leaders of Afghanistan, Pakistan, and Nigeria, where polio is still to be eradicated.

By 2004, some people wrongly believed that the UN was instrumental in spreading polio and were so angry that UNICEF vaccinators in northern Nigeria had to tape over the familiar emblem so their cars were not ambushed. Vaccinators in the tribal areas of Pakistan were routinely attacked and often killed. In parts of Afghanistan, families just hid their children.

When I became secretary-general, four countries still had active polio outbreaks. I visited them all, on health or other business, and always spoke of the importance of wiping out polio, a frighteningly contagious disease. India was declared polio-free in January 2014, but otherwise, we were in danger of falling victim to our own success. The vast majority of today's population has never seen polio, and many pockets have grown lax about the vaccines. Even doctors in some developed countries may not be able to diagnose a disease that has not been seen in forty-five years. When the virus strikes under those conditions, the impact can be devastating.

My wife Yoo Soon-taek and I did our part. Whenever we went to one of the affected countries, we would try to leave the capital and visit a village where polio was still endemic. In an effort to show how safe the vaccine is, we would carefully squeeze a few sweet drops onto a child's tongue as the neighbors watched and, we hoped, lined up for their own dose. Even if people didn't know the secretary-general, it was clear by the village elders, security, and religious officials with us that our example was to be followed.

I continue to be awed by the world's global commitment to kick out polio. UNICEF's strategists and field staff, in particular, deserve our gratitude for stalking the virus to isolated villages, persevering when communities violently resist, and finding creative solutions to problems ranging from unreliable refrigeration to deadly misinformation. Our successes would not be possible without the coordination of half a dozen UN agencies and long-term support from outside partners, now consolidated as the Global Polio Eradication Initiative. In particular, I am grateful for three decades of global fund-raising by Rotary International. Rotary members contributed more than $2 billion for their polio-eradication campaign. I visited the headquarters office in Chicago and thanked them for their strong support.

If the world could meet the SDG targets for sanitation, we would be on track to curb polio, malaria, cholera, and other water-borne diseases. Proper water management would greatly reduce the amount of standing water that plays host to malarial mosquitos and a stew of other germs and viruses.

LESSONS LEARNED, LESSONS FORGOTTEN

The earliest recorded virus outbreaks probably predate the Old Testament's ten plagues. We have learned a great deal from studying all the outbreaks throughout history, but I'm not sure we have remembered our lessons. No doubt we will learn many more lessons over the next century. Let me add my voice to so many others: We have not learned from our failures; we are not prepared.

The year 2020 started with a gloomy tone as a novel coronavirus spread with terrifying speed from central China to every corner of the world. By the time it reached Korea, in February 2020, the virus had a name: Covid-19. At this moment, millions of vaccine doses have been delivered and hundreds of millions more are on the way. But too many people are falling back into poverty after rising with the help of the Sustainable Development Goals. So many children missed school that Secretary-General Antonio Guterres warned of a "generational catastrophe." These consequences are real and are worldwide, and they will linger long after the vaccine contains the virus, or it goes dormant.

The coronavirus casualties quickly surpassed those from Ebola, SARS, MERS, and the bird and swine flus combined, and the end is not yet in sight. Could this plague have been prevented? Probably not. Could its deadly effects have been blunted? Undoubtedly.

The pandemic changed the spectrum of our lives. Countrywide lockdowns were necessary, but they stranded billions of people, often far from family and jobs. As many people as possible stayed out of the workplace, and essential workers were faced with daily decisions that could affect their health. The rituals that shape our lives—weddings and funerals and religious practices—changed in ways that emphasize isolation rather than community. Xenophobia skyrocketed as the virus spurred travel bans, froze immigration, and stalled international cooperation.

The United Nations celebrated its seventy-fifth anniversary in September 2020 with world leaders' video addresses to a nearly empty General

Assembly chamber. Many of the speakers pleaded for international assistance to cope with the virus. In fact, the very first resolution passed by the General Assembly called the coronavirus "a wake-up call for improving our preparedness for not only health related crises but also other challenges and crises. We need to strengthen international cooperation, coordination, and solidarity. It is important to learn and share experiences and information to reduce risks and make our systems more resilient."

On January 31, 2020, at the onset of Covid-19, I telephoned WHO Director General Tedros Adhanom Ghebreyesus and urged him to closely coordinate with Secretary-General Guterres to mobilize all resources. I do not want to undermine the capacity and authority of the WHO or the office of the secretary-general, but I believe earlier and more powerful UN strategies could have contained or lessened this epidemic and many others. There is no better platform than the United Nations to address global pandemics and mobilize the political, financial, and logistical resources that may yet contain this plague.

Safe, affordable vaccines are being developed with amazing speed, and they must be produced in sufficient quantities for a world in need. I call on all leaders to ensure these vaccines are distributed justly and swiftly. Many governments seem concerned only about their own citizens, but they should be seeking a coordinated response to a microscopic enemy that leaps international borders with a single sneeze.

I am alarmed that it took four months for the Security Council to pass its first coronavirus resolution, one that called for a ninety-day cease-fire in conflict areas around the world to allow humanitarian teams to access areas under siege. This resolution did not break new ground, nor did it contain the danger. By contrast, the Security Council wasted no time in declaring the 2014 Ebola outbreak was a threat to international security. In the United States, President Donald Trump mocked the "China virus," and withdrew the United States from the WHO.

I have always emphasized the importance of tackling global challenges with global solutions. This is the essence of the SDGs and the force behind our collective response to the climate crisis. Every country must improve international public health by engaging in ongoing surveillance, early detection and control, and dissemination of honest, depoliticized information.

Korea was an early battlefield. The virus exploded unexpectedly in the southern city of Daegu in late February of 2020 after a religious sect persisted in holding secret meetings and misrepresented the infections even as the scope of its culpability was clear. The Korean Medical Association criticized Seoul's weak response in the first weeks of the crisis and its reluctance to ban flights from China. We even had an early shortage of face masks. Nonetheless, the country quickly tested tens of thousands of people and imposed powerful movement restrictions that were ultimately effective. Korea is recognized by the world's medical communities and media as a pioneer in Covid-19 response. When we were nonetheless inundated by a second wave of cases, other countries continued to look to Seoul to adapt our successes and learn from some missteps.

More than one hundred countries have sought advice and medical support from Korea, and we are sharing our resources as best we can. I hope that Korea's example will continue to be an inspiration to the global community when we are faced with the pandemics to come.

PART IV

Our Future

The UN and the World Move Forward

Chapter Twenty-One

ACCOUNTABILITY

No Justice, No Peace

Accountability is vital across the board and around the world, not only in building peace but in repairing ruptured relationships. To heal from a culture of repression, violence, and human rights abuses, society must begin by addressing the vast emotional and physical wounds. The pain, loss, humiliation, and fear must be acknowledged and atoned for if there is ever to be a genuine peace. As we have seen, people who cannot get past this history are likely to repeat it.

Relations between nations are no different. A commitment to justice is ingrained in Korean culture, and it is very important to me. When the Korean government was established in 1948, it created a special committee to try "Chinilpas," the Koreans accused of collaborating with the Japanese during the colonial period, but few traitors were punished. In 2003, newly elected President Roh Moo-hyun established a presidential committee to investigate pro-Japanese actions before and during the Japanese colonial era. Many Koreans said that this wasn't necessary after six decades, but the government wanted to show the people that justice will prevail. As a diplomat and later as secretary-general, I took considerable inspiration from my home country's approach to accountability and reconciliation.

There are many ways to achieve reconciliation, including public acknowledgment of wrongdoing or even prosecutions in the International Criminal Court. I am disappointed that so many governments and people are growing less trusting of justice and more resistant to accountability. The path to an enduring peace is long and rocky, but in my experience, lasting peace rests on a foundation of accountability.

SPECIAL TRIBUNAL FOR LEBANON

On February 14, 2005, a 2,200-pound truck bomb detonated beside the motorcade carrying Lebanese Prime Minister Rafik Hariri—a blast so powerful that it left a meteor-sized crater in Beirut's seaside Corniche promenade. The explosion injured 231 people and killed twenty-one in addition to Prime Minister Hariri, a Sunni construction magnate who vigorously opposed Syria's destabilizing influence. He was determined to end Syria's support of Hezbollah, the Shia political party and its vast military organization. His assassination marked a dangerous reset in the tortured relationship between Lebanon and its dominating neighbor to the north, Syria.

I was the Korean foreign minister at the time and was shocked by the audacity and the magnitude of the attack. The carnage was breathtaking during peacetime. I could barely take my eyes off the shooting flames news networks looped over and over. No one doubted that this was the work of Damascus. The attack quickly ignited a widespread and vigorous rejection of Syria's thirty-year interference in Lebanese affairs. The Cedar Revolution predated the Arab Spring by nearly five years, but it set the template for what was to follow. Hundreds of thousands of people were drawn into the streets in a spontaneous demonstrations in the capital that demanded political transformation. Unlike so many of the protests that followed, the Lebanese rebellion was successful. Syrian troops began withdrawing within weeks. Sunnis and Christians took to the streets, but most Shia Muslims lived in the southern half of the country and remained loyal to Damascus.

Hamstrung by the Shia-Sunni hostilities, the Lebanese government was unable to undertake its own investigation of the bombing. After a year of deadlock, Beirut and its patron France asked the UN Security Council to create an international court to try the suspects under Lebanese law. French President Jacques Chirac—possibly motivated by his long friendship with Prime Minister Hariri—was a passionate proponent and pressed the Security Council to create the Special Tribunal for Lebanon (STL) in May 2007;[1] it was my first major initiative as secretary-general. This case inspired me to focus on justice and accountability throughout my tenure.

I appointed Serge Brammertz, a Belgian federal prosecutor, as prosecutor of the STL. Damascus strenuously opposed the UN Special Tribunal for

Lebanon, and its obstruction rendered the international court useless. Not one relatively low-level defendant ever sat in the dock. The court returned only one guilty verdict after fifteen years of operation, and found no evidence tying Hezbollah's leadership or the Syrian government to the bomb.

The cost: almost $1 billion. Although justice often requires significant and sustained support, this unconscionably high expense was borne by some two dozen member states and the people of Lebanon, who split the budget 51:49. The court sat empty for years, and most of its budget went to salaries. I was furious that this much money was being syphoned from development and other budgets that could have been spent improving lives in Lebanon and dozens of other countries. As secretary-general, I did not put my emotion on the record; instead my office released status reports twice each year with dishearteningly little information. Often the only fact that needed to be updated was the amount of money spent. Contributions to the STL were voluntary, and I hated collecting money each year from Beirut, a country that could not easily afford this gold-plated justice, especially after the disastrous 2006 war between Hezbollah and Israel.

Lebanon was my first major undertaking to promote accountability and justice, and its proceedings outlasted my tenure by four years. The judicial process was the best we could have possibly created, but without Syrian cooperation the STL was a disappointment for human rights advocates, Middle East experts, and the Lebanese people.

COTE D'IVOIRE: FROM DICTATOR TO DEFENDANT

When I began my term in 2007, I wanted to visit Côte d'Ivoire, which had been ruled by President Laurent Gbagbo since he won a junta-backed and violence-plagued election in 2000. Gbagbo's eleven-year presidency was marked by factional battles, corruption, and crushing poverty, causing domestic tensions to rise as quickly as his critics' demands for him to step down.

I knew this would require a strong hand, and I needed a skilled diplomat to handle this volatile situation. I decided to replace Secretary-General Kofi Annan's Special Representative to Cote d'Ivoire, Swedish diplomat Pierre Schori, with my own choice, Choi Young-jin, a very able Korean diplomat who worked for me as vice foreign minister and later as ambassador to the UN. President Gbagbo objected and asked me to appoint an African on whom he could have more influence. I persisted and asked President Blaise Compaore of Burkina Faso, Economic Community of West African States' mediator for Cote d'Ivoire, to exercise his influence. President Gbagbo finally relented under Compaore's persuasion and agreed to my choice when we spoke during the General Assembly in September 2007. Although the special representative speaks for me alone, there is no point in designating an envoy that the government will not accept.

France, the former colonial power of the country, still had close ties to Côte d'Ivoire and was particularly concerned. President Nicolas Sarkozy was adamant that I not pay an official visit, saying this would "legitimize" Gbagbo's regime. "Mr. Secretary-General, why do you want to visit Côte d'Ivoire? President Gbagbo is a liar."

"*Il est un menteur*" (He is a liar), I agreed. I added that I wanted to speak with the president in straight and direct language about the need to hold credible elections. I flew to Abidjan on April 23, 2008, with the hope of moving the political process forward, and President Gbagbo met with me immediately. "Mr. President, you have been in power for a long time and you have made economic and political stability," I told him. "Why don't you hold an election to legitimize your presidency?" I was delighted when President Gbagbo, a union activist, later agreed.

This was my first visit to Côte d'Ivoire, a relatively small country with a long Atlantic Ocean coastline and the world's largest cocoa exports. The United Nations Operation in Côte d'Ivoire (UNOCI) had maintained a significant presence in the country since the 2002–2007 civil war with a cluster of development programs and a compact peacekeeping mission. France, the former colonial power, supplemented our 9,600 Blue Helmets with a separate command, *Opération Licorne*, comprised of more than a thousand troops plus heavy weapons, logistical experts, and air power.

In Abidjan, I held a meeting with scores of small political parties whose leaders pledged to engage in a fair election. President Gbagbo made the same vow to me as rival candidates and the media looked on. He was fully confident of his victory, but we all knew the real challenger was Alassane Ouattara, a former International Monetary Fund economist who had served as prime minister in the early 1990s.

On October 31, 2010, Ivoirians voted for their president for the first time in a decade. It was a deeply divisive two-round election in which Gbagbo received the most votes in the first round but fell short of the simple majority required to win outright. Ouattara won the November 28 runoff with 54 percent to 46 percent, according to the independent Ivorian Electoral Commission. The African Union, the UN, the United States, and the EU accepted these results, but President Gbagbo did not. Instead, he brought his case to Côte d'Ivoire's Constitutional Court, whose members—all appointed by Gbagbo—declared him the winner.

Certifying a winner became an extraordinarily delicate process involving several branches of the government and judiciary as well as the UN and the African Union. Special Representative Choi recommended that I endorse the decision by the Ivoirian Electoral Commission and confirm Ouattara the winner. I did, and it was one of the most dramatic and critical decisions I had ever made.

President Gbagbo continued to claim victory and refused to leave the Presidential Palace. This was simply untenable. I publicly urged the president to accept the election results, and he demanded that the Blue Helmets leave his country. He refused and I refused, and the standoff created a tense confrontation between the UN and the Ivorian government. In late March, as the conflict entered a new, more deadly phase and UNOCI facilities were targeted, I stressed that the United Nations was not a party to the conflict but there only to stem hostilities. The Security Council reiterated its condemnation of hostilities on March 30, 2011.[2]

None of this curbed the violence against us. In fact, Gbagbo's soldiers seemed to target UN staff now. Government forces began attacking our civilians and shelling peacekeepers' positions, escalating the barrages into mid-April. Gbagbo's forces initiated a sustained attack on UNOCI's Sebroko Hotel headquarters, firing high-caliber mortars and rocket-propelled grenades from its Gallieni barracks, a large military installation atop a nearby hill. The projectiles became so numerous that scores of peacekeepers, Special Representative Choi, and the whole civilian staff donned helmets and took shelter in an underground bunker, eating biscuits and drinking rationed water for ten days. Four peacekeepers were injured, but it could have been much worse.

Most of the peacekeepers were scattered in other parts of the country, and the contingent in the capital was unable to hold its own against an army of fifty thousand troops. In addition, Special Forces of the UNOCI had to rescue diplomats from China, Japan, Korea, and other countries. This stretched our capacities even thinner and made a very dangerous situation even riskier.

Government soldiers and Ouattara's army took to the streets, and inevitably it was the general population that paid the heaviest price. By the end of the sixteen-week civil war, three thousand Ivoirians had lost their lives and nearly one million had lost their homes. I watched with horror from New

York as both sides battled to solidify their power: Sexual violence, abductions, executions, and torture roiled towns and neighborhoods for four months. I sternly urged President Gbagbo to accept his loss and called on both leaders to end the fighting for the sake of their country and the people they both wanted to lead. These appeals for calm were amplified by the Security Council, the Human Rights Council, and other UN bodies as well as world capitals.

Finally, I called Paris. "Mr. President," I said on April 3, "can you mobilize some air support?" Sarkozy quickly agreed, and French pilots took to the air even before I could send an official written request for military assistance to neutralize the heavy weapons deployed against UNOCI and the Ivoirian people. It was no secret that Paris favored the Francophile Ouattara; while mayor of Neuilly-Sur-Seine, Sarkozy had officiated at Ouattara's 1990 wedding. I was uneasy that UNOCI's more robust rules of engagement appeared to advance France's political agenda. Indeed Moscow immediately announced it would look into the legitimacy of the UN's use of force.[3]

"He has to be mindful of the well-being, safety, and prosperity of his people," I told reporters on April 7, 2011. "This is Gbagbo's last opportunity to gracefully exit." But government forces continued to shell our position. On April 10, UNOCI, the French Licorne helicopter unit, and Ouattara's ground forces surrounded Gbagbo's residence and other sites in Abidjan under his control. Days later the former president and his wife were found in a bunker below their home and immediately arrested. I gave firm instructions to the UN commander that Gbagbo should be arrested solely by Ivoirians, not UN peacekeepers, to avoid any unnecessary political or legal problems.

President Sarkozy was enthusiastic about the handover to Ouattara and insisted that we go together to the May 21, 2011, inauguration ceremony. "Mr. Secretary-General, you and I worked for this and we must go," he insisted. I usually turn down these requests. If I attended the swearing-in ceremonies of 192 nations, I would rarely be in New York! But Côte d'Ivoire was special to me because of the role the UN played in the fair elections and, later, in halting the violence. The ceremony was opulent and attended by more than two dozen African leaders. They had come to show solidarity with the new president and to celebrate Côte d'Ivoire's emergence from political chaos and civil war. As I looked around the room, I hoped that none of them would hold onto power as tenaciously as Gbagbo had if their own time came to an end.

President Ouattara spoke about healing, peace, and the importance of development to the future of Côte d'Ivoire. He also promised to transfer Gbagbo to the International Criminal Court, where he had been indicted on four counts of crimes against humanity.[4] This was a message the continent needed to hear, but African leaders had unexpectedly begun to reject the ICC, saying that the court disproportionately targeted African leaders and failed to respect their sovereignty. It is true that by May 2011 nearly all of the Court's formal investigations concerned African situations. But I was frustrated that so many African leaders worked to discredit the ICC. It was easy for some leaders to dismiss it as a "Western" invention. Worse, several of these governments were engaging in the kind of abuses the court was created to punish. This buttressed the decisions of many governments not to cooperate with the international tribunal, making prosecutions close to impossible by preventing witnesses from testifying and investigators from gathering evidence. Despite my intense lobbying, in 2017 the African Union passed a nonbinding resolution calling on African states to withdraw from the ICC. I wish they could see that poisoning the name of the ICC and undermining justice will not benefit Africans now or in the future.

I wondered how many of the African leaders were particularly preoccupied with Gbagbo's fate. More than a few of these men had seized power by force, and others held onto power through sham elections and violence. Were any of them worried that they would be turned over to international justice? Were they thinking about how they would answer to gruesome allegations? The room held a fair number of autocrats. I wondered how many of them assumed that they could end their days in the peace of exile and immunity.

On January 15, 2019, I was startled to learn that the International Criminal Court had acquitted Gbagbo of crimes against humanity, a remarkable loss for one of its highest-profile prosecutions. I trusted the ICC procedures, but in this case justice was a bitter disappointment. A guilty verdict and a jail sentence would have shown the cocoa farmers, parliamentarians, and world leaders that the rule of law is one of the strongest anchors of a stable society.

RWANDA'S LEVERAGE

What is the right balance between peace and justice in the quest for accountability? This is an important question for any country emerging from conflict.

The United Nations' three pillars—peace, human rights, and development—are interlocking, overlapping, and co-equal. Equal progress may not be possible on all three simultaneously, but they must remain interlinked or our guiding principles will be lost.

I wanted to discuss with my senior staff the relationship between accountability and justice, and their unique roles in postconflict societies. It was early September 2010, and I had been preparing my response to a particularly delicate report from Navi Pillay, high commissioner for human rights, on her examination of hundreds of atrocities committed in Congo (then Zaire) between 1993 and 2003. The five-hundred-fifty-page Democratic Republic of Congo mapping report contains a detailed accounting of the systematic attacks against ethnic Hutus that resulted in the massacre of tens of thousands. Although the report also implicated Angola, Burundi, Congo, and Uganda, it found Rwanda's actions "could be characterized as crimes of genocide."[5]

The mapping report was so controversial that the French draft was leaked to the media by a senior human rights official to ensure that the language was not softened under international pressure. The government of Rwanda threatened to withdraw its four battalions from the UN-African Union Mission in Darfur (UNAMID) in retaliation if the report was published. But I was also embarrassed and angry by this intentional leak. I flew straight to Rwanda to meet personally with President Paul Kagame. On my way to Kigali, I had to transit through Brussels, and Belgian Foreign Minister Steven Vanackere met me at the airport. Rwanda is a former Belgian colony, and the two countries still share a close relationship. Brussels was seriously concerned about the repercussions of the mapping report, and Minister Vanackere expressed strong support for my diplomatic initiative.

I arrived in Kigali in the evening on September 7, 2010, and was received by Foreign Minister Louise Mushikiwabo, who hosted a working dinner that adjourned at midnight. Rwandan Justice Minister Tharcisse Karugarama and Presidential Defense and Security Advisor Brigadier-General Richard Rutatina were also there. I was accompanied by Alain Le Roy, head of the UN Department for Peacekeeping Operations, Assistant Secretary General for Human Rights Ivan Šimonović, and Deputy Chief of Staff Kim Won-soo.

The three-hour dinner was very tense. The Rwandan foreign and justice ministers argued that the mapping report was "flawed" and tantamount to "double genocide," meaning that Rwandan Tutsis committed war crimes of about the same scale as the Hutus did in 1994. The Tutsis, they argued, were the victims, and their response was not illegal. The ministers showed their anger during the dinner. As I expected, they repeated their government's threat to withdraw peacekeepers from Darfur if the mapping exercise was released. This was terrible, and it was not only the numbers that mattered. Rwandan troops are among our most reliable, and pulling 3,300 from a ten-thousand-person force meant that the Rwandan mission would collapse.

I calmly explained the UN positions. The mapping report was never intended to accuse Rwanda of "double genocide." If Kigali thought the report was "illegal and flawed," it should submit its own position to the UN, and it would be added to the report and released simultaneously. Pulling the troops from UNAMID would have seriously dangerous implications for Darfur and, implicitly, for neighboring countries. It would also negatively affect Rwanda's international reputation; member states would view this as a retaliatory measure motivated by short-term political considerations. I had a two-hour meeting with President Paul Kagame the next morning, and I used the same points to make my case. "If you withdraw Rwandan peacekeepers, you will cripple UNAMID," I told him. After a long and tense but mutually respectful conversation, President Kagame agreed to honor his peacekeeping commitment. I felt a sigh of relief that this crisis was over.

President Kagame and I had worked together since 2005 when I was still foreign minister. It is unusual for a president to receive a foreign minister at night in his residence, but he had a special affinity for Korea and had studied our economic and social development program, the New Community Movement. President Park Chung-hee introduced the initiative in 1969, and it was remarkably successful. President Kagame, who was rebuilding his country after the 1994 genocide, had studied the program on his own and had instructed his ministers to apply what the Korean government had practiced. "I am doing what your people have done," he said. I was touched by his trust in and respect for Korea.

Our relationship deepened after I became secretary-general. President Kagame invited me to attend a cabinet meeting where I encouraged the officials to enact social and economic initiatives. Today Rwanda and Korea are among the few nations that have connected the whole country to the internet. In fact, I was touched to learn that several African countries (Ethiopia and Uganda) were following the Korean campaigns.

This relationship was especially important two years later, when Spanish judge Fernando Andreu Merelles issued an arrest warrant for Rwandan Lieutenant General Emmanuel Karenzi Karake, alleging crimes against humanity in connection with his orders of political assassinations and massacres after the Tutsi genocide. At this time, Spanish law recognized its universal jurisdiction to pursue human rights cases around the world. To our embarrassment, at the time General Karake was the deputy force commander for UNAMID. I tried to relieve him of his post immediately, but President Kagame insisted I keep him or replace him with another Rwandan general. I reluctantly extended Gen. Karake's service by several months, until April 2010, when he made a scheduled graceful exit. It was a difficult decision, but the Rwanda contingent stayed put.

The secretary-general doesn't have the luxury of focusing on a single problem but must balance many related issues. Leaking the mapping report set a big fire, and I had to put out the fire because it would have burned down the Darfur mission, and we could not jeopardize its fragile security. Diplomacy helped maintain the peace in that troubled region, and my personal relationship with President Kagame helped both of us reach an agreement under which justice would prevail. People must trust that even when justice is delayed it will surely prevail.

President Kagame came to New York in September for the 2010 General Assembly Debate. Some of my senior advisors counseled me not to meet him again, but I insisted because I wanted to make sure he would not change his mind about withdrawing troops from Darfur. The Rwandan leader was still bitterly angry about the mapping report. From the General Assembly podium, he accused the United Nations of operating a double standard and, implicitly, criticized the hypocrisy of many Western states. "It has become clear that the UN has evolved into a two-tiered organization, reflecting a world that seems to be divided into two categories: one with inherent laudable values, rights, and liberties, and another that needs to be taught and coached on these values."

I reject this view. Some leaders are not yet committed to the principles of justice and accountability, but many have made this commitment, and many more may still. As I have publicly stated, justice will prevail, if not today, then surely tomorrow.

Chapter Twenty-Two

UN REFORM

Making Room for the Future

I was alone in my peaceful study in our Seoul apartment in 2006 when the enormity of my election as secretary-general hit me hard. The United Nations needed to be modernized, but even after months of study and campaigning, I hadn't registered how ambitious that undertaking would be. Every system from the subbasement printing press to the General Assembly's leaking roof needed to be repaired or updated. There was asbestos in the Secretariat and corruption in at least one country office. Global field operations from humanitarian relief in the Asia-Pacific to peacekeeping missions in Central Africa were inefficient, and our environmental footprint was shameful. The UN's problems were financial, physical, political, and environmental.

I felt a shiver of apprehension at having to address a learning curve that was nearly vertical. Was there another world leader anywhere whose mandate was so broad? The secretary-general takes responsibility for every far-flung crisis, manages a multibillion dollar budget, negotiates contracts, renovates the Secretariat building, improves interdepartmental cooperation between scores of duty stations, raises funds, helps run more than a dozen concurrent military missions, represents the organization at thousands of meetings and dozens of receptions and luncheons, monitors complex humanitarian disaster relief, and understands the ecological implications of high asbestos loads and low-flow flush toilets.

In 2007, as demands on the organization increased, the United Nation's \$3.9 billion core budget was creeping upward, and there seemed to be nothing left to cut. Yet, I thought, the New York City Police Department budget was nearly three times larger. Waste needed to be addressed. The Security Council's authority had been undermined, probably permanently, by its sixty-year-old power dynamic. Peacekeepers were increasingly resented by the people they were deployed to protect. Campaigning for the secretary-general's office over the previous year, I had firm ideas about reforms in the United Nations. Now, I realized, *overhaul* would be a better word.

I pored over confidential reports, briefing books, internal assessments, and other material dominating a corner of the room. Every page felt like a new priority! My stomach lurched to think of all the legal, political, and financial disasters the United Nations had somehow managed to avoid. That combination of global goodwill and a tablespoon of luck, I decided, was nothing we could count on forever. "If the United Nations were a business," I used to tell UN staff, "it would have gone bankrupt fifty years ago." I didn't know where to start.

But I did know how the organization worked, a legacy of my year as chief of staff to Han Seung-soo, president of the General Assembly from September 2001 to September 2002. And I knew which nations were influential on particular issues. During my sixteen-month campaign for secretary-general, I also figured out which ambassadors got things done. Yes, I could do this.

UPENDING "BUSINESS AS USUAL"

I had already begun plotting the most sweeping reform effort in the history of the organization. Previous agendas had addressed the symptoms, not the causes, of our present situation. We needed to muster our institutional, financial, intellectual, and human resources and be willing to shake them up. It was a daunting task, especially because many of the innovations were interlocking and had to be made simultaneously. These efforts were frequently compared to painting a battleship on the high seas.

Above all, we had to delink UN reform from the blunt demand by the United States to cut the UN budget. The host country, the largest contributor, and the loudest critic demanded *reform*. Reform had become a one-word referendum on whether the UN still deserved taxpayers' dollars, or even whether the United States should remain a member. The R-word could still make member states defensive or angry, and some even obstructed cost-cutting measures in protest.

I knew the issue was far more subtle than cutting our operating budget by an arbitrary amount. We needed to do a lot more with the staff and resources we already had, and we had to do it better. It was time for a top-to-bottom assessment. "We reform not to please others but because we value what the organization stands for," I said, accepting a second term in June 2011. "We reform because we believe in its future."

When I took office on January 1, 2007, the organization was still reeling from the oil-for-food scandal. Many Western countries, but chiefly the United States, complained that the UN office overseeing Iraqi oil sales had allowed Saddam's cronies to skim billions of dollars meant to be spent on relief for Iraqi families impoverished by mandated Security Council sanctions.

In 2004, Kofi Annan persuaded Paul Volker, the respected former chairman of the U.S. Federal Reserve, to head a commission looking into the hydra-headed scandal. I respected his appointment. Volker, a legend in U.S. economic circles, would run a thorough and impartial inquiry. The investigation lasted more than a year and produced a hefty five-volume report filled with a detailed accounting of Iraq's oil income and expenditures, contracts awarded to favored businesses, and even the grocery list for the regime's illicit spending sprees. Few escaped unscathed, most for making questionable decisions or because they didn't know about irregularities but should have. The episode reminded critics why they didn't trust the United Nations and rattled supporters who didn't understand how the Secretariat, Security Council, and the office overseeing the Iraq sanctions could have missed so many signs of impropriety or mismanagement. As the scandal unfolded in the early 2000s, I watched from Korea, dismayed to see how badly the United Nations had failed.

TRANSPARENCY, ACCOUNTABILITY, AND EFFICIENCY

I knew from experience that the first step in reforming the United Nations was building a culture of transparency and fairness. I was driven to make the UN an organization that earned the trust of its staff, member states, partners, and the public. The United Nations must once again be seen by the world's people and their governments as a positive force, an organization that improves lives and enforces peace. That confidence is important for our staff members' safety in the field, and it also enhanced our stature and reassured member states.

One of my first acts as secretary-general was to ask all senior UN officials—roughly 250 people above the rank of under secretaries general and assistant secretaries general—to submit financial disclosure forms, which would be made public. I led by example, telling reporters on December 14, 2006—two weeks before I assumed office—that I would declare my own financial assets. Five weeks later, I did.[1] One Confucian teaching was especially relevant for me: "To put the world in order, we must first put the nation in order; to put the nation in order, we must first put the family in order; to put the family in order, we must first cultivate our personal life; we must first set our hearts right."

Financial disclosure faced a lot of resistance at the UN, including from some people in my office. There were many reasons for this. One UN official wouldn't make his holdings public because of a pending divorce. Another feared that his distant relatives would ask for money if they saw that he had some. And a female official said she would happily disclose her holdings to the Secretariat but could not allow them to be published because women are not supposed to inherit property in her country. A Dutch man dying of cancer wanted to be exempted. I looked at these requests individually and did grant a few exceptions. Finally, I was able to convince nearly all senior staff to submit their financial declarations, but most remained confidential.

The United Nations would be nothing without a committed and motivated staff. But the organization wasn't easy to get into and could be deeply unfair to individual employees. While studying the organization's administration and management, I was astounded to discover no less than eleven job classifications, creating a system in which two employees would receive different compensation for the same work. It was complex to administer and demoralizing all around. It took years for my management team to reorganize positions into only three types of contracts and to harmonized pay as best we could. In the annals of UN reform, that was a huge victory.

I also emphasized mobility, which I believed was crucial to the health of this or any organization. So many staffers, particularly at headquarters buildings, had been doing the same work for ten or even twenty years. Some had grown sluggish, failing to bring fresh ideas to their work. Many needed stimulation, and I thought going into the field would energize them. On the flipside, we were losing excellent staff members because the existing system marooned them in hardship duty stations. These were devoted employees who had earned the opportunity to move to a headquarters building, to walk about freely and enjoy their surroundings. When asked, many complained that they wanted to live with their families and plant their roots. As I expected, the mobility initiative was more popular in the field than at headquarters. Few volunteered to leave Manhattan, Geneva, or Vienna, and we were never able to rotate enough staff to see the payoff I knew was possible. Member states, too, were wary of the project. Some countries thought of their citizens at headquarters as a source of national pride or even a potential conduit of inside information. They did not want to lose this advantage.

I recall with frustration the many meetings I logged with UN ambassadors and staff unions around the world. There was little support for this measure at first because they were reluctant to share their privileges. One day at a meeting with all the UN ambassadors I appealed to them, "You are here as part of your government's rotation systems. Nobody is expected to serve in one duty station permanently. I want all the UN staff to have a fair and equitable opportunity and to learn from different experiences. If a staff member stays too long in one station, it not only deprives opportunities for other staff but allows people to become complacent in their work."

It took seven years to overcome the truculent staff unions and various other interests and get a resolution from the General Assembly endorsing mobility.[2] I don't know how much weight that resolution would have had if passed earlier in my tenure, but at that late date it did little to change the system. As soon as I left the United Nations, my successor, António Guterres, decided not to implement it. Many staff members must have worked hard to persuade the new secretary-general that a personnel upheaval was not in the organization's best interests. Most foreign ministries rotate staff and so should the United Nations.

To improve fairness, in July 2009 my administration established a new avenue for staff members with complaints against the organization or its management. I, as secretary-general, was the defendant in every case that came before the UN Dispute Tribunal and the UN Appeals Tribunal. It was necessary to create an internal justice system, in part because the United Nations has a unique international status and cannot be sued in national courts. I worked with the legal department to strengthen whistleblower protections and to provide a mechanism to discipline any staff members who violated their contracts or their trust.

The UN was not nearly as efficient as it should be; it was losing millions to overlapping responsibilities, fragmented procurement, and duplicative record-keeping. Despite its reputation, the UN system wasn't so much bloated as disorganized. As I studied UN meetings and briefing papers before I took up my responsibilities, I knew we needed to integrate a dozen systems that were shockingly out of date. The redundant efforts and last-minute fixes were costing the organization millions of dollars.

In 2008, staff worked with a contractor to develop the Umoja project to streamline our operations from accounting to inventory. Named for the Swahili word for unity, the system was developed to automate payroll and purchasing, budgeting, travel and other expenses, and improved coordination between thirty thousand staff in hundreds of duty stations. When deployed in November 2015, we thought Umoja would make the global organization more modern, flexible, and efficient. And I still believe it will. Unfortunately, we rolled out the $400 million program before adequately training employees, which resulted in delays and widespread frustration among UN staff. Difficult to use and prone to glitches, many found the system confusing and did not trust it. I did everything I could to build support.

PERMANENT POWER

Of all the inconsistencies and frustrations in the UN system, I think the inability to modernize Security Council membership has been the most damaging. The UN member states elect ten representatives to the council, but they are not equal to the five permanent members. The United States, the United Kingdom, France, Russia, and China (the P5) make most decisions among themselves because each can veto any council position for any reason. This unchecked power has so undermined the Security Council's credibility that rogue nations routinely shrug off its criticism as illegitimate.

There are two problems here, and neither is going away on its own. First, it is egregious when a government vetoes a resolution because of domestic or strategic considerations rather than because of its effect on international peace and security. Some countries have been given free rein to violate international law, and dictators with an ally in the P5 have been allowed to violate human rights. Was there any acceptable reason for China and Russia to veto council measures in the early days of the Syrian conflict? Both were backing Syrian President al-Assad in a brutal proxy war against the West.

The second problem is that the P5 reflects the global power structure from 1945, not today's. Scores of nations point out that the Arab, Latin, and African nations still do not have a permanent seat, a void that diminishes their contribution to the organization. This is unlikely to change—ever. The entire P5 has to agree, first, whether to expand their club and, second, which countries should be added. The five nations ruling the horseshoe table will always veto a proposal that dilutes their power. The remaining nations, meanwhile, will ultimately have to choose which nations will represent their regions.

Brokering a compromise between the P5 and the rest of the UN membership would be a lasting legacy, I thought, but I knew that wasn't going to change during my tenure. Despite my frequent criticism, the UN Charter does not give the secretary-general power in this matter.

THE MOST TRAGIC LESSON

The United Nations has always been active in tumultuous environments. Those who work with refugees, emergency relief, or peace operations, for example, are on the frontline in every type of humanitarian emergency. This life can be dangerous, dirty, stressful, exhausting, exhilarating, and rewarding—sometimes all at once. Today the blue and white UN flag is more of a target than a shield. We should have learned this in Baghdad when Islamic terrorists detonated a truck bomb on the access road right next to our headquarters on the outskirts of the capital on August 19, 2003. Twenty-two people were killed in the Canal Hotel bombing, including UN Special Representative for Iraq Sérgio Vieira de Mello, a battle-tested Brazilian diplomat and a hero of the humanitarian community.

Special Representative Vieira de Mello made a crucial decision to refuse the Coalitional Provisional Authority's offer to protect the compound, believing it would shatter our neutrality and prevent many Iraqis from visiting the office. It was a tragic mistake by the veteran of a dozen duty postings in a stellar thirty-four-year career. His death was a significant loss for the United Nations and for the Iraqi people. The entire organization was plunged into grief by what was to that point the deadliest assault in the UN's history. I admired Vieira de Mello and was shocked and sickened by the attack.

Secretary-General Kofi Annan soon reorganized the UN security department, but the measures did not overcome its structural weaknesses. The United Nations was attacked again on December 11, 2007, one year into my term. A suicide bomber aligned with Al Qaida in the Maghreb slammed a truck bomb into the UN office in Algiers, killing seventeen civilian staff, including fourteen Algerians. It was a despicable attack. The explosion was so strong that it almost leveled the UN refugee office across the street and killed twenty-seven Algerians who lived nearby. At least one hundred injuries were reported.

I was in Bali for the annual international conference on climate change and learned about the bombing only minutes ahead of the media. I was so shaken by the news that I could barely remember to condemn the attack and praise our colleagues for their brave work. My voice was low, and I heard my words shake as I told the journalists we had no details yet. "Were any UN staff killed?" a reporter asked gently.

"I have received that information," I said. I was in shock, but even as my head cleared, words could not express my outrage at the cowardly attack on the men and women who chose to serve the people of Algeria. It was a gruesome wake-up call to the UN to take security even more seriously. I was furious when I learned that the head of security in Algiers, Babacar Ndiaye of Senegal, had repeatedly warned our Department of Safety and Security about the high probability of an attack. Inexplicably, officials did not respond to his suggestions to fortify the building or to exfiltrate our foreign nationals. I was certain that better security could have lessened the impact of the explosion or even prevented the bombing. We had let this happen.

I quickly flew to the Algerian capital and drove directly to the site. My stomach lurched at the destruction and my eyes were wet. I walked over a field of broken concrete and stepped over twisted iron. The scene was awful; blackened, caved-in walls revealed furniture and personal possessions. The bodies had been removed, but bits of clothing, broken objects, and papers were strewn throughout the debris. The damage was unbearable. The memorial service took place on an overcast day near our splintered offices. I delivered brief remarks but could barely hold back my tears. I was so overwhelmed at a gathering with the survivors that I could barely talk. Instead I hugged victims and their families.

My meeting with Algerian President Abdelaziz Bouteflika was strained. I had already made it clear that I would raise the threat level the UN assigned to the Algerian office. But the president resisted, noting that businesses and tourists stay away from countries that are not considered safe. He was very demanding and expected me to give him this point because he was an early and active supporter of my election bid. But after seeing the scale of the attack, I knew I had to protect my staff first. I flew home for the first time—but not the last—holding a tattered UN flag in my hands.

Other attacks on UN staff during my tenure have triggered grief and anger that never goes away. On August 28, 2009, three gunmen in police uniforms stormed the staff residence in Kabul. We had kept a very low profile, living in several guesthouses in a quiet Kabul neighborhood. UN security guards, nearly all Afghan, suffered losses as they tried to fight off the incursion. We quickly learned that an elite Afghan security unit responded to our call for help but returned to base when they realized our building was not the home of President Karzai's brother. Five international UN staff and three Afghans were killed in that assault, which felt like a direct attack on the United Nations. It was also a rejection of collective aid and international assistance for this severely underdeveloped country. I felt horrified, grief-stricken, angry, and defiant. The Taliban claimed responsibility; it was yet another slaughter in their campaign to rule or ruin this shattered country.

I flew to Kabul and demanded that President Karzai reinforce UN security or I would withdraw our staff. He assured me that there would be no further problems. I remained concerned but recognized how deeply the country needed UN support and agreed to stay. Sometimes we ordered nonessential staff to take holidays during elections and on other symbolic days. We also moved many international staff to better-fortified quarters.

On August 26, 2011, the Islamic militant group Boko Haram drove an explosives-filled sedan past two checkpoints and crashed into the lobby of our headquarters in Nigeria, killing eighteen civilian staff members. The group had been waging a struggle against Jonathan's government, and we were merely collateral damage, attacked to prove that even foreigners were not safe.

Attacks on peacekeepers have escalated over the past decade, rendering their operations less feasible for financial and troop contributing countries and diminishing the respect and support of local populations. When political missions are undermined, they become less respected, less effective. Today aid workers are increasingly being targeted by both militants and governments as a symbol of international meddling.

MAKING THE ELEPHANT MORE NIMBLE

My study of the Department of Peacekeeping Operations (DPKO) while preparing to assume my post as secretary-general left me with the impression that the department was lumbering like an elephant. The undersecretary general for peacekeeping operations was overseeing everything: military strategy and planning, administrative duties, information technology, logistics, personnel management, and everything else that keeps a mission running. All these necessary functions were taking time away from consulting with commanders in the field and senior staff at headquarters. Clearly the department should be concerned with carrying out peace operations, not keeping track of jet fuel or paychecks. The solution came to me almost as quickly as the size of the problem. I would split peacekeeping in two: DPKO would oversee all military affairs, and a new Department of Field Support would handle all the logistical and back-office functions.

The numbers were compelling. Between peace operations and the largely civilian UN special political missions, the UN maintained 245 duty stations in thirty countries. Roughly 150,000 civilian and military personnel were serviced by two hundred aircraft, fourteen thousand vehicles, and three hundred medical facilities. They consumed ten million liters of water and one million liters of fuel every day. In all, the missions accounted for 85 percent of the entire UN procurement process and half of its CO_2 emissions.

I am not a military expert, although I volunteered for military service in my early twenties and later served as national security advisor to Korean President Kim Young-sam. But the armed forces did shape my ideas, and I approached these problems with a military, not a civilian, perspective.

The Department of Field Support (now Operational Support) was created to oversee personnel, budget and finance, logistics, and information technology—nearly all of which can be handled from New York or from a regional office rather than within the mission itself. The department ensures that peacekeeping missions are more resilient, which is especially important as so many duty postings are the very picture of hardship: austere regions either isolated or overpopulated by desperately displaced people. Sometimes the area is also home to people who may be hostile to the peacekeeping operations.

The resistance should not have surprised me, but it did. I shared my plan with Undersecretary General for Peacekeeping Jean-Marie Guéhenno, whom I thought would be enthusiastic about having so many nonmilitary tasks taken off his shoulders. He wasn't. I suspected a turf war, and I was right. French diplomats were the first to object to the new department, a particularly delicate negotiation because French nationals had run the peacekeeping department since 1997. Paris fiercely guards this position, and the United Nations complies because France historically contributed more troops to peacekeeping than the other permanent Security Council members. I told Foreign Minister Phillippe Douste-Blazy that hiving off the support functions did not undermine the head of peacekeeping but would in fact give military experts more time to do their jobs and reduce the possibility of important decisions falling through the cracks. The second department would actually streamline operations. Eventually he agreed.

The United States was on board from the beginning, as were the other countries that paid the bulk of peacekeeping expenses. But it was not easy to change the mindset of the people who had been accustomed to the existing system for decades. Indian Ambassador Nirupam Sen even criticized me publicly, telling a *New York Times* journalist, "the secretary-general is not the king and the member states are not the subjects of the king." Upon my complaint, Prime Minister Manmohan Singh later sent his senior advisor to apologize, and he recalled Ambassador Sen soon afterward.

I appointed my former chief of staff Susana Malcorra of Argentina to head the new department. She had trained as an electrical engineer and had served as chief operating officer for the World Food Programme. I trusted her completely, and I knew she would quickly get the new department on its feet. She was rational and diplomatic, and I counted on her to find creative strategies to change entrenched procedures and reduce our environmental impact.

GREENING THE BLUE

Our peace operations are most often set in fragile environments where water, pastureland, and other resources are so scarce that they may be the cause of the conflict itself. Mission impact is not a new problem. Every agency, fund, and program, and especially the DPKO, knows how big an environmental footprint we leave. When I began studying this issue, I was dismayed that so little had been done about it. No—I was shocked! A single UN peace operation can bring tens of thousands of people into a region that can't support the meager needs of those who already live there. It is morally indefensible to divert water, land, or food from the people we are trying to help. It is wrong to pollute their air with Co_2 from our planes, generators, and vehicles, and there is no excuse for draining waste into their fields or waterways.

It was clear that we needed to reassess our physical impact. We had already begun the conversion to cleaner generators, solar power, water filtration, closed incinerators, and waste disposal systems. Each innovation yielded concrete savings that encouraged the next. In East Timor, the mission saved $360,000 by analyzing how long our vehicles idled and improving traffic flow. In Haiti, peacekeepers shredded cardboard and paper into charcoal pellets that local people used for cooking fuel. In southern Lebanon, UNIFIL converted its fleet to electric cars and introduced recycling into nearby communities. We installed solar panels at nearly every mission.

RESTORING THE LANDMARK

I had been in office for five months when Donald Trump, then a New York City real estate developer, called and demanded to speak to me. I didn't know him personally, but I called him back. We were in the middle of a $1.8 billion, seven-year renovation of the Secretariat and General Assembly building, and he abruptly told me he wanted to take over the project. "I can do it for exactly half price," said the future president. "The Americans will like it because it will save them so much money. And I'll make it much nicer, just beautiful."

I explained that this was impossible. Secretary-General Annan spent more than two years negotiating the costs, logistics, and timeline with member states, who would be footing the bill. I told Trump "no" more than once, but he didn't hear me. "Let me do this for you!" he repeated. "Same time frame, same design, same materials, and much better construction."

"I don't have room to consider your proposal," I said with finality. "If the Americans want this, please have them contact me directly." We never spoke again.

I did have a connection to him, though. When I was chief of staff to the president of the General Assembly in 2001–2002, my wife and I rented a two-bedroom apartment on the sixteenth floor in the brand new Trump World apartment building. The entire neighborhood opposed the skyscraper, which cast a shadow over some very expensive residences nearby. The United Nations, of course, did not choose sides in the fight, which the citizens of Turtle Bay finally lost.

The Secretariat renovation was messy, dangerous, and logistically nearly impossible, but necessary. The building was hopelessly, dangerously outdated. The glass and marble facade, which resembles a gigantic green ice cube tray, was hemorrhaging heat in the winter and trapping sun in the summer, causing unconscionable energy use. Deferred maintenance had eroded parts of the structure. Private offices left too little space for the five thousand people who now worked there. The phone system was ancient, and we had to retrofit for internet connectivity. I was shocked to learn how much water our toilets wasted.

The Secretariat renovation would let us shatter-proof thirty-eight floors of glass curtain walls in case someone fired a mortar from across the East River (as happened after Che Guevara's speech to the General Assembly in December 1964) or ploughed a truck bomb through the First Avenue bollards meant to deter vehicles from driving into our building. The original plan called for construction to be carried out ten floors at a time, with the remaining twenty-nine floors occupied. I was concerned about exposure to so much asbestos and the possibility of accidents. The largest contractors assured me that the construction would not be harmful to those still working in the buildings during construction, but I was not convinced. I ultimately hired Michael Adlerstein, an architect who specialized in historic preservation, and he agreed that we should renovate the entire Secretariat in one pass, instead of by thirds. He had recently overseen the restoration of the Statue of Liberty, and I trusted him.

That decision meant renegotiating the payment schedule and time frame. That was the hard part but, after several rounds of negotiations, member states finally approved the plan. By renovating the building in one shift, we shortened the construction to five years from the original seven years without altering the schedule of payments. It took many, many meetings, but finally everyone supported my idea. The global recession of 2008–2009 created a surfeit of vacant office space in midtown Manhattan, so it was suddenly feasible to move five thousand staff members at one time.

The United Nations is legally international territory and exempt from landmarking. However, the architecture and interiors were considered valuable examples of midcentury modern architecture, designed by nearly a dozen international architects. American Wallace Harrison, the Rockefeller family's architect, led the design team, which included Swiss architect and painter le Corbusier, then near the height of his fame. The Nordic countries, which designed and built the organization's instantly recognizable assembly halls, paid for those renovations. Brazil, proud of architect Oscar Niemeyer's contribution, would not consider any alterations to the exterior and could likely persuade other Latin American nations to join them in opposition. Gentle restoration and heavy construction were undertaken with care. Nonetheless, I would have been tempted to tear the Secretariat down because a new building would better suit our purposes and be less expensive than the renovation.

Another important factor was the protection of "high value targets" such as the secretary-general and scores of world leaders who attend the annual General Assembly. The U.S. Secret Service refused to let us move into a commercial building because it would be impossible to guarantee our safety. Keeping us on campus was the only option. Member states agreed to build a block-long three-story temporary office building on the UN lawn along the East River. To prove to critics and ourselves that this extra office space really was only temporary, we chose the cheapest possible option, a prefabricated white box about the size of a Walmart. Of course, that's how everyone jokingly referred to it. My office was in a Walmart! It wasn't elegant; in fact, it didn't even have an elevator. Many breathless world leaders called the climb to my office "Ban's gym." I hadn't known at the time that quite a few people were wagering that the Walmart would become permanent. In fact, when the building was dismantled for scrap, the *New York Times* called the demolition "a marvel."[3]

I am proud that the renovation, which spanned half my time in office, emphasized environmental efficiencies. Repairs, replacements, and innovations, such as electricity that automatically shuts off in empty offices, have already brought the Secretariat's total energy costs down by 65 percent, reduced carbon emissions by 86 percent, and saved an astounding 80 percent on water. Using new technology and best practices, the Secretariat, a symbol of the United Nations, turned out to be more energy efficient and less expensive to maintain than we'd hoped.

I hope the delegates and UN staff enjoy working in the beautifully renovated building and appreciate its energy efficiency, connectivity, and comfort. The restoration sets an important global example, and I hope all real estate developers will notice.

Chapter Twenty-Three

MISSION POSSIBLE

It's Our World, Nourish It

I believe humanity has the power and motivation to save itself. Threats range from superbugs to superpowers to superstorms, but if we act quickly and together, we can get ahead of these challenges. The work is daunting, but our missions are achievable. A lifetime of diplomatic problem-solving has shown me a way forward, and I tried to share this vision every day I served as secretary-general: use less, care more, think long term, look beyond borders, build communities, foster empathy, work for peace.

I've been working on behalf of my country and my world for more than fifty years, and I hope this memoir will motivate and inspire others to work for peace. Our world is growing more polarized, militarized, and carbonized—this is an unsustainable trajectory. Our survival depends on a universal commitment from all of us to save the planet and ourselves. It won't be easy. We must act with urgency but practice patience because the road ahead is long. The necessary commitment will be different from one continent to the next, one country to the next, one culture and one community and one person to the next. One thing is sure: You have a moral responsibility to act wherever you are and however you define your place on this Earth. I call that global citizenship.

World leaders: Commit to prosecuting corruption, pursue peace, empower women, invest in young people, cooperate with other nations for effective collective action, ensure equitable development and inclusive human rights, establish laws and policies that serve all of your people, and stop fighting proxy wars.

Business executives: Commit to challenging graft and corruption, change your culture to value human rights, dramatically reduce your carbon emissions, remember that you are accountable to many more people beyond your shareholders, and join the UN Global Compact for responsible corporate citizenship.

Global citizens: Commit to raising your voices to demand change without violence, hold your leaders accountable, overcome grievances with compassion, unite for peace, and join with others to address the climate crisis.

We have the resources to provide food, education, medical care, and opportunity to all by fully implementing the UN's Sustainable Development Goals. The SDGs, designed to eradicate the most extreme poverty by 2030, are ambitious and audacious—but so are we. Although I am deeply troubled by the Covid-19 pandemic and sputtering economy, I believe we can work past these calamities to achieve better lives.

In my heart, I am still the boy who was saved by the United Nations, and I continue to repay this debt of gratitude by working to advance its mission for peace, development, and human rights. I remain focused on the SDGs, the Paris Climate Agreement, and the empowerment of women and young people because these are all engines of our prosperity and peace.

I have noticed a profound and encouraging shift in global attitudes since 2007. Many more people, particularly the young, are taking responsibility and fighting for global good. Forceful and eloquent, Malala Yousafzai and Greta Thunberg are motivating us to build a better world, one that values education and confronts the climate crisis. I am overjoyed that these young women are claiming their place in the conversation and providing such powerful role models. The youth-driven response to the climate crisis is the most powerful movement I have ever witnessed, and it gives me hope for our own future as well as the planet.

Many children born today will live to be at least one hundred, my grandchildren—Seoyon, Seojin, Jai, and Hyunjin—among them. What will their world look like in 2121? If we do not act now, I fear it could be even further destabilized by violence, poverty and environmental degradation. Our young people are inheriting a planet too hot and dry to sustain fragile life. Hundreds of thousands of plants and animals are already extinct, and voracious deserts, uncontrollable fires, and rising seas are destroying habitable land. The biggest powers—also the biggest polluters—have pledged to attain carbon neutrality by mid-century, a goal I hope will not be too late.

Since leaving the United Nations, I have been offered a number of international and national positions, many of which I have accepted because they clearly point toward expanding understanding and cooperation.

I am deeply honored to join The Elders, a small corps of former world leaders and distinguished figures founded by Nelson Mandela to prevent conflict and encourage development. I was humbled in 2018 to be elected deputy chair of this group.

As the chair of the Boao Forum, often called the Davos of Asia, I work with world leaders and innovators to seek political, economic, and principled responses to global problems. I am also the chair of the Ethics Commission of the International Olympic Committee, a position I value because it reinforces the importance of accountability and unity through sport. In addition, I head of a number of organizations, including the Global Green Growth Institute, the Global Center on Adaptation, the National Council on Climate and Air Quality of Korea, the UN Global Compact Korea Network, and the Sustainable Development Solutions Network, Korea. I established the Ban Ki-moon Centre for Global Citizens in Vienna to train new leaders to promote inclusion and opportunity for all. I am deeply grateful to President Heinz Fischer of Austria (2004–2016), the cochair of the BKM Centre, which was inaugurated in January 2018. This organization works with the The Seoul-based Ban Ki-moon Foundation for a Better Future.

I also hold distinguished professorships at Yonsei University, the oldest university in Korea, which has established the Ban Ki-moon Institute for Global Engagement and Empowerment. I am deeply honored that the Handong Global University built a home for the Ban Ki-moon Institute for Global Education.

I admit, my natural optimism is tempered by the wave of populism that threatens to roll back human rights and democracy. We've seen strong powers and key players become increasingly insular. Once a beacon of international cooperation, the United States under President Biden has returned to multilateral political and financial commitments such as the Paris Climate Agreement and the World Health Organization.

Trygve Lie, the first UN secretary-general, warned his successor, Dag Hammarskjold, that he was taking on "the most impossible job on this Earth." We cannot expect our leaders alone to make this world a better place. This book is, in part, a rebuke to the notion that unilateralism will benefit anyone in the long run. Global problems require global solutions, and I will continue to work for global cooperation for succeeding generations. Every man, woman, and child shares responsibility for the future. Together, our mission is possible.

—Ban Ki-moon

ACKNOWLEDGMENTS

I am immensely grateful to my wife, Soon-taek, who has been with me for more than fifty years. With a sense of devotion, patience, and trust, she has always supported me. Whenever I was faced with difficulties, she encouraged me to overcome them. I also appreciate my loving children, Seon-yong, Woo-hyun, and Hyun-hee, together with their spouses and children, who all had to endure personal difficulties just because they are my family.

I offer my sincere gratitude to writer Betsy Pisik, without whose dedication and tireless work this book would not have been possible.

I am grateful to my senior advisors, starting with two deputy secretaries-general, Asha-Rose Migiro of Tanzania and Jan Eliasson of Sweden, as well as my three chefs de cabinet, Vijay Nambiar of India, Susana Malcorra of Argentina, and Edmond Mulet of Guatemala. In addition, I thank many undersecretaries and assistant secretaries general and their hard-working staffs. My special thanks go to Ambassador Yoon Yeocheol and to Chang Wook-jin, Elisabeth Weidmann, Elena Stroganova, Isabelle Kim, Gian Dean, and many others for their dedicated service through many sleepless nights helping to make my work possible.

I also thank Ambassador Kim Won-soo, who was my deputy chef de cabinet and later under-secretary general for disarmament. I am grateful to former Korean Foreign Minister Kang Kyung-hwa who has served the UN with distinction in several senior positions. Korean ambassadors to the United Nation Choi Young-jin, Kim Hyun-jong, Park In-gook, Kim Sook, Oh Joon, and Cho Tae-yul provided me with professional and personal support during the past ten years.

I would like to express my gratitude to those who have taken time to review this book: Ambassadors Vijay Nambiar, Lynn Pascoe, Jeffrey Feltman, Ivan Simonowic, Kim Sook, Chung Rae-Kwon, Yoon Yeo-cheol, and Professor Robert Orr.

My deep appreciation also goes to my security detail led by Captain Bernard Robinson, Lieutenant Thomas Bryant, and all the courageous, hardworking officers of the Department of Security and Safety for their dedicated support around the clock.

I thank researchers Dali ten Hove and Janet Naylor Vandenabeele, whose knowledge, curiosity, and determination brought depth to this account.

Last but not least, I take this opportunity to express my deep appreciation to Jennifer Lyons of the Jennifer Lyons Literacy Agency for her hard work on my behalf. I am grateful to publisher Jennifer Crewe and editor Caelyn Cobb of the Columbia University Press for their kind guidance and full support for this book. I also thank Chairman YS Chi of Elsevier for his professional guidance.

Finally, I dedicate this book with humble appreciation to the many staff and peacekeepers who paid the ultimate price for their service, upholding the values and principles of the United Nations around the world.

NOTES

1. EARLY LIFE: FROM TRAGEDY TO STRENGTH

1. Allan R. Millett, "Korean War: 1950–1953," *Britannica*, May 4, 1999, last updated September 10, 2020, https://www.britannica.com/event/Korean-War.

2. DIPLOMATIC LIFE: SHARING KOREA'S TRADITIONAL VALUES

1. United Nations Security Council Resolution 82, S/RES/82, June 25, 1950, https://undocs.org/S/RES/82(1950).
2. Patrick E. Tyler, "South Korean President Sides with Russia on Missile Defense," *New York Times*, February 27, 2001, https://www.nytimes.com/2001/02/27/world/south-korean-president-sides-with-russia-on-missile-defense.html.

3. ELECTION OF THE SECRETARY-GENERAL: SEEKING A MANDATE TO LEAD

1. "Preamble," United Nations Charter, https://www.un.org/en/sections/un-charter/preamble/index.html.
2. Ban Ki-moon, "Address on Taking the Oath of Office in the General Assembly," United Nations Secretary-General, December 14, 2006, https://www.un.org/sg/en/content/sg/speeches/2006-12-14/address-taking-oath-office-general-assembly.
3. Roh Moo-hyun, "Address by President Roh Moo-hyun of the Republic of Korea at the High-Level Plenary Meeting of the 60th Session of the United Nations General Assembly," September 14, 2005, https://www.un.org/webcast/summit2005/statements/rok050914eng.pdf.

4. Association of Southeast Asian Nations, "Chairman's Statement of the 10th ASEAN Summit Vientiane, 29 November 2004," November 29, 2004, https://asean.org/?static_post=chairman-s-statement-of-the-10th-asean-summit-vientiane-29-november-2004.
5. Park Song-wu, "Minister Ban to Run for Top UN Job," *Korea Times*, February 14, 2006.
6. "Bolton Pushing for Female UNSG?," unsg.org, April 10, 2006, http://www.unsg.org/wordpress/2006/04/bolton-looking-for-woman-unsg/.
7. "Ban Takes 1st Straw Poll," unsg.org, July 24, 2006, http://www.unsg.org/wordpress/2006/07/ban-takes-1st-straw-poll/.
8. "Ban Firms Up Lead in Second Straw Poll," unsg.org, September 14, 2006, unsg.org/wordpress/2006/09/ban-firms-up-lead-in-second-straw-poll/.
9. "Ban Slips but Holds, Vike Freiberga Pushes Into Third," unsg.org, September 28, 2006, http://www.unsg.org/wordpress/2006/09/ban-slips-but-holds-vike-freiberga-pushes-into-third/.
10. "Ban Ki Moon Wins," unsg.org, October 2, 2006, http://www.unsg.org/wordpress/2006/10/first-color-coded-straw-poll-results/.

5. NEGOTIATION: FLOW LIKE WATER

1. Zeid Ra'ad Al Hussein, *Denial of Access and Lack of Cooperation with UN Bodies Will Not Diminish Scrutiny of a State's Human Rights Record*, Human Rights Council, Thirty-Fifth Session, Opening Statement by United Nations High Commissioner for Human Rights, June 6, 2017, https://www.ohchr.org/EN/NewsEvents/Pages/DisplayNews.aspx?NewsID=21687&LangID=E.
2. United Nations Security Council, *Report of the Secretary-General on His Mission of Good Offices in Cyprus*, July 8, 2016, https://undocs.org/en/S/2016/599.

6. NORTH KOREA: THE DIFFICULT COUSINS

1. United Nations Security Council Resolution 83, S/RES/83, June 25, 1950, https://undocs.org/S/RES/83(1950).
2. Allan R. Millett, "Korean War: 1950–1953," *Britannica*, last updated September 10, 2020, https://www.britannica.com/event/Korean-War.
3. "Joint Declaration of the Denuclearization of the Korean Peninsula," January 20, 1992, https://peacemaker.un.org/sites/peacemaker.un.org/files/KR%20KP_920120_Joint-DeclarationDenuclearizationKoreanPeninsula.pdf.
4. Korean Peninsula Energy Development Organization, "Nuclear Threat Initiative," October 26, 2011, https://www.nti.org/learn/treaties-and-regimes/korean-peninsula-energy-development-organization-kedo/.
5. George W. Bush, "The President's State of the Union Address," January 29, 2002, https://georgewbush-whitehouse.archives.gov/news/releases/2002/01/20020129-11.html.
6. United Nations Office for Disarmament Affairs, "Treaty on the Non-Proliferation of Nuclear Weapons," https://www.un.org/disarmament/wmd/nuclear/npt/text; see also International Atomic Energy Agency, "Safeguards and Verification," https://www.iaea.org/topics/safeguards-and-verification.

7. United Nations Security Council, "Statement by the President of the Security Council," April 13, 2009, https://www.un.org/en/ga/search/view_doc.asp?symbol=S/PRST/2009/7.
8. "UN Chief Announces Rare Visit to DPR Korea, Aiming to Help Boost Cooperation on Peninsula," *UN News*, May 19, 2015, https://news.un.org/en/story/2015/05/499112-un-chief-announces-rare-visit-dpr-korea-aiming-help-boost-cooperation-peninsula.
9. "Secretary-General's Remarks at the Seoul Digital Forum," United Nations, May 20, 2015, https://www.un.org/sg/en/content/sg/statement/2015-05-20/secretary-generals-remarks-seoul-digital-forum.
10. "U.N. Chief Ban Ki-moon to Visit Pyongyang This Week," *Yonhap News Agency*, November 16, 2015, https://en.yna.co.kr/view/AEN20151116001453315.
11. John Hudson and Josh Dawsey, "Trump Botches North Korea Sanctions Announcement, Sparking Widespread Confusion," *Washington Post*, March 22, 2019, https://www.washingtonpost.com/world/national-security/trump-cancels-some-sanctions-aimed-at-north-korea-contradicting-treasury-dept/2019/03/22/6ecb2732-4cd0-11e9-93d0-64dbcf38ba41_story.html.
12. Choonsik Yoo, "North Korea's Economy Tanks as Sanctions, Drought Bite: South Korea," *Reuters*, updated July 25, 2019, https://www.reuters.com/article/us-northkorea-economy-gdp/north-koreas-economy-tanks-as-sanctions-drought-bite-south-korea-idUSKCN1UL08G.
13. Edith M. Lederer, "US Opposes Lifting Key Sanctions Against North Korea," *Associated Press*, December 18, 2019, https://apnews.com/article/8692b877d6c22548622056e263f25ec7.
14. Christy Lee, "Will Kim's Claim in Constitution Weaken Efforts to Denuclearize?," *Voice of America*, July 21, 2019, https://www.voanews.com/east-asia-pacific/will-kims-claim-constitution-weaken-efforts-denuclearize.
15. United Nations Security Council, *Report of the Panel of Experts Established Pursuant to Resolution 1874 (2009)*, August 30, 2019, https://undocs.org/S/2019/691.

7. SEPTEMBER 11, 2001: THE COMPLEXITY OF CONSENSUS

1. "Condemnation of Terrorist Attacks in the United States of America," Resolution A/RES/56/1, adopted by the UN General Assembly, September 18, 2001, https://digitallibrary.un.org/record/448065?ln=en.

8. PEACEKEEPING: WITHOUT 360° AGREEMENT, EVERY STEP IS A BATTLE

1. For a full list of UN peace operations, see "List of Peacekeeping Operations 1948–2019," United Nations Peacekeeping, https://peacekeeping.un.org/sites/default/files/unpeacekeeping-operationlist_3_1_0.pdf.
2. "Fatalities," United Nations Peacekeeping, https://peacekeeping.un.org/en/fatalities.
3. " 'Intervention Brigade' Authorized as Security Council Grants Mandate Renewal for United Nations Mission in Democratic Republic of Congo" (press release), United Nations, March 28, 2013, https://www.un.org/press/en/2013/sc10964.doc.htm.

9. SUDAN: WAR CRIMINALS, REFUGEES, AND A COW CALLED BAN KI-MOO--

1. United Nations Security Council Resolution 1769, S/RES/1769, July 31, 2007, https://undocs.org/en/S/RES/1769(2007).
2. United Nations Security Council Resolution 1740, S/RES/1740, January 23, 2007, https://www.un.org/ga/search/view_doc.asp?symbol=S/RES/1740(2007).
3. "Secretary-General Appoints Geir O. Pedersen of Norway Special Coordinator for Lebanon" (press release), February 16, 2007, https://www.un.org/press/en/2007/sga1056.doc.htm.
4. United Nations Security Council Resolution 1778, S/RES/1778, September 25, 2007, https://undocs.org/en/S/RES/1778(2007).
5. United Nations Security Council Resolution 1996, S/RES/1996, July 8, 2011, https://undocs.org/S/RES/1996(2011).
6. International Criminal Court, "Situation in Darfur, Sudan: *The Prosecutor v. Omar Hassan Ahmad Al Bashir*," Case Information Sheet, updated April 2018, https://www.icc-cpi.int/CaseInformationSheets/AlBashirEng.pdf.
7. UNMIS became UNMISS in 2011.

10. GAZA: CONVEYOR BELT DIPLOMACY

1. United Nations Security Council Resolution 1860, S/RES/1860, January 8, 2009, https://undocs.org/S/RES/1860(2009).
2. "Data on Casualties," United Nations Office for the Coordination of Humanitarian Affairs in Occupied Palestinian Territory, https://www.ochaopt.org/data/casualties.
3. United Nations Human Rights Council, *Human Rights in Palestine and Other Occupied Arab Territories: Report of the United Nations Fact-Finding Mission on the Gaza Conflict*, A/HRC/12/48, September 25, 2009, https://www2.ohchr.org/english/bodies/hrcouncil/docs/12session/A-HRC-12-48.pdf.
4. United Nations Relief and Works Agency for Palestine Refugees in the Near East, *Updated Quick Response Plan for Gaza: An Assessment of Needs Six Months After the War*, July 2009, https://www.unrwa.org/sites/default/files/20100119144213.pdf.
5. "Data on casualties."

11. ARAB SPRING: SEASON OF DISCONTENT

1. Associated Press, "Tunisia: 11 Die in New Clashes After Weeks of Unrest," *Guardian*, January 9, 2011, https://www.theguardian.com/world/2011/jan/09/tunisia-clashes-weeks-unrest.
2. Hélène Mulholland, "David Cameron Condemns 'Despicable' Violence in Egypt," *Guardian*, February 2, 2011, https://www.theguardian.com/politics/2011/feb/02/egypt-transition-of-power-david-cameron.
3. "Arab League Suspends Libya Delegation—TV," *Reuters*, February 22, 2011, https://www.reuters.com/article/libya-protests-league/arab-%C3%82%C2%ADleague-suspends-libya-delegation-tv-idUSLDE71L2GK20110222.
4. United Nations Security Council Resolution 1973, S/RES/1973, March 17, 2011, https://www.undocs.org/S/RES/1973(2011).

5. "Syria Death Toll: UN Envoy Estimates 400,000 Killed," *Al Jazeera*, April 23, 2016, https://www.aljazeera.com/news/2016/04/23/syria-death-toll-un-envoy-estimates-400000-killed/.
6. United Nations Office for the Coordination of Humanitarian Affairs, "UN Secretary-General Pays Tribute to Kuwaiti Amir for Humanitarian Leadership" Relief Web, https://reliefweb.int/sites/reliefweb.int/files/resources/Kuwait%20humanitarian%20award_press%20release%209%20Sept%202014.pdf.

12. IRAN: THE IMPORTANCE OF PROMISES

1. "Statements by President Obama, French President Sarkozy, and British Prime Minister Brown on Iranian Nuclear Facility," The White House, September 25, 2009, https://obamawhitehouse.archives.gov/the-press-office/2009/09/25/statements-president-obama-french-president-sarkozy-and-british-prime-mi.
2. "Inflation, Consumer Prices (Annual %)—Iran, Islamic Rep.," The World Bank, accessed October 10, 2020, https://data.worldbank.org/indicator/FP.CPI.TOTL.ZG?end=2015&locations=IR&start=2000.
3. "Unemployment, Youth Total (% of Total Labor Force Ages 15–24) (National Estimate)," The World Bank, accessed October 4, 2020, https://data.worldbank.org/indicator/SL.UEM.1524.NE.ZS?end=2015&locations=IR&start=2000.
4. Ban Ki-moon, "Secretary-General's Remarks to the High-Level Segment of the 16th Non-Aligned Movement Summit," United Nations, August 30, 2012, https://www.un.org/sg/en/content/sg/statement/2012-08-30/secretary-generals-remarks-high-level-segment-16th-non-aligned.
5. "The World Factbook: Middle East: Iran," United States Central Intelligence Agency, last updated September 24, 2020, https://www.cia.gov/library/publications/the-world-factbook/geos/ir.html#People.
6. "Implementation of the Joint Plan of Action at a Glance," Arms Control Association, last updated August 2017, https://www.armscontrol.org/Implementation-of-the-Joint-Plan-of-Action-At-A-Glance.
7. Barack Obama, "Statement by the President on Iran," The White House, July 14, 2015, https://obamawhitehouse.archives.gov/the-press-office/2015/07/14/statement-president-iran.
8. United Nations Security Council Resolution 2231, S/RES/2231, July 20, 2015, https://www.undocs.org/S/RES/2231(2015).
9. Gardiner Harris and Jack Ewing, "U.S. to Restore Sanctions on Iran, Deepening Divide with Europe," *New York Times*, August 6, 2018, https://www.nytimes.com/2018/08/06/us/politics/iran-sanctions-trump.html.

13. MYANMAR: CYCLONE NARGIS OPENS THE HERMIT NATION

1. Knut Ostby, "Statement by the United Nations Resident and Humanitarian Coordinator in Myanmar, Knut Ostby, Ten Years After Cyclone Nargis," May 2, 2018, https://myanmar.un.org/en/21807-statement-united-nations-resident-and-humanitarian-coordinator-myanmar-knut-ostby-ten-years.
2. "UKAID in Burma," Department for International Development, accessed November 12, 2020, https://reliefweb.int/sites/reliefweb.int/files/resources/B6115C470BC0B96D852576EF0058D317-Full_Report.pdf.

3. Ban Ki-moon, "Address to Union Assembly of the Republic of the Union of Myanmar," April 30, 2012, https://www.un.org/sg/en/content/sg/speeches/2012-04-30/address-union-assembly-republic-union-myanmar.

14. SRI LANKA: ACCESS AND INACTION

1. Navanethem Pillay, "Serious Violations of International Law Committed in Sri Lanka Conflict: UN Human Rights Chief," Office of the United Nations High Commissioner for Human Rights, March 13, 2009, https://newsarchive.ohchr.org/en/NewsEvents/Pages/DisplayNews.aspx?NewsID=9499&LangID=E.
2. United Nations Security Council, "Press Statement on Sri Lanka" (press release), May 13, 2009, https://www.un.org/press/en/2009/sc9659.doc.htm.
3. Sri Lankan Ministry of Defence, "LTTE Defeated; Sri Lanka Liberated from Terror," May 18, 2009, https://web.archive.org/web/20090521113622/http:/www.defence.lk/new.asp?fname=20090518_10.
4. "Ban Arrives in Sri Lanka for First-Hand Look at Post-Conflict Situation," *UN News*, May 22, 2009, https://news.un.org/en/story/2009/05/300982.
5. "Joint Statement by United Nations Secretary-General, Government of Sri Lanka" (press release), May 26, 2009, https://www.un.org/press/en/2009/sg2151.doc.htm.
6. "Secretary-General Names Panel of Experts to Advise on Accountability for Possible Rights Violations During Sri Lanka Conflict" (press release), June 22, 2010, https://www.un.org/press/en/2010/sgsm12967.doc.htm.
7. "Secretary-General Releases Expert Panel's Report on Accountability with Respect to Final Stages of Sri Lanka Conflict" (press release), April 25, 2011, https://www.un.org/press/en/2011/sgsm13524.doc.htm.
8. United Nations Human Rights Council Resolution 25/1, A/HRC/RES/25/1, April 9, 2014, https://undocs.org/A/HRC/RES/25/1.
9. United Nations Human Rights Council Document 30/61, *Comprehensive Report of the Office of the United Nations High Commissioner for Human Rights on Sri Lanka*, A/HRC/30/61, September 28, 2015, https://undocs.org/A/HRC/30/61.
10. Ban Ki-moon, "Secretary-General's Remarks at Youth Event in Galle, Sri Lanka: Reconciliation and Coexistence: The Role of Youth," September 1, 2016, https://www.un.org/sg/en/content/sg/statement/2016-09-01/secretary-general's-remarks-youth-event-galle-sri-lanka.

15. HAITI: FROM EARTHQUAKE TO HEARTBREAK

1. United Nations Peacekeeping, "UN Mission's Contributions by Country—Month of Report: 31-Dec-09," December 31, 2009, https://peacekeeping.un.org/sites/default/files/dec09_5.pdf.
2. "Haitians in UN's Cash-for-Work Scheme Earn Income as They Help Their Country," *UN News*, January 26, 2010, https://news.un.org/en/story/2010/01/327652-haitians-uns-cash-work-scheme-earn-income-they-help-their-country.
3. "Billions Pledged at Donors' Conference as Ban Calls for Wholesale Rebuilding of Haiti," *UN News*, March 31, 2010, https://news.un.org/en/story/2010/03/334242-billions-pledged-donors-conference-ban-calls-wholesale-rebuilding-haiti.

4. United Nations General Assembly Document, *New Approach to Cholera in Haiti: Report of the Secretary-General*, A/71/895, May 3, 2017, https://undocs.org/A/71/895.
5. "U.N. Haiti Cholera Panel Avoids Blaming Peacekeepers," *Reuters*, May 5, 2011, https://www.reuters.com/article/us-haiti-cholera-panel/u-n-haiti-cholera-panel-avoids-blaming-peacekeepers-idUSTRE74457Q20110505.
6. David Ingram, "U.S Judge Rules Haitians Cannot Sue U.N. for Cholera Epidemic," *Reuters*, January 10, 2015, https://www.reuters.com/article/us-un-haiti-lawsuit-idUSKBN0KJ0PX20150110.

16. HUMAN RIGHTS: BORN FREE AND EQUAL

1. "Secretary-General's Encounter with the UN Press Corp" (statement), January 2, 2007, https://www.un.org/sg/en/content/sg/press-encounter/2007-01-02/secretary-generals-encounter-un-press-corps.
2. "A Status Quo Secretary General" (editorial), *New York Times*, January 6, 2007, https://www.nytimes.com/2007/01/06/opinion/06sat3.html.
3. "General Assembly Adopts Landmark Text Calling for Moratorium on Death Penalty" (press release), General Assembly, December 18, 2007, https://www.un.org/press/en/2007/ga10678.doc.htm.
4. Ban Ki-moon, "Secretary-General Defends, Clarifies 'Responsibility to Protect' at Berlin Event on 'Responsible Sovereignty: International Cooperation for a Changed World'" (press release), Secretary-General, July 15, 2008, https://www.un.org/press/en/2008/sgsm11701.doc.htm.
5. Francis Deng, Sadikiel Kimaro, Terrence Lyons, Donald Rothchild, and I. William Zartman, *Sovereignty as Responsibility: Conflict Management in Africa* (Washington, DC: Brookings Institution Press, 1996).
6. Ban Ki-moon, "Implementing the Responsibility to Protect: Report of the Secretary-General," United Nations General Assembly Document, A/63/677, January 12, 2009, https://undocs.org/en/A/63/677.
7. "Security Council Approves 'No-Fly Zone' Over Libya, Authorizing 'All Necessary Measures' to Protect Civilians, by Vote of 10 in Favour with 5 Abstentions" (press release), Security Council, March 17, 2011, https://www.un.org/press/en/2011/sc10200.doc.htm.
8. Mabvuto Banda, "Malawi Pardons Gay Couple During UN Chief's Visit," *Reuters*, May 29, 2010, https://www.reuters.com/article/idINIndia-48907720100530.
9. "Ban Calls for End to Violence and Discrimination Against Lesbian, Gay, Bisexual, and Transgender People," *UN News*, December 11, 2012, https://news.un.org/en/story/2012/12/428052-ban-calls-end-violence-and-discrimination-against-lesbian-gay-bisexual-and.
10. "Stand Up for Equal Rights & Fair Treatment for Lesbian, Gay, Bi, Trans, & Intersex People Everywhere," UN Free & Equal (website), accessed November 12, 2020, https://www.unfe.org/.
11. Rose Troup Buchanan, "Robert Mugabe Tells UN General Assembly: 'We Are Not Gays!'," *Independent*, September 29, 2015, https://www.independent.co.uk/news/people/robert-mugabe-tells-un-general-assembly-we-are-not-gays-a6671316.html.
12. Office of the High Commissioner on Human Rights, "Independent Expert on Sexual Orientation and Gender Identity," accessed June 30, 2019, https://www.ohchr.org/EN/Issues/SexualOrientationGender/Pages/Index.aspx.

17. WOMEN: OUR MOST IMPORTANT RESOURCE

1. UN Women, *Beijing Declaration and Platform for Action* (New York: United Nations, 1995, repr, 2014), https://beijing20.unwomen.org/~/media/headquarters/attachments/sections/csw/pfa_e_final_web.pdf.
2. "Goal 1: End Poverty in All Its Forms Everywhere," *United Nations Sustainable Development Goals*, accessed October 5, 2020, https://www.un.org/sustainabledevelopment/poverty/.
3. United Nations Security Council Resolution 1325, S/RES/1325, October 31, 2000, https://undocs.org/en/S/RES/1325(2000).
4. "Gender," United Nations Peacekeeping, accessed October 5, 2020, https://peacekeeping.un.org/en/gender.

18. THE SUSTAINABLE DEVELOPMENT GOALS: TOWARD DIGNITY FOR ALL

1. Harlem Brundtland, *Our Common Future* (Geneva, Switzerland: World Commission on Environment and Development, 1987).
2. *The Future We Want*, United Nations Conference on Sustainable Development, Rio de Janeiro, Brazil, June 20–22, 2012, https://sustainabledevelopment.un.org/content/documents/733FutureWeWant.pdf.
3. *The Road to Dignity by 2030: Ending Poverty, Transforming All Lives and Protecting the Planet*, United Nations, December 4, 2014, https://www.un.org/ga/search/view_doc.asp?symbol=A/69/700&Lang=E.
4. *Investing in the SDGs: An Action Plan for Promoting Private Sector Contributions*, World Investment Report, chap. 4, 2014, https://unctad.org/en/PublicationChapters/wir2014ch4_en.pdf.
5. Global Commission on Adaptation, *Adapt Now: A Global Call for Leadership on Climate Resilience*, updated September 13, 2019, https://cdn.gca.org/assets/2019-09/GlobalCommission_Report_FINAL.pdf.
6. "Malala Yousafzai Urges World Leaders at UN to Promise Safe, Quality Education for Every Child," *UN News*, September 25, 2015, https://news.un.org/en/story/2015/09/509752-malala-yousafzai-urges-world-leaders-un-promise-safe-quality-education-every.

20. GLOBAL HEALTH: PREVENTING, CONTAINING, AND CURING TOGETHER

1. Michael R. Snyder, "What Role for UN Peacekeepers in Tackling Ebola?," International Peace Institute Global Observatory, September 8, 2014, https://theglobalobservatory.org/2014/09/role-un-peacekeepers-unmil-tackling-ebola/.
2. World Bank Group, "World Bank Group Pledges Additional $100 Million to Speed New Health Workers to Ebola-Stricken Countries," October 30, 2014, https://www.worldbank.org/en/news/press-release/2014/10/30/world-bank-group-additional-100-million-new-health-workers-ebola-stricken-countries.
3. World Health Organization, "Poliomyelitis," July 22, 2019, https://www.who.int/en/news-room/fact-sheets/detail/poliomyelitis.

21. ACCOUNTABILITY: NO JUSTICE, NO PEACE

1. United Nations Security Council Resolution 1757, S/RES/1757, May 30, 2007, https://undocs.org/S/RES/1757(2007).
2. United Nations Security Council Resolution 1975, S/RES/1975, March 30, 2011, https://undocs.org/S/RES/1975(2011).
3. "Lavrov Questions Use of Force in Ivory Coast," *Moscow Times*, April 5, 2011, https://www.themoscowtimes.com/2011/04/05/lavrov-questions-use-of-force-in-ivory-coast-a6104.
4. International Criminal Court, "Situation in Côte d'Ivoire: *The Prosecutor v. Laurent Gbagbo and Charles Blé Goudé*" (Case Information Sheet), September 2019, https://www.icc-cpi.int/CaseInformationSheets/gbagbo-goudeEng.pdf.
5. Office of the High Commissioner for Human Rights, *Democratic Republic of the Congo, 1993–2003*, United Nations, August 2010, https://www.ohchr.org/Documents/Countries/CD/DRC_MAPPING_REPORT_FINAL_EN.pdf.

22. UN REFORM: MAKING ROOM FOR THE FUTURE

1. "Secretary-General Makes Public His Financial Disclosure Statement," *UN News*, January 26, 2007, https://news.un.org/en/story/2007/01/206992-secretary-general-makes-public-his-financial-disclosure-statement.
2. Ban Ki-moon, *Towards a Global, Dynamic and Adaptable Workforce Mobility*, United Nations General Assembly Document 68/358, September 3, 2013, https://undocs.org/en/A/68/358.
3. David W. Dunlap, "Retiring a U.N. Building Not Quite Fit for the World Stage," *New York Times*, January 6, 2016, https://www.nytimes.com/2016/01/07/nyregion/retiring-a-un-building-not-quite-fit-for-the-world-stage.html.

INDEX

ABOUT THE AUTHOR

BAN KI-MOON is a South Korean diplomat and former foreign minister who served as the eighth secretary-general of the United Nations from January 2007 to December 2016. Throughout his career, Ban worked to mobilize international efforts against a slate of global pressures including climate change, extreme poverty, and armed conflict to make the world a safer and more equitable place.